THE
FOUCAULT
EFFECT

THE
FOUCAULT
EFFECT

STUDIES IN
GOVERNMENTALITY

WITH TWO LECTURES BY AND AN INTERVIEW WITH

MICHEL FOUCAULT

Edited by
Graham Burchell, Colin Gordon
and Peter Miller

THE UNIVERSITY OF CHICAGO PRESS

The University of Chicago Press, Chicago 60637
© 1991 Editors and Contributors
All rights reserved. Published 1991
Printed in the United States of America
07 06 05 04 03 02 01 00   3 4 5 6

ISBN: 0-226-08045-5 (paperback)

Library of Congress Cataloging-in-Publication Data

The Foucault effect : studies in governmentality : with two lectures
  by and an interview with Michel Foucault / edited by Graham
  Burchell, Colin Gordon, and Peter Miller.
       p.   cm.
  Includes bibliographical references and index.
  ISBN 0-226-08044-7 (cloth). — ISBN 0-226-08045-5 (pbk.)
  1. Reason of state. 2. Welfare state. I. Foucault, Michel.
II. Burchell, Graham. III. Gordon, Colin. IV. Miller, Peter, Ph.
D.
JC131.F63   1991
320′.01′1—dc20
                                                              91–10456
                                                              CIP

♾ The paper used in this publication meets the minimum
requirements of the American National Standard for
Information Sciences—Permanence of Paper for Printed
Library Materials, ANSI Z39.48-1992.

Contents

Acknowledgements

Chapter 2 originally appeared in the French journal *Esprit*, no. 371 (May 1968) pp. 850–874. An English translation first appeared in the journal *Salmagundi*, no. 20 (Summer–Fall, 1972) pp. 225–48. A revised translation by Colin Gordon originally appeared in *Ideology and Consciousness*, no. 3 (Spring, 1978). The present version has been further extensively revised.

Chapter 3 originally appeared in Michelle Perrot, ed., *L'impossible prison: Recherches sur le système pénitentiare au XIXe siecle* (éditions du Seuil, Paris, 1980). The translation by Colin Gordon, reproduced here with minor corrections, originally appeared in *I&C*, no. 8, *Power and Desire: Diagrams of the Social* (Spring 1981).

Chapter 4 is a lecture given at the Collège de France, February 1978. The first publication was in an Italian translation by Pasquale Pasquino, in the journal *Aut . . . aut*, no. 167–8 (September – December 1978). An English translation by Rosi Braidotti originally appeared in *I&C*, no. 6 (Autumn 1979). A French version, re-translated from the Italian, appeared in *Actes* No. 54 (été 1986) pp. 7–15. The present version was revised by Colin Gordon.

Chapter 5 was given as a paper to a seminar organized at the Collège de France by Michel Foucault in 1978. A translation by Colin Gordon originally appeared in *Ideology and Consciousness*, no. 4 (Autumn 1978). The present translation has been extensively revised.

Chapter 7 originally appeared in *Aut . . . aut*, no. 167–8 (September–December 1978). A translation from the Italian by Jennifer Stone originally appeared in *Ideology and Consciousness*, no. 4 (Autumn 1978). The present version has been extensively revised by Colin Gordon.

Chapter 8 was written for a conference on neo-social democracy held in 1982. The translation by Colin Gordon appears here for the first time.

Chapter 9 originally appeared in *I&C* no. 8 (Spring 1981). The text and notes for this version have been revised by the author.

Chapter 12 was written for a seminar organized at the Collège de France in 1979 by Michel Foucault. The translation by Colin Gordon, reproduced here with minor modifications originally appeared in *I&C* no. 7, *Technologies of the Human Sciences* (Autumn 1980). The present version has been further revised.

Chapter 13 originally appeared in Jean Carpentier, Robert Castel, Jacques Donzelot, Jean Marie Lacrosse, Anne Lovell and Giovanna Procacci, *Résistances à la médecine et démultiplication du concept de santé* (C.O.R.D.E.S./Commisariat Géneral du Plan, Paris 1980). The translation by Colin Gordon originally appeared in *I&C* no. 9, *Life, Labour and Insecurity* (Winter 1981–1982).

Chapters 1, 6, 10, 11 and 14 are published here for the first time.

Preface

An effect of this kind is by no means an appearance or an illusion. It is a product which spreads or distends itself over a surface; it is strictly co-present to, and co-extensive with, its own cause, and determines this cause as an immanent cause, inseparable from its effects, pure *nihil* or *x*, outside of the effects themselves. Such effects, or such a product have usually been designated by a proper or singular name. A proper name can be considered fully as a sign only to the extent that it refers to an effect of this kind. (Gilles Deleuze, *The Logic of Sense*, p. 70)

Michel Foucault's contemporary and friend Gilles Deleuze glosses here a practice in scientific nomenclature, the naming of certain special physical phenomena, such as the Kelvin effect or the Compton effect. He is also hinting something about individuality: that its fullest achieved form can embody the same kind of impersonal singularity as that designated by the physicists' name for an 'effect'. Our title for this collection of studies invokes this idea. The 'Foucault effect' documented here is – briefly stated – the making visible, through a particular perspective in the history of the present, of the different ways in which an activity or art called *government* has been made thinkable and practicable.

Our title also intends justly to convey what, personal connection aside, our authors have in common, something rather different from membership of a school or subscription to a manifesto. What they share is a particular exploratory passion, a striving to capture and analyze, across a range of its modern manifestations (reason of state, police, liberalism, security, social economy, insurance, *solidarisme*, welfare, risk management and others) a dimension of historical existence which Michel Foucault, perhaps, did most to isolate and describe.

We think there is something in this work which is still new, which has not been digested or staled by the intellectual trends of the past decade, and which can help us to understand, to respond to and perhaps even to look beyond our present. Foucault wrote in 1976 that in political analysis we have still not cut off the king's head – meaning that thought about politics is trapped by the antitheses of despotism and legitimation, repression and rights. In Britain, critical political culture now espouses the aims of a written constitution and a Bill of Rights. Certainly Foucault did not mean that these were futile objectives. But government is not just a power needing to be tamed or an authority needing to be legitimized. It is an activity and an art which concerns all and which touches each. And it is an art which presupposes thought. The sense and object of governmental acts do not fall from the sky or emerge ready formed from social practice. They are things which have had to be – and which have been – invented. Foucault observed that there is a parcel of thought in even the crassest and most obtuse parts of social reality, which is why criticism can be a real power for change, depriving some practices of their self-evidence, extending the bounds of the thinkable to permit the invention of others. The 'Foucault effect' may, or such is our hope, contribute to a renewal of these powers of critique.

CHAPTER ONE

Governmental rationality: an introduction
Colin Gordon

Between 1970 and 1984, Michel Foucault delivered thirteen annual courses of lectures at the Collège de France in Paris. Foucault's duties at the college, as professor in a specially created Chair in the History of Systems of Thought, were not to teach a syllabus but to report on the results of his own researches. Several of these lecture series, Foucault's own official summaries of which have been republished as a volume by the Collège de France,[1] are preliminary explorations of themes taken up in various of Foucault's later books. But others contain rich seams of material which he never chose or had time to work up in a final written form. Perhaps the two most remarkable annual courses of which this is true were those of 1978 and 1979, entitled respectively 'Security, territory and population', and 'The birth of biopolitics'. One of the 1978 lectures was published (although not in French) in Foucault's lifetime, and is reprinted in this volume (Chapter 4). A provision in Foucault's will has been interpreted by his literary executors as precluding posthumous publication of the complete lecture series; but the exceptional interest of the 1978 and 1979 courses has been recognized by the recent publication on cassette tape of the initial lectures of the two series, and a complete tape edition of the two series is currently under consideration. Complete recordings of these lectures are available to researchers in the Foucault archive at the Bibliothèque du Saulchoir in Paris.

In these lectures Foucault defined and explored a fresh domain of research into what he called 'governmental rationality', or, in his own neologism, 'governmentality'. This work was not carried out single-handedly. A group of fellow researchers, several of whom are among the contributors to this volume, took part in seminars held at the Collège de France which paralleled and complemented the programme of the lectures. In the subsequent lecture courses in Paris, Foucault shifted his attention away from these governmental themes in the direction of the topics of his final volumes of the *History of Sexuality*. But he continued to teach and organize research seminars on questions of government on his frequent visits to the United States, particularly at Berkeley. A number of lectures, essays and interviews published in the USA during these later years provide valuable documentation of this area of Foucault's work.

1

In the present essay I shall attempt a brief outline of the meaning of the theme of 'governmentality' in Foucault's work and the studies which he and others carried out under this heading, constructing a composite picture of the kinds of political and philosophical analysis which this style of working produces in the hands of a number of different and independent researchers. In some ways this is a problematic and even a foolhardy undertaking. A condensed, syncretic account may risk glossing over important differences of perspective between different individual contributions. One is describing a zone of research, not a fully formed product (although happily, it is now possible to refer to major subsequent publications by many of this volume's authors).[2] The inaccessibility and the informal oral structure of the lecture materials makes summarization at once an indispensable and an uncomfortable task. I can only hope that the richness of the material itself will encourage the reader to tolerate these presentational obstacles and their attendant irritations.

As well as summarizing, I shall attempt to connect and to contextualize. We are only gradually becoming aware of, and are still far from having fully documented access to, the astounding range of Foucault's intellectual enterprises, especially in the later years from 1976 to 1984. The governmental theme has a focal place in Foucault's later philosophy; an effort needs to be made to locate this as accurately as possible. To understand the theme's wider resonance, something needs to be said about the interactions between a research agenda and a contemporary political world. To help to situate its distinctive value – and on grounds of good sense – it will be advisable to resist doctrinaire overstatement of this work's unique and unprecedented character, and instead to try to establish lines of communication with twentieth-century enquiries into allied areas of political philosophy and the history of political ideas. Such points of fruitful connection are, as Graham Burchell illustrates (Chapter 6), encouragingly numerous. Finally, and taking due account of widespread extant discussion of Foucault's later published work, something ought to be said about the ethical and political considerations (if any) implicit in this way of working and thinking.

What did Foucault have in mind by the topic 'governmental rationality'? Foucault understood the term 'government' in both a wide and a narrow sense. He proposed a definition of the term 'government' in general as meaning 'the conduct of conduct': that is to say, a form of activity aiming to shape, guide or affect the conduct of some person or persons. 'The government of one's self and of others' was Foucault's title for his last two years' lectures, and for a projected, unpublished book. Government as an activity could concern the relation between self and self, private interpersonal relations involving some form of control or guidance, relations within social institutions and communities and, finally, relations concerned with the exercise of political sovereignty. Foucault was crucially interested in the interconnections between these different forms and meanings of government; but in his lectures specifically on governmental rationality he concerned himself principally with government in the political domain.

Foucault used the term 'rationality of government' almost interchangeably with 'art of government'. He was interested in government as an activity or practice, and in arts of government as ways of knowing what that activity consisted in, and how it might be carried on. A rationality of government will thus mean a way or system of thinking about the nature of the practice of government (who can govern; what governing is; what or who is governed), capable of making some form of that activity thinkable and practicable both to its practitioners and to those upon whom it was practised. Here, as elsewhere in his work, Foucault was interested in the philosophical questions posed by the historical, contingent and humanly invented existence of varied and multiple forms of such a rationality.

In these two years' lectures, Foucault applied this perspective of analysis to three or four different historical domains: the theme, in Greek philosophy and more generally in antiquity and early Christianity, of the nature of government, and the idea of government as a form of 'pastoral power'; doctrines of government in early modern Europe associated with the idea of reason of state and the police state; the eighteenth-century beginning of liberalism, considered as a conception of the art of government; and, lastly, post-war forms of neo-liberal thought in Germany, the USA and France, considered as ways of rethinking the rationality of government. These different and discontinuous forays were linked together for Foucault by a common focus of interest, encapsulated in the formula of one of his lecture titles: 'Omnes et singulatim' (all and each).[3] Foucault saw it as a characteristic (and troubling) property of the development of the practice of government in Western societies to tend towards a form of political sovereignty which would be a government of all and of each, and whose concerns would be at once to 'totalize' and to 'individualize'.

We can better locate this preoccupation of Foucault's by reconstructing some of the moves which took him there. In his preceding book *Discipline and Punish*, he had famously proposed and expounded a kind of political analysis called the 'microphysics of power', exemplified by the study of the application of disciplinary techniques as part of the invention of the modern penitentiary prison. A whole aspect of modern societies, Foucault was suggesting here, could be understood only by reconstructing certain 'techniques of power', or of 'power/knowledge', designed to observe, monitor, shape and control the behaviour of individuals situated within a range of social and economic institutions such as the school, the factory and the prison. These ideas encountered considerable interest and extensive criticism. Foucault's responses to some of these criticisms can be read as giving some of the key directions to his subsequent work.

One objection frequently raised by the Marxist left was that this new attentiveness to the specifics of power relations and the detailed texture of the particular techniques and practices failed to address or shed light on the global issues of politics, namely the relations between society and the state. Another was that Foucault's representation of society as a network of omnipresent relations of subjugating power seemed to preclude the possibility of meaningful individual freedom. A third complaint was that Foucault's markedly bleak account of the effects of humanitarian penal reformism corresponded to an overall political philosophy of nihilism and despair.

Foucault introduced his lectures on governmentality as being, among other things, an answer to the first of these objections. The same style of analysis, he argued, that had been used to study techniques and practices addressed to individual human subjects within particular, local institutions could also be addressed to techniques and practices for governing populations of subjects at the level of a political sovereignty over an entire society. There was no methodological or material discontinuity between three respective, microphysical and macrophysical approaches to the study of power. At the same time, moving from the former to the latter meant something different from returning to the theory of the state in the form demanded and practised by Foucault's Marxist critics. Foucault acknowledged the continuing truth of the reproach that he refrained from the theory of the state, 'in the sense that one abstains from an indigestible meal'. State theory attempts to deduce the modern activities of government from essential properties and propensities of the state, in particular its supposed propensity to grow and to swallow up or colonize everything outside itself. Foucault holds that the state has no such inherent propensities; more generally, the state has no essence. The nature of the institution of the state is, Foucault thinks, a function of changes in practices of government, rather than the converse. Political theory attends too much to institutions, and too little to practices. Foucault takes the same methodological course here as in *Discipline and Punish*, where changes in the rationale and meaning of the practice of punishing are prioritized over transformations in the structure of penal institutions.

Foucault had already begun to develop his view of the links between the microphysics and the macrophysics of power in the final chapter of *The History of Sexuality*, volume 1 (1976). Here he had introduced the term 'biopower', to designate forms of power exercised over persons specifically in so far as they are thought of as living beings: a politics concerned with subjects as members of a *population*, in which issues of individual sexual and reproductive conduct interconnect with issues of national policy and power. Foucault reintroduced this theme of biopower or biopolitics in his 1978 lectures, in a way linking it intimately with his approach to the theme of government. One of the key connections here was the perception that modern biopolitics generates a new kind of counter-politics. As governmental practices have addressed themselves in an increasingly immediate way to 'life', in the form of the individual detail of individual sexual conducts, individuals have begun to formulate the needs and imperatives of that same life as the basis for political counter-demands. Biopolitics thus provides a prime instance of what Foucault calls here the 'strategic reversibility' of power relations, or the ways in which the terms of governmental practice can be turned around into focuses of resistance: or, as he put it in his 1978 lectures, the way the history of government as the 'conduct of conduct' is interwoven with the history of dissenting 'counter-conducts'.

In these matters Foucault had some important clarifications to offer, notably in his American essays and interviews, on his views about power, freedom and hope. Foucault seems to have found fault afterwards at least with his rhetoric in *Discipline and Punish*, where this may have seemed to give an impression of certain uses of power as having an almost absolute capability to tame and subject individuals. In his 1982 essay 'The subject and power', Foucault affirms, on the contrary, that power is only power (rather than mere physical force or violence) when addressed to individuals who are free to act in one way or another. Power is defined as 'actions on others' actions': that is, it presupposes rather than annuls their capacity as agents; it acts upon, and through, an open set of practical and ethical possibilities.[4] Hence, although power is an omnipresent dimension in human relations, power in a society is never a fixed and closed regime, but rather an endless and open strategic game:

> At the very heart of the power relationship, and constantly provoking it, are the recalcitrance of the will and the intransigence of freedom. Rather than speaking of an essential freedom, it would be better to speak of an 'agonism' – of a relationship which is at the same time reciprocal incitation and struggle; less of a face-to-face confrontation which paralyzes both sides than a permanent provocation.[5]

Perhaps, then, what Foucault finds most fascinating and disturbing in the history of Western governmental practice and its rationalities is the idea of a kind of power which takes freedom itself and the 'soul of the citizen', the life and life-conduct of the ethically free subject, as in some sense the correlative object of its own suasive capacity. This was one of the crucial points where Foucault found himself among the inheritors of Max

Weber.[6] In the fresh way it re-poses the conjunction of the history of politics and the history of ethics, Foucault's later work rejoins a great theme of modern political sociology.

A little more needs to be said about the political and critical value orientation of this work of Foucault's, beginning with a note on its place and time of gestation. Foucault's 1978 course overlapped with an unexpected defeat in French parliamentary elections of an alliance of Socialist and Communist parties. His 1979 course ended a few weeks before Margaret Thatcher's election as British Prime Minister. This work was being done at a time of the fading in France of the multitudinous blossomings of post-1968 social militancy, at a time when the intellectual prestige of Marxism was about to undergo a rapid collapse (partly stimulated by the influence of Eastern European dissidents, with whose welcome and reception in France Foucault was actively involved), and when the spreading influence of neo-liberal political thought, from the Germany of Helmut Schmidt to the France of Giscard and Barre and the Britain of Callaghan and Healey, had begun to present a challenge to the post-war orthodoxies of governmental thought.

One of the conspicuous attributes of Foucault's governmentality lectures is their serene and (in a Weberian sense) exemplary abstention from value judgements. In a pithy preamble he rejects the use of an academic discourse as a vehicle of practical injunction ('love this; hate that; do this; refuse that . . .'), and dismisses the notion that practical political choices can be determined within the space of a theoretical text as trivializing the act of moral decision to the level of a merely aesthetic preference. The terms of Foucault's accounts of governmental rationalities are devoid of the implicit pejorative sarcasm which Foucault's Nietzschean affiliations have so often led readers to hear in his writing. Foucault's accounts of the liberal and neo-liberal thinkers indeed often evince a sense of (albeit value-neutral) intellectual attraction and esteem. The perspective may be libertarian, but it is not anarchist. His reproach, if there is one, is addressed to critical culture itself. Foucault does not eschew practical maxims where the obligations of thought are concerned. In a nutshell, he suggests that recent neo-liberalism, understood (as he proposes) as a novel set of notions about the art of government, is a considerably more original and challenging phenomenon than the left's critical culture has had the courage to acknowledge, and that its political challenge is one which the left is singularly ill equipped to respond to, the more so since, as Foucault contends, socialism itself does not possess and has never possessed its own distinctive art of governing. The conclusion from this exercise in critical attentiveness to the present lies in the affirmation of the possibility and necessity, for those who wish to pursue certain ends and values, of fresh acts of inventiveness.

Some of these views are well attested in Foucault's later years. In an interview in 1981 where he candidly welcomes the election of a Socialist government, Foucault expressed the hope of seeing a new 'logique de gauche' in the conduct of the regime, replacing the tutelary arrogance of its predecessor towards the governed with a practice of free dialogue between government and governed, 'debout et en face' (upright and face to face). He himself showed willingness to engage in discussion about problems and contradictions in social policy, notably in a long dialogue with a CFDT trade union representative on health funding issues and the need to devise new welfare policy mechanisms capable of providing the means of individual autonomy as well as the means of security. In the course of this discussion Foucault makes an emphatic plea for a renewal of inventiveness in political culture. Foucault also retained a continuing practical concern with the problems of the prisons which had so much occupied him in the 1970s. It is a matter of record that Foucault gave private advice to one governmental figure, the Minister of Justice Robert Badinter, his longstanding ally in the 1970s campaign against the death penalty.[7] Foucault is said also to have been on friendly terms with Michel Rocard, whose subsequent written references to 'le gouvernment des hommes' seem reminiscent of some of our present material. On the whole, however, Foucault seems to have been disappointed by the Socialists and their preferred role for intellectuals as a supporting ideological chorus line rather than as interlocutors in a discussion about how to govern. Paul Veyne recently wrote that, at the time of his death in 1984, Foucault was 'preparing a book against the Socialists'.

I will return below to the practical philosophy contained in Foucault's later work. We must now look more closely at the 'governmentality' lectures. We have seen how Foucault distinguished his topic from that of certain forms of state theory. How does it relate to the more classic domain of political philosophy? Perhaps a classic distinction can be used to draw a doubtless oversimplified contrast. A major part, at least, of classical political philosophy, in its central concern with the legitimate foundations of political sovereignty and political obedience, is about 'the best government'. Governmentality is about how to govern. Foucault continues here his predilection for 'how' questions, for the immanent conditions and constraints of practices. The choice does not carry any immediate polemical implication. Foucault does not say that legitimation theory is empty (though in a lecture he does call the social contract a bluff and civil society a fairy story); but only that a theory of the legitimate basis of sovereignty cannot be relied upon as a means of describing the ways in which power is actually exercised under such a sovereignty.

Even here, though, the concern with 'how' is not a concern with the domain of the purely expedient or factual. Firstly, Foucault's topic is quite as much about critique, problematizations, invention and imagination, about the changing shape of the thinkable, as it is about the 'actually existing'. Secondly, the perceived internal constraints of the activity of governing are no less capable of carrying normative meaning and content than the principles of legitimation. Thirdly, as we have already seen, the content and object of governing as biopolitics, as the conduct of living and the living, is itself already ethical. Fourthly, Foucault goes on to develop (in the first lecture of his 1980 course), the idea that government in Western cultures carries with it a concern with truth which exceeds the merely utilitarian relationship postulated in his earlier schema of power-knowledge. Extending the idea that sovereignty is seldom grounded on pure violence alone, Foucault advances the thesis of a regular, though variously actualized interdependence between the 'government of men' and what he calls the 'manifestation of truth'. One Western version of the art of government, accordingly, is 'government in the name of the truth'.

EARLY MODERN

Beginning his lectures in 1978 on the topic of 'pastoral power' in ancient culture, Foucault was returning in a new way to a classic theme in his own work. In *The Birth of the Clinic*, Foucault retraces the difficult origins of a style of medical knowledge structured around the interpretation of the individual case. Earlier medicine, he showed, had obeyed an Aristotelian interdict on a science of the individual: science concerned itself with genus and species; the individual difference was infra-scientific. Plato's dialogue, *The Statesman*, concerning the nature of the art of government, discusses the possibility that the ruler's art is like the shepherd's who cares for each individual sheep in his flock. In Plato, this idea is dismissed as impracticable: a ruler's knowledge and attentiveness could never extend so far as to minister to each individual: 'only a god could act thus'. Greek politics chooses the game of citizen and laws, rather than the pastoral game. The pastoral model is adopted and vastly elaborated by Christianity, as the care of souls. In Western Christianity, however, the roles of sacerdotal pastor and secular ruler never come to be unified. The focus of Foucault's interest in modern governmental rationalities consists, precisely, in the realization of what he calls the 'daemonic' coupling of 'city-game' and 'shepherd-game': the invention of a form of secular political pastorate which couples 'individualization' and 'totalization'.

Foucault singles out the emergence of doctrines of reason of state in sixteenth-century Europe as the starting point of modern governmentality, as an *autonomous* rationality. The principles of government are no longer part of and subordinate to the divine, cosmo-theological order of the world. The principles of state are immanent, precisely, in the state itself. To know how to govern, one must know the state and the secret springs of its *interests*, a knowledge which in part may not and cannot be accessible to the ruled, and is liable to dictate governmental acts of a singular, unforeseeable and drastic character. These are the key inter-locking terms of the French *politique* theorists of the early seventeenth century: *raison d'état; intérêt d'état; mystère d'état; coup d'état*. As Etienne Thuau has written:

> The notion of state ceases to be derived from the divine order of the universe. The point of departure for political speculation is no longer the Creation in its entirety, but the sovereign state. Reason of state seems to have perverted the old order of values . . . Born of the calculation and ruse of men, a knowing machine, a work of reason, the state encompasses a whole heretical substrate . . . Set above human and religious considerations, the state is thus subject to a particular necessity . . . Obeying its own laws, *raison d'état* appears as a scandalous and all-powerful reality, whose nature escapes the intelligence and constitutes a mystery.[8]

The state has its reasons which are known neither to sentiment nor to religion.

A contemporary synonym of *raison d'état* (condemned by a Pope as 'the devil's reason') was 'civil prudence': part of its genealogy has been seen to lie in the transformation of the Christian doctrine of prudence, con-sidered as the virtue displayed by a ruler capable of just action in circumstances which are singular and specific: the governor as helmsman – another of Plato's metaphors – preserving ship and passengers from the hazards of reef and storm. The meaning of prudence evolves from a context where it can be identified with a knowledge of apt precedent (the singular is never the wholly unprecedented) to a context, as in Machiavellian Italy, where the uncertain and the unexpected come to be perceived as the norm of Fortune's empire. The Machiavellian political art invented in response to this observation has, as Foucault remarks, its own inherent limit: a doctrine whose focus is merely to 'hold out', to retain one's sovereignty, however acquired, can scarcely provide assur-ance of holding out indefinitely. The importance of shifting the seat of political reason from prince to state is that the latter is capable of being credited with a form of secular perpetuity (itself a notion with complex Christian antecedents, explored by Kantorowicz:) 'States are realities which must needs hold out for an indefinite length of time.'[9] 'The art of governing is rational', Foucault writes, 'if reflexion causes it to observe the nature of what is governed – here, the *state*': reason of state is 'government in accordance with the state's strength'.[10]

9

Foucault suggests that the style of political thinking which enables continental European *raison d'état* to outgrow its Machiavellian limitations and to become a knowledge of 'the state's strength' can be found most fully embodied and articulated in the corpus of theory, pedagogy and codification developed in German territories after the Thirty Years War, under the rubric of *Polizeiwissenschaft*, or 'science of police' (although the English word 'policy' is arguably a better equivalent to this meaning of *Polizei*). Perhaps one could say, very formulaically, that reason of state's problem of calculating detailed actions appropriate to an infinity of unforeseeable and contingent circumstances is met by the creation of an exhaustively detailed knowledge of the governed reality of the state itself, extending (at least in aspiration) to touch the existences of its individual members. The police state is also termed the 'state of prosperity'. The idea of prosperity or happiness is the principle which identifies the state with its subjects. Police theory shares the mercantilist economic policy of striving to maximize the quantity of bullion in the sovereign's treasury. But it emphasizes that the real basis of the state's wealth and power lies in its population, in the strength and productivity of all and each. This, Foucault writes, is 'the central paradox of police': the aim of the modern art of government, viz., to develop those elements of individual lives in such a way that their development also fosters the strength of the state.' [11] The police state, we might say in other terms, strives towards the prudential by cultivating the pastoral.

Some citations and paraphrases from *Polizeiwissenschaft* writers by Foucault and Pasquino are eloquent on this topic. 'Life is the object of police: the indispensable, the useful, and the superfluous. That people survive, live, and even do better than just that, is what the police has to ensure.' Police 'sees to living': 'the objects which it embraces are in some sense indefinite'. 'The police's true object is man.' Police 'sees to everything pertaining to man's happiness'. 'The sole purpose of police is to lead to the utmost happiness in this life.' [12] Police is a science of endless lists and classifications; there is a police of religion, of customs, of health, of foods, of highways, of public order, of sciences, commerce, manufactures, servants, poverty . . . Police science seems to aspire to constitute a kind of omnivorous espousal of governed reality, the sensorium of a Leviathan. It is also (again in aspiration) a knowledge of inexhaustibly detailed and continuous control. Foucault (borrowing the title of an anti-Gaullist polemic by François Mitterrand) describes government in the police state as a 'permanent coup d'état'. Police government does not limit its action on the governed to the general form of laws: it works by the means of specific, detailed regulation and decree. The exponents of reason of state described its executive actions as those of a 'special justice'; Foucault notes as a defining characteristic of the police state the marginalization of the distinction between government by law and government by decree.

What kind of a rationality of government is this? Perhaps one may usefully refer here to Max Weber's vocabulary of reflection on the varieties of rationality and rationalization in world history and modern history. Somewhat as Weber remarks of Chinese Confucianism, police is a 'rationalism of order', which conceptually amalgamates the ordered course of the world and the ordering activity of administration.[13] But police resituates both these notions within a secular, non-traditional ethos, under a reign of artifice. Meinecke, in his *Macchiavellism*, evokes the view of the state of Turkey in the writings of the Italian reason of state theorist Trajano Boccalini (1556–1613):

> Turkey brought to life and exemplified what the political thought of the Renaissance had always been striving after: an artificial construction which had been consciously and purposely built up, a State mechanism which was arranged like a clock, and which made use of the various species and strengths and qualities of men as its springs and wheels.[14]

In a somewhat similar sense, the assurance of order in the police state is the assurance of an order which it itself has created. If the problem of Macchiavelli's prince is the securing of a new and non-legitimate sovereignty, the equivalent characteristic problem of police, in the German states newly demarcated by the Treaty of Westphalia, is, as Pasquino shows, to create a polity, as it were *ex nihilo*, out of a war-devastated no man's land. What the social market economy was for the Germany of 1945, the police state was for the Germany of 1648.

Police science, or 'Cameralism', is also, in conjunction with the allied knowledge of mercantilism and political arithmetic, the first modern system of *economic sovereignty*, of government understood as an economy. The economy emerges here, as Pasquino has put it, as a *specific*, but not yet (as for liberalism) an *autonomous* form of rationality. The economy of a functioning whole is a machine which has to be continuously made, and not merely operated, by government. This governmental theme of economy retains here from the ancient context of the *oikos* all its implications of possession, domestication and controlling action. In German, *Wirtschaft* (economy) has as its cognates the terms *Wirt* (householder/smallholder) and *Wirtschaften* (economic activity, the conduct of the *Wirtschaft*). Max Weber signalled an equivalent feature of a concept which has a key relevance for the antecedents of Cameralism, the *Stadtwirtschaft* (city economy): this was a term which, as Weber critically observed, signifies indiscriminately both a mode of *economic organization* and an *organism regulating the economy*. If it is possible for Cameralists to speak of the state as being identical with the 'whole body of society', this is so largely by virtue of the state's corresponding oeconomic properties: the identity of state and society here is, in some senses, equivalent to the unity of the *Wirt* and the *Wirtschaft* – or possibly, in a later vocabularly, to that of the entrepreneur and the enterprise (Otto Hintze argues that the 'spirit of state' in early modern Prussia is one and the same thing as Weber's Protestant spirit of capitalism).

Police government, finally, is in Foucault's terms a form of pastoral power, a government which defines itself as being 'of all and of each': a universal assignation of subjects to an economically useful life. Police government is also an oeconomy, through its way of equating the happiness of its individual subjects with the state's strength. Police is therefore a kind of *economic pastorate* (cf. Foucault's gloss in his lecture reprinted in Chapter 4, on the idea of a government 'of men and of things'), or a secular hierocracy, albeit somewhat different in its regime from the Catholic pastorate which had placed its obstacles in the path of the early capitalists. The state does not sacrifice itself for the individual: the individual (as Richelieu declares) must sometimes be sacrificed for the state. The ruler is a shepherd (German *Hirt*), but also a husbandman (German *Wirt*). The population of the governed is likened to a herd as well as to a flock: welfare is conjoined to exploitation, as the police thinkers are coolly capable of recognizing. Mercantilism, Weber remarks, means 'running the state like a set of enterprises'.[15]

Alongside the moral ambivalences of the police state, however, it is necessary to recognize also the emergence of changing forms of ethical culture. Beside the startlingly ambitious promises current in this period on behalf of the new science of state, the second remarkable feature of early modern political culture is the sense of a profound connectedness between the principles of political action and those of personal conduct. As Foucault observes, it is possible that never before or since has the activity of government been perceived as so essentially interdependent with the government of self, on the part of ruler and ruled alike. The problem of government, it has been said, was posed in terms of a 'language of persons'. Foucault was aware of his precursors in this domain of study, especially in German political sociology since Weber. There is also, as Pasquale Pasquino has rightly noted, a striking complementarity here between Foucault's work and the concurrent research of Gerhard Oestreich on the role of neo-stoicism in the early modern state.[16]

Why was 'conduct' such an important theme at this time? The answer has to do with the same broad antecedents as those of reason of state: the erosion of a feudal order in which personal identity was anchored in a hereditary status and an associated network of loyalties and dependences; the impact of the Reformation, in terms of the religious problematization of the individual, and the demand for a renovated and invigorated structure of pastoral guidance; and the pervasive dislocation of public and private life by religious wars. In France, *raison d'état* had its origin in the choice made, notably by the *politiques*, for a 'detheologization' (Oestreich) of politics, in preference to a religious path of mutual annihilation. The development of a secularized manner of reflection on personal ethics is a close corollary of this shift. The trend should not be mistaken for a move towards irreligion. It provided, as well, an instrument of active mobilization on each side of the confessional battle lines: Catholic, Calvinist, Lutheran – a kind of competition in moral armaments.

The rediscovery and renewal of Stoic ethics studied by Oestreich owes its influence in early modern political thought to an elective affinity with these conditions. The Roman Stoics were read with especial attention because of a perceived similarity between the public disturbances of ancient Rome and those of modern Europe. Philosophy was studied here in a search for resources for the recovery of moral and ethical orientation out of outward chaos and inner confusion, as a weapon and a medicine. This neo-Stoic culture regarded its philosophy above all as a pragmatic, practical form of knowledge, a methodology of order. The Stoic style postulates a world-order, the 'police of this world', yet is at the same time hospitable to, and consonant with, artifice and technique: hence its affinity, certain appearances notwithstanding, to the thought of *raison d'état*. One of its main moral and technical virtues was the promise, developed notably in the extremely influential writings of Justus Lipsius, of a common prudential ethic of 'constancy' (*constantia*) for ruler and ruled: both were required to cultivate in their separate stations the same basic virtues of life-conduct. Neo-stoicism provided perhaps the first distinct secular ethic of command and obedience: to obey meant not a mere abnegation or servitude of the will, but an active form of life-conduct: Oestreich cites here testimonies to the spirit of almost religious zeal among the executant personnel of French *raison d'état*.

By relating these developments to the 'regulation-mania' of the police state, Oestreich helps to convey better the moral tenor of the latter's global regulatory endeavours, particularly relative to newly urbanized populations:

> Greater social complexity brought a greater deployment of authority. People had to be 'coached', as it were, for the tasks created by the more populous society and the claims which it made on its citizens . . . a start was made on educating people to a discipline of work and frugality and on changing the spiritual, moral and psychological make-up of political, military and economic man.[17]

At the same time, Oestreich usefully remarks, of the disciplines of Court life, that 'All social intercourse was governed by strict order: this, however severe, was not seen as slavery, but as a moral stiffening which prevented one from falling.' Or, as Hobbes writes at the beginning of his *De Cive*, 'Man is not fitted for society by nature, but by discipline.' [18]

REAL LIBERALISM

Economic Government

As we have seen, Foucault sees the early modern conjunction of *raison d'état* and science of police as momentously original in both an epistemological and an ethical sense. It constitutes the activity of government as an art with its own distinctive and irreducible form of rationality; and it gives to the exercise of sovereignty the practical form of a political pastorate, a government of all and each for the purposes of secular security and prosperity.

Some of the attributes of the contemporary welfare state can, or so this seems to suggest, be seen as originating with the *Polizeistaat*. But only some. Foucault's lectures on modern governmental rationality attach equally close attention to the other great intervening mutation in the history of his topic, namely the advent of liberalism.

In some respects (as Graham Burchell shows in Chapter 6), Foucault's approach to this subject converges with some recent moves in the study of early liberal thought by English-speaking historians: the rejection of a narrowly anachronistic reading of the origins of political economy solely within the co-ordinates of a historical autobiography of present-day economic science; an emphasis on the unity of economic, social and governmental reflection in the work of Adam Smith and his contemporaries; and a scepticism about the Marxist interpretation of eighteenth-century liberals as conveniently prescient apologists of nineteenth-century industrial capital. What is distinctive, albeit not unique, about Foucault's perspective here is his concern to understand liberalism not simply as a doctrine, or set of doctrines, of political and economic theory, but as a style of thinking quintessentially concerned with the art of governing.

Foucault sees Adam Smith's *The Wealth of Nations* as effecting not only a transformation in political and economic thinking but also a transformation in the relationship between knowledge and government. For Cameralist thinkers, police science and state action are isomorphous and inseparable; the notion of 'science' carries here an immediately pragmatic connotation, akin, as Foucault puts it, to the calculating know-how of diplomacy. For political economy, on the other hand, scientific objectivity depends on the maintenance of relative distance and autonomy from the standpoint and preoccupations of state, while the content of economic science affirms the necessary finitude and frailty of the state considered as a knowing subject. Liberalism can thus be accurately characterized in Kantian terms as a *critique of state reason*, a doctrine of limitation and wise restraint, designed to mature and educate state reason by displaying to it the intrinsic bounds of its power to know. Liberalism undertakes to determine how government is possible, what it can do, and what ambitions it must needs renounce to be able to accomplish what lies within its powers.

Foucault distinguishes two stages in this politico-epistemological revolution. In France, the Physiocratic sect of *économistes* inverts the once scandalous heresy propagated by the earlier sect of *politiques*, the initial proponents of *raison d'état*. The artificial, invented reason of Leviathan is rebutted by the proclaimed discovery that the affairs of human society constitute a quasi-nature. Society and its economy can and must only be governed in accordance with, and in respect for, the laws of that nature, the autonomous capability of civil society to generate its own order and its own prosperity. In Physiocratic doctrine, this version of a *laissez-faire* policy is associated with a specific technical proposal, Quesnay's economic 'Table', a device intended to permit a sovereign to monitor the totality of economic processes within the state. Here the ruler is in a position to permit economic subjects freedom of action just because, through the Table, the sovereign can still know what is happening in the economy, and how. There is here, in Foucault's terms, a relation of adequation between the sovereign's knowledge and his subjects' liberty, a kind of transparent superposition of the political and the economic.

Adam Smith's 'invisible hand' represents, for Foucault, an oblique but radical criticism of the technique of the Table: it means that the Physiocratic model of economic sovereignty is an impossibility; the knowledge intended to be compiled in the Table is, even in principle, impossible for a sovereign reliably to obtain.

Of the choices and calculations of the individual economic agent, Smith writes that 'he intends only his own gain, and he is in this, as in many other cases, led by an invisible hand to promote an end which was no part of his intention':[19] an end which serves the public good. Smith also makes it clear that the workings of the invisible hand are possible only *because* it is invisible; little good would follow if an individual were so perverse as to attempt to trade for the public good.[20] Foucault notes that this thesis of the benign opacity of economic processes holds good not only for the individual citizen but also for government; it is not as though the workings of the 'invisible hand', while remaining inaccessible to the common citizen, could yet become transparently intelligible when seen within a totalizing scientific perspective, comparable to God's knowledge of the operations of Providence. To endeavour to constrain individual economic actions towards the public good is an undertaking no more feasible for the sovereign than for the subject: it is 'a duty, in the attempting to perform which he must always be exposed to innumerable delusions, and for the proper performance of which no human wisdom or knowledge could ever be sufficient'.[21] The finitude of the state's power to act is an immediate consequence of the limitation of its power to know. Kant, soon after Smith, was to declare the unknowability for man of the cosmos as totality: political economy announces the unknowability for the sovereign of the totality of the economic process and, as a consequence, the *impossibility of an economic sovereignty*. Political economy is a form of scientific knowledge of which government must needs, in its own interest, take cognizance: what political economy cannot do for government is to generate a detailed, deductive programme for state action. Political economy assumes the role of a knowledge which is, as Foucault puts it, 'lateral to', or 'in *tête-à-tête* with' the art of governing: it cannot, however, in itself constitute that art.[22]

Thus the immediate unity of knowledge and government which typifies *raison d'état* and police science now falls apart. The regularities of economic or commercial society display a rationality which is fundamentally different in kind from that of calculative state regulation. The new objectivity of political economy does not consist solely in its occupation of a politically detached scientific standpoint: more profoundly, it inaugurates a new mode of objectification of governed reality, whose effect is to resituate governmental reason within a newly complicated, open and unstable politico-epistemic configuration. The whole subsequent governmental history of our societies can be read in terms of the successive topological displacements and complications of this liberal problem-space.

This complex event cannot, however, properly be understood if it is thought of as a moment of total discontinuity in governmental thought: this would also, one might add, be quite foreign to Foucault's usual methodological practice.[23] As many commentators have emphasized, *The Wealth of Nations* is not an ivory-tower edifice of theory, any more than it is a propaganda tract on behalf of the rising bourgeois class. *The Wealth of Nations* is, among other things, a collection of arguments for a series of quite specific policy recommendations addressed to the state. Smith, for all his scorn of the insidious and crafty race of politicians, does not disdain to enter into pragmatic calculations of particular questions of state security, such as those of military policy. Smith's Edinburgh lectures introduce the topic of political economy as falling within a branch of the art of legislation, namely *police*: 'The objects of police are the cheapness of commodities, public security, and cleanliness, if the two last were not too minute for a lecture of this kind. Under this head we will consider the opulence of a state.' [24] In contrast to the Cameralists (some at least of whose writings Smith appears to have been acquainted with), but in common with many of the Cameralists' own jurisprudential colleagues and rivals, Smith swiftly dispatches the extra-economic concerns of police science: 'the proper method of carrying dirt from the streets' and 'the method of keeping a city guard' are 'though useful . . . too mean to be considered in a general discourse of this kind'.[25] This is not, as we shall see, the whole story so far as liberalism is concerned. But in any case, and even though Smith represents modern levels of 'public opulence' as having been attained largely despite, rather than because of, the endeavours of rulers, this does not mean that he does not still place this opulence, or 'cheapness', 'plenty' and 'prosperity', in precisely the same spirit as did the Cameralists, at the heart of the objectives of state policy. Only the method espoused is different.

A further complexity emerges when one examines that method itself, or its most celebrated slogan-formula, *laissez-faire*. *Laissez-faire* is a way of acting, as well as a way of not acting. It implies, in Foucault's words, an injunction 'not to impede the course of things, but to ensure the play of natural and necessary modes of regulation, to make regulations which permit natural regulation to operate': 'manipuler, susciter, faciliter, laissez-faire'.[26] The permissive meaning of *laissez-faire* needs to be understood in an activist, enabling sense no less than in its character of passive abstentionism. Albert Hirschman has drawn a contrast between the liberalisms of Adam Smith and James Steuart which perhaps bears on this point. Steuart likens the 'modern economy' to a watch mechanism, in two respects. 'On the one hand, the watch is so delicate that it is immediately destroyed if . . . touched by any but the gentlest hand'; this means that the penalty for old-fashioned arbitrary *coups d'autorité* is so stiff that they will simply have to cease. On the other hand, these same watches 'are continually going wrong; sometimes the spring is found too weak, at other times too strong for the machine . . . and the workman's hand becomes necessary to set it right'.[27] Steuart thus argues 'both the impossibility of arbitrary and careless handling and the need for frequent corrective moves by the solicitous and expert "statesman" '.[28] In Adam Smith's thinking, on the other hand, the accent appears to fall on the need not so much to augment governmental expertise as to set a limit on its ineptitude: Smith seeks 'less a state with minimal functions than one whose capacity for folly would have some ceiling'.[29]

Steuart appears to present liberal government as entailing an order of skill more exacting than that of government by police; Smith's somewhat lower expectation of the talents of rulers backhandedly emerges in his commendation of the ease and convenience of *laissez-faire*. Can liberalism be both more and less difficult than its alternative? Perhaps: one may opt to read the difference between Steuart and Smith as largely one of tactic and temper, and their underlying objective as effectively the same; but one also senses here one of the elements of an enduring puzzle of liberalism, the conundrum of how to establish a viable boundary between the objects of necessary state action and those of necessary state inaction, or between what Smith's disciple Jeremy Bentham designates as the *agenda* and the *non-agenda* of government.

Liberal theory problematizes the methods of government no less than it does the nature of the reality which government has to address. It is by their examination of these methods, together with their attendant problems, that Foucault and his co-researchers help to show how liberalism has functioned historically not so much as a web of inveterate contradiction (reverie of a minimal state, as background music to a real state that ceaselessly grows), but as a prodigiously fertile problematic, a continuing vector of political invention. Here lies the force of Foucault's stress on the theoretical originality of liberalism: 'Liberalism is not a dream which clashes with reality and fails to insert itself there. It constitutes – and this is the reason both for its polymorphic character and for its recurrences – an instrument for the criticism of reality.' [30] The theoretical closure of the world, the conception of reality as the scene of a potentially total effectuation of political doctrine, is the very essence of what liberalism, in contradistinction both to the science of police and to scientific socialism, denounces and abjures. This is not, of course, to say that liberal ideas have no real effects. If there nowhere exists a truly liberal society, this is not because liberalism is a utopian doctrine. We now accept that there is (or has been) not only socialist thought, but also an 'actually existing socialism' which can be something rather different. What some of our authors are undertaking could be described as collating and analyzing the phenomena of what might be termed 'real liberalism' – undeterred by their complex, diagonal and often disconcerting relationship with what conventional wisdom recognizes as 'true' liberal precepts.

Foucault – in common with other recent authors – takes issue with the neo-Marxist thesis of a kind of pre-established liberal harmony between Lockean political jurisprudence (civil society, the social contract and the sanctity of individual property rights) and the political economists' conception of a commercial society, as a kind of casuistic synthesis whereby eighteenth-century liberalism prepares the philosophical legitimation for the capitalist appropriation of surplus value. The formation and development of liberalism as a governmental method can only be properly grasped when one recognizes that its constituent elements are far less mutually cohesive than ideology-critics have been apt to suppose.

Foucault sees the neo-Marxist interpretation as a misconception of the place of law in liberal thinking. Liberalism, Foucault argues, 'was not born out of the idea of a political society founded on a contractual relationship': if it proposes to recast and constrain regulatory acts of state into a predominantly legislative format, this is:

> not at all because of liberalism's affinity for the juridical as such, but because law provides general forms of intervention which preclude particular, individual exceptional measures, and because the participation of the governed in the elaboration of such law through a parliament constitutes the most effective system for a governed economy.[31]

It is a concern with the adequate technical form of governmental action (the form of expertise of Steuart's watchmender), rather than with the legitimation of political sovereignty (and, by extension, of economic exploitation), which determines the specific importance of the rule of law for economic liberalism.

Foucault suggests that this mode of technical reflection and elaboration needs to be envisaged in terms of a further category, distinct alike from the purely legal and the purely economic: that of security. And it is here that a certain dialectical interleaving of the universe of police with that of political economy becomes crucial to Foucault's account.

The preoccupation with security, with a 'holding out' of the state over an indefinite span of time, is both a founding and a universally mediating principle of the Cameralist 'state of prosperity'. Prosperity is the necessary condition of the state's own security, and prosperity in itself is nothing if not the capacity to preserve and hold on to, and where possible even to enhance, a certain global level of existence. Bentham's legislative science is as categorical on this matter as is the science of police:

> Among the objects of the law, security is the only one which embraces the future; subsistence, abundance, equality, may be regarded for a moment only; but security implies extension in point of time with respect to all the benefits to which it is applied. Security is therefore the principal object.[32]

Bentham says as well that 'if we are to have clear notions, we must mean by liberty a branch of security'.[33] Foucault adds that, for liberal government, the converse is also true: liberty is a condition of security. The active meaning of *laissez-faire*, the devising of forms of regulation which permit and facilitate natural regulation, comprises what Foucault terms:

> the setting in place of mechanisms of security . . . mechanisms or modes of state intervention whose function is to assure the security of those natural phenomena, economic processes and the intrinsic processes of population: this is what becomes the basic objective of governmental rationality. Hence liberty is registered not only as the right of individuals legitimately to oppose

the power, the abuses and usurptions of the sovereign, but also now as an indispensable element of governmental rationality itself.[34]

Liberty is the circumambient medium of governmental action: disrespect of liberty is not simply an illegitimate violation of rights, but an ignorance of how to govern.

The contrast between this new figure of liberty–security and the security of police is not an absolute one. Police disciplines, compartmentalizes, fixes: but this gridwork of order watched over by the agents of a geometer-king is also a network of movements and flows. Urbanization and police are, Foucault notes, almost synonymous ideas in eighteenth-century France. One formulation of the objective of police was that of organizing the whole royal territory like one great city. Public spaces, bridges, roads and rivers are prominent among the objects of police attention: this physical infrastructure of connection and mobility is seen by the police-theorist Jean Domat as the means whereby the policed city can function as a place of assembly and *communication*, a term whose meaning embraces all the processes of human intercourse, exchange, circulation and cohabitation within a governed population.[35] Liberalism discards the police conception of order as a visible grid of communication; it affirms instead the necessarily opaque, dense autonomous character of the processes of population. It remains, at the same time, preoccupied with the vulnerability of these same processes, with the need to enframe them in 'mechanisms of security'.

Foucault's discussion of security is one of his most important subsequent extensions to the framework of analysis he uses in *Discipline and Punish*.[36] He treats security here not just as a broad, self-evident requisite of political power, but as a specific principle of political method and practice, distinct alike from those of law, sovereignty and discipline, and capable of various modes of combination with these other principles and practices within diverse governmental configurations.

Foucault characterizes the method of security through three general traits. It deals in series of possible and probable events; it evaluates through calculations of comparative cost; it prescribes not by absolute binary demarcation between the permitted and the forbidden, but by the specification of an optimal mean within a tolerable bandwidth of variation. Whereas sovereignty has as its object the extended space of a territory, and discipline focuses on the body of the individual (albeit treated as a member of a determinate collectivity), security addresses itself distinctively to 'the ensemble of a population'. Foucault suggests that, from the eighteenth century onwards, security tends increasingly to become the dominant component of modern governmental rationality: we live today not so much in a *Rechtsstaat* or in a disciplinary society as in a society of security.

Foucault locates a major source of what is specific and original in the liberal treatment of population – and hence of security – in a discovery of British empirical philosophy, that of economic man as a *subject of interest*, a subject of individual preferences and choices which are both irreducible (personal sentiment cannot finally be explained from any other, more fundamental causal principle) and non-transferable (no external agency can supplant or constrain the individual determination of preferences). As Hume puts it: 'It is not contrary to reason for me to prefer the destruction of the whole world to the scratching of my finger.'[37] This conception of interest founds, in Foucault's view, the arguments of Hume and Bentham which demolish both the Lockean social contract theory and Blackstone's attempt to reconcile the social contract with the principle of interest. The postulate in social contract theory of an inaugural act of delegation and renunciation whereby the individual is constituted as a political and juridical subject is one which interest can never countenance as definitive: nothing can, in principle, exclude the possibility that interest will dictate the repudiation of such a contract. The subject of interest perpetually outflanks the scope of the act of self-imposed limitation which constitutes the subject of law.

This postulate of a radical discord between the economic and the juridical register is not, of course, a wholly novel notion in the discussion of liberalism. Halevy identified the problem in Bentham's philosophy of an apparent contradiction between the 'natural harmonisation of interests' which it attributes to the economy, and the 'artificial harmonisation of interests' which is the objective of Benthamite legislation.[38] Halevy points to a discrepancy of logic: Foucault identifies something more like a dissonance of rationalities, one which affects not only the principles of subjective individuation and the foundations of sovereignty, but also the processes of collective totalization and the determinability of governmental action.

Political economy and Smith's conception of an 'invisible hand' characterize the private determination of individual interests and their effective harmonization within society as proceeding in a modality entirely different from the universality and transcendence ascribed to the principles of law and juridical sovereignty, working instead, Foucault suggests, through a 'dialectic of spontaneous multiplication' which unfolds in a condition of radical immanence, of inextricable circumstance and accident, incapable in principle of becoming accessible to the totalizing scrutiny of subject or sovereign. This conception of a domain of political sovereignty populated by economic subjects of interest is, accordingly, very far from providing a complement or a completion of Lockean political jurisprudence: it amounts, rather, to a disqualification of economic sovereignty.

Liberalism's real moment of beginning is, for Foucault, the moment of formulation of 'this incompatibility between the non-totalizable multiplicity which characterizes subjects of interest, and the totalizing unity of the juridical sovereign'. This means that liberalism's main task must be that of devising a new definition of the governmental domain which can avert the hazardous alternatives (equally prejudicial to the integrity of governmental reason) of either excising the market from the field of sovereignty, or downgrading the economic sovereign into a mere functionary of political economy. To identify the economic subject with the subject of law is, according to Foucault, a rigorous impossibility not only for early liberalism but for all its posterity: there has never been and cannot be such a thing as a juridico-economic science. What liberalism undertakes is something different: the construction of a complex domain of governmentality, within which economic and juridical subjectivity can alike be situated as relative moments, partial aspects of a more englobing element. The key role which it comes to play in this effort of construction and invention is, for Foucault, the characteristic trait of the liberal theory of *civil society*.[39]

For Locke, as for his predecessors, 'civil society' is in effect a straightforward synonym of political or juridical society. In the later eighteenth century this term takes on a quite new dimension of meaning, one which Foucault sees as most fully and suggestively expounded in Adam Ferguson's *History of Civil Society*, a work close in spirit and complementary in argument to *The Wealth of Nations*. Here, the quality of radical immanence which Smith's thinking attributes to private economic interest as the motor of public prosperity is extended to cover the general constitution of society. For Ferguson, society makes itself. There is no historical act which founds it: groups of men possess and exercise a capacity to organize themselves and divide their labour (which includes political labour, specialized tasks of command being allocated to those best endowed for them), no less naturally and spontaneously than in their exercise of their sense organs and the power of speech. Society makes its own history out of its 'self-rending unity' (*unité déchirante*): that is to say, the intrinsic tension between the centrifugal forces of economic egoisms and a centripetal force of non-economic interest, that feeling of sympathy or 'disinterested interest' whereby individuals naturally espouse the well-being of their proximate family, clan or nations (and take comfort in the adversities of others). The existence of society is an inherently historic process, in which society is continually tearing itself apart and thereby at the same time endlessly remaking its own fabric. The activity of government, as an organic component of the evolving social bond, participates in this historic passage through a range of distinct, consecutive social forms.

The early liberals' conception of civil society needs, Foucault suggests, to be understood first of all as an instrument or correlate of a technology of government. What it makes possible is, so to speak, a social government which is an economy of the transeconomic, a methodology which straddles the formal bounds of the market:

> *Homo economicus* is, so to speak, the abstract, ideal, purely economic point which populates the real density, fullness and complexity of civil society; or alternatively, civil society is the concrete ensemble within which these abstract points, economic men, need to be positioned in order to be made adequately manageable.[40]

Civil society is therefore not to be taken, primarily or fundamentally, as an aboriginal nature which repels and contests the will of government: it is (like police, or sexuality) a 'réalité de transaction', a vector of agonistic contention over the governmental relation, of 'the common interplay of relations of power and everything which never ceases to escape their grasp'.[41] This perspective on liberalism illuminates its history. The nineteenth century is haunted by the quest for a *social government*, a government which can elicit for itself, amid the contending forces of modernity, a vocation and functionality anchored in the troubled element of the social.

How do these notions about civil society shape the development of liberalism as political practice, as the elaboration of 'mechanisms of security' for an economic government? A strikingly pertinent treatment of this question can be found, nearly two decades prior to the lectures summarized here, in Foucault's *Histoire de la Folie*, which includes an analysis of late eighteenth-century mutations in policies for social assistance and public medicine. One can recognize here the different traits of what Foucault later identifies as the methodology of security.

The principles of security, Foucault suggests, address themselves to a series of possible and probable events. This frame of reference is evident in Turgot's criticisms of the immobilization of public capital in charitable foundations. The needs of society are subject to innumerable circumstantial and conjunctural modifications: 'the definitive character of the foundations contradicts the variable and floating quality of the accidental needs they are supposed to answer'.[42]

The French economists strive to re-inscribe the institutions of assistance within the element of civil society (in Ferguson's understanding of the term). Public assistance is the manifestation of a feeling of compassion intrinsic to human nature and hence coeval with, if not anterior to, society and government. This purely human dimension retains its primacy even in political societies: the *social duty* of assistance is understood by the economists as *a duty of man in society*, rather than as *a duty of society*:[43]

> To establish which forms of assistance are possible, it will be necessary to define for social man the nature and limits of the feelings of pity, compassion and solidarity which can unite him to his fellows. The theory of assistance must be founded on this semi-moral, semi-psychological analysis, rather than on a definition of contractual group obligations.[44]

Such sentiments, it is argued (following Hume and Ferguson), are real, but finite and local in range. The organization of assistance needs to be integrated into a kind of discontinuous geography of social sympathies: 'active zones of psychological vivacity; inactive and neutral zones of distance and the heart's inertia'.[45] This prompts an argument for the replacement of a hospitalizing medicine by a method of domiciliary assistance which combines the security principles of minimized cost and protection of an optimal norm: the directing of assistance to the sick person's family will reinforce existing natural ties and affections, while requiring less than half the cost of a system of general hospitalization.

The perspective of civil society induces a new governmental analysis of the collective human substance of population. The idea of an 'economic government' has, as Foucault points out, a double meaning for liberalism: that of a government informed by the precepts of political economy, but also that of a government which economizes on its own costs: a greater effort of technique aimed at accomplishing more through a lesser exertion of force and authority.

Over this same period, in absolutist and constitutional European regimes alike, a closely similar rationale can be seen at work in the renewal, from Beccaria to Bentham and Anselm Feuerbach, of the principles of criminal and penal law. As is shown in *Discipline and Punish*, these programmes of reform centre on an effort to improve the intrinsic effectiveness of penal law and to ensure the greater adequacy of legal institutions to the conditions of a commercial society (to which concerns there may be added the further topic, discussed in *The Wealth of Nations*, of the 'expense of justice' and its funding).[46] The penal reformers' criticisms of traditional, violent and spectacular forms of punishment and their emphasis on the application to the law itself of new standards of operational regularity and reliability is entirely consonant with Steuart's strictures on 'old fashioned *coups d'autorité*' in the domain of economic policy proper. Bentham's deployment of a utilitarian calculus of pleasures and pains is the example *par excellence* of an applied rationality of security, in Foucault's sense of the term; *homo economicus*, the man of interest, of pleasures and pains, functions here not just as the abstract, elusive atom of market economics, but as a theme for political inventiveness.

It is again necessary here to give close attention to the precise similarities and differences between liberal government and the older practices of police. Foucault's discussion in *Discipline and Punish* on

Bentham's invention, the Inspection House or Panopticon, encapsulates this issue. There is no doubt that, as Foucault's book shows at length, Bentham's idea has affiliations to the disciplinary techniques character-istic of the police state. One of the Panopticon's immediate inspirations came from the Crimean naval labour colony administered by Bentham's brother Samuel on behalf of the Russian government; Bentham himself for a time entertained hopes that the Empress Catherine might be a sympathetic promoter of his own legislative ambitions. Foucault calls the Cameralist political technique an *étatisation*, a taking into state control, of discipline: a continuous network of power connecting the vigilance of the sovereign to the minute regulation and supervision of individual conduct: 'Police power must bear "upon everything" . . . the dust of events, actions, behaviour, opinions – "everything that happens"; police's object is "the things of each moment", the "little things" of which Catherine II spoke in her Great Instruction.' [47] In *Discipline and Punish*, Foucault places this style of thinking within what he calls 'a History of Detail in the Eighteenth century, presided over by Jean-Baptiste de la Salle, touching on Leibniz and Buffon, via Frederick II, covering pedagogy, medicine, military tactics and economics', and climaxing in the regime of Napoleon, who 'wished to arrange around him a mechanism of power that would enable him to see the smallest event that occurred in the state he governed'.[48]

That history also culminates, one might readily think, in the idea of the Panopticon. And yet on closer study, both Bentham's idea and some parallel trends of post-Revolutionary government in France can be seen to mark a profound mutation in this political history of detail. Jacques Donzelot cites, in illustration of this change, a draft law on factory regulations, commissioned by the Interior Ministry of the Consulate:

> since it would be a vain ambition to attempt to provide for all the details of production through regulations issuing from the public power . . . in view of the varied nature of industrial occupations, the best expedient is to authorize those in charge of the conduct of labour to regulate everything that relates to it.[49]

As Donzelot shows, this system of delegated, legally mandated private authority which this unpublished document envisages for the sphere of economic production does in fact accurately foreshadow both reality and the rationale of the French industrial system for most of the nineteenth century:

> The contractual economic relation between worker and employer is coupled with a sort of contractual tutelage of employer over worker, by virtue of the employer's total freedom in determining the code of factory regulations, among which he may include – as is most often the case – a whole series of disciplinary and moral exigencies reaching well outside the sphere of

production proper, to exercise control over the habits and attitudes, the social and moral behaviour of the working class outside of the enterprise . . . The reason given for this exclusive responsibility on the part of the employer, the pretext for this particular reinforcement of his powers, is the *singular* character of each enterprise.[50]

Just as, for political economy, the intricate workings of the market ineluctably exceed the omniscient aspirations of the police state, so the detailed exigencies of order in the sphere of production are recognized by a liberal government as capable of being grasped and determined, not just (as in the words of the police-scientist Delamare) 'only by a sufficiently detailed examination', but furthermore only by a delegation of regulatory oversight (and power) to the proximate, distributed micro-level of the individual enterprise and employer. Rather than seek to enforce order by encyclopaedic decree, the French government confers the *de facto* force of public law on the private jurisdiction of the entrepreneur. Liberal security means here not so much a bonfire of controls as a recoding of the politics of order.

In its different, elaborately artificial and unrealized manner, the Panopticon follows a similar logic: the function of control by inspection and surveillance passes from the political sovereign to the individual, entrepreneurial manager of the Inspection House, constrained only by the incentive of private profit and the republican sanction of exposure to public scrutiny. In its initial, penal target area of application, Bentham's offer personally to build and operate a Panopticon met, after lengthy deliberation and delay, with refusal by the British government. Michael Ignatieff has called this decision 'a major event in the history of imprisonment'.[51] This may be so: modern penal history does indeed attest (although not exclusively or unequivocally) to the force of political resistance to the liberal privatization and commercialization of certain state functions, including notably that of punishment. But perhaps this point indicates a need to distinguish between two different, albeit overlapping tendencies within liberalism as 'economic government': on the one hand, an effort to reduce governmental functions to a set of economically regulated structures and institutions (making economy, to invert Steuart's image, into the regulator of the governmental clock-work), and on the other, an effort to endow existing economic structures and institutions (those of the enterprise, as well as those of the market) with certain of the functions of a governmental infrastructure. Bentham's personal reverse (itself compensated by the immense subsequent influence of his idea) indicates the limits of the former tendency; Donzelot's evidence shows the importance of the second. François Ewald cites another example. A Napoleonic edict of 1810 made the concession of national mineral rights to private enterprise conditional on the obligation of the entrepreneur to ensure 'good order and security' (*sûreté et sécurité*) among the 'mass of men, women and children' needed for their exploitation. Ewald writes:

> A mining company was as much an enterprise of pacification, even of regional colonization, as a commercial undertaking . . . These spaces of private enterprise are, from the standpoint of common law, strictly speaking illegal. The law, nevertheless, allows them, so long as they properly fulfil their task of order and security; they do not lie outside the sphere of public order just because, on the contrary, they maintain that order by producing docile individuals.

'This strategy of power', Ewald concludes, 'might be called *liberalism*, provided that one regards liberalism not just as an economic form but as the functioning principle of power in capitalist societies.'[52]

This Imperial precedent can, no doubt, be read partly as indicative of the enduring admixture in French liberalism of certain structures of police administration. Yet Engels and Marx document, within the more informal and decentralized politico-legal environment of early nineteenth-century England, a *de facto* situation not very dissimilar to the French one, where local magistrates' courts regularly confer legal enforceability on the sanctions exacted by factory owners' private penal codes. Such phenomena perhaps evidence the extent and intensity of concern with the interdependence of economic order and public order which liberalism inherits from the police state.

This suggests one answer to those who sense in *Discipline and Punish* an elision of the question of the state. It is in fact vain to look for the hand of the state everywhere pulling the strings of micro-disciplinary power in nineteenth-century societies. But, on the other hand, these largely privatized micro-power structures none the less participate, from the viewpoint of government, in a coherent general policy of order. Furthermore, if liberalism halts the Cameralist tendency towards the *étatisation* of discipline, liberal government also pursues, in parallel to the elaboration elsewhere within 'civil society' of systems of privatized order, a policy which Foucault terms the 'disciplinarization of the state',[53] that is to say, a focusing of the state's immediate interest in disciplinary technique largely on the organization of its own staffs and apparatuses. As Karl Polanyi observes, Bentham's Panoptic principle of 'inspectability' had its applications not only to prisons and convicts, but also to ministries and civil servants.[54]

Government of the social

This dual-tier structure of public order and private order may serve, if only in extremely schematic terms, to characterize a first form of 'real liberalism', liberalism as an effective practice of security.

The most obvious limitation of this system was that the governmental virtues it invested in the economy were, at best, constrained in their effectiveness by the performance of the economy itself; but that economy, by accelerating the formation of a precarious mass population of the urban poor, could be seen to provide neither for the political security of the state, nor for the material security of the population. This situation tended to expose an underlying duality in the liberal idea of civil society, which C. B. Macpherson has traced to the political philosophy of Locke:[55] in one sense property makes everyone a citizen, since everyone is at least owner of his or her own body and labour; but in another sense it makes the labourer a member of society only through the mediation of his or her master, the owner of the means of production.[56]

In his book *L'Invention du social*, Jacques Donzelot suggests how this tension in liberal political jurisprudence, unresolved by the intervening innovations of 'economic government', emerged in the events of 1848 as a radical fracturing in the republican idea of right, an explosive clash between two incompatible notions of economic citizenship: citizenship as the right to work, or the obligation of the state to ensure for its citizens the minimum conditions of their economic existence, and citizenship as the right of property, affirmed against the feared violation of economic citizenship by confiscatory nationalizations.[57] What made this situation an utterly untenable one for government was that both parties to this argument moreover viewed the legitimacy of the republican regime as absolutely conditional on its satisfaction of one or other version of the criterion of social right.

The meaning of the idea of civil society became, in the course of this same conflict, subject to new and conflicting interpretations. The post-1815 French constitutions of qualified franchise, mirrored in the unilateral powers conferred within industry on the industrial entrepreneur, have been described as implementing a nakedly dualistic version of Lockean civil society, designed to maintain the labouring population politically in a 'virtual state of nature'.[58] 1848 and the Commune of 1871 can, for their part, no doubt justly be interpreted as countervailing attempts by that excluded population to construct a new civil society on their own terms.

But this same set of themes was, as Giovanna Procacci shows (Chapter 7), also being mobilized at the same period by other, bourgeois forces which can by no means be relegated from political history as mere vulgar moralizers: the liberal 'social economists' and philanthropists who, from a different direction, denounced the condition of the pauperized masses as that of a virtual anti-society, a 'state of nature' in a menacing and regressive understanding of that term, a radical deficiency in the moral and human fabric of civil society. Their plans for the reclamation and recolonization of this terrain were to be no less momentous in their sequel than the popular memory of insurrections.

Conflict over the meaning of social rights and civil society also meant conflict over the role of the state. The central issue of the civil warfare of 1848 was, precisely, one of the *agenda* and *non-agenda* of the state. As Donzelot points out, the mid-nineteenth century, the supposed heyday of liberalism, witnesses not a withering away of the question of the state, but an unprecedented intensification in debate and struggle over the state, its duties and its dangers. The paradox here, if there is one, is easily explained: the generalized anxiety and contention over the *question of the state* coincides with a common recognition of the demise of *reason of state*, of a rationality intrinsic to the state's actions. This is, decidedly, not a domain whose analysis can be grounded in a theory of the state, or in a view of the 'bourgeois state' as the subject of modern history.

Donzelot remarks on a certain noticeable parallelism, cutting across the battle over social rights, between liberal–conservative and revolutionary Marxian attacks on a French state perceived at this time as a crushing, alien burden on the social body, one which, either through the revolutionary suppression of 'intermediary bodies' (craft corporations, religious congregations) mediating between the individual citizen and the state, or through the parcellization of peasant property by bourgeois inheritance laws, pulverizes the structures of social community into a mass of anonymous and impotent individuals.[59] Both in 1848 and 1871, Marx interprets popular revolts in France as (among other things) revolts of civil society against the state, an idea which has been enthusiastically revived in recent years by sections of the French and British left. From the *18th Brumaire* to the *Critique of the Gotha Programme*, the language of Marx's treatment of the state is consistent in its violence (a violence which is, perhaps, the major distinctive feature of Marx's views in this matter): a 'supernaturalist abortion', a 'parasitic body', an 'incubus', an 'excrescence of civil society' which illicitly strives to detach itself from its social basis. Marx not only abstains from, but expressly prohibits, any generalized theory of existing states: unlike capitalist society, which can be analyzed as a universal form variously actualized in all civilized societies, 'the "present state" changes with each country's border . . . "*The* present state" is thus a fiction.'[60] States are a major concern for Marx only in those countries (Imperial Germany and France, but not Britain, Holland or the USA) where the proletariat is called upon to win political battles which a national bourgeoisie has previously lost. The significance of states correlates with cases of the obstruction of normal historical progress; Marx's language so powerfully expresses the sense of the perversity, the intrinsic irrationality, of the state's existence, that the method of historical materialism seems, in confronting it, already close to its own breaking point.

Conversely, if Marx shares with Paine or Godwin a certain idea of the virtuous nature of civil society, this is not of course out of any esteem for its present character, but because of its potential as the terrain of development of the contradictory logic of the economy, ultimately to be resolved in the advent of communist society. The Paris Commune, having effected the 'reabsorption of state power by society' and dissipated the spurious mystiques of state administration, restores the integrity of society as 'the rational medium in which the class struggle can run through its different phases in the most rational and humane way'.[61] If there is a strand of liberal–utopian rationalism to be found in Marx's thought, this may be located less, or less crucially, in his vision of communist society than in his prospectus for the class struggle within the open public space of bourgeois society.

The factor which, as Foucault and his co-workers help to show, tends to elude the Marxian critique, is the quite overt and conscious degree to which, for liberal thinkers (however oblivious they may be of the deeper strata of contradiction uncovered by Marx), the propositions of political economy and their implications immediately problematize the determination of governmental. At *this* level, liberalism is, to a very large degree, well apprized of its own perplexity. The very idea of a capitalist rationale of government may well, from a scientifically Marxian viewpoint, be judged a fundamentally incoherent one: modern Marxist theories of the capitalist state tend to confirm rather than refute this reading. Foucault does not offer an opinion as to whether the judgement itself is true or false: what he does signal is the danger of allowing its supporting logic to preclude a sufficient analysis of the historically formidable, elaborately innovatory and still persisting attempts which have been made to construct such a rationale.

Each of the major contested terms of the mid-nineteenth-century governmental crisis – society, state, property, right – is affected by a profound strategic realignment during the course of subsequent decades. As Pasquale Pasquino has suggested, following Reinhart Koselleck, one needs to look to other, less titanically influential thinkers of the period than Marx for the most prescient anticipations of the direction this process takes.[62] Marx's contemporary, the German historian and liberal reformist Lorenz von Stein, envisages a historical trend towards what he terms a 'social state'; he views the governmental problem in Prussia as the existence of an 'economic society' which has yet to become a civil society or 'society of state-citizenship'.[63] For Stein, this discrepancy springs from a lack of social homogeneity, by which he means not the class struggle, but the survival of an archaic and fragmented polity of estates (*Stände*): he calls upon the state to accelerate the retarded national evolution from a society of estates to a society of classes. (Something of this scenario for the state as an unavoidable participant in social evolution later emerges as the object of Marx's appalled revulsion in his attack on the German Social Democrats' Gotha Programme.) Several of these points have a relevance extending beyond their distinctively German context: the vision of a liberal state as active historic partner in the making of civil society; an exacting appraisal of the inner consistency of the social fabric; and, perhaps most strikingly, a tabling of the question of class formation as part of the state's agenda – a condition, one might add, of the state's security.

Reinhart Koselleck links Stein's notable preoccupation with long-term political prognoses to a broader mutation in the historical sensibilities of his time. We noted earlier how the problem of security extended out for the police state over the span of a secular perpetuity. But the thinkers of the Cameralist era still had recourse to the notion of *historia magistrae vitae*, history as the teacher of life: the record of past events seen as a repertory of instructive example and precedent for rulers. With the Enlightenment, the Revolution and the advent of the idea of progress, there emerges a new perception of present events as following a trajectory which is both radically unprecedented and constantly accelerating. Koselleck quotes Tocqueville on this penalty of progress, the loss to political reflection of the didactic resources of history: 'As the past ceases to illuminate the future, the mind moves forward in darkness'.[64] At the same date, the *Communist Manifesto* speaks of the 'everlasting uncertainty and agitation' characteristic of the bourgeois epoch.[65] And yet, in general, Marxism credits liberal thought with little share of this spirit of unease and uncertainty.

The process of class formation is in fact very far from being foreign to the preoccupations of liberal government. On the contrary, the question of class, as the problem of making an industrial market economy *socially* possible, becomes, from the bourgeois point of view, an essential part of the politics of security. Others besides Marx address themselves to the articulation of the open spaces of industrial sociability with the closed spaces of industrial discipline. By the latter part of the nineteenth century, the relegation of propertyless labour to a political 'state of nature' has become a demonstrably untenable expedient. 1848 and 1871 make spectacularly evident to an anxious bourgeoisie the danger represented by the indiscipline, the asocial autonomy, of the pauperized urban masses. Urgent efforts are addressed to the reconstruction of the population of the poor according to a model of collective economic citizenship: the social incorporation of the working class as an element of the body politic. The process of proletarian class formation becomes a major vector of bourgeois class struggle.[66] The encounter on this terrain between liberalism and socialism is, in its way, no less subtle and redoubtably ambiguous than liberalism's preceding relationship with the world of *Polizei*.

In France, the Third Republic was the setting for the deciding stages of this process.[67] The Republic began its life confronting the same questions of political sovereignty on which its predecessor had been wrecked in 1848, in the dual context of a sovereign legislature elected by universal (male) franchise, and a mounting popular intolerance of the older industrial order of private entrepreneurial despotism. A contemporary writes of 'the shocking contrast between man as voter and man as worker. In the polling-booth he is a sovereign; in the factory, he is under the yoke.'[68] The Third Republic departs, however, from the example of the Second by eschewing from the outset the political language of rights: its constitution refrains from endorsing the Declaration of Human Rights. Instead there is an effort to eliminate the fateful republican confrontation between individual and state, in which the former demands benefactions from the latter in the name of right, under threat of the exercise of his sovereign right to rebel. The end of the nineteenth century witnesses a radical recasting of liberalism's politico-juridical heritage, a quiet legal revolution whose discretion and apparent technical neutrality is, arguably, a measure of its strategic strength and influence.

The new republican jurists, influenced here by their German colleagues, incriminate the 'Rousseauist' framework of natural right as an engine of civil war. The transcendence of the law, of which the state is cast as the revocable custodian, is dissolved; law now becomes the historically relative emanation and expression of society. At the same time, both legal theory (administrative, civil and criminal) and the human sciences (psychology, criminology, sociology) question the founding legal status of the autonomous individual will, emphasizing instead its evanescent, intermittent and generally problematic character. Thirdly, mediating between the poles of state and individual, law and sociology together strive to construct a governable legal status for the 'intermediary bodies' suppressed by the Revolution: this is the purpose of Maurice Hauriou's theory of the institution.[69] Institutions – familial, commercial, professional, political, religious – make up the empirical texture of civil society. In each institution there is a partial source of social right; the seat of a *de facto* founding authority; a certain task or enterprise; and a postulated, *a priori* consensus. The durability of the institution contrasts with the ephemeral life of its individual members; the individual only becomes a citizen and subject of right through and thanks to the institution; the citizen's obligations to it are logically anterior to his or her rights. But the state, too, figures here only in a relativized role, as one institution among others, the special institution which acts for the *general interest*, and according to the principles of *public service*.

The Third Republic transforms the strictly juridical relationship between individual and state by constructing an administrative law which explicitly dispenses with natural right. The citizen is accorded the entitlement under this law to compensation for the accidental infringement by the state of his or her private interest: what the citizen is disqualified from doing is to inculpate the state at the level of its sovereignty. The juridical self-limitation and 'self-control' of the executive power is balanced by the designation of a range of 'governmental acts' which are immune to legal challenge.[70] This juridical reserve area of executive power is, Donzelot suggests, the qualification which – in the French situation – calculations of security impose as a condition of the political feasibility of a liberal democracy.

This simultaneous relativization of state and individual is accompanied by a new attenuation of the opposition between the public and the private. Sociological thought and social law regard the private domain as a 'virtual' public sphere. Authority in the sphere of private enterprise and private institutions is assimilated to, and (partially and indirectly) juridically integrated with, the 'public-service' preoccupation of the state. The disciplinary 'private law' of the factories is in part subordinated to the public norms prescribed in health and safety legislation, in part opened up to collective negotiation with organized labour, and, for the rest, underwritten in the interest of public order as a necessary branch of public law.[71] At the same time, the state's new role in industrial security as the provider of workers' accident insurance permits it to emulate the standing of its private commercial forerunners as a new kind of 'public institution'.

This new political jurisprudence reorganizes some of the basic terms of classical political theory. The (Lockean) principle of property, with its perturbing connotations of irreducible prerogative, is now made subordinate to the (Fergusonian) category of interest, which in turn is now considered itself in a primarily collectivist perspective, mediated through institutions and associations. Social right now becomes, in the terms of the German jurist Jhering, the stake and resultant of a continuous process of collective struggle.[72] While the right of civil resistance is suppressed, the right of social struggle and *revendication* is endorsed as necessary and even obligatory. In the France of 1900, this conjunction expresses the political rationale of a regime which accepts the role of organized labour, while mobilizing armed force to suppress workers' meetings: a political incorporation of the class struggle.

It is also the beginning of the end of a certain idea of civil society: the historical point from which it becomes decreasingly plausible to think of civil society as an autonomous order which confronts and experiences the state as an alien, incursive force. This is not because society is swallowed up by some new avatar of the police state. Rather, the activities of government themselves begin to acquire something of the density and complexity formerly attributed by liberal thinkers to the object of government, namely commercial society or the market. What entitles us to think of this as a transmutation, rather than a liquidation or betrayal, of liberal government is that it proceeds not by the institution of a new reason of state but by the invention, out of a range of extraneous sources, of a set of new roles *for* the state. The state of the mid-nineteenth-century crisis, variously perceived as at once minimal and monstrous, gives way to a state which is at once activist and disengaged, interventionist and neutral.

The new discipline of sociology, Donzelot argues, plays a catalytic part in this new settlement, by providing the basis for a principled resolution of the liberal riddle of the state's *agenda* and *non-agenda*. The concept of *solidarity*, developed by Durkheim and elaborated into a political doctrine by Duguit and Léon Bourgeois, prescribes, in competition and complementarity with Hauriou's doctrine of the institution, a framework and mode of state intervention which is to address itself to 'the forms of the social bond, rather than the structure of society itself'.[73] *Solidarisme*, which in the France of the 1900s becomes something approaching a dominant ideology (not unlike the British liberal collectivism of the same era) provides a political rationale for a series of radical innovations in social administration.[74] Solidarity is often cited today as the basic, enduring value of socialist ethics. But, as with civil society, it is advisable also to keep in mind the history of this term's *instrumental* value.

Foucault's comment on the concept of civil society as a 'transactional' one, an encoding of the mobile interface of the game between government and governed, has its amplest verification in the new universe of what Donzelot has called 'the social'. 'The social' designates a field of governmental action operating always within and upon the discrepancies between economy and society, principles each of which comes to be envisaged in terms of its incipient prejudice to the other, so that the politics of prosperity (Keynes, Beveridge) centres on the effort to establish positive feedbacks for their reciprocal correction.

This is a situation where 'the state itself is no longer at stake in social relations, but stands outside them and becomes their guarantor of progress':[75] the focal question of politics is now not so much the justification of state action as the governability of the social. Here is one kind of relevance of a study of the police state to the characterization of the modern situation. The police state posited an immediate identity between the state and 'the whole body of civil society'; twentieth-century government postulates not an identity but an isomorphism, an intimate symbiosis between the cares of government and the travails of a society exposed to the conflicts and crises of the liberal economy. The self-perception of society takes the form of a catalogue of problems of government.

During the early decades of the twentieth century, the modified legal-governmental armature of capitalist production is caught up in a mutation of economic class relations, namely the 'Taylorist' transaction by which the working class concedes increased productivity and the abandonment of the syndicalist demands for self-management in return for improved wages and working conditions and a dismantling of the old, carceral methods of factory discipline.[76] This historic transaction has been interpreted by some as marking a reformist stalemate of the class struggle within the labour process, compensated, however, by a shifting of the terrain of struggle to the sphere of the state and the issues of social rights and the social wage, vehicles (at least implicitly) for more radically insurrectionist objectives. In different ways, this appreciation of events seems both incontestable and profoundly misleading. The new governmental system which culminates in Keynesianism and the welfare state is indeed characterized by permanent contention among all political forces over the manner in which the state should most beneficially fulfil its socioeconomic vocation: a debate punctuated by warnings from both left and right, nourished by the cautionary totalitarian lessons of the century, against the perversion of that vocation. And yet, as Donzelot points out, the dramatically conflicting terms in which this argument is pursued stand in inverse proportion to the relatively narrow bandwidth of effective dissent over the adjustment and management of this socio-economic system.

In suggesting that the society we now live in has become, pre-eminently, a 'society of security', part of what Foucault no doubt has in mind is that our government involves a distinctive circuit of inter-dependence between *political security* and *social security*. It is misleading to envisage the dimension of the social as the state's antagonist or its prey. In modern liberal societies the social is, *characteristically*, the field of governmental security considered in its widest sense; the register of government forms, in return, the surface of inscription of the security problems of society. A certain vital dimension of this situation is masked by the model of a total sociopolitical system (benign or otherwise) within which state action performs as a determined servo-mechanism. The rationality of security is, in Foucault's rendering, as inherently open-ended one: it deals not just in closed circuits of control, but in calculations of the possible and the probable. The relation of government with which it corresponds is not solely a functional, but also a 'transactional' one: it structures government as a practice of problematization, a zone of (partially) open interplay between the exercise of power and everything that escapes its grip.

Foucault contrasts to the somewhat monolithic object postulated by theories of the state the perspective of a 'multiple regime of governmentality': this phrase might serve as the rubric for an analysis of a range of distinct *modes of pluralization* of modern government which contribute towards the relativization of the notional boundary line between state and society. Among these processes might be numbered the initiating roles of private individuals and organizations in the exploring and defining of new governmental tasks (many aspects of social hygiene and medicine, social work, the collection of statistics, etc.); the cross-fertilizing interplay between different agencies and expertises, public and private alike (criminal anthropology and accident insurance; industrial sociology and psychotherapy); the propensity of the public institutions of government to secrete within themselves their own multiple spaces of partly autonomous authority; the different forms of delegation represented by the 'quango', municipal privatization and the renewed mobilization of the voluntary sector in social services; the function accorded to representative organizations of capital and labour as 'social partners' engaged in tripartite dialogue with the state, bodies whose function as (to use Keith Middlemas's apt term)[77] governing institutions rests on their positioning exterior to the state apparatus.

In what sense can this state of affairs still be called a form of 'real liberalism'? One rough and tentative answer might be the following. The fulfilment of the liberal idea in government consists – over and above the economic market in commodities and services, whose existence founds the classic liberal attribution of an autonomous rationality to the processes of civil society – in a recasting of the interface between state and society in the form of something like a second-order market of governmental goods and services. It becomes the ambition of neo-liberalism to implicate the individual citizen, as player and partner, into this market game.

PASSAGES FROM CIVIL SOCIETY TO THE SOCIAL MARKET

Modern governmental rationality, Foucault has said, is simultaneously about individualizing and totalizing: that is, about finding answers to the question of what it is for an individual, and for a society or population of individuals, to be governed or governable. Different ways of posing and answering these questions compete and coexist with one another. Here I will look at some of our contributors' reconstructions of these different modern governmental problems and techniques. Taken together, they can perhaps be read as chapters in a genealogy of the welfare state – and of neo-liberalism.

In his *Histoire de la Folie*, nearly two decades prior to his lectures on liberalism, Foucault had dealt with the effect on thinking about the treatment of the insane of the eighteenth century's concern with devising a form of social citizenship appropriate to a bourgeois political and economic culture. Adam Ferguson's notion of civil society can be read, as we have seen, as being concerned with the task of inventing a wider political framework than that of the juridical society of contract, capable of encompassing individual economic agency within a governable order. The new mental medicine of the same era addresses the problem of grounding a para-legal jurisdiction over persons who could no longer acceptably be disposed of through the police-internment institutions of the *ancien régime*. 'It was one of the eighteenth century's constant endeavours', Foucault writes here, 'to adjust with the old juridical notion of the "subject of law" the contemporary experience of social man . . . Nineteenth-century positivist medicine is the heir to this effort of the Enlightenment.' [78] Our modern conception of 'normal man' is a construct dating from this era; 'its conceptual space lies not within the space of nature, but in a system which identifies the *socius* with the subject of law. The abnormal person of mental illness, 'a slowly constituted product representing the mythical union of the juridically incompetent subject with the man who is perceived as perturber of a group', emerges in conjunction with a new style of public sensibility towards the socially irregular. Foucault notes how in the civil society of the first French republic, where the transparent realm of public opinion is instituted as the seat of sovereignty, the political citizen is called upon to assume, in the place of the bureaucracy and police of despotism, the combined role of 'man of law' and 'man of government'. The postulation of an interior domain of mental norms parallels and presupposes this promotion of an alert public sensorium of civil vigilance.

Among the most active subsequent proponents of this style of civic conscience might be numbered the 'social economists' of the first half of the nineteenth century, whose neglected contribution to the political thought of early industrial society is examined in Chapter 7 by Giovanna Procacci. Social economy is a critique of political economy. To enable the wealth-creating mechanisms of the economy to work, it is not enough to remove the obstacles of obsolete privileges and the restrictive policies of mercantilism. It is (in one sense) society itself, or the *social* problem, which represents the main obstacle to economic progress: the very existence of (in another sense) an economic society, of that form or order which is a necessary condition for freedom, is something which has yet to be realized and made secure, and which, as the social economists argue, cannot be realized merely through the institution of a proletarianized production process. The amoral, pre-industrial solidarities of the poor come to be perceived as the purest form of *social danger*, not only as the obvious political threat of riot and sedition, but also, and more profoundly, as the danger of an anti-society, a zone of unchecked instinct incompatible with truly social being, blocking the free circulation of labour and capital which is the *sine qua non* of liberal welfare. The unaided logic of the economy cannot suffice to make a *homo economicus* out of the Malthusian pauper's chronic deficit of interest, his 'refusal to make the passage from penury to well-being'.[79] Indeed, the personality and mentality of economic man cannot be implanted among the populations of the poor except as part of a broader strategy, a political technology designed to form, out of the recalcitrant material of the 'dangerous classes', something more than economic man: a social citizen.

'There is a strange paradox here: if it is claimed that crime is a phenomenon with a social aetiology, how is it possible to say that the criminal has an asocial nature?'[80] By the mid-nineteenth century, the Enlightenment configuration of society, nature and history has been turned inside out. In psychiatry, the insane are regarded less and less as casualties of progress and modern living, and more and more as the detritus of social evolution. Madness, Foucault wrote in *Histoire de la Folie*:

> becomes the stigmata of a class which has abandoned the forms of social ethics; and just at the moment when the philosophical concept of alienation acquires a historical significance through the economic analysis of labour, the medical and psychological concept of alienation totally detaches itself from history, becoming a moral critique conducted in the name of the compromised salvation of the species.[81]

Pasquale Pasquino (Chapter 12) places the beginnings of criminology within the same conjuncture of thought:

> In the midst of social evolution and by virtue of its progress, archaic residues can be identified comprising those individuals and groups who, outpaced and left behind by the proper rate of evolution, endanger by their existence the orderly functioning of the whole.[82]

While the social economists discover that the utilitarian calculus of interests is an instilled rather than a natural habit, jurists begin to question the utilitarian theory of deterrence as the basis of criminal law. The failure of deterrent punishment is attributed to the fact that the criminal, being an *ipso facto* abnormal being, is inaccessible to normal measures of rational dissuasion. The social contract theory of the juridical foundation of society is inverted: law is now simply one of the manifestations of a historically mutable society; criminal jurisprudence must contribute to the service and defence of society's vital interests by adapting the law to the dictates of evolutionary progress. The criminal is not an erring individual but a specimen of a dangerous biological milieu, a separate race. The task of justice, as social defence, accordingly consists on this view not so much in deterrence as in neutralization and prophylaxis. In this respect, social defence joins hands with social economy and social hygiene.

Social defence has another modern corollary: social security. One of the conditions which François Ewald suggests has made possible the modern world of 'sociopolitics' within which these strategies cohabit is the entry into social thought of the *philosophy of risk* (see Chapter 10). Risk, enterprise, progress and modernity are genealogically interdependent social ideas. The constellations they have formed are often, to a retrospective gaze, paradoxical ones. One of Ewald's most striking *aperçus* is that risk is a capital, not a spirit of capitalism. The very terms 'risk' and 'risk taking' are products of insurance techniques. The insurer 'takes' the risk of the client entrepreneur: capitalism's Faustian daring depends on this capability of taking the risk out of risk. Risk becomes in the nineteenth century, as Ewald shows, a kind of omnivorous, encyclopaedizing principle for the objectification of possible experience – not only of the hazards of personal life and private venture, but also of the common venture of society. The rhetoric of daring modernity and its risk-pledged soul seems, on this account, to have been mobilized in the nineteenth century largely for the purpose of exhorting the working class to adopt the bourgeois ethic of individual life, conceived as an enterprise which providently reckons with its chances of death and disablement as 'professional risks' of human existence. But these ideas of prudence and enterprise themselves undergo a considerable mutation at the hands of later nineteenth-century jurisprudence.

Daniel Defert and François Ewald (Chapters 10 and 11) study the nodal role played in this story by the problem of industrial accidents (a topic, alongside the struggles in the prisons, of intense concern in French left-wing politics in the early 1970s). Read alongside Ian Hacking's parallel epistemological survey of statistical thinking over the same period (Chapter 9), their chapters present a picture of an epoch-making mutation of metaphysical ideas catalyzed around the middle of the nineteenth century by the techniques of insurance: a statistically grounded conception of social causality, a philosophy of civil law as the redistribution of *social risk*, rather than the retribution of private culpability, and a novel notion of faultless civil responsibility. Michel Foucault, in an important essay on the notion of the dangerous individual, has suggested that this latter idea may also have helped to make the criminologists' new preventative doctrines juridically feasible:

In a rather strange way, this depenalization of civil liability offered a model for a penal law based on the idea of the criminal anthropologists. After all, what is a born criminal or degenerate or a criminal personality, if not a person who, by reason of a causal chain which is difficult to reconstruct, carries a particularly high index of criminal probability, and is, himself, a criminal risk?[83]

The concept of social risk makes it possible for insurance technologies to be applied to social problems in a way which can be presented as creative simultaneously of social justice and social solidarity. One of the important strengths of the insurance technique is its use of *expertise* as the technical basis of a form of security which can dispense with recourse to continuous surveillance:

> Insurance contributes in a large degree to the solidarization of interests . . . Insurance is one of the main ties of what we call – to use a favourite phrase of the jurists – *real solidarity, or solidarity through things*, as contrasted with personal or moral solidarity.[84]

The idea which Foucault notes as characteristic of the science of police, the distinctive concern with governing 'men and things', acquires a new dimension here. 'Solidarity through things' corresponds to a double process of social capitalization. As Daniel Defert points out, it is the worker's own life, rather than his labour power, which first enters into commercial calculation as an economic form of *human capital*. The forms of welfare with which the new institutions of social security concern themselves are precisely those human assets which are capable of capitalization as *risks*; while the premiums which serve to insure those capitals provide an efficient channel for storing proletarian savings in capitalist institutions.

The apprehension of social laws, of a specifically sociological order of causality, is one of the preconditions for social legislation and labour law. If society is in some sense the general subject of human enterprises, then the form of the industrial enterprise and labour relations within the enterprise can no longer plausibly be consigned in law to regulation solely by the private provisions of the contract of employment. The progressive conquest through industrial legislation of protective rights for workers and unions signifies, in Jacques Donzelot's formulation, 'enlarging the sphere of the *statutory* at the expense of the *contractual* in the definition of the employment contract'. 'We move from a situation in which man defines himself as a worker confronting capital to a situation in which he is an employee of society (whether in work or not).' [85]

While this measure of economic socialization is still designed to leave society 'free' of direct responsibility for running the economy and guaranteeing work, the vocation assumed by society as the taker of risk *par excellence* confers a new guarantee of security on the state. For if the state is the only institution within society possessed of that degree of solidity requisite in a provider of certain kinds of insurance, it then follows that the continued survival of the state will itself become a peculiarly social imperative. The existence of insurance is, as Ewald puts it, an insurance against revolution. The corresponding political principle of solidarity, shaped by insurance practice and refined as sociological theory by Durkheim and others,[86] forms the core of the historic governmental compromise implemented in France under the Third Republic around the turn of the century. Other scholars have documented the shaping presence of similar and analogous ideas in British politics and society of the same period.[87]

VERSIONS OF NEO-LIBERALISM

In his Collège de France lectures of 1979, Foucault followed his discussion of the liberal art of government as initially propounded in the eighteenth century with a review of the post-war currents of thought which present the most radical challenges to the system of the welfare state, some of whose derivations have been outlined above. Foucault discussed neo-liberalism in three post-war Western countries: West Germany, the United States and France.

A group of jurists and economists who came collectively to be known (from their participation in the journal *Ordo*) as the *Ordoliberalen* played a significant role as architects of the post-war West German state and attributed a novel governmental meaning to the idea of a market. For them, the market is no longer to be thought of as being a spontaneous (albeit historically conditioned) quasi-natural reality, recognition of whose existence constrains government to the practice of *laissez-faire*. The market is not a natural social reality at all; and what is incumbent on government is to conduct a policy towards society such that it is possible for a market to exist and function. For the *Ordoliberalen*, the political and economic disasters of recent memory are not to be attributed to a flaw or contradiction in a market economy, for, while the market is not a natural phenomenon, neither is it subject to an essential logical incoherence: it is not that liberalism has been tried and found wanting in modern Germany; it has been found inexpedient and not been tried.

In Adenauer's embryonic republic, these thinkers' conception of the open space of the market and the artificial game of its competitive freedom functions as the principle of a possible new political legitimacy. Prosperity, Foucault suggests, has a meaning in the West German state which is comparable to the meaning for Weber's Protestant capitalists of worldly wealth as a mark of divine election: prosperity is the engine for creation, out of national political annihilation, of a new basis of civil adhesion and prospective sovereignty.

For the *Ordoliberalen*, the major problem of social politics within this framework is not the anti-social effects of the economic market, but the anti-competitive effects of society. To enable competition to function in the real world, a certain framework of positive institutional and juridical forms is required: a capitalist *system*. West German neo-liberalism, Foucault remarks, stands within the sociological heritage of Max Weber in accepting, albeit only tacitly, the justice of the Marxian critique of classical political economy in regard to the latter's failure to take account of the legal and institutional dimensions of the market. Capitalism's prospects of survival depend on a broadening of economic thinking so as to make proper provision for these systemic historic contingencies. Not only is the juridical domain not to be regarded as a mere superstructure of the economic, but an economic government conducted in the name of the market must accord a central role to a new kind of legal activism, a 'conscious notion of economic right'.

There is an important transmutation here in the received liberal notion of the 'rule of law' as the form of government most consonant with the workings of a market economy. Whereas for the eighteenth century the formalism of law was a recipe for minimal intervention (*laissez-faire*, in its more passive sense), the *Ordoliberalen* envisage an extensive juridical interventionism with a vocation to further the game of enterprise as a pervasive style of conduct, diffusing the enterprise-form throughout the social fabric as its generalized principle of functioning. One of their number, Alexander von Rüstow, significantly terms this policy a *Vitalpolitik*, or 'vital policy'. He proposes that the whole ensemble of individual life be structured as the pursuit of a range of different enterprises: a person's relation to his or her self, his or her professional activity, family, personal property, environment, etc., are all to be given the ethos and structure of the enterprise-form. This 'vital policy' will foster a process of 'creation of ethical and cultural values' within society.[88]

As Foucault points out, Rüstow's thinking here seems almost to make an admission that the principle of enterprise bears its own seeds of contradiction, since the idea of *Vitalpolitik* (so evocative of the strain of statist edification which distinguishes the West German polity) seems in large part designed to palliate the disaggregating effects of market competition on the social body. An altogether more radical consistency is manifested, Foucault suggests, in the work of the post-war American school of neo-liberal economists centred at Chicago. Whereas the West Germans propound a government of the social conducted in the name of the economic, the more adventurous among the Americans (Foucault looks in particular at the ideas of Gary C. Becker) propose a global redescription of the social as a form of the economic.

This operation works by a progressive enlargement of the territory of economic theory by a series of redefinitions of its object, starting out from the neo-classical formula that economics concerns the study of all behaviours involving the allocation of scarce resources to alternative ends. Now it is proposed that economics concerns all purposive conduct entailing strategic choices between alternative paths, means and instruments; or, yet more broadly, *all rational conduct* (including rational thought, as a variety of rational conduct); or again, finally, all conduct, rational or irrational, which responds to its environment in a non-random fashion, or 'recognizes reality'.

Economics thus becomes an 'approach' capable in principle of addressing the totality of human behaviour, and, consequently, of envisaging a coherent, purely economic method of programming the totality of governmental action. The neo-liberal *homo economicus* is both a reactivation and a radical inversion of the economic agent as conceived by the liberalism of Smith, Hume or Ferguson. The reactivation consists in positing a fundamental human faculty of *choice*, a principle which empowers economic calculation effectively to sweep aside the anthropological categories and frameworks of the human and social sciences. Foucault shows this consequence emerging very strikingly in Becker's economic analysis of crime and crime prevention, which manages to dispense entirely with the psychological or biological presuppositions common in this domain; here *homo economicus* drives out the nineteenth-century *homo criminalis*. Likewise, the category of order is dethroned from its usual ruling role in legal thought, by being reinterpreted as meaning a *supply of law-abiding behaviour*: that is to say, of a commodity whose price is determined by a level of effective social demand. Becker thinks that it is reasonable to calculate the quantity of crimes which it is worth a society's while to tolerate.

But the great departure here from eighteenth-century precedent is that, whereas *homo economicus* originally meant that subject the springs of whose activity must remain forever untouchable by government, the American neo-liberal *homo economicus* is *manipulable man*, man who is perpetually responsive to modifications in his environment. Economic government here joins hands with behaviourism.

This is only part of the story. American neo-liberalism also claims to effect a decisive enrichment of the economic understanding of human work, here again inspired by its overall view of economic activity as a discriminating use of available resources. The abstract appearance of labour in industrial society is not, as Marxism supposes, a real effect of the logic of capital, but rather a misperception caused by political economy's failure to produce a concrete qualitative analysis of labour, an account of 'what work is for the worker'. Work for the worker means, according to the neo-liberals, the use of resources of skill, aptitude and competence which comprise the worker's human capital, to obtain earnings which constitute the revenue on that capital. Human capital is composed of two components, an innate component of bodily and genetic equipment, and an acquired component of aptitudes produced as a result of investment in the provision of appropriate environmental stimuli: nurture, education, etc. Economically, an aptitude is defined as a quasi-machine for the production of a value; this applies not only to the production of commodities, but also to the production of satisfactions. As one neo-liberal thinker puts it, an education which, for example, confers on its possessor the capacity for such satisfactions as logical discourse or the appreciation of works of art can be considered economically akin to a consumer durable which has the peculiarity of being inseparable from its owner. From this point of view, then, the individual producer-consumer is in a novel sense not just an enterprise, but the entrepreneur of himself or herself.

However one assesses these schools of neo-liberal thought and the extent of their influence, there are a number of signs that a neo-liberal rationality of government is beginning to play a part in the life of several Western societies. To begin with a simple indicator, it would seem that a part of the unexpected political acceptability of renewed mass unemployment can be plausibly attributed to the wide diffusion of the notion of the individual as enterprise. The idea of one's life as the enterprise of oneself implies that there is a sense in which one remains always continuously employed in (at least) that one enterprise, and that it is a part of the continuous business of living to make adequate provision for the preservation, reproduction and reconstruction of one's own human capital. This is the 'care of the self' which government commends as the corrective to collective greed. It is noticeable that where, as in the tentatively neo-liberal France of the 1970s, the 'right to permanent retraining' has been translated into a kind of institutional reality, its technical content has relied heavily on the contributions of the 'new psychological culture', that cornucopia of techniques of the self which symbiotize aptitude with self-awareness and performance with self-realization (not to mention self-presentation). What some cultural critics diagnose as the triumph of auto-consuming narcissism can perhaps be more adequately understood as a part of the managerialization of personal identity and personal relations which accompanies the capitalization of the meaning of life.

Closely allied to these developments is the move which Jacques

Donzelot describes in Chapter 13 towards a modified conception of social risk, which shifts the emphasis from the principle of collective indemnification of ills and injuries attendant on life in society, towards a greater stress on the individual's civic obligation to moderate the burden of risk which he or she imposes on society, by participating, for example, in preventive health-care programmes. In Donzelot's terms, the shift from contract to status in social welfare relations begins to go into reverse. It is not that social guarantees are annulled or their mechanisms dismantled, but that these henceforth become, as it were, a part of each player's stakes in the game of socioeconomic negotiations. There is a kind of generalized floating of currencies. Even the idea of progress, that guarantee of guarantees, loses its overarching virtue. The notion of the social body as a collective subject committed to the reparation of the injuries suffered by its individual members gives place to a role for the state as a custodian of a collective reality-principle, distributing the disciplines of the competitive world market throughout the interstices of the social body. The state presents itself as the referee in an ongoing transaction in which one partner strives to enhance the value of his or her life, while another endeavours to economize on the cost of that life.

Robert Castel in Chapter 14 shows how this new regime of concerted action in risk prevention is capable of extension into a prospective new sector of socio-environmental interventionism. Computerization and administrative rationalization begin to make possible for the first time a 'real' government of population which, by co-ordinating appropriate forms of expertise and assessment, is capable of identifying all those individual members of society who can be deemed, by manifesting some combination of a specified range of 'factors', to present a significant, albeit involuntary, risk to themselves or to the community. The classic techniques of carceral and tutelary management of the deviant or asocial, developed over the past 150 years by psychiatry and social work, begin to be displaced by a form of management based instead on non-custodial guidance. *Handicap* (defined in a newly extended sense) serves as a focal category for the rationalization of individual destinies. Following the precedent of British wartime achievements in mobilizing previously neglected sources of manpower, a method of risk management is devised which consists in contriving not special spaces of neutralizing containment for the abnormal, but special circuits of protected mobility for handicapped individuals, within the greater game of the social market. Daniel Defert notes in Chapter 11 how, in the development of the techniques of insurance, differential methods of actuarial analysis make possible the subdivision, out of an insurable population, of various specific strata of 'marginal risk'. Castel suggests that 'marginality itself, instead of remaining an unexplored or dangerous territory, can become an organized zone within the social, towards which those persons will be directed who are incapable of following more competitive pathways'.

Even a marginal or 'handicapped' majority is in this sense by no means an impossible prospect, especially given the way that the ethos of continued retraining is capable of sanctioning a regime of downward mobility. The priority for a neo-liberal government here is not indeed to annul, but rather to dissipate and disperse the mass of handicaps present in a given society. Where this objective cannot be achieved, the alternative may be what is called in English a 'community' solution: that is to say, a specialized regime of environmental intervention designed to contain high local concentrations of risk.

FOUCAULT'S POLITICS

The kinds of political analysis presented in this volume are not liable or designed to inspire and guide new political movements, transform the current agendas of political debate, or generate new plans for the organization of societies. Their claim would be, at most, to help political thought to grasp certain present realities, thus perhaps providing a more informed basis for practical choice and imagination. But this would already be more than a modest service. It would be fair to add that, notwithstanding the scandalously subversive image which has often been presented of Foucault's philosophy, the ideas put forward by this current of work – above all, and most simply, the idea that a fresh effort of thought has to be made in order to understand our times – are not wildly at odds with some parts of received contemporary political wisdom, albeit ones which they may in places claim to have slightly anticipated, and to which they may still be able to contribute a distinctive critical and analytical edge.

The formulae of politics have changed. The phobic representation of a potentially totalitarian state, which is at the same time made the addressee of unlimited social demands, loses it credibility. Government itself assumes the discourse of critique, challenging the rigidities and privileges of a blocked society. Promises of expanded individual autonomy and responsibility become electoral necessities. Our authors do not share a common assessment of the value and consequences of these changes. I shall limit myself here, by way of a conclusion, to drawing out some connections between aspects of Foucault's own later philosophy and his comments on political matters.

Foucault said in an interview that nothing is an evil in itself, but everything is dangerous, with the consequence that things are always liable to go wrong, but also that there is always the possibility of doing something to prevent this, since disaster is never ineluctable. The position is avowedly a somewhat pessimistic, but also an activist one.[89] This statement fits in well with Foucault's comments in his discussions of modern Western forms of government. Foucault denied that the welfare state is either a variant or an incipient version of the modern totalitarian (or Party) state, Stalinist, national socialist or fascist; on this point Foucault seems to find the critiques of neo-liberal thinkers like Hayek less than convincing. On the other hand, Foucault also found some of the law and order policy tendencies of French government in the 1970s (under the regime which was at the same time experimenting with neo-liberal ideas) to present a dangerous new elaboration of doctrines of social defence dating from the nineteenth-century antecedents of the welfare state.[90]

These views went with a distinctive political attitude to reality. Foucault advocated in political culture a lowered threshold of acceptance of governmental abuses, but also an accompanying reduction in the level of political paranoia (particularly paranoia in the service of revolutionary militancy): the fear (and hope) that the existing state will finally show its true colours as a police state blunts, he argued, our ability to perceive and refuse the unacceptable in what actually exists.

Foucault was, one might say, sufficiently respectful of the historical effectiveness of liberalism as an art of government to doubt the liberal (and Marxist) nightmare of an ever-expansionist and despotic tendency within the state. Although not enamoured of minimalist anarcho-liberal individualism in the manner of Robert Nozick, Foucault does seem to have been (at least) intrigued by the properties of liberalism as a form of knowledge calculated to limit power by persuading government of its own incapacity; by the notion of the rule of law as the architecture of a pluralist social space;[91] and by the German neo-liberals' way of conceiving the social market as a game of freedom sustained by governmental artifice and invention.

His basic objection is to the project (neo-liberal or socialist) of a guaranteed freedom or a definitive Enlightenment:

> Liberty is a *practice* . . . The liberty of men is never assured by the institutions and laws that are intended to guarantee them. This is why almost all of these laws and institutions are quite capable of being turned around. Not because they are ambiguous, but simply because 'liberty' is what must be exercised . . . I think it can never be inherent in the structure of things to guarantee the exercise of freedom. The guarantee of freedom is freedom.[92]

Uncertainty, however, does not imply absence of rigour:

> I do not say that power, by its nature, is an ill; I say that power, by its mechanisms, is infinite (which is not to say that it is all-powerful; on the contrary). The rules that limit it can never be sufficiently rigorous; to

deprive it of the occasions it seizes on, universal principles can never be made sufficiently strict. Against power there must always be opposed unbreakable laws and unrestrictable rights.[93]

There is a kind of Sisyphean optimism in the later Foucault, or perhaps one can say there are two different strands of optimism, which promise to converge in his thinking about government. One is contained in the very idea of governmental rationality, in the sense that Foucault seems to think that the very possibility of an activity or way of governing can be conditional on the availability of a certain notion of its rationality, which may in turn need, in order to be operable, to be credible to the governed as well as the governing: here, the notion of rationality seems clearly to exceed the merely utilitarian bounds of a technique or know-how, as in Foucault's earlier thinking about the relations between power and knowledge. The second is the thought that ideas which go without saying, which make possible existing practices and our existing conceptions of ourselves, may be more contingent, recent and modifiable than we think. The two themes connect because government is a 'conduct of conduct': because the relation between government and the governed passes, to a perhaps ever-increasing extent, through the manner in which governed individuals are willing to exist as subjects. One might see the consequent meaning of the relation of government for Foucault as a kind of moral judo (or 'agonism'): to the extent that the governed are engaged, in their individuality, by the propositions and provisions of government, government makes its own rationality intimately their affair: politics becomes, in a new sense, answerable to ethics.

In 1981 Foucault thought that a governmental 'logic of the left' could be developed on this kind of basis, involving a way for the governed to work with government, without any assumption of compliance or complicity, on actual and common problems. 'To work with a government implies neither subjection nor global acceptance. One can simultaneously work and be restive. I even think that the two go together.' [94] In the event, these hopes seem to have been disappointed. But we have no reason to think that they were abandoned.

NOTES

1. Michel Foucault, *Résumés des cours*, Collège de France, Paris, 1989.
2. Jacques Donzelot, *L'Invention du Social*, Paris, 1984; Francois Ewald, *L'Etat Providence*, Paris, 1986; Ian Hacking, *The Taming of Chance*, Cambridge, 1990; Giovanna Procacci's book on the government of poverty will be published in 1991.
3. 'Omnes et singulatim: Towards a Critique of "Political Reason" ', in *The Tanner Lectures of Human Values II*, ed. Sterling McMurrin, Utah, 1981.

4. I attempt to address this point in my 'Afterword' to Michel Foucault, *Power/Knowledge*, Brighton, 1980, p. 245ff.
5. 'The Subject and Power', in Hubert L. Dreyfus and Paul Rabinow, *Michel Foucault, Beyond Structuralism and Hermeneutics*, Brighton, 1982, pp. 221–2.
6. I discuss this in 'The Soul of the Citizen', in *Max Weber, Rationality and Modernity*, eds. Sam Whimster and Scott Lash, London, 1987, pp. 293–316.
7. Robert Badinter, 'Au nom des mots', in *Michel Foucault, Une histoire de la vérité*, Syros, Paris, 1985, pp. 73–5.
8. Etienne Thuau, *Raison d'Etat et pensée politique à l'époque de Richelieu*, Paris, 1966, pp. 360ff.
9. Michel Foucault, *Tanner Lectures*; cf. Ernst Kantorowicz, 'Christus-Fiscus', in *The King's Two Bodies*, pp. 164–92.
10. Foucault, 'Omnes et singulatim', p. 246.
11. *Ibid.*, pp. 251–2.
12. Foucault, Lecture, Collège de France, 1978; Pasquino, this volume, p. 109.
13. Max Weber, *The Religion of China*, New York, 1951, pp. 169, 181–3.
14. Friedrich Meinecke, *Machiavellism: The Doctrine of Raison d'Etat and its Place in Modern History*, London, 1957.
15. Max Weber, *General Economic History*, London, 1927.
16. Pasquale Pasquino, 'Michel Foucault 1926–84: The will to knowledge', *Economy and Society*, vol. 15, no. 1, 97–101. Gerhard Oestreich, *Neo-Stoicism and the Early Modern State*, trans. D. McLintock, Cambridge, 1983.
17. Oestreich ibid, p. 157.
18. Thomas Hobbes, *De Cive* 1.1., in *Man and Citizen*, Brighton, 1972.
19. Adam Smith, *Wealth of Nations*, Chicago, 1976, p. 477.
20. *Ibid.*, p. 478.
21. *Ibid.*, p. 208.
22. Lecture, Collège de France, 28 March 1979.
23. See Foucault's discussion of this point in 'Questions of Method', this volume, p. 75ff.
24. Adam Smith, *Lectures on Jurisprudence*, ed. R. C. Meek, D. D. Raphael, P. G. Stein, Oxford, 1978, p. 349.
25. *Ibid.*, p. 486.
26. Lecture, Collège de France, 5 April 1978.
27. Albert O. Hirschman, *The Passions and the Interests: Political Arguments for Capitalism before its Triumph*, Princeton, 1977, pp. 86–7.
28. *Ibid.*, p. 87.
29. *Ibid.*, p. 104.
30. Michel Foucault, 'History of Systems of Thought, 1979', trans. James Bernauer, *Philosophy and Social Criticism* vol. 8, no. 3 (Fall, 1981), pp. 355–6.
31. *Ibid.*, p. 357.
32. Jeremy Bentham, *The Civil Code*, Part I, Ch. 2..
33. *Ibid.*
34. Lecture, Collège de France, 5 April 1978.
35. *Ibid.*
36. *Ibid.*
37. David Hume, *Treatise on Human Nature*, Oxford, 1978, Book 2, p. 416.
38. Halévy, *The Growth of Philosophical Radicalism*, London, 1972, p. 118.
39. Lecture, Collège de France, 4 April 1979.
40. *Ibid.*
41. Lecture, Collège de France, 4 April 1979.

42. Michel Foucault, *Histoire de la Folie*, Paris, 1972, p. 431.
43. *Ibid.*, p. 435.
44. *Ibid.*, p. 435.
45. *Ibid.*, p. 436.
46. Adam Smith, *Wealth of Nations*, Book V, Part II, Chapter I.
47. Michel Foucault, *Discipline and Punish*, Harmondsworth, 1979, p. 213.
48. Ibid. p. 140f.
49. Jacques Donzelot, *L'invention du social*, p. 144.
50. *Ibid.*, pp. 145–6.
51. Michael Ignatieff, *A Just Measure of Pain*, Harmondsworth, 1989, p. 112. (This reprinting omits a comment on Foucault present in the 1978 original edition.)
52. Francois Ewald, 'Présentation', *Les Temps Modernes*, 354, January 1979, pp. 974–5.
53. Lecture, Collège de France, 1978.
54. Karl Polanyi, *The Great Transformation* Boston, 1957, p. 140.
55. C. B. Macpherson, *The Political Theory of Possessive Individualism*, Oxford, 1962.
56. Cf. Jacques Donzelot, *L'invention du social*.
57. *Ibid.*, Ch. 1.
58. *Ibid.*
59. *Ibid.*
60. Karl Marx, 'Critique of the Gotha Program', in *The First International and After*, Harmondsworth, 1974, p. 355.
61. Karl Marx, First Draft of 'The Civil War in France', in *The First International and After*, Harmondsworth, 1974, p. 253.
62. Pasquale Pasquino, 'Lorenz von Stein' and Karl-Herman Kästner, 'From the social question to the social state' trans. Keith Tribe, *Economy and Society* vol. 10, no. 1, February 1981, pp. 1–25.
63. Reinhardt Koselleck, *Vergangene Zukunft, Zur Semantik geschichtlicher Zeiten*, Suhrkamp, 1979, trans. Keith Tribe as *Futures Past* . . .
64. Alexis de Tocqueville, *De la démocratie en Amerique*, Part 4, Chapter 8, cited in Reinhardt Koselleck, ibid.
65. Karl Marx and Friedrich Engels, *The Communist Manifesto*, in *The Revolutions of 1848*, Harmondsworth, 1973, p. 70.
66. Cf. Chs. 7 and 11 below.
67. Jacques Donzelot, *L'invention du social*, Ch. 11.
68. Catherine Mével, 'Du droit public au droit disciplinaire', in C. Mével, J. Donzelot, J.-D. Grousson, *Introduction aux transformations des rapports de pouvoir dans l'entreprise*, Contrat de recherches, Ministère de Travail, December 1979, p. 45. This quotation is by Viviani (French Minister of Labour), *le temps*, 25 February 1908.
69. Jacques Donzelot, *L'invention du social*, pp. 86–103.
70. Cf. Catherine Mével, 'Du droit public', p. 52; Hauriou, *La science sociale traditionelle*, 1986.
71. Jacques Donzelot, *L'invention du social*, pp. 141ff.
72. Cf. Catherine Mével, 'Du droit public'.
73. Jacques Donzelot, this volume, p. 173.
74. Jacques Douzelot, *L'invention du social*, ch. 2.
75. Jacques Donzelot, this volume, p. 173.
76. *Ibid.*, pp. 254–5.
77. Keith Middlemas, *Politics in Industrial Society*, London, Deutsch 1979.
78. *Histoire de la Folie*, p. 146.

79. Giovanna Procacci, this volume, p. 155.
80. Pasquale Pasquino, this volume, p. 242.
81. *Histoire de la Folie*, p. 399.
82. Pasquale Pasquino, this volume, p. 242.
83. 'About the concept of the "dangerous individual" in 19th century legal psychiatry', trans. Alan Baudot and Jane Couchman, *International Journal of Law and Psychiatry*, 1978, p. 16.
84. A. Chauffon, *Les assurances, leur passé, leur présent, leur avenir*, Paris, 1884, p. 303. Cited by François Ewald, this volume, p. 207.
85. Jacques Donzelot, 'The poverty of political culture', *Ideology and Consciousness*, vol. 5, Spring 1979, p. 81.
86. Cf above, pp. 32–4.
87. Notably Michael Freeden, *The New Liberalism*, Oxford, 1978.
88. Cf. my 'The Soul of the Citizen', p. 314f, and A. von Rüstow, *Rede und Antwort*, Ludwigsburg, 1963, pp. 36, 82.
89. 'On the Genealogy of Ethics: An Overview of Work in Progress', interview with Hubert Dreyfus and Paul Rabinow, in *The Foucault Reader*, ed. Paul Rabinow, Harmondsworth, 1986, (reprinted from 2nd edition of Dreyfus and Rabinow, op. cit.) p. 343.
90. 'La stratégie du pourtoir', *Nouvel observateur*, 759, 28 May 1979, p. 57. 'Le citron et le lait', *Le Monde*, 21 October 1979, p. 14. The title of Foucault's Collège de France lectures for 1976 was 'Il faut défendre la société', in Michel Foucault, *Résumé des cours 1970–82*, Paris, 1989.
91. Robert Badinter, 'Au nom des mots', in *Michel Foucault. Une histoire de la vérité*, Syros, Paris, 1985, p. 73–5.
92. 'Space, Knowledge and Power', in *The Foucault Reader*, op. cit., p. 245.
93. 'Inutile de se soulever?', *Le Monde*, 11 May 1979, pp. 1–2, trans. James Bernauer as 'Is it useless to revolt?', *Philosophy and Social Criticism*, Spring 1981, pp. 1–9.
94. 'Est-il donc nécessaire de penser?', *Libération*, 30–31 May 1981, p. 21. trans., with an afterword, by Thomas Keenan as 'Is it really important to think?', *Philosophy and Social Criticism*, vol. 9, no. 1, Spring 1982, pp. 29–40.

CHAPTER TWO

Politics and the study of discourse
Michel Foucault

Does a mode of thought which introduces discontinuity and the constraints of system into the history of the mind not remove all basis for a progressive political intervention? Does it not lead to the following dilemma: either the acceptance of the system or the appeal to an unconditioned event, to an irruption of exterior violence which alone is capable of upsetting the system?

I have chosen the last of the questions put to me (not without regret for abandoning the other ones) firstly, because at first sight it surprised me, and because I quickly became convinced that it concerned the very heart of my work; because it allowed me to locate at least a few of the answers which I would have liked to give to the other questions; because it posed the challenge which no theoretical work can today avoid.

I must admit that you have characterized with extreme accuracy what I have undertaken to do, and that you have at the same time identified the point of inevitable discord: 'to introduce discontinuity and the constraints of system into the history of the mind'. Yes, I accept this diagnosis almost entirely. Yes, I recognize that this is scarcely a justifiable move. With diabolical pertinence you have succeeded in giving a definition of my work to which I cannot avoid subscribing, but for which no one would ever reasonably wish to assume responsibility. I suddenly sense how bizarre my position is, how strange and illegitimate. And I now perceive how far this work, which was no doubt somewhat solitary, but always patient, with no other law but its own, and sufficiently diligent, I thought, to be able to stand up for itself, has deviated from the best-established norms, how jarring it was bound to seem. However, two or three details in the very accurate definition which you propose bother me, preventing me from (perhaps allowing me to avoid) agreeing completely with it.

First of all you use the word *system* in the singular. Now, I am a pluralist. What I mean is this. (You will allow me, I think, to speak not only of my last book, but also of those which preceded it; this is because together they form a cluster of researches whose themes and chrono-logical reference points are quite adjacent; also because each one constitutes a descriptive experiment which contrasts with and therefore relates to the other two in certain of its traits.) I am a pluralist: the problem which I have set myself is that of the *individualization* of discourses. There exist criteria for individualizing discourses which are known and reliable (or almost): the linguistic system to which they belong, the identity of the subject which holds them together. But there are other criteria, no less familiar but much more enigmatic. When one speaks in the singular of *psychiatry*, or of *medicine*, or of *grammar*, or of *biology*, or of *economics*, what is one speaking of? What are these curious entities which one believes one can recognize at first glance, but whose limits one would have some difficulty in defining? Some of them seem to date back to the dawn of history (medicine, mathematics), whereas others have appeared quite recently (economics, psychiatry), and still others have perhaps disappeared (casuistry). Each discourse undergoes constant change as new utterances (*énoncés*) are added to it (consider the strange entities of sociology or psychology which have been continually making fresh starts ever since their inception). There are:

1. Criteria of *formation*. What individualizes a discourse such as political economy or general grammar is not the unity of its object, nor its formal structure; nor the coherence of its conceptual architecture, nor its fundamental philosophical choices; it is rather the existence of a set of rules of formation for *all* its objects (however scattered they may be), *all* its operations (which can often neither be superposed nor serially connected), *all* its concepts (which may very well be incompatible), *all* its theoretical options (which are often mutually exclusive). There is an individualized discursive formation whenever it is possible to define such a set of rules.

2. Criteria of *transformation* or of *threshold*. I shall say natural history or psychopathology are units of discourse, if I can define the set of conditions which must have been jointly fulfilled at a precise moment of time, for it to have been possible for its objects, operations, concepts and theoretical options to have been formed; if I can define what internal modifications it was capable of; finally if I can define at what threshold of transformation new rules of formation came into effect.

3. Criteria of *correlation*. I will say that clinical medicine is an autonomous discursive formation if I can define the set of relations which define and situate it among other types of discourse (such as biology, chemistry, political theory or the analysis of society) and in the non-discursive context in which it functions (institutions, social relations, economic and political conjuncture).

These criteria make it possible to substitute differentiated analyses for the theme of totalizing history ('the progress of reason', 'the spirit of a century'). They make it possible to describe, as the *episteme* of a period, not the sum of its knowledge, nor the general style of its research, but the divergence, the distances, the oppositions, the differences, the relations of its various scientific discourses: the *episteme* is not *a sort of grand underlying theory*, it is a space of *dispersion*, it is an *open and doubtless indefinitely describable field of relationships*. They make it possible furthermore to describe not a universal history which sweeps along all the sciences in a single common trajectory, but the kinds of history – that is to say, of remanences and transformation – characteristics of different discourses (the history of mathematics does not follow the same model as the history of biology, which itself does not share the same model as psychopathology): *the episteme is not a slice of history* common to all the sciences: it is *a simultaneous play of specific remanences*. Lastly, they make it possible to establish the respective siting of different sorts of threshold: for nothing proves in advance (and nothing demonstrates after examination either) that their chronology will be the same for all types of discourses; the thresholds which one can describe for the analysis of language at the beginning of the nineteenth century has doubtless no counterpart in the history of mathematics; and, what is more paradoxical, the threshold of formation for political economy (marked by Ricardo) does not coincide with the constitution – by Marx – of an analysis of society and of history.[1] *The episteme is not a general developmental stage of reason, it is a complex relationship of successive displacements.*

Nothing, you see, is more foreign to me than the quest for a sovereign, unique and constraining form. I do not seek to detect, starting from diverse signs, the unitary spirit of an epoch, the general form of its consciousness, a kind of *Weltanschauung*. Nor have I described the emergence and eclipse of a formal structure destined to reign for a time over all the manifestations of thought: I have not written the history of a syncopated transcendental. Nor, finally, have I described the thoughts and sensibilities of centuries coming to life, stammering their first words, battling and fading away like vast phantoms acting out their shadow-play on the backdrop of history. I have studied, in turn, ensembles of discourse: I have characterized them; I have defined the play of rules, of transformations, of thresholds, of remanences. I have collated different discourses and described their clusters and relations. Wherever it seemed necessary, I have been prepared to add to the *plurality* of distinguishable systems.

Mine is, you say, a thought which 'emphasizes discontinuity'. This, indeed, is a notion whose importance today – for historians as much as for linguists – cannot be underestimated. But the use of the singular does not appear to me to be entirely suitable. Here again, I am a pluralist. My problem is to substitute the analysis of *different types of transformation* for the abstract, general and monotonous form of 'change' which so easily serves as our means for conceptualizing succession. This has two implications: first, bracketing all the old forms of strained continuity which ordinarily serve to attenuate the raw fact of change (tradition, influence, habits of thought, broad mental forms, constraints of the human mind), and insistently making plain instead all the intensity of difference, establishing a painstaking record of deviation; second, bracketing all psychological explanations of change (the genius of great inventors, crises of conscience, the appearance of a new cast of mind), and turning instead to define as carefully as possible the transformation which, I do not say provoked, but *constituted* change. In short, substituting for the theme of *becoming* (general form, abstract element, first cause and universal effect, a confused mixture of the identical and the new) an analysis of *transformations* in their specificity.

1. *Within* a given discursive formation, detecting the changes which affect its objects, operations, concepts, theoretical options. Thus, one can distinguish (I limit myself to the example of *general grammar*): changes by deduction or implication (the theory of the verb as copula implied the distinction between a substantive root and a verbal inflexion); changes by generalization (extension to the verb of the theory of the noun as designation, with the consequent disappearance of the verb-copula theory); changes by limitation (the concept of attribute is specified by the syntactical notion of the complement); changes by shift between complementary objectives (from the project of constructing a universal and transparently intelligible language to the search for the secrets hidden in the most primitive of languages); changes by passing to the other term of a pair of alternatives (primacy of vowels or primacy of consonants in the constitution of roots); changes through permutation of dependencies (one can found the theory of the verb on the theory of the noun, or the other way round); changes by exclusion or inclusion (the analysis of languages as systems of representative signs supersedes the investigation of their marks of kinship, a task which, however, is then reactivated by the quest for a primitive language). These different types of change together constitute the set of *derivations* characteristic of a discursive formation.

2. Detecting the changes which affect the discursive formations *themselves*:

(a) the displacement of boundaries which define the field of possible objects (the medical object at the beginning of the nineteenth century ceases to be positioned on a surface of classification; it is mapped out in the three-dimensional space of the body);

(b) the new position and role occupied by the speaking subject in discourse (the subject in the discourse of eighteenth-century naturalists becomes exclusively a subject *looking* according to a grid of perceptions, and *noting* according to a code; it ceases to be a listening, interpreting, deciphering subject);

(c) a new mode of functioning of language with respect to objects (beginning with Tournefort the role of naturalists' discourse is not to penetrate into things, to capture the language which they secretly enclose, to reveal it to the light of day; but to provide a surface of transcription where the form, the number, the size and the disposition of elements can be translated in a univocal manner);

(d) a new form of localization and circulation of discourse within society (clinical discourse is not formulated in the same places, it does not go through the same process of inscription, it is not diffused, amassed, conserved or contested in the same way as the medical discourse of the eighteenth century).

All these changes of a type superior to the preceding ones define the transformations which affect the discursive areas themselves: their *mutations*.

3. Lastly, there are changes which simultaneously affect several discursive formations:

(a) the inversion of a diagram of hierarchy (during the classical period the analysis of language had a leading role which it lost, in the first years of the nineteenth century, to biology);

(b) change in the nature of the directing principle (classical grammar, as a general theory of signs, provided an analytical tool guaranteed to be transposable to other areas; in the nineteenth century, certain concepts in biology become available for 'metaphorical' importation: organism, function, life thus engender social organization, social function, the life of words and languages);

(c) functional displacements; the theory of the continuity of beings which in the eighteenth century belonged to philosophical discourse is taken over in the nineteenth century by the discourse of science.

These transformations, which operate at a higher level than the two preceding groups, typify changes peculiar to the *episteme* itself, its *redistributions*.

There you have a small collection of perhaps fifteen or so different kinds of recognizable modification affecting discourses. You see why I would rather it were said that I have stressed not *discontinuity*, but *discontinuities* (that is to say, the different transformations which it is possible to describe concerning two states of discourse). But the important thing for me, now, is not to establish an exhaustive typology of these transformations.

57

1. The important thing is to give the monotonous and empty concept of 'change' a content, that of the play of specified modifications. The history of 'ideas' or 'sciences' must no longer be written as a mere checklist of innovations, it must be a descriptive analysis of the different transformations effectuated.[2]

2. What is important to me is to avoid mixing up such an analysis with a procedure of psychological diagnosis. It is legitimate to ask whether a person whose work manifests a certain set of modifications was a genius, whether he or she underwent certain significant experiences in early childhood, etc. But it is another thing to describe the field of possibilities, the forms of operations, the types of transformation which characterize that person's discursive practice.

3. What is important to me is to show that there are not on the one hand inert discourses, which are already more than half dead, and on the other hand, an all-powerful subject which manipulates them, overturns them, renews them; but that discoursing subjects form a part of the discursive field – they have their place within it (and their possibilities of displacements) and their function (and their possibilities of functional mutation). Discourse is not a place into which the subjectivity irrupts; it is a space of differentiated subject-positions and subject-functions.

4. What is important to me above all is to define the play of dependencies between all these transformations:

(a) *intradiscursive* dependencies (between the objects, operations and concepts of a single formation);
(b) *interdiscursive* dependencies (between different discursive formations: such as the correlations which I studied in *The Order of Things* between natural history, economics, grammar and the theory of representation);
(c) *extradiscursive* dependencies (between discursive transformations and transformations outside of discourse: for example, the correlations studied in *Histoire de la Folie* and *Birth of the Clinic* between medical discourse and a whole play of economic, political and social changes).

I would like to substitute the study of this whole play of dependencies for the uniform, simple activity of allocating causality; and by suspending the indefinitely renewed privileges of cause, to render apparent the polymorphous interweaving of correlations. As you see, there is absolutely no question here of substituting the category of the 'discontinuous' for the no less abstract and general one of the 'continuous'. I am attempting, on the contrary, to show that discontinuity is not a monotonous and unthinkable void between events, which one must hasten to fill with the dim plenitude of cause or by the nimble bottle-imp of mind (the one solution being the symmetrical twin of the other), but that it is a play of specific transformations, each one different from the next (with its own conditions, rules and level of impact), linked together according to schemes of dependence. History is the descriptive analysis and the theory of these transformations.

There is one final point on which I hope I can be more brief. You use the expression: 'history of the mind'. In fact, I intended rather to write a history of discourse. You'll ask: 'What's the difference? You do not study the texts which you take as raw material according to their grammatical structure: you do not describe the semantic field which they cover: it is not language which is your object. What then? What do you seek if not to discover the thought which animates them, to reconstitute the representations of which they are a durable, but doubtless unfaithful, transcription? What are you aiming for if not to rediscover behind them the intention of the men who formulated them, the meanings which, deliberately or unknowingly, they set down, that imperceptible supplement to the linguistic system which is something like the beginning of liberty or the history of the mind?'

Therein lies, perhaps, the essential point. You are right: what I am analyzing in discourse is not the system of its language, nor, in a general sense, its formal rules of construction: for I am not concerned about knowing what makes it legitimate, or makes it intelligible, or allows it to serve in communication. The question which I ask is not about codes but about events: the law of *existence* of statements, that which rendered them possible – them and none other in their place: the conditions of their singular emergence; their correlation with other previous or simultaneous events, discursive or otherwise. But I try to answer this question without referring to the consciousness, obscure or explicit, of speaking subjects; without referring the facts of discourse to the will – perhaps involuntary – of their authors; without having recourse to that intention of saying which always goes beyond what is actually said; without trying to capture the fugitive unheard subtlety of a word which has no text.

What I am doing is thus neither a formalization nor an exegesis, but an *archaeology*: that is to say, as its name indicates only too obviously, the description of an *archive*. By this word, I do not mean the mass of texts gathered together at a given period, those from some past epoch which have survived erasure. I mean the set of rules which at a given period and for a given society define:

1. The limits and forms of the *sayable*. What is it possible to speak of? What is the constituted domain of discourse? What type of discursivity is assigned to this or that domain (what is allocated as matter

59

for narrative treatment; for descriptive science; for literary formulation)?

2. The limits and forms of *conservation*. Which utterances are destined to disappear without any trace? Which are destined, on the other hand, to enter into human memory through ritual recitation, pedagogy, amusement, festival, publicity? Which are marked down as reusable, and to what ends? Which utterances are put into circulation, and among what groups? Which are repressed and censored?

3. The limits and forms of *memory* as it appears in different discursive formations. Which utterances does everyone recognize as valid, or debatable, or definitely invalid? Which have been abandoned as negligible, and which have been excluded as foreign? What types of relationship are established between the system of present statements and the body of past ones?

4. The limits and forms of *reactivation*. Among the discourses of previous epochs or of foreign cultures, which are retained, which are valued, which are imported, which are attempts made to reconstitute? And what is done with them, what transformations are worked upon them (commentary, exegesis, analysis), what system of appreciation are applied to them, what role are they given to play?

5. The limits and forms of *appropriation*. What individuals, what groups or classes have access to a particular kind of discourse? How is the relationship institutionalized between the discourse, speakers and its destined audience? How is the relationship of the discourse to its author indicated and defined? How is struggle for control of discourses conducted between classes, nations, linguistic, cultural or ethnic collectivities?

This is the context within which the analyses I am undertaking have their identity and direction. Thus, what I am writing is not a history of the mind which follows the succession of its forms or the density of its sedimented significations: I do not question discourses about their silently intended meanings, but about the fact and the conditions of their manifest appearance; not about the contents which they may conceal, but about the transformations which they have effected; not about the sense preserved within them like a perpetual origin, but about the field where they coexist, reside and disappear. It is a question of an analysis of the discourses in the dimension of their exteriority. From this there follow three consequences:

1. To treat discourse not as a theme of reviving *commentary*, but as a *monument*[3] to be described in its intrinsic configuration.
2. To investigate not the laws of construction of discourse, as is done by those who use structural methods, but its conditions of existence.[4]

3. To relate the discourse not to a thought, mind or subject which engendered it, but to the practical field in which it is deployed.

Excuse me for being so lengthy and laborious, just to propose three slight changes in your definition and to request your agreement that we speak of my work as an attempt to introduce 'the diversity of *systems* and the play of *discontinuities* into the history of *discourses*'. Do not think that I want to fudge the issue; or that I seek to avoid the point of your question by endlessly quibbling about its terms. But this preliminary understanding was necessary. Now I have my back to the wall. I must answer.

The question I will try to answer is not, to be sure, that of whether *I* am a reactionary; nor whether my texts are (in themselves, intrinsically, by virtue of a certain number of clearly coded signs). You ask me a much more serious question, the only one, I believe, which can legitimately be asked. You question me on the *relationships* between what I say and a certain political practice.

It seems to me that two kinds of answer can be made to this question. One answer concerns the critical operations which my discourse carries out in its own domain (the history of ideas, of sciences, of thought, of knowledge . . .): was what it tries to remove from circulation indispensable to a progressive politics? The other answer concerns the field of analysis and the realm of objects which my discourse attempts to make visible: how can these ideas be articulated with the effective practice of a progressive politics?

I shall sum up as follows the critical operations which I have undertaken.

1. *To establish limits* where the history of thought, in its traditional form, posited an unbounded space. In particular:

(a) to challenge the great interpretative postulate that the realm of discourse admits of no assignable frontiers, that dumb objects and silence itself are peopled with words, and that where no word is heard any more one can still hear the deep buried murmur of meaning, that what men do not say is a continuation of their speaking, that a world of slumbering texts awaits us even in the empty pages of our history. Against this kind of thinking, I would like to put forward the notion that the discourses are limited practical domains which have their boundaries, their rules of formation, their conditions of existence: the historical base of discourse is not some other, more profound discourse, at once identical and different;

(b) to challenge the idea of a sovereign subject which arrives from elsewhere to enliven the inertia of linguistic codes, and sets down in discourse the indelible trace of its freedom; to challenge the idea of a subjectivity which constitutes meanings and then transcribes them into discourse. Against these ideas I would advocate a procedure which maps the roles and operations exhausted by different 'discoursing' subjects;

(c) to challenge the idea of an indefinitely receding origin, and the idea that, in the realm of thought, the role of history is to reawaken that which has been forgotten, to uncover the occluded, to rejoin what has been blocked from us. Against this, I would propose an analysis of historically definite discursive systems for which it is possibe to assign thresholds and conditions of birth and disappearance.

To establish such limits, to question these three themes of origin, subject and implicit meaning, is to undertake (a difficult task, as the intensity of the resistance demonstrates) to liberate the discursive field from the historical–transcendental structure which nineteenth-century philosophy imposed on it.

2. *To eliminate certain ill-considered oppositions.* Here are a few of these in increasing order of importance: the opposition between the vitality of innovations and the dead weight of tradition, the inertia of acquired knowledge, the old beaten tracks of thought; the opposition between average forms of knowledge (representing its everyday mediocrity) and deviant forms (which manifest the singularity or solitude of genius); the opposition between periods of stability and universal convergence, and moments of effervescence when minds enter into crisis, when sensibilities are metamorphosed, when all notions are revised, overturned, revivified or cast into indefinite desuetude. For these dichotomies I would like to substitute the analysis of a field of simultaneous differences (which define at a given period the possible dispersal of knowledge) and of successive differences (which define a set of transformations, their hierarchy, their dependence, their level). Where previously the history was told of traditions and invention, of the old and the new, of the dead and the living, of the closed and the open, of the static and the dynamic, I would set out to tell the history of perpetual differences; more precisely, to tell the history of ideas as a set of specified and descriptive forms of non-identity. And thus I would like to free it of the triple metaphor which has encumbered it for more than a century: the evolutionist metaphor which imposes on it a subdivision into regressive and adaptive forms; the biological metaphor, which distinguishes the inert from the living; the dynamic metaphor which opposes movement and immobility.

3. *To end the denegation* of discourse in its specific existence (and this for me is the most important of the critical operations I have undertaken). This denegation comprises several aspects:

(a) that of never treating discourse except as an indifferent element devoid of intrinsic consistency or inherent laws: a pure surface of translation for mute objects; a simple site of expression for thoughts, imaginings, knowledges, unconscious themes;

(b) that of only ever recognizing in discourse patternings which are psychological and individualizing (the *oeuvre* of an author, and – why not, indeed? – his youthful and mature output), linguistic or rhetorical (a genre, a style), or semantic (an idea, a theme);

(c) that of supposing that all operations are conducted prior to discourse and outside of it, in the ideality of thought or the silent gravity of practices; that discourse, consequently, is no more than a meagre additive, an almost impalpable fringe surrounding things and thought; a surplus which *goes without saying*, since it does nothing else except say what is said.

To this denial, I would object that discourse is not nothing or almost nothing. And what it is – what defines its intrinsic consistence, what makes it available to historical analysis – is not what was 'meant' (that obscure and heavy charge of intentions, imagined as carrying far more weight, in its shadowy way, than what is said); it is not what has remained mute (those imposing things which do not speak, but leave their traceable marks, their dark profile set off against the light surface of what is said): discourse is constituted by the difference between what one could say correctly at one period (under the rules of grammar and logic) and what is actually said. The discursive field is, at a specific moment, the law of this difference. It thus defines a certain number of operations which are not of the order of linguistic construction or formal deduction. It deploys a 'neutral' domain in which speech and writing may vary the system of their opposition and the difference of their functioning. It consists of a whole group of regulated practices which do not merely involve giving a visible outward embodiment to the agile inwardness of thought, or providing the solidity of things with a surface of manifestation capable of duplicating them. At the bottom of this denegation imposed on discourse (in favour of the polarities of thought and language, history and truth, speech and writing, words and things), there was the refusal to recognize that in discourse something is formed, according to clearly definable rules; that this something exists, subsists, changes, disappears, according to equally definable rules; in short, that alongside everything a society can produce (alongside: that is to say, in a determinate relationship with) there is the formation and transformation of 'things said'. It is the history of these 'things said' that I have undertaken to write.

4. Finally, the last of these critical tasks (one which sums up and embraces all the others): *freeing from their uncertain status* that set of disciplines which we call history of ideas, history of sciences, history of

thought, history of knowledge, concepts or consciousness. This uncertainty manifests itself in several ways:

(a) difficulties about demarcating domains. Where does the history of sciences end, where does the history of opinions and beliefs begin? How are the history of concepts and the history of notions or themes to be separated? Where does the boundary lie between the history of knowledge and the history of imagination?

(b) the difficulty of defining the objects of study: is one writing the history of what has been known, learned, forgotten, or the history of mental forms, or the history of their interference? Is one writing the history of characteristic mental traits shared by people of one period or one culture? Is one describing a collective mind? Is one analyzing the (teleological or genetic) history of reason?

(c) the difficulty of establishing a relationship between these facts of thought or knowledge and other areas of historical analysis: must one treat them as signs of something else (a social relation, a political situation, an economic determination)? Or as its result? Or as its refraction through a consciousness? Or as the symbolic expression of its total form?

In place of all these uncertainties, I would like to put the analysis of discourse itself in its conditions of formation, in its serial modification, and in the play of its dependencies and correlations. Discourses would thus be seen in a describable relationship with a set of other practices. Instead of having to deal with an economic, social or political history which encompasses a history of thought (which would be its expression and something like its duplicate), instead of having to deal with a history of ideas attributed (through a play of signs and expressions, or by relations of causality) to extrinsic conditions, one would be dealing with a history of discursive practices in the specific relationships which link them to other practices. It is not a matter of composing a *global history* – which would regroup all its elements around one principle or one form – but rather of opening out a field of *general history* within which one could describe the singularity of practices, the play of their relations, the form of their dependencies. In the space of such a general history, the historical analysis of discursive practices could be circumscribed as a specific discipline.

These are more or less the critical operations that I have undertaken. And now may I ask you to attest the question I would put to those who may be getting alarmed: 'Is progressive politics tied (in its theoretical reflexion) to the themes of meaning, origin, constituent subject, in short, to all the themes which guarantee in history the inexhaustible presence of a Logos, the sovereignty of a pure subject, the deep teleology of a primeval destination? Is progressive politics tied to such a form of analysis – rather than to one which questions it? And is such politics bound to all the dynamic, biological, evolutionist metaphors that serve to mask the difficult problem of historical change – or, on the contrary, to their meticulous destruction? And further: is there some necessary kinship between progressive politics and refusing to recognize discourse as anything more than a shallow transparency which shimmers for a moment at the margins of things and of thoughts, and then vanishes? Can one believe that such a politics has an interest in rehashing one more time the theme – from which I would have thought that the existence and practice of the revolutionary discourse in Europe for more than 200 years might by now have freed us – that words are just air, extraneous matter, a fluttering of wings scarcely audible among the earnestness of history and the silence of thought? Finally, must one think that progressive politics must be linked to the devaluation of discursive practices, so that the history of the mind, consciousness, reason, knowledge, ideas or opinions can be assured of triumph in its uncertain ideality?'

It seems to me that I can see, on the contrary, quite clearly the perilous ease which the politics you speak of would accord itself, if it assumed the guarantee provided by a primitive foundation or a transcendental teleology, if it habitually exploited the metaphorization of time through images of life or models of movement, if it abandoned the difficult task of a general analysis of practices, their relations and transformations, and instead took refuge in a global history of totalities, expressive relationships, symbolic values and secret significations invested in thoughts and things.

You are entitled to say to me: 'This is all very well: the critical operations you are making are not as blameworthy as they might seem at first glance. But, after all, how can grubbing about in the origins of philology, economics or pathological anatomy be of concern for politics, or be counted among the problems which matter to it today? There was a time when philosophers did not display such zeal in devoting themselves to the dust of archives . . .' Here, roughly, is what I would say in reply. There exists at present a problem which is not without importance for political practice: that of the status, of the conditions of exercise, functioning and institutionalization of scientific discourses. That is what I have undertaken to analyze historically – choosing the discourses which possess not the strongest epistemological structure (mathematics or physics), but the densest and most complex field of positivity (medicine, economics, the human sciences).

Take a simple example: the formation of clinical discourse characteristic of medicine roughly from the early nineteenth century to the present. I choose it because we are dealing with a very definite, historical fact, and because one cannot backdate its emergence to some remote primeval ur-form; because it would be extremely frivolous to denounce it as a 'pseudo-science'; and above all because it is easy to grasp 'intuitively' the relationship between this scientific mutation and a certain number of precise political events: those which one groups – even on the European scale – under the title of the French Revolution. The problem is to give to this still vague relationship an analytical content.

First hypothesis: the consciousness of men changed under the influence of other economic, social, political changes, and their perception of disease thereby altered: they recognized its political consequences (social malaise, discontent, revolt in populations whose health is deficient); they saw its economic implications (the desire of employers to have at their disposal a healthy workforce; the wish of the bourgeoisie in power to transfer to the state the costs of assistance); they superimposed on the medical question their conception of society (a single medicine with universal value, with two distinct fields of application: the hospital for the poor classes; liberal, competitive practice for the rich); they transcribed their new conception of the world (desacralization of the corpse, enabling autopsies to be performed; a greater importance accorded the living body as an instrument of work; concern for health replacing preoccupation with salvation). In all this, there are many things which are true; but, on the one hand, they do not account for the formation of a scientific discourse; and, on the other, these changed attitudes and the effects that follow from them were themselves only possible to the extent that the medical discourse achieved a new status.

Second hypothesis: the fundamental notions of clinical medicine can be derived, by transposition, from a political practice or at least from the theoretical forms in which it is reflected. The ideas of organic solidarity, of functional cohesion, of tissulary communication, the abandonment of the principle of classification in favour of an analysis of the whole body corresponded to a political practice which revealed, beneath surface strata which were still feudal, social relationships of a functional and economic type. Or again, does not the rejection of the earlier conception of diseases as a great family of quasi-botanical species, and the effort to understand illness as a pathological process with its point of insertion, its mechanism of development, its cause and, ultimately, its therapy, correspond to the project current among the ruling social class of mastering the world not just by means of theoretical knowledge, but also by a set of applicable knowledges, and its decision to accept no longer as natural that which imposed itself as a limit and an ill? Such analyses do not appear to me to answer the problem either, because they avoid the essential question: in the midst of other discourses, and in a general way, of other practices, what must the mode of existence and function of medical discourse be, in order for such transpositions or correspondence to be produced?

That is why I would displace my investigative point of attack from those addressed by traditional analyses. If indeed there is a link between political practice and medical discourse, it is not, it seems to me, because this practice first changed men's consciousness, their way of perceiving things or conceiving of the world, and then finally the form of their knowledge and its content; nor is it because it was initially reflected, in a more or less clear and systematic manner, in concepts, notions or themes which were subsequently imported into medicine. The link is much more direct: political practice did not transform the meaning or form of medical discourse, but the conditions of its emergence, insertion and functioning; it transformed the mode of existence of medical discourse. And this came about through a certain number of operations which I have described elsewhere and will summarize here: new criteria to designate those who receive by law the right to hold a medical discourse; a new delineation of the medical object through the application of another scale of observation which is superimposed on the first without erasing it (sickness observed statistically on the level of a population); a new law of assistance which makes the hospital into a space for observation and medical intervention (a space which is organized furthermore, according to an economic principle, since the sick person who benefits from care must compensate through the medical lesson which he provides; he pays for the right of being cared for by the obligation of being examined, up to the moment of death); a new mode of recording, preserving, accumulating, diffusing and teaching medical discourse (which is no longer so much a manifestation of a physician's experience as, primarily, a document of disease); a new mode of functioning of medical discourse as part of a system of administrative and political control of the population (society as such is considered and 'treated' according to the categories of health and pathology).

Now – and this is where the analysis becomes complex – these transformations in the conditions of existence and functioning of the discourse are not 'reflected', 'transposed' or 'expressed' in the concepts, methods and utterances of medicine. They modify their rules of formation. What is transformed by political practice is not medical 'objects' (it is quite evident that political practice does not change 'morbid species' into 'lesional infections'), but the system which provides a possible object for medical discourse (a population surveyed and listed; a total pathological evolution in an individual whose antecedents are ascertained and whose disturbances or their remissions are daily observed; an autopsied anatomical space); what is transformed by political practice is not the methods of analysis but the system of their formation (administrative recordings of illness, deaths, their causes, admissions and discharges from hospital; the establishment of medical archives; relations between medical personnel and patients in the hospital); what is transformed by political practice is not the concepts but their system of formation (the substitution of the concept of 'tissue' for that of 'solid' is obviously not the result of a political change; but what political practice modifies is the system of formation of concepts: for the intermittent notation of the effects of illness, and for the hypothetical assignment of a functional cause, it allowed the substitution of a close-textured, almost unbroken, grid of deep anatomical observation, with the localization of anomalies, their field of dispersion and their eventual routes of diffusion). The haste with which one ordinarily relates the contents of a scientific discourse to a political practice obscures, to my mind, the level at which the articulation can be described in precise terms.

It seems to me that, starting from such an analysis, one can understand the following.

1. How to describe a set of relations between a scientific discourse and a political practice, the details of which it is possible to follow and whose forms of subordination one can grasp. These are very direct relations in the sense that they no longer have to pass through the consciousness of speaking subjects or the efficacy of thought. But they are indirect to the extent that the statements of a scientific discourse can no longer be considered as the immediate expression of a social relation or of an economic situation.

2. How to assign its proper role to political practice in relation to a scientific discourse. Political practice does not have a thaumaturgic creative role: it does not bring forth sciences out of nothing; it transforms the conditions of existence and systems of functioning of discourse. These changes are neither arbitrary nor 'free': they operate in a domain which has its own configuration and consequently does not offer unlimited possibilities of modification. Political practice does not reduce to insignificance the consistency of the discursive field in which it operates. Nor does it have a universal, critical role. The scientificity of a science is not a matter on which judgement can be passed in the name of political practice (unless the latter claims to be, in one way or another, a theory of politics). One can, however, question the mode of existence and the functioning of a science in the name of political practice.

3. How the relations between a political practice and a discursive field can be articulated in turn on relations of another order. Thus medicine, at the beginning of the nineteenth century, is linked at once to a political practice (in a manner which I analyzed in *The Birth of the Clinic*), and to a whole group of 'interdiscursive' changes which occurred simultaneously

in several disciplines (replacing an analysis of order and of taxonomical characters with an analysis of solidarities, functionings and successive series, which I described in *The Order of Things*).

4. How phenomena which are customarily highlighted (influence, communication of models, transfer and metaphorization of concepts) have their historical condition of possibility in these prior modifications: for example, the importation into the analysis of society of biological concepts such as those of organism, function, evolution, even sickness, was able to play the role we know it had in the nineteenth century (a much more important, much more ideologically charged role than the 'naturalist' comparisons of preceding periods) only by virtue of the status accorded to medical discourse by political practice.

This protracted illustration is all intended to convey one point, but one that particularly matters to me: to show how what I am attempting to bring out through my analysis – the *positivity* of discourses, their conditions of existence, the systems which regulate their emergence, functioning and transformation – can concern political practice; to show what political practice can make of them; to convince you that, by sketching this theory of scientific discourse as an ensemble of regulated practices which are articulated in an analyzable fashion upon other practices, I am not just amusing myself by making the game more complicated, a diversion for a few lively minds. I am trying to define how, to what extent, at what level discourses, particularly scientific discourses, can be objects of a political practice, and in what system of dependence they can exist in relation to it.

Allow me once more to put before you the question I am posing. Are we all not too familiar with the kind of politics which answers in terms of thought or consciousness, in terms of pure ideality or psychological traits, when one speaks to it of a practice, of its conditions, of its rules, of its historical transformations? Are we all not too familiar with the kind of politics which, since the beginning of the nineteenth century, obstinately insists on seeing in the immense domain of practice only an epiphany of triumphant reason, or deciphering in it only the historico-transcendental destiny of the West? And more precisely, does not the refusal to analyze, in both their specificity and their dependence, the conditions of existence and rules of formation of scientific discourses condemn all politics to a perilous choice: either to postulate, in a style which one can, if one likes, call 'technocratic', the validity and efficacy of a scientific discourse as a universal rule for all other practices, without taking account of the fact that it is itself a regulated and conditioned practice; or else to intervene directly in the discursive field, as if it had no consistency of its own, using it as raw material for a psychological inquisition (judging what is said by who says it, or vice versa), or practising symbolic evaluations of ideas (distinguishing within a science between concepts which are 'reactionary' and those which are 'progressive')?

I should like to conclude by putting to you a few hypotheses:

1. A progressive politics is one which recognizes the historic conditions and the specific rules of a practice, whereas other politics recognize only ideal necessities, one-way determinations or the free-play of individual initiatives.
2. A progressive politics is one which sets out to define a practice's possibilities of transformation and the play of dependencies between these transformations, whereas other politics put their faith in the uniform abstraction of change or the thaumaturgical presence of genius.
3. A progressive politics does not make man or consciousness or the subject in general into the universal operator of all transformations: it defines the different levels and functions which subjects can occupy in a domain which has its own rules of formation.
4. A progressive politics does not hold that discourses are the result of mute processes or the expression of a silent consciousness; but rather that – whether as science, literature, religious utterance or political discourse – they form a practice which is articulated upon the other practices.
5. A progressive politics does not adopt an attitude towards scientific discourse of 'perpetual demand' or of 'sovereign criticism', but seeks to understand the manner in which diverse scientific discourses, in their positivity (that is to say, as practices linked to certain conditions, obedient to certain rules, susceptible to certain transformations) are part of a system of correlations with other practices.

This is the point where what I have been trying to do for about ten years now comes up against the question you are asking me. I ought to say: that is the point where your question – which is so legitimate and pertinent – reaches the heart of my own undertaking. If I were to reformulate this undertaking – under the pressure of your questioning which has not ceased to occupy me for almost two months – here is, more or less, what I would say: 'To determine, in its diverse dimensions, what the mode of existence of discourses and particularly of scientific discourses (their rules of formation, with their conditions, their dependencies, their transformations) must have been in Europe, since the seventeenth century, in order that the knowledge which is ours today could come to exist, and, more particularly, that knowledge which has taken as its domain this curious object which is man.'

I know as well as anyone how 'thankless' such research can be, how irritating it is to approach discourses not by way of the gentle, silent and intimate consciousness which expresses itself through them, but through an obscure set of anonymous rules. I know how unpleasing it must be to reveal the limits and necessities of a practice, in places where it has been customary to see the play of genius and freedom unfolding in their pure transparency. I know how provoking it is to treat as a bundle of transformations this history of discourses which, until now, was animated by the reassuring metamorphoses of life or the intentional continuity of lived experience. Finally I know, considering how each person hopes and believes he put something of 'himself' into his own discourse, when he takes it upon himself to speak, how intolerable it is to cut up, analyze, combine, recompose all these texts so that now the transfigured face of their author is never discernable. So many words amassed, so many marks on paper offered to numberless eyes, such zeal to preserve them beyond the gesture which articulates them, such a piety devoted to conserving and inscribing them in human memory – after all this, must nothing remain of the poor hand which traced them, of that disquiet which sought its calm in them, of that ended life which had nothing but them for its continuation? Are we to deny that discourse, in its deepest determination, is a 'trace', and that its murmur can be a seat of insubstantial immortality? Must we think that the time of discourse is not the time of consciousness extended into the dimension of history, nor the time of history present in the form of consciousness? Must I suppose that, in my discourse, it is not my own survival which is at stake? And that, by speaking, I do not exorcise my death, but establish it; or rather, that I suppress all interiority, and yield my utterance to an outside which is so indifferent to my life, so *neutral*, that it knows no difference between my life and my death?

I can well understand those who feel this distress. They have doubtless had difficulty enough in recognizing that their history, their economy, their social practices, the language they speak, their ancestral mythology, even the fables told them in childhood, obey rules which are not given to their consciousness; they hardly wish to be dispossesed, in addition, of this discourse in which they wish to be able to say immediately, directly, what they think, believe or imagine; they prefer to deny that discourse is a complex and differentiated practice subject to analyzable rules and transformations, rather than be deprived of this tender, consoling certainty, of being able to change, if not the world, if not life, at least their 'meaning', by the sole freshness of a word which comes only from them and remains forever close to its source. So many things, in their language, have already escaped them; they do not mean to lose, in addition, *what they say*, that little fragment of discourse – speech or writing, it matters little – whose frail and uncertain existence is necessary to prolong their life in time and space. They cannot bear – and one can understand them a little – to be told: discourse is not life; its time is not yours; in it you will not reconcile yourself with death; it is quite possible that you have killed God under the weight of all that you have said; but do not think that you will make, from all that you are saying, a man who will live longer than he. In each sentence that you pronounce – and very precisely in the one that you are busy writing at this moment, you who have been so intent, for so many pages, on answering a question in which you felt yourself personally concerned and who are going to sign this text with your name – in every sentence their reigns the nameless law, the blank indifference: 'What matter who is speaking; someone has said: what matter who is speaking.'

NOTES

1. This fact, already pointed out by Oscar Lange, explains at once the limited and perfectly circumscribed place which the concepts of Marx occupy in the epistemological field which extends from Petty to contemporary econometrics, and the founding character of these same concepts for a theory of history. I hope that I will have time to analyze the problems of historical discourse in a forthcoming work, which will be called something like *The Past and the Present: Another archeology of the human sciences*.
2. In which I follow the examples of this method given on several occasions by Georges Canguilhem.
3. I borrow this word from Georges Canguilhem. It describes, better than I have done myself, what I have wanted to do.
4. Is it necessary to point out yet again that I am not what is called a 'structuralist'?

CHAPTER THREE

Questions of method

Michel Foucault

WHY THE PRISON?

Question: Why do you see the birth of the prison, and in particular this process you call 'hurried substitution' which in the early years of the nineteenth century establishes the prison at the centre of the new penal system, as being so important?

Aren't you inclined to overstate the importance of the prison in penal history, given that other quite distinct modes of punishment (the death penalty, the penal colonies, deportation) remained in effect too? At the level of historical method, you seem to scorn explanations in terms of causality or structure, and sometimes to prioritize a description of a process which is purely one of events. No doubt it's true that the preoccupation with 'social history' has invaded historians' work in an uncontrolled manner, but, even if one does not accept the 'social' as the only valid level of historical explanation, is it right for you to throw out social history altogether from your 'interpretative diagram'?

Michel Foucault: I wouldn't want what I may have said or written to be seen as laying any claims to totality. I don't try to universalize what I say; conversely, what I don't say isn't meant to be thereby disqualified as being of no importance. My work takes place between unfinished

The discussion translated here was published in a volume edited by Michelle Perrot, entitled *L'impossible prison: Recherches sur les système pénitentiaire au XIXe siècle* (éditions du Seuil, Paris 1980). This book is an enlarged version of a set of essays in *Annales historiques de la Révolution française*, 1977:2, in which a group of historians reflect on Michel Foucault's *Discipline and Punish* and explore a number of complementary aspects of nineteenth-century penal history.

This interview is based on a round-table debate involving Michel Foucault and Maurice Agulhon, Nicole Castan, Catherine Duprat, François Ewald, Arlette Farge, Allesandro Fontana, Carlo Ginzburg, Remi Gossez, Jacques Léonard, Pasquale Pasquino, Michelle Perrot and Jacques Revel. In *L'impossible prison* it is preceded by two preliminary texts, 'L'historien et le philosophe', an essay on *Discipline and Punish* by Jacques Léonard, and 'La poussière et le nuage', a reply by Michel Foucault. As Michelle Perrot explains, the transcript of the discussion is extensively recast in its published form, Michel Foucault having revised his own contributions and the other historians' interventions having been rearranged into a series of questions by 'a collective Historian'.

abutments and anticipatory strings of dots. I like to open up a space of research, try it out, and then if it doesn't work, try again somewhere else. On many points – I am thinking especially of the relations between dialectics, genealogy and strategy – I am still working and don't yet know whether I am going to get anywhere. What I say ought to be taken as 'propositions', 'game openings' where those who may be interested are invited to join in; they are not meant as dogmatic assertions that have to be taken or left en bloc. My books aren't treatises in philosophy or studies of history: at most, they are philosophical fragments put to work in a historical field of problems.

I will attempt to answer the questions that have been posed. First, about the prison. You wonder whether it was as important as I have claimed, or whether it acted as the real focus of the penal system. I don't mean to suggest that the prison was the essential core of the entire penal system; nor am I saying that it would be impossible to approach the problems of penal history – not to speak of the history of crime in general – by other routes than the history of the prison. But it seemed to me legitimate to take the prison as my object, for two reasons. First, because it had been rather neglected in previous analyses; when people had set out to study the problems of 'the penal order' (*pénalité*) – a confused enough term in any case – they usually opted to prioritize one of two directions: either the sociological problem of the criminal population, or the juridical problem of the penal system and its basis. The actual practice of punishment was scarcely studied except, in the line of the Frankfurt school, by Rusche and Kirchheimer. There have indeed been studies of prisons as institutions, but very few of imprisonment as a general punitive practice in our societies.

My second reason for wanting to study the prison was the idea of reactivating the project of a 'genealogy of morals', one which worked by tracing the lines of transformation of what one might call 'moral technologies'. In order to get a better understanding of what is punished and why, I wanted to ask the question: *how* does one punish? This was the same procedure as I had used when dealing with madness: rather than asking *what*, in a given period, is regarded as sanity or insanity, as mental illness or normal behaviour, I wanted to ask *how* these divisions are operated. It's a method which seems to me to yield, I wouldn't say the maximum of possible illumination, but at least a fairly fruitful kind of intelligibility.

There was also, while I was writing this book, a contemporary issue relating to the prison and, more generally, to the numerous aspects of penal practice which were being brought into question. This development was noticeable not only in France but also in the United States, Britain and Italy. It would be interesting incidentally to consider why all these problems about confinement, internment, the penal dressage of individuals and their distribution, classification and objectification through forms of knowledge came to be posed so urgently at this time, well in advance of May 1968: the themes of anti-psychiatry were formulated around 1958 to 1960. The connection with the matter of the concentration camps is evident – look at Bettelheim. But one would need to analyze more closely what took place around 1960.

In this piece of research on the prisons, as in my other earlier work, the target of analysis wasn't 'institutions', 'theories' or 'ideology', but *practices* – with the aim of grasping the conditions which make these acceptable at a given moment; the hypothesis being that these types of practice are not just governed by institutions, prescribed by ideologies, guided by pragmatic circumstances – whatever role these elements may actually play – but possess up to a point their own specific regularities, logic, strategy, self-evidence and 'reason'. It is a question of analyzing a 'regime of practices' – practices being understood here as places where what is said and what is done, rules imposed and reasons given, the planned and the taken for granted meet and interconnect.

To analyze 'regimes of practices' means to analyze programmes of conduct which have both prescriptive effects regarding what is to be done (effects of 'jurisdiction'), and codifying effects regarding what is to be known (effects of 'veridiction').

So I was aiming to write a history not of the prison as an institution, but of the *practice of imprisonment*: to show its origin or, more exactly, to show how this way of doing things – ancient enough in itself – was capable of being accepted at a certain moment as a principal component of the penal system, thus coming to seem an altogether natural, self-evident and indispensable part of it.

It's a matter of shaking this false self-evidence, of demonstrating its precariousness, of making visible not its arbitrariness, but its complex interconnection with a multiplicity of historical processes, many of them of recent date. From this point of view I can say that the history of penal imprisonment exceeded my wildest hopes. All the early nineteenth-century texts and discussions testify to the astonishment at finding the prison being used as a general means of punishment – something which had not at all been what the eighteenth-century reformers had had in mind. I did not at all take this sudden change – which was what its contemporaries recognized it as being – as marking a result at which one's analysis could stop. I took this discontinuity, this in a sense 'phenomenal' set of mutations, as my starting point and tried, without eradicating it, to account for it. It was a matter not of digging down to a buried stratum of continuity, but of identifying the transformation which made this hurried transition possible.

As you know, no one is more of a continuist than I am: to recognize a discontinuity is never anything more than to register a problem that needs to be solved.

EVENTALIZATION

Question: What you have just said clears up a number of things. All the same, historians have been troubled by a sort of equivocation in your analyses, a sort of oscillation between 'hyper-rationalism' and 'infra-rationality'.

Michel Foucault: I am trying to work in the direction of what one might call 'eventalization'. Even though the 'event' has been for some while now a category little esteemed by historians, I wonder whether, understood in a certain sense, 'eventalization' may not be a useful procedure of analysis. What do I mean by this term? First of all, a breach of self-evidence. It means making visible a *singularity* at places where there is a temptation to invoke a historical constant, an immediate anthropological trait, or an obviousness which imposes itself uniformly on all. To show that things 'weren't as necessary as all that'; it wasn't as a matter of course that mad people came to be regarded as mentally ill; it wasn't self-evident that the only thing to be done with a criminal was to lock him up; it wasn't self-evident that the causes of illness were to be sought through the individual examination of bodies; and so on. A breach of self-evidence, of those self-evidences on which our knowledges, acquiescences and practices rest: this is the first theoretico-political function of 'eventalization'.

Secondly, eventalization means rediscovering the connections, encounters, supports, blockages, plays of forces, strategies and so on which at a given moment establish what subsequently counts as being self-evident, universal and necessary. In this sense one is indeed effecting a sort of multiplication or pluralization of causes.

Does this mean that one regards the singularity one is analyzing simply as a fact to be registered, a reasonless break in an inert continuum? Clearly not, since that would amount to treating continuity as a self-sufficient reality which carries its own *raison d'être* within itself.

This procedure of causal multiplication means analyzing an event according to the multiple processes which constitute it. So to analyze the practice of penal incarceration as an 'event' (not as an institutional fact or ideological effect) means to determine the processes of 'penalization' (that is, progressive insertion into the forms of legal punishment) of already existing practices of internment; the processes of 'carceralization'

76

of practices of penal justice (that is, the movement by which imprisonment as a form of punishment and technique of correction becomes a
central component of the penal order); and these vast processes need
themselves to be further broken down: the penalization of internment
comprises a multiplicity of processes such as the formation of closed
pedagogical spaces functioning through rewards and punishments, etc.

As a way of lightening the weight of causality, 'eventalization' thus
works by constructing around the singular event analyzed as process a
'polygon' or rather a 'polyhedron' of intelligibility, the number of whose
faces is not given in advance and can never properly be taken as finite.
One has to proceed by progressive, necessarily incomplete saturation.
And one has to bear in mind that the further one breaks down the
processes under analysis, the more one is enabled and indeed obliged to
construct their external relations of intelligibility. (In concrete terms: the
more one analyzes the process of 'carceralization' of penal practice down
to its smallest details, the more one is led to relate them to such practices
as schooling, military discipline, etc.). The internal analysis of processes
goes hand in hand with a multiplication of analytical 'salients'.

This operation thus leads to an increasing polymorphism as the analysis
progresses:

1. A polymorphism of the elements which are brought into relation:
   starting from the prison, one introduces the history of pedagogical
   practices, the formation of professional armies, British empirical
   philosophy, techniques of use of firearms, new methods of division of
   labour.
2. A polymorphism of relations described: these may concern the
   transposition of technical models (such as architectures of
   surveillance), tactics calculated in response to a particular situation
   (such as the growth of banditry, the disorder provoked by public
   tortures and executions, the defects of the practice of penal banish-
   ment), or the application of theoretical schemas (such as those
   representing the genesis of ideas and the formation of signs, the
   utilitarian conception of behaviour, etc.).
3. A polymorphism of domains of reference (varying in their nature,
   generality, etc.), ranging from technical mutations in matters of detail
   to the attempted emplacement in a capitalist economy of new
   techniques of power designed in response to the exigencies of that
   economy.

Forgive this long detour, but it enables me better to reply to your
question about hyper- and hypo-rationalisms, one which is often put to
me.

It is some time since historians lost their love of events, and made 'de-eventalization' their principle of historical intelligibility. The way they work is by ascribing the object they analyze to the most unitary, necessary, inevitable and (ultimately) extra-historical mechanism or structure available. An economic mechanism, an anthropological structure or a demographic process which figures the climactic stage in the investigation – these are the goals of de-eventalized history. (Of course, these remarks are only intended as a crude specification of a certain broad tendency.)

Clearly, viewed from the standpoint of this style of analysis, what I am proposing is at once too much and too little. There are too many diverse kinds of relations, too many lines of analysis, yet at the same time there is too little necessary unity. A plethora of intelligibilities, a deficit of necessities.

But for me this is precisely the point at issue, both in historical analysis and in political critique. We aren't, nor do we have to put ourselves, under the sign of a unitary necessity.

THE PROBLEM OF RATIONALITIES

Question: I would like to pause for a moment on this question of eventalization, because it lies at the centre of a certain number of misunderstandings about your work. (I am not talking about the misguided portrayal of you as a 'thinker of discontinuity'.) Behind the identifying of breaks and the careful, detailed charting of these networks of relations that engender a reality and a history, there persists from one book to the next something amounting to one of those historical constants or anthropologico-cultural traits you were objecting to just now: this version of a general history of rationalization spanning three or four centuries, or at any rate of a history of one particular kind of rationalization as it progressively takes effect in our society. It's not by chance that your first book was a history of reason as well as of madness, and I believe that the themes of all your other books, the analysis of different techniques of isolation, the social taxonomies, etc., all this boils down to one and the same meta-anthropological or meta-historical process of rationalization. In this sense, the 'eventalization' which you define here as central to your work seems to me to constitute only one of its extremes.

Michel Foucault: If one calls 'Weberians' those who set out to take on board the Marxist analyses of the contradictions of capital, treating these contradictions as part and parcel of the irrational rationality of capitalist society, then I don't think I am a Weberian, since my basic preoccupation isn't rationality considered as an athropological invariant. I don't believe one can speak of an intrinsic notion of 'rationalization' without on the one hand positing an absolute value inherent in reason, and on the other taking the risk of applying the term empirically in a completely arbitrary way. I think one must restrict one's use of this word to an instrumental and relative meaning. The ceremony of public torture isn't in itself more irrational than imprisonment in a cell; but it's irrational in terms of a type of penal practice which involves new ways of envisaging the effects to be produced by the penalty imposed, new ways of calculating its utility, justifying it, graduating it, etc. One isn't assessing things in terms of an absolute against which they could be evaluated as constituting more or less perfect forms of rationality, but rather examining how forms of rationality inscribe themselves in practices or systems of practices, and what role they play within them, because it's true that 'practices' don't exist without a certain regime of rationality. But, rather than measuring this regime against a value-of-reason, I would prefer to analyze it according to two axes: on the one hand, that of codification/prescription (how it forms an ensemble of rules, procedures, means to an end, etc.), and on the other, that of true or false formulation (how it determines a domain of objects about which it is possible to articulate true or false propositions).

If I have studied 'practices' like those of the sequestration of the insane, or clinical medicine, or the organization of the empirical sciences, or legal punishment, it was in order to study this interplay between a 'code' which rules ways of doing things (how people are to be graded and examined, things and signs classified, individuals trained, etc.) and a production of true discourses which serve to found, justify and provide reasons and principles for these ways of doing things. To put the matter clearly: my problem is to see how men govern (themselves and others) by the production of truth (I repeat once again that by production of truth I mean not the production of true utterances, but the establishment of domains in which the practice of true and false can be made at once ordered and pertinent).

Eventalizing singular ensembles of practices, so as to make them graspable as different regimes of 'jurisdiction' and 'veridiction': that, to put it in exceedingly barbarous terms, is what I would like to do. You see that this is neither a history of knowledge-contents (*connaissances*) nor an analysis of the advancing rationalities which rule our society, nor an anthropology of the codifications which, without our knowledge, rule our behaviour. I would like in short to resituate the production of true and false at the heart of historical analysis and political critique.

Question: It's not an accident that you speak of Max Weber. There is in your work, no doubt in a sense you wouldn't want to accept, a sort of 'ideal type' which paralyzes and mutes analysis when one tries to account for reality. Isn't this what led you to abstain from all commentary when you published the memoir of Pierre Rivière?

Michel Foucault: I don't think your comparison with Max Weber is exact. Schematically one can say that the 'ideal type' is a category of historical interpretation; it's a structure of understanding for the historian who seeks to integrate, after the fact, a certain set of data: it allows him to recapture an 'essence' (Calvinism, the state, the capitalist enterprise), working from general principles which are not at all present in the thought of the individuals whose concrete behaviour is nevertheless to be understood on their basis.

When I try to analyze the rationalities proper to penal imprisonment, the psychiatrization of madness, or the organization of the domain of sexuality, and when I lay stress on the fact that the real functioning of institutions isn't confined to the unfolding of this rational schema in its pure form, is this an analysis in terms of 'ideal types'? I don't think so, for a number of reasons.

The rational schemas of the prison, the hospital or the asylum are not general principles which can be rediscovered only through the historian's retrospective interpretation. They are explicit *programmes*; we are dealing with sets of calculated, reasoned prescriptions in terms of which institutions are meant to be reorganized, spaces arrranged, behaviours regulated. If they have an ideality, it is that of a programming left in abeyance, not that of a general but hidden meaning.

Of course this programming depends on forms of rationality much more general than those which they directly implement. I tried to show that the rationality envisaged in penal imprisonment wasn't the outcome of a straightforward calculation of immediate interest (internment turning out to be, in the last analysis, the simplest and cheapest solution), but that it arose out of a whole technology of human training, surveillance of behaviour, individualization of the elements of a social body. 'Discipline' isn't the expression of an 'ideal type' (that of 'disciplined man'); it's the generalization and interconnection of different techniques themselves designed in response to localized requirements (schooling; training troops to handle rifles).

These programmes don't take effect in the institutions in an integral manner; they are simplified, or some are chosen and not others; and things never work out as planned. But what I wanted to show is that this difference is not one between the purity of the ideal and the disorderly impurity of the real, but that in fact there are different strategies which are mutually opposed, composed and superposed so as to produce permanent and solid effects which can perfectly well be understood in terms of their rationality, even though they don't conform to the initial programming: this is what gives the resulting apparatus (*dispositif*) its solidity and suppleness.

Programmes, technologies, apparatuses – none of these is an 'ideal type'. I try to study the play and development of a set of diverse realities articulated on to each other; a programme, the connection which explains it, the law which gives it its coercive power, etc., are all just as much realities – albeit in a different mode – as the institutions that embody them or the behaviours that more or less faithfully conform to them.

You say to me: nothing happens as laid down in these 'programmes'; they are no more than dreams, utopias, a sort of imaginary production that you aren't entitled to substitute for reality. Bentham's *Panopticon* isn't a very good description of 'real life' in nineteenth-century prisons.

To this I would reply: if I had wanted to describe 'real life' in the prisons, I wouldn't indeed have gone to Bentham. But the fact that this real life isn't the same thing as the theoreticians' schemas doesn't entail that these schemas are therefore utopian, imaginary, etc. One could only think that if one had a very impoverished notion of the real. For one thing, the elaboration of these schemas corresponds to a whole series of diverse practices and strategies: the search for effective, measured, unified penal mechanisms is unquestionably a response to the inadequation of the institutions of judicial power to the new economic forms, urbanization, etc; again, there is the attempt, very noticeable in a country like France, to reduce the autonomy and insularity of judicial practice and personnel within the overall workings of the state; there is the wish to respond to emerging new forms of criminality; and so on. For another thing, these programmes induce a whole series of effects in the real (which isn't of course the same as saying that they take the place of the real): they crystallize into institutions, they inform individual behaviour, they act as grids for the perception and evaluation of things. It is absolutely true that criminals stubbornly resisted the new disciplinary mechanism in the prison; it is absolutely correct that the actual functioning of the prisons, in the inherited buildings where they were established and with the governors and guards who administered them, was a witches' brew compared to the beautiful Benthamite machine. But if the prisons were seen to have failed, if criminals were perceived as incorrigible, and a whole new criminal 'race' emerged into the field of vision of public opinion and 'justice', if the resistance of the prisoners and the pattern of recidivism took the forms we know they did, it's precisely because this type of programming didn't just remain a utopia in the heads of a few projectors.

These programmings of behaviour, these regimes of jurisdiction and veridiction aren't abortive schemas for the creation of a reality. They are fragments of reality which induce such particular effects in the real as the distinction between true and false implicit in the ways men 'direct', 'govern' and 'conduct' themselves and others. To grasp these effects as historical events – with what this implies for the question of truth (which is the question of philosophy itself) – this is more or less my theme. You see that this has nothing to do with the project – an admirable one in itself – of grasping a 'whole society' in its 'living reality'.

The question which I won't succeed in answering here but have been asking myself from the beginning is roughly the following: 'What is history, given there is continually being produced within it a separation of true and false?' By that I mean four things. Firstly, in what sense is the production and transformation of the true/false division characteristic and decisive for our historicity? Secondly, in what specific ways has this relation operated in 'Western' societies which produce scientific knowledge whose forms are perpetually changing and whose values are posited as universal? Thirdly, what historical knowledge is possible of a history which itself produces the true/false distinction on which such knowledge depends? Fourthly, isn't the most general of political problems the problem of truth? How can one analyze the connection between ways of distinguishing true and false and ways of governing oneself and others? The search for a new foundation for each of these practices, in itself and relative to the other, the will to discover a different way of governing oneself through a different way of dividing up true and false – this is what I would call 'political *spiritualité*'.

THE ANAESTHETIC EFFECT

Question: There is a question here about the way your analyses have been transmitted and received. For instance, if one talks to social workers in the prisons, one finds that the arrival of *Discipline and Punish* had an absolutely sterilizing, or rather anaesthetizing effect on them, because they felt your critique had an implacable logic which left them no possible room for initiative. You said just now, talking about eventalization, that you want to work towards breaking up existing self-evidences to show both how they are produced and how they are nevertheless always unstable. It seems to me that the second half of the picture – the aspect of instability – isn't clear.

Michel Foucault: You're quite right to pose this problem of anaesthesis, one which is of capital importance. It's quite true that I don't feel myself capable of effecting the 'subversion of all codes', 'dislocation of all orders of knowledge', 'revolutionary affirmation of violence', 'overturning of all contemporary culture', these hopes and prospectuses which currently underpin all those brilliant intellectual ventures which I admire all the more because the worth and previous achievements of those who undertake them guarantees an appropriate outcome. My project is far from being of comparable scope. To give some assistance in wearing away certain self-evidences and commonplaces about madness, normality, illness, crime and punishment; to bring it about, together with many others, that certain phrases can no longer be spoken so lightly, certain acts no longer, or at least no longer so unhesitatingly, performed; to contribute to changing certain things in people's ways of perceiving and doing things; to participate in this difficult displacement of forms of sensibility and thresholds of tolerance – I hardly feel capable of attempting much more than that. If only what I have tried to say might somehow, to some degree, not remain altogether foreign to some such real effects . . . And yet I realize how much all this can remain precarious, how easily it can all lapse back into somnolence.

But you are right, one has to be more suspicious. Perhaps what I have written has had an anaesthetic effect. But one still needs to distinguish on whom.

To judge by what the psychiatric authorities have had to say, the cohorts on the right who charge me with being against any form of power, those on the left who call me the 'last bulwark of the bourgeoisie' (this isn't a 'Kanapa phrase'; on the contrary), the worthy psychoanalyst who likened me to the Hitler of *Mein Kampf*, the number of times I've been 'autopsied' and 'buried' during the past fifteen years – well, I have the impression of having had an irritant rather than anaesthetic effect on a good many people. The epidermi bristle with a constancy I find encouraging. A journal recently warned its readers in deliciously Pétainist style against accepting as a credo what I had had to say about sexuality ('the importance of the subject', 'the personality of the author' rendered my enterprise 'dangerous'). No risk of anaesthesis in that direction. But I agree with you, these are trifles, amusing to note but tedious to collect. The only important problem is what happens on the ground.

We have known at least since the nineteenth century the difference between anaesthesis and paralysis. Let's talk about paralysis first. Who has been paralyzed? Do you think what I wrote on the history of psychiatry paralyzed those people who had already been concerned for some time about what was happening in psychiatric institutions? And, seeing what has been happening in and around the prisons, I don't think the effect of paralysis is very evident there either. As far as the people in prison are concerned, things aren't doing too badly. On the other hand, it's true that certain people, such as those who work in the institutional setting of the prison – which is not quite the same as being in prison – are not likely to find advice or instructions in my books that tell them 'what is to be done'. But my project is precisely to bring it about that they 'no longer know what to do', so that the acts, gestures, discourses which up until then had seemed to go without saying become problematic, difficult, dangerous. This effect is intentional. And then I have some news for you: for me the problem of the prisons isn't one for the 'social workers' but one for the prisoners. And on that side, I'm not so sure what's been said over the last fifteen years has been quite so – how shall I put it? – demobilizing.

But paralysis isn't the same thing as anaesthesis – on the contrary. It's in so far as there's been an awakening to a whole series of problems that the difficulty of doing anything comes to be felt. Not that this effect is an end in itself. But it seems to me that 'what is to be done' ought not to be determined from above by reformers, be they prophetic or legislative, but by a long work of comings and goings, of exchanges, reflections, trials, different analyses. If the social workers you are talking about don't know which way to turn, this just goes to show that they're looking, and hence are not anaesthetized or sterilized at all – on the contrary. And it's because of the need not to tie them down or immobilize them that there can be no question for me of trying to tell 'what is to be done'. If the questions posed by the social workers you spoke of are going to assume their full amplitude, the most important thing is not to bury them under the weight of prescriptive, prophetic discourse. The necessity of reform mustn't be allowed to become a form of blackmail serving to limit, reduce or halt the exercise of criticism. Under no circumstances should one pay attention to those who tell one: 'Don't criticize, since you're not capable of carrying out a reform.' That's ministerial cabinet talk. Critique doesn't have to be the premise of a deduction which concludes: this then is what needs to be done. It should be an instrument for those who fight, those who resist and refuse what is. Its use should be in processes of conflict and confrontation, essays in refusal. It doesn't have to lay down the law for the law. It isn't a stage in a programming. It is a challenge directed to what is.

The problem, you see, is one for the subject who acts – the subject of action through which the real is transformed. If prisons and punitive mechanisms are transformed, it won't be because a plan of reform has found its way into the heads of the social workers; it will be when those who have to do with that penal reality, all those people, have come into collision with each other and with themselves, run into dead-ends, problems and impossibilities, been through conflicts and confrontations;

when critique has been played out in the real, not when reformers have realized their ideas.

Question: This anaesthetic effect has operated on the historians. If they haven't responded to your work it's because for them the 'Foucauldian schema' was becoming as much of an encumbrance as the Marxist one. I don't know if the 'effect' you produce interests you. But the explanations you have given here weren't so clear in *Discipline and Punish*.

Michel Foucault: I really wonder whether we are using this word 'anaesthetize' in the same sense. These historians seemed to me more to be 'aesthetized', 'irritated' (in Broussais' sense of the term, of course). Irritated by what? By a schema? I don't believe so, because there is no schema. If there is an 'irritation' (and I seem to recall that in a certain journal a few signs of this irritation may have been discreetly manifested), it's more because of the absence of a schema. No infra- or superstructure, no Malthusian cycle, no opposition between state and civil society: none of these schemas which have bolstered historians' operations, explicitly or implicitly, for the past hundred or hundred and fifty years.

Hence no doubt the sense of malaise and the questions enjoining me to situate myself within some such schema: 'How do you deal with the state? What theory do you offer us of the state?' Some say I neglect its role, others that I see it everywhere, imagining it capable of minutely controlling individuals' everyday lives. Or that my descriptions leave out all reference to an infrastructure – while others say that I make an infrastructure out of sexuality. The totally contradictory nature of these objections proves that what I am doing doesn't correspond to any of these schemas.

Perhaps the reason why my work irritates people is precisely the fact that I'm not interested in constructing a new schema, or in validating one that already exists. Perhaps it's because my objective isn't to propose a global principle for analyzing society. And it's here that my project has differed since the outset from that of the historians. They – rightly or wrongly, that's another question – take 'society' as the general horizon of their analysis, the instance relative to which they set out to situate this or that particular object ('society, economy, civilization', as the *Annales* have it). My general theme isn't society but the discourse of true and false, by which I mean the correlative formation of domains and objects and of the verifiable, falsifiable discourses that bear on them; and it's not just their formation that interests me, but the effects in the real to which they are linked.

I realize I'm not being clear. I'll take an example. It's perfectly legitimate for the historian to ask whether sexual behaviours in a given period were supervised and controlled, and to ask which among them were heavily disapproved of. (It would of course be frivolous to suppose that one has explained a certain intensity of 'repression' by the delaying of the age of marriage; here one has scarcely even begun to outline a problem: why is it that the delay in the age of marriage takes effect thus and not otherwise?) But the problem I pose myself is a quite different one: it's a matter of how the rendering of sexual behaviour into discourse comes to be transformed, what types of jurisdiction and 'veridiction' it's subject to, and how the constitutive elements are formed of the domain which comes – and only at a very late stage – to be termed 'sexuality'. Among the numerous effects the organization of this domain has undoubtedly had, one is that of having provided historians with a category so 'self-evident' that they believe they can write a history of sexuality and its repression.

The history of the 'objectification' of those elements which historians consider as objectively given (if I dare put it thus: of the objectification of objectivities), this is the sort of circle I want to try and investigate. It's a difficult tangle to sort out: this, not the presence of some easily reproducible schema, is what doubtless troubles and irritates people. Of course this is a problem of philosophy to which the historian is entitled to remain indifferent. But if I am posing it as a problem within historical analysis, I'm not demanding that history answer it. I would just like to find out what effects the question produces within historical knowledge. Paul Veyne saw this very clearly:[1] it's a matter of the effect on historical knowledge of a nominalist critique itself arrived at by way of a historical analysis.

NOTES

1. Cf. 'Foucault révolutionne l'histoire', in Paul Veyne, *Comment on écrit l'histoire* 2nd edn, Paris, 1978.

CHAPTER FOUR

Governmentality

Michel Foucault

In a previous lecture on 'apparatuses of security', I tried to explain the emergence of a set of problems specific to the issue of population, and on closer inspection it turned out that we would also need to take into account the problematic of government. In short, one needed to analyze the series: security, population, government. I would now like to try to begin making an inventory of this question of government.

Throughout the Middle Ages and classical antiquity, we find a multitude of treatises presented as 'advice to the prince', concerning his proper conduct, the exercise of power, the means of securing the acceptance and respect of his subjects, the love of God and obedience to him, the application of divine law to the cities of men, etc. But a more striking fact is that, from the middle of the sixteenth century to the end of the eighteenth, there develops and flourishes a notable series of political treatises that are no longer exactly 'advice to the prince', and not yet treatises of political science, but are instead presented as works on the 'art of government'. Government as a general problem seems to me to explode in the sixteenth century, posed by discussions of quite diverse questions. One has, for example, the question of the government of oneself, that ritualization of the problem of personal conduct which is characteristic of the sixteenth century Stoic revival. There is the problem too of the government of souls and lives, the entire theme of Catholic and Protestant pastoral doctrine. There is government of children and the great problematic of pedagogy which emerges and develops during the sixteenth century. And, perhaps only as the last of these questions to be taken up, there is the government of the state by the prince. How to govern oneself, how to be governed, how to govern others, by whom the people will accept being governed, how to become the best possible governor – all these problems, in their multiplicity and intensity, seem to me to be characteristic of the sixteenth century, which lies, to put it schematically, at the crossroads of two processes: the one which, shattering the structures of feudalism, leads to the establishment of the

This lecture, given at the Collège de France in February 1978, is translated from the Italian version, transcribed and edited by Pasquale Pasquino, published in *Aut Aut* 167–8, September–December 1978.

great territorial, administrative and colonial states; and that totally different movement which, with the Reformation and Counter-Reformation, raises the issue of how one must be spiritually ruled and led on this earth in order to achieve eternal salvation.

There is a double movement, then, of state centralization on the one hand and of dispersion and religious dissidence on the other: it is, I believe, at the intersection of these two tendencies that the problem comes to pose itself with this peculiar intensity, of how to be ruled, how strictly, by whom, to what end, by what methods, etc. There is a problematic of government in general.

Out of all this immense and monotonous literature on government which extends to the end of the eighteenth century, with the transformations which I will try to identify in a moment, I would like to underline some points that are worthy of notice because they relate to the actual definition of what is meant by the government of the state, of what we would today call the political form of government. The simplest way of doing this is to compare all of this literature with a single text which from the sixteenth to the eighteenth century never ceased to function as the object of explicit or implicit opposition and rejection, and relative to which the whole literature on government established its standpoint: Machiavelli's *The Prince*. It would be interesting to trace the relationship of this text to all those works that succeeded, criticized and rebutted it.

We must first of all remember that Machiavelli's *The Prince* was not immediately made an object of execration, but on the contrary was honoured by its immediate contemporaries and immediate successors, and also later at the end of the eighteenth century (or perhaps rather at the very beginning of the nineteenth century), at the very moment when all of this literature on the art of government was about to come to an end. *The Prince* re-emerges at the beginning of the nineteenth century, especially in Germany, where it is translated, prefaced and commented upon by writers such as Rehberg, Leo, Ranke and Kellerman, and also in Italy. It makes its appearance in a context which is worth analyzing, one which is partly Napoleonic, but also partly created by the Revolution and the problems of revolution in the United States, of how and under what conditions a ruler's sovereignty over the state can be maintained; but this is also the context in which there emerges, with Clausewitz, the problem (whose political importance was evident at the Congress of Vienna in 1815) of the relationship between politics and strategy, and the problem of relations of force and the calculation of these relations as a principle of intelligibility and rationalization in international relations; and lastly, in addition, it connects with the problem of Italian and German territorial unity, since Machiavelli had been one of those who tried to define the conditions under which Italian territorial unity could be restored.

This is the context in which Machiavelli re-emerges. But it is clear that, between the initial honour accorded him in the sixteenth century and his rediscovery at the start of the nineteenth, there was a whole 'affair' around his work, one which was complex and took various forms: some explicit praise of Machiavelli (Naudé, Machon), numerous frontal attacks (from Catholic sources: Ambrozio Politi, *Disputationes de Libris a Christiano detestandis*; and from Protestant sources: Innocent Gentillet, *Discours sur les moyens de bien gouverner contre Nicolas Machiavel*, 1576), and also a number of implicit critiques (G. de La Perrière, *Miroir politique*, 1567; Th. Elyott, *The Governor*, 1580; P. Paruta, *Della Perfezione della Vita politica*, 1579).

This whole debate should not be viewed solely in terms of its relation to Machiavelli's text and what were felt to be its scandalous or radically unacceptable aspects. It needs to be seen in terms of something which it was trying to define in its specificity, namely an art of government. Some authors rejected the idea of a new art of government centred on the state and reason of state, which they stigmatized with the name of Machiavellianism; others rejected Machiavelli by showing that there existed an art of government which was both rational and legitimate, and of which Machiavelli's *The Prince* was only an imperfect approximation or caricature; finally, there were others who, in order to prove the legitimacy of a particular art of government, were willing to justify some at least of Machiavelli's writings (this was what Naudé did to the *Discourses* on Livy; Machon went so far as to attempt to show that nothing was more Machiavellian than the way in which, according to the Bible, God himself and his prophets had guided the Jewish people).

All these authors shared a common concern to distance themselves from a certain conception of the art of government which, once shorn of its theological foundations and religious justifications, took the sole interest of the prince as its object and principle of rationality. Let us leave aside the question of whether the interpretation of Machiavelli in these debates was accurate or not. The essential thing is that they attempted to articulate a kind of rationality which was intrinsic to the art of government, without subordinating it to the problematic of the prince and of his relationship to the principality of which he is lord and master.

The art of government is therefore defined in a manner differentiating it from a certain capacity of the prince, which some think they can find expounded in Machiavelli's writings, which others are unable to find; while others again will criticize this art of government as a new form of Machiavellianism.

This politics of *The Prince*, fictitious or otherwise, from which people sought to distance themselves, was characterized by one principle: for Machiavelli, it was alleged, the prince stood in a relation of singularity and externality, and thus of transcendence, to his principality. The prince acquires his principality by inheritance or conquest, but in any case he does not form part of it, he remains external to it. The link that binds him to his principality may have been established through violence, through family heritage or by treaty, with the complicity or the alliance of other princes; this makes no difference, the link in any event remains a purely synthetic one and there is no fundamental, essential, natural and juridical connection between the prince and his principality. As a corollary of this, given that this link is external, it will be fragile and continually under threat – from outside by the prince's enemies who seek to conquer or recapture his principality, and from within by subjects who have no *a priori* reason to accept his rule. Finally, this principle and its corollary lead to a conclusion, deduced as an imperative: that the objective of the exercise of power is to reinforce, strengthen and protect the principality, but with this last understood to mean not the objective ensemble of its subjects and the territory, but rather the prince's relation with what he owns, with the territory he has inherited or acquired, and with his subjects. This fragile link is what the art of governing or of being prince espoused by Machiavelli has as its object. As a consequence of this the mode of analysis of Machiavelli's text will be twofold: to identify dangers (where they come from, what they consist in, their severity: which are the greater, which the slighter), and, secondly, to develop the art of manipulating relations of force that will allow the prince to ensure the protection of his principality, understood as the link that binds him to his territory and his subjects.

Schematically, one can say that Machiavelli's *The Prince*, as profiled in all these implicitly or explicitly anti-Machiavellian treatises, is essentially a treatise about the prince's ability to keep his principality. And it is this *savoir-faire* that the anti-Machiavellian literature wants to replace by something else and new, namely the art of government. Having the ability to retain one's principality is not at all the same thing as possessing the art of governing. But what does this latter ability comprise? To get a view of this problem, which is still at a raw and early stage, let us consider one of the earliest texts of this great anti-Machiavellian literature: Guillaume de La Perrière's *Miroir Politique*.

This text, disappointingly thin in comparison with Machiavelli, prefigures a number of important ideas. First of all, what does La Perrière mean by 'to govern' and 'governor': what definition does he give of these terms? On page 24 of his text he writes: 'governor can signify monarch, emperor, king, prince, lord, magistrate, prelate, judge and the like'. Like La Perrière, others who write on the art of government constantly recall that one speaks also of 'governing' a household, souls, children, a province, a convent, a religious order, a family.

These points of simple vocabulary actually have important political implications: Machiavelli's prince, at least as these authors interpret him, is by definition unique in his principality and occupies a position of externality and transcendence. We have seen, however, that practices of government are, on the one hand, multifarious and concern many kinds of people: the head of a family, the superior of a convent, the teacher or tutor of a child or pupil; so that there are several forms of government among which the prince's relation to his state is only one particular mode; while, on the other hand, all these other kinds of government are internal to the state or society. It is within the state that the father will rule the family, the superior the convent, etc. Thus we find at once a plurality of forms of government and their immanence to the state: the multiplicity and immanence of these activities distinguishes them radically from the transcendent singularity of Machiavelli's prince.

To be sure, among all these forms of government which interweave within the state and society, there remains one special and precise form: there is the question of defining the particular form of governing which can be applied to the state as a whole. Thus, seeking to produce a typology of forms of the art of government, La Mothe Le Vayer, in a text from the following century (consisting of educational writings intended for the French Dauphin), says that there are three fundamental types of government, each of which relates to a particular science or discipline: the art of self-government, connected with morality; the art of properly governing a family, which belongs to economy; and finally the science of ruling the state, which concerns politics. In comparison with morality and economy, politics evidently has its own specific nature, which La Mothe Le Vayer states clearly. What matters, notwithstanding this typology, is that the art of government is always characterized by the essential continuity of one type with the other, and of a second type with a third.

This means that, whereas the doctrine of the prince and the juridical theory of sovereignty are constantly attempting to draw the line between the power of the prince and any other form of power, because its task is to explain and justify this essential discontinuity between them, in the art of government the task is to establish a continuity, in both an upwards and a downwards direction.

Upwards continuity means that a person who wishes to govern the state well must first learn how to govern himself, his goods and his patrimony, after which he will be successful in governing the state. This ascending line characterizes the pedagogies of the prince, which are an important issue at this time, as the example of La Mothe Le Vayer shows: he wrote for the Dauphin first a treatise of morality, then a book of economics and lastly a political treatise. It is the pedagogical formation of the prince, then, that will assure this upwards continuity. On the other hand, we also have a downwards continuity in the sense that, when a state is well run, the head of the family will know how to look after his family, his goods and his patrimony, which means that individuals will, in turn, behave as they should. This downwards line, which transmits to individual behaviour and the running of the family the same principles as the good government of the state, is just at this time beginning to be called *police*. The prince's pedagogical formation ensures the upwards continuity of the forms of government, and police the downwards one. The central term of this continuity is the government of the family, termed *economy*.

The art of government, as becomes apparent in this literature, is essentially concerned with answering the question of how to introduce economy – that is to say, the correct manner of managing individuals, goods and wealth within the family (which a good father is expected to do in relation to his wife, children and servants) and of making the family fortunes prosper – how to introduce this meticulous attention of the father towards his family into the management of the state.

This, I believe, is the essential issue in the establishment of the art of government: introduction of economy into political practice. And if this is the case in the sixteenth century, it remains so in the eighteenth. In Rousseau's *Encyclopedia* article on 'Political economy' the problem is still posed in the same terms. What he says here, roughly, is that the word 'economy' can only properly be used to signify the wise government of the family for the common welfare of all, and this is its actual original use; the problem, writes Rousseau, is how to introduce it, *mutatis mutandis*, and with all the discontinuities that we will observe below, into the general running of the state. To govern a state will therefore mean to apply economy, to set up an economy at the level of the entire state, which means exercising towards its inhabitants, and the wealth and behaviour of each and all, a form of surveillance and control as attentive as that of the head of a family over his household and his goods.

An expression which was important in the eighteenth century captures this very well: Quesnay speaks of good government as 'economic government'. This latter notion becomes tautological, given that the art of government is just the art of exercising power in the form and according to the model of the economy. But the reason why Quesnay speaks of 'economic government' is that the word 'economy', for reasons that I will explain later, is in the process of acquiring a modern meaning, and it is at this moment becoming apparent that the very essence of government – that is, the art of exercising power in the form of economy – is to have as its main objective that which we are today accustomed to call 'the economy'.

The word 'economy', which in the sixteenth century signified a form of government, comes in the eighteenth century to designate a level of reality, a field of intervention, through a series of complex processes that I regard as absolutely fundamental to our history.

The second point which I should like to discuss in Guillaume de La Perrière's book consists of the following statement: 'government is the right disposition of things, arranged so as to lead to a convenient end'.

I would like to link this sentence with another series of observations. Government is the right disposition of things. I would like to pause over this word 'things', because if we consider what characterizes the ensemble of objects of the prince's power in Machiavelli, we will see that for Machiavelli the object and, in a sense, the target of power are two things, on the one hand the territory, and on the other its inhabitants. In this respect, Machiavelli simply adapted to his particular aims a juridical principle which from the Middle Ages to the sixteenth century defined sovereignty in public law: sovereignty is not exercised on things, but above all on a territory and consequently on the subjects who inhabit it. In this sense we can say that the territory is the fundamental element both in Machiavellian principality and in juridical sovereignty as defined by the theoreticians and philosophers of right. Obviously enough, these territories can be fertile or not, the population dense or sparse, the inhabitants rich or poor, active or lazy, but all these elements are mere variables by comparison with territory itself, which is the very foundation of principality and sovereignty. On the contrary, in La Perrière's text, you will notice that the definition of government in no way refers to territory. One governs things. But what does this mean? I do not think this is a matter of opposing things to men, but rather of showing that what government has to do with is not territory but rather a sort of complex composed of men and things. The things with which in this sense government is to be concerned are in fact men, but men in their relations, their links, their imbrication with those other things which are wealth, resources, means of subsistence, the territory with its specific qualities, climate, irrigation, fertility, etc.; men in their relation to that other kind of things, customs, habits, ways of acting and thinking, etc.; lastly, men in their relation to that other kind of things, accidents and misfortunes such as famine, epidemics, death, etc. The fact that government concerns things understood in this way, this imbrication of men and things, is I believe readily confirmed by the metaphor which is inevitably invoked in these treatises on government, namely that of the ship. What does it mean to govern a ship? It means clearly to take charge of the sailors, but also of the boat and its cargo; to take care of a ship means also to reckon with winds, rocks and storms; and it consists in that activity of establishing a relation between the sailors who are to be taken care of and the ship which is to be taken care of, and the cargo which is to be brought safely to port, and all those eventualities like winds, rocks, storms and so on; this is what characterizes the government of a ship. The same goes for the running of a household. Governing a household, a family, does not essentially mean safeguarding the family property; what concerns it is the individuals that compose the family, their wealth and prosperity. It means to reckon with all the possible events that may intervene, such as births and deaths, and with all the things that can be done, such as possible alliances with other families; it is this general form of management that is characteristic of government; by comparison, the question of landed property for the family, and the question of the acquisition of sovereignty over a territory for a prince, are only relatively secondary matters. What counts essentially is this complex of men and things; property and territory are merely one of its variables.

This theme of the government of things as we find it in La Perrière can also be met with in the seventeenth and eighteenth centuries. Frederick the Great has some notable pages on it in his *Anti-Machiavel*. He says, for instance, let us compare Holland with Russia: Russia may have the largest territory of any European state, but it is mostly made up of swamps, forests and deserts, and is inhabited by miserable groups of people totally destitute of activity and industry; if one takes Holland, on the other hand, with its tiny territory, again mostly marshland, we find that it nevertheless possesses such a population, such wealth, such commercial activity and such a fleet as to make it an important European state, something that Russia is only just beginning to become.

To govern, then, means to govern things. Let us consider once more the sentence I quoted earlier, where La Perrière says: 'government is the right disposition of things, arranged so as to lead to a convenient end'. Government, that is to say, has a finality of its own, and in this respect again I believe it can be clearly distinguished from sovereignty. I do not of course mean that sovereignty is presented in philosophical and juridical texts as a pure and simple right; no jurist or, *a fortiori*, theologian ever said that the legitimate sovereign is purely and simply entitled to exercise his power regardless of its ends. The sovereign must always, if he is to be a good sovereign, have as his aim, 'the common welfare and the salvation of all'. Take for instance a late seventeenth-century author. Pufendorf says: 'Sovereign authority is conferred upon them [the rulers] only in order to allow them to use it to attain or conserve what is of public utility'. The ruler may not have consideration for anything advantageous for himself, unless it also be so for the state. What does this common good or general salvation consist of, which the jurists talk about as being the end of sovereignty? If we look closely at the real content that jurists and theologians give to it, we can see that 'the common good' refers to a state of affairs where all the subjects without exception obey the laws, accomplish the tasks expected of them, practise the trade to which they are assigned, and respect the established order so far as this order conforms to the laws imposed by God on nature and men: in other words, 'the common good' means essentially obedience to the law, either that of their earthly sovereign or that of God, the absolute sovereign. In every case, what characterizes the end of sovereignty, this common and general good, is in sum nothing other than submission to sovereignty. This means that the end of sovereignty is circular: the end of sovereignty is the exercise of sovereignty. The good is obedience to the law, hence the good for sovereignty is that people should obey it. This is an essential circularity which, whatever its theoretical structure, moral justification or practical effects, comes very close to what Machiavelli said when he stated that the primary aim of the prince was to retain his principality. We always come back to this self-referring circularity of sovereignty or principality.

Now, with the new definition given by La Perrière, with his attempt at a definition of government, I believe we can see emerging a new kind of finality. Government is defined as a right manner of disposing things so as to lead not to the form of the common good, as the jurists' texts would have said, but to an end which is 'convenient' for each of the things that are to be governed. This implies a plurality of specific aims: for instance, government will have to ensure that the greatest possible quantity of wealth is produced, that the people are provided with sufficient means of subsistence, that the population is enabled to multiply, etc. There is a whole series of specific finalities, then, which become the objective of government as such. In order to achieve these various finalities, things must be disposed – and this term, *dispose*, is important because with sovereignty the instrument that allowed it to achieve its aim – that is to say, obedience to the laws – was the law itself; law and sovereignty were absolutely inseparable. On the contrary, with government it is a question not of imposing law on men, but of disposing things: that is to say, of employing tactics rather than laws, and even of using laws themselves as tactics – to arrange things in such a way that, through a certain number of means, such and such ends may be achieved.

I believe we are at an important turning point here: whereas the end of sovereignty is internal to itself and possesses its own intrinsic instruments in the shape of its laws, the finality of government resides in the things it manages and in the pursuit of the perfection and intensification of the processes which it directs; and the instruments of government, instead of being laws, now come to be a range of multiform tactics. Within the perspective of government, law is not what is important: this is a frequent theme throughout the seventeenth century, and it is made explicit in the eighteenth-century texts of the Physiocrats which explain that it is not through law that the aims of government are to be reached.

Finally, a fourth remark, still concerning this text from La Perrière: he says that a good ruler must have patience, wisdom and diligence. What does he mean by patience? To explain it, he gives the example of the king of bees, the bumble-bee, who, he says, rules the bee-hive without needing a sting; through this example God has sought to show us in a mystical manner that the good governor does not have to have a sting – that is to say, a weapon of killing, a sword – in order to exercise his power; he must have patience rather than wrath, and it is not the right to kill, to employ force, that forms the essence of the figure of the governor. And what positive content accompanies this absence of sting? Wisdom and diligence. Wisdom, understood no longer in the traditional sense as knowledge of divine and human laws, of justice and equality, but rather as the knowledge of things, of the objectives that can and should be attained, and the disposition of things required to reach them; it is this knowledge that is to constitute the wisdom of the sovereign. As for his diligence, this is the principle that a governor should only govern in such a way that he thinks and acts as though he were in the service of those who are governed. And here, once again, La Perrière cites the example of the head of the family who rises first in the morning and goes to bed last, who concerns himself with everything in the household because he considers himself as being in its service. We can see at once how far this characterization of government differs from the idea of the prince as found in or attributed to Machiavelli. To be sure, this notion of governing, for all its novelty, is still very crude here.

This schematic presentation of the notion and theory of the art of government did not remain a purely abstract question in the sixteenth century, and it was not of concern only to political theoreticians. I think we can identify its connections with political reality. The theory of the art of government was linked, from the sixteenth century, to the whole development of the administrative apparatus of the territorial monarchies, the emergence of governmental apparatuses; it was also connected to a set of analyses and forms of knowledge which began to develop in the late sixteenth century and grew in importance during the seventeenth, and which were essentially to do with knowledge of the state, in all its different elements, dimensions and factors of power, questions which were termed precisely 'statistics', meaning the science of the state; finally, as a third vector of connections, I do not think one can fail to relate this search for an art of government to mercantilism and the Cameralists' science of police.

To put it very schematically, in the late sixteenth century and early seventeenth century, the art of government finds its first form of crystallization, organized around the theme of reason of state, understood not in the negative and pejorative sense we give to it today (as that which infringes on the principles of law, equity and humanity in the sole interests of the state), but in a full and positive sense: the state is governed according to rational principles which are intrinsic to it and which cannot be derived solely from natural or divine laws or the principles of wisdom and prudence; the state, like nature, has its own proper form of rationality, albeit of a different sort. Conversely, the art of government, instead of seeking to found itself in transcendental rules, a cosmological model or a philosophico-moral ideal, must find the principles of its rationality in that which constitutes the specific reality of the state. In my subsequent lectures I will be examining the elements of this first form of state rationality. But we can say here that, right until the early eighteenth century, this form of 'reason of state' acted as a sort of obstacle to the development of the art of government.

This is for a number of reasons. Firstly, there are the strictly historical ones, the series of great crises of the seventeenth century: first the Thirty Years War with its ruin and devastation; then in the mid-century the peasant and urban rebellions; and finally the financial crisis, the crisis of revenues which affected all Western monarchies at the end of the century. The art of government could only spread and develop in subtlety in an age of expansion, free from the great military, political and economic tensions which afflicted the seventeenth century from beginning to end. Massive and elementary historical causes thus blocked the propagation of the art of government. I think also that the doctrine formulated during the sixteenth century was impeded in the seventeenth by a series of other factors which I might term, to use expressions which I do not much care for, mental and institutional structures. The pre-eminence of the problem of the exercise of sovereignty, both as a theoretical question and as a principle of political organization, was the fundamental factor here so long as sovereignty remained the central question. So long as the institutions of sovereignty were the basic political institutions and the exercise of power was conceived as an exercise of sovereignty, the art of government could not be developed in a specific and autonomous manner. I think we have a good example of this in mercantilism. Mercantilism might be described as the first sanctioned efforts to apply this art of government at the level of political practices and knowledge of the state; in this sense one can in fact say that mercantilism represents a first threshold of rationality in this art of government which La Perrière's text had defined in terms more moral than real. Mercantilism is the first rationalization of the exercise of power as a practice of government; for the first time with mercantilism we see the development of a *savoir* of state that can be used as a tactic of government. All this may be true, but mercantilism was blocked and arrested, I believe, precisely by the fact that it took as its essential objective the might of the sovereign; it sought a way not so much to increase the wealth of the country as to allow the ruler to accumulate wealth, build up his treasury and create the army with which he could carry out his policies. And the instruments mercantilism used were laws, decrees, regulations: that is to say, the traditional weapons of sovereignty. The objective was sovereign's might, the instruments those of sovereignty: mercantilism sought to reinsert the possibilities opened up by a consciously conceived art of government within a mental and institutional structure, that of sovereignty, which by its very nature stifled them.

Thus, throughout the seventeenth century up to the liquidation of the themes of mercantilism at the beginning of the eighteenth, the art of government remained in a certain sense immobilized. It was trapped within the inordinately vast, abstract, rigid framework of the problem and institution of sovereignty. This art of government tried, so to speak, to reconcile itself with the theory of sovereignty by attempting to derive the ruling principles of an art of government from a renewed version of the theory of sovereignty – and this is where those seventeenth-century jurists come into the picture who formalize or ritualize the theory of the contract. Contract theory enables the founding contract, the mutual pledge of ruler and subjects, to function as a sort of theoretical matrix for deriving the general principles of an art of government. But although contract theory, with its reflection on the relationship between ruler and subjects, played a very important role in theories of public law, in practice, as is evidenced by the case of Hobbes (even though what Hobbes was aiming to discover was the ruling principles of an art of government), it remained at the stage of the formulation of general principles of public law.

On the one hand, there was this framework of sovereignty which was too large, too abstract and too rigid; and on the other, the theory of government suffered from its reliance on a model which was too thin, too weak and too insubstantial, that of the family: an economy of enrichment still based on a model of the family was unlikely to be able to respond adequately to the importance of territorial possessions and royal finance.

How then was the art of government able to outflank these obstacles? Here again a number of general processes played their part: the demographic expansion of the eighteenth century, connected with an increasing abundance of money, which in turn was linked to the expansion of agricultural production through a series of circular processes with which the historians are familiar. If this is the general picture, then we can say more precisely that the art of government found fresh outlets through the emergence of the problem of population; or let us say rather that there occurred a subtle process, which we must seek to reconstruct in its particulars, through which the science of government, the recentring of the theme of economy on a different plane from that of the family, and the problem of population are all interconnected.

It was through the development of the science of government that the notion of economy came to be recentred on to that different plane of reality which we characterize today as the 'economic', and it was also through this science that it became possible to identify problems specific to the population; but conversely we can say as well that it was thanks to the perception of the specific problems of the population, and thanks to the isolation of that area of reality that we call the economy, that the problem of government finally came to be thought, reflected and calculated outside of the juridical framework of sovereignty. And that 'statistics' which, in mercantilist tradition, only ever worked within and for the benefit of a monarchical administration that functioned according to the form of sovereignty, now becomes the major technical factor, or one of the major technical factors, of this new technology.

In what way did the problem of population make possible the derestriction of the art of government? The perspective of population, the reality accorded to specific phenomena of population, render possible the final elimination of the model of the family and the recentring of the notion of economy. Whereas statistics had previously worked within the administrative frame and thus in terms of the functioning of sovereignty, it now gradually reveals that population has its own regularities, its own rate of deaths and diseases, its cycles of scarcity, etc.; statistics shows also that the domain of population involves a range of intrinsic, aggregate effects, phenomena that are irreducible to those of the family, such as epidemics, endemic levels of mortality, ascending spirals of labour and wealth; lastly it shows that, through its shifts, customs, activities, etc., population has specific economic effects: statistics, by making it possible to quantify these specific phenomena of population, also shows that this specificity is irreducible to the dimension of the family. The latter now disappears as the model of government, except for a certain number of residual themes of a religious or moral nature. What, on the other hand, now emerges into prominence is the family considered as an element internal to population, and as a fundamental instrument in its government.

In other words, prior to the emergence of population, it was impossible to conceive the art of government except on the model of the family, in terms of economy conceived as the management of a family; from the moment when, on the contrary, population appears absolutely irreducible to the family, the latter becomes of secondary importance compared to population, as an element internal to population: no longer, that is to say, a model, but a segment. Nevertheless it remains a privileged segment, because whenever information is required concerning the population (sexual behaviour, demography, consumption, etc.), it has to be obtained through the family. But the family becomes an instrument rather than a model: the privileged instrument for the government of the population and not the chimerical model of good government. This shift from the level of the model to that of an instrument is, I believe, absolutely fundamental, and it is from the middle of the eighteenth century that the family appears in this dimension of instrumentality relative to the population, with the institution of campaigns to reduce mortality, and to promote marriages, vaccinations, etc. Thus, what makes it possible for the theme of population to unblock the field of the art of government is this elimination of the family as model.

In the second place, population comes to appear above all else as the ultimate end of government. In contrast to sovereignty, government has as its purpose not the act of government itself, but the welfare of the population, the improvement of its condition, the increase of its wealth, longevity, health, etc.; and the means that the government uses to attain these ends are themselves all in some sense immanent to the population; it is the population itself on which government will act either directly through large-scale campaigns, or indirectly through techniques that will make possible, without the full awareness of the people, the stimulation of birth rates, the directing of the flow of population into certain regions or activities, etc. The population now represents more the end of government than the power of the sovereign; the population is the subject of needs, of aspirations, but it is also the object in the hands of the government, aware, *vis-à-vis* the government, of what it wants, but ignorant of what is being done to it. Interest at the level of the consciousness of each individual who goes to make up the population, and interest considered as the interest of the population regardless of what the particular interests and aspirations may be of the individuals who compose it, this is the new target and the fundamental instrument of the government of population: the birth of a new art, or at any rate of a range of absolutely new tactics and techniques.

Lastly, population is the point around which is organized what in sixteenth-century texts came to be called the patience of the sovereign, in the sense that the population is the object that government must take into account in all its observations and *savoir*, in order to be able to govern effectively in a rational and conscious manner. The constitution of a *savoir* of government is absolutely inseparable from that of a knowledge of all the processes related to population in its larger sense: that is to say, what we now call the economy. I said in my last lecture that the constitution of political economy depended upon the emergence from among all the various elements of wealth of a new subject: population. The new science called political economy arises out of the perception of new networks of continuous and multiple relations between population, territory and wealth; and this is accompanied by the formation of a type of intervention characteristic of government, namely intervention in the field of economy and population. In other words, the transition which takes place in the eighteenth century from an art of government to a political science, from a regime dominated by structures of sovereignty to one ruled by techniques of government, turns on the theme of population and hence also on the birth of political economy.

This is not to say that sovereignty ceases to play a role from the moment when the art of government begins to become a political science; I would say that, on the contrary, the problem of sovereignty was never posed with greater force than at this time, because it no longer involved, as it did in the sixteenth and seventeenth centuries, an attempt to derive an art of government from a theory of sovereignty, but instead, given that such an art now existed and was spreading, involved an attempt to see what juridical and institutional form, what foundation in the law, could be given to the sovereignty that characterizes a state. It suffices to read in chronological succession two different texts by Rousseau. In his *Encyclopaedia* article on 'Political economy', we can see the way in which Rousseau sets up the problem of the art of government by pointing out (and the text is very characteristic from this point of view) that the word 'oeconomy' essentially signifies the management of family property by the father, but that this model can no longer be accepted, even if it had been valid in the past; today we know, says Rousseau, that political economy is not the economy of the family, and even without making explicit reference to the Physiocrats, to statistics or to the general problem of the population, he sees quite clearly this turning point consisting in the fact that the economy of 'political economy' has a totally new sense which cannot be reduced to the old model of the family. He undertakes in this article the task of giving a new definition of the art of government. Later he writes *The Social Contract*, where he poses the problem of how it is possible, using concepts like nature, contract and general will, to provide a general principle of government which allows room both for a juridical principle of sovereignty and for the elements through which an art of government can be defined and characterized. Consequently, sovereignty is far from being eliminated by the emergence of a new art of government, even by one which has passed the threshold of political science; on the contrary, the problem of sovereignty is made more acute than ever.

As for discipline, this is not eliminated either; clearly its modes of organization, all the institutions within which it had developed in the seventeenth and eighteenth centuries – schools, manufactories, armies, etc. – all this can only be understood on the basis of the development of the great administrative monarchies, but nevertheless, discipline was never more important or more valorized than at the moment when it became important to manage a population; the managing of a population not only concerns the collective mass of phenomena, the level of its aggregate effects, it also implies the management of population in its depths and its details. The notion of a government of population renders all the more acute the problem of the foundation of sovereignty (consider Rousseau) and all the more acute equally the necessity for the development of discipline (consider all the history of the disciplines, which I have attempted to analyze elsewhere).

Accordingly, we need to see things not in terms of the replacement of a society of sovereignty by a disciplinary society and the subsequent replacement of a disciplinary society by a society of government; in reality one has a triangle, sovereignty–discipline–government, which has as its primary target the population and as its essential mechanism the apparatuses of security. In any case, I wanted to demonstrate the deep historical link between the movement that overturns the constants of sovereignty in consequence of the problem of choices of government, the movement that brings about the emergence of population as a datum, as a field of intervention and as an objective of governmental techniques, and the process which isolates the economy as a specific sector of reality, and political economy as the science and the technique of intervention of the government in that field of reality. Three movements: government, population, political economy, which constitute from the eighteenth century onwards a solid series, one which even today has assuredly not been dissolved.

In conclusion I would like to say that on second thoughts the more exact title I would like to have given to the course of lectures which I have begun this year is not the one I originally chose, 'Security, territory and population': what I would like to undertake is something which I would term a history of 'governmentality'. By this word I mean three things:

1. The ensemble formed by the institutions, procedures, analyses and reflections, the calculations and tactics that allow the exercise of this very specific albeit complex form of power, which has as its target population, as its principal form of knowledge political economy, and as its essential technical means apparatuses of security.
2. The tendency which, over a long period and throughout the West, has steadily led towards the pre-eminence over all other forms (sovereignty, discipline, etc.) of this type of power which may be termed

government, resulting, on the one hand, in the formation of a whole series of specific governmental apparatuses, and, on the other, in the development of a whole complex of *savoirs*.
3. The process, or rather the result of the process, through which the state of justice of the Middle Ages, transformed into the administrative state during the fifteenth and sixteenth centuries, gradually becomes 'governmentalized'.

We all know the fascination which the love, or horror, of the state exercises today; we know how much attention is paid to the genesis of the state, its history, its advance, its power and abuses, etc. The excessive value attributed to the problem of the state is expressed, basically, in two ways: the one form, immediate, affective and tragic, is the lyricism of the *monstre froid* we see confronting us; but there is a second way of overvaluing the problem of the state, one which is paradoxical because apparently reductionist: it is the form of analysis that consists in reducing the state to a certain number of functions, such as the development of productive forces and the reproduction of relations of production, and yet this reductionist vision of the relative importance of the state's role nevertheless invariably renders it absolutely essential as a target needing to be attacked and a privileged position needing to be occupied. But the state, no more probably today than at any other time in its history, does not have this unity, this individuality, this rigorous functionality, nor, to speak frankly, this importance; maybe, after all, the state is no more than a composite reality and a mythicized abstraction, whose importance is a lot more limited than many of us think. Maybe what is really important for our modernity – that is, for our present – is not so much the *étatisation* of society, as the 'governmentalization' of the state.

We live in the era of a 'governmentality' first discovered in the eighteenth century. This governmentalization of the state is a singularly paradoxical phenomenon, since if in fact the problems of governmentality and the techniques of government have become the only political issue, the only real space for political struggle and contestation, this is because the governmentalization of the state is at the same time what has permitted the state to survive, and it is possible to suppose that if the state is what it is today, this is so precisely thanks to this governmentality, which is at once internal and external to the state, since it is the tactics of government which make possible the continual definition and redefinition of what is within the competence of the state and what is not, the public versus the private, and so on; thus the state can only be understood in its survival and its limits on the basis of the general tactics of governmentality.

And maybe we could even, albeit in a very global, rough and inexact fashion, reconstruct in this manner the great forms and economies of power in the West. First of all, the state of justice, born in the feudal type of territorial regime which corresponds to a society of laws – either customs or written laws – involving a whole reciprocal play of obligation and litigation; second, the administrative state, born in the territoriality of national boundaries in the fifteenth and sixteenth centuries and corresponding to a society of regulation and discipline; and finally a governmental state, essentially defined no longer in terms of its territoriality, of its surface area, but in terms of the mass of its population with its volume and density, and indeed also with the territory over which it is distributed, although this figures here only as one among its component elements. This state of government which bears essentially on population and both refers itself to and makes use of the instrumentation of economic *savoir* could be seen as corresponding to a type of society controlled by apparatuses of security.

In the following lectures I will try to show how governmentality was born out of, on the one hand, the archaic model of Christian pastoral, and, on the other, a diplomatic–military technique, perfected on a European scale with the Treaty of Wesphalia; and that it could assume the dimensions it has only thanks to a series of specific instruments, whose formation is exactly contemporaneous with that of the art of government and which are known, in the old seventeenth- and eighteenth-century sense of the term, as *police*. The pastoral, the new diplomatic–military techniques and, lastly, police: these are the three elements that I believe made possible the production of this fundamental phenomenon in Western history, the governmentalization of the state.

CHAPTER FIVE

Theatrum politicum: The genealogy of capital - police and the state of prosperity

Pasquale Pasquino

To begin, an extended quotation from an English writer who published in 1821, under the pseudonym of Piercy Ravenstone, a work entitled: *A Few Doubts as to the Correctness of Some Opinions Generally Entertained on the Subjects of Population and Political Economy.* I cite from it at length, even if what particularly interests me is towards the end, because I find the whole passage remarkable: we are, I repeat, in 1821. The following remarks come from the opening of a chapter entitled 'Capital'.

> But it would be taking a very imperfect view of the effects of rent and taxes, if we were to overlook the consequences which result from the creation of capital. Capital is their child, their confederate, their constant ally, in all their encroachments on industry. It is indeed the pioneer which opens the way for their approaches. It is the great operative cause in swelling the numbers of idle men, in loading society with their burthen.
>
> It is not a very easy matter, however, to acquire an accurate idea of the nature of capital. It is quite another sort of being from its confederates. Rent and taxes have an open and avowed existence; we see the manner in which they operate. In calculating their amount we are able to compute their effects. Their motions are in open day, their pretensions are not concealed. They are visible and tangible substances. Their properties may be ascertained in the crucible of experience. They may be submitted to the test of their consequences. But it is not so with capital. It has none but a metaphysical existence. Though its effects be everywhere felt, its presence can nowhere be detected. Its incorporeal nature for ever eludes our grasp. No man hath seen its form; none can tell its habitation. Its power resides not within itself, it never acts but by borrowed means. Its treasures are not real wealth, they are only representations of wealth. They may be increased to any imaginable amount without adding to the real riches of a nation. Capital is like the subtle ether of the older philosophers; it is around us, it is about us, it mixes in every thing we do. Though itself invisible, its effects are but too apparent. It is no less useful to our economists than that was to the philosophers.
>
> It serves to account for whatever cannot be accounted for in any other way. Where reason fails, where argument is insufficient, it operates like a talisman to silence all doubts. It occupies the same place in their theories, which was held by darkness in the mythology of the ancients. It is the root of all their genealogies, it is the great mother of all things, it is the cause of every event that happens in the world. Capital, according to them, is the parent of industry, the forerunner of all improvements. It builds our towns, it cultivates our fields, it restrains the vagrant waters of our rivers, it covers our barren mountains with timber, it converts our deserts into gardens, it

bids fertility arise where all before was desolation. It is the deity of their idolatry which they have set up to worship in the high places of the Lord; and were its powers what they imagine, it would not be unworthy of their adoration.[1]

Very good. This text is directed, it seems to me, against at least two targets. On the one hand, against a discourse of the choristers of the benefits of capital, 'it builds our towns, etc.'. Now by this approach it seems to hint at a rebuttal which had, however, been invented by the very economists against whom the text is directed: 'It is by labour that all the wealth of the world was originally purchased.'[2] On the other hand – and this to my mind is far more interesting – it attacks what it calls capitalist genealogies, where capital figures as the great mother of all things, the cause of all events which happen in the world, the talisman which silences all doubt. It is true that for quite some time our understanding of recent history has been made to turn on the axis of capital and of its correlate, the bourgeoisie, and that the history of knowledges and institutions has begun to be made to revolve around these concepts. People thought they had found a simple, and hence all the more seductive, principle to make sense of and give an explanation for all those great figures of oppression and revolt which have perturbed the surface of our social history for about the past two centuries. A strange paradox: capital, a metaphysical substance, had in addition what was or came to be the privilege of materiality. Everything else was mere shadow-play.

The prison, the asylum and all the knowledge which had instigated and accompanied the emplacement of these institutions represented nothing but the 'hidden hand', the omnipresence of the bourgeoisie (or of capital), which needed progressively to subject, intern or banish everything which opposed its advance along the royal road of accumulation and proletarianization – for this is the only kind of opposition one encounters in this history – and which had therefore, one way or another, to be put out of the way; even though a day may come when it is said that this is socialism.

For twenty years now this schema has begun to be called in question, as being theoretically unsatisfactory and politically untenable. Theoretically unsatisfactory, in that as soon as it was sought to apply this schema in a detailed analysis, it revealed itself to be false, that is, incapable of accounting for problems that formed the crux of these analyses: consider the realities of the prison or of confinement in general. Politically untenable, because it failed to account for a great number of struggles which, since the sixties at least, have traversed our Western societies. It could only do so at the cost of imposing an interpretation on them which gradually became intolerable to the very people who were engaged in struggle. The result of this questioning was the discovery of the whole submerged part of an iceberg. Behind the monotonous, uninterrupted and omnipresent genealogy of capital, there appeared the polymorphous universe of what we have since begun to call technologies of power. There was a sense of astonishment which brought philosophizing for once to a halt, and prompted, in its place, a new attentiveness to history.

But this is a disquieting universe for our thought, in so far as it clearly cannot be subordinated to the simple form of grand binary confrontations, nor explained by recourse to an essential unitary principle. Now, it seems to me that among all the forms of knowledge, all the social sciences which the last two centuries have engendered, it is indeed political economy which has formed the key element of what I have called the bourgeois, capitalist genealogy of history. And this for two reasons, and in two senses:

1. Precisely because it is viewed as the 'science' which, it is often said, dawns in England and France with the rise of the modern bourgeoisie, whether industrial or agrarian.
2. But also because it was political economy which, well before Marx, even if this is less often noted, invented what formed the basis for bourgeois or capitalist history: that is to say, what later came to be called historical materialism, and which in its most simple and general form was formulated in Scotland in the second part of the eighteenth century, by such writers as Smith, Millar, Ferguson, etc.[3]

When I speak of capitalist history, this must not be misunderstood; I do not want to imply that there might be some other history, or rather another way of writing history, which would be Marxist, proletarian, from below, from the side of the people, of the marginals, or what you will. What I mean, or what I would like at least to suggest, is exactly the opposite: what I term 'capitalist' or 'bourgeois' is a way of presenting history – one can locate oneself on one or other side of the imaginary barricade, that does not alter the basic question – which takes as the privileged object of its discourse, as the axis of all events, as trajectory of development and at the same time principle of explication, capital and the bourgeoisie, their positive nature, their negation, their origins, their evolution or transcendence, their transformations or metamorphoses.

Shortly after the birth of historical materialism in Scotland, towards the end of the eighteenth century, there emerged out of political thought in Germany a discourse which staged a grand *pièce de résistance* which is still being revived today and perhaps has a long time yet to run in the *theatrum politicum*: I mean that combat of good and evil which goes under the name of the conflict between society and the state. With Kant and Humboldt (notably in the latter's essay on the limits of state intervention),[4] a political discourse is born which ranges over a wide spectrum of positions, from anarchists like William Godwin to liberals like Benjamin Constant,[5] and including certain variants of Marxism. It is a discourse which, speaking in the name of the individual and of civil society, announcing the political maturity of subjects, demands an end to the long tutelage imposed on men by the state, an end to what the German authors in particular saw as the 'paternalist regimen'[6] of the territorial states. But the feature of this discourse which most concerns us here is the way it presents the state as a small, all-powerful apparatus which obstructs the freedom of individuals and threatens the development of social forces. The state, in this context, is an instance separate from, and exercising a repressive, negative power over, the social body, which, for its part, is endowed with an originally virtuous essence.

Yet, if one chose to think that this theatre in which from time immemorial these two dramas have been performed, either in repertory or as a double bill, of the genealogy of capital and the combat between society and the state, if one happened to decide that this theatre is empty, its actors dummies and the lines they speak absurd, and if instead one were to take a look behind its scenery, then whereas on the stage they sing the songs of Keynes and Marx ('The Modern Age opened, I think, with the accumulation of capital'),[7] behind the scenes I think one would be more likely to hear the words of Frégier, who wrote in 1850 (two years, that is to say, after Marx's *Manifesto*): 'It can be affirmed without fear of contradiction that police is the most solid basis of civilisation.'[8]

Please do not think that it was a passion for the sordid and ignoble that led me to the science of police. On the contrary, I was searching for the origin – the *Entstehung*, in Nietzsche's sense – of what is doubtless the noblest, at least in its theoretical rigour (think of Quesnay, Ricardo, Marx), of all the social sciences: political economy. Reading J. A. Schumpeter's *History of Economic Analysis*, I came upon these titles of works by Von Justi: *Foundations of the Power and Happiness of States, or an Exhaustive Presentation of the Science of Public Police* (1760–1), and Von Sonnenfels: *Foundations of the Science of Police, Commerce and Finance* (1765).[9] Studying these writings, I gradually came to realize that the 'science of police' is only the culmination of a whole vast literature, today largely neglected, which traverses the whole of the modern period, accompanying and supporting the construction of the social order we have known since the century of Enlightenment, whose beginnings we might guess to lie considerably further back in time. This literature, or rather body of knowledge, of *police*, known in the eighteenth century as both 'the science of happiness' and 'the science of government', which constitutes society as the object of a knowledge and at the same time as the target of political intervention, seems to me to speak to us about our history and our present much more eloquently today than do the genealogies of capital.

Here is what Beccaria says in his *Elements of Public Economy*, which are the notes of lectures given in Milan in 1769, at the Chair of Political Economy and Science of Police created for him by Maria Theresa of Austria:

> But neither the products of the earth, nor those of the work of the human hand, nor mutual commerce, nor public contributions can ever be obtained from men with perfection and constancy if they do not know the moral and physical laws of the things upon which they act, and if the increase of bodies is not proportionately accompanied by the change of social habits; if, among the multiplicity of individuals, works and products one does not at each step see shining the light of order, which renders all operations easy and sure. Thus, the sciences, education, good order, security and public tranquillity, objects all comprehended under the name of police, will constitute the fifth and last object of public economy.[10]

Police and civilization, as Frégier puts it less than a century later. Clearly we are not talking here about police in the present-day sense of the term, the 'police' whose purpose – officially at least – is the 'maintenance of order and prevention of dangers'. This latter notion of police is a relatively late invention, dating from the late eighteenth or early nineteenth century. Police begins to be defined in this rather negative sense in Sagnier's *Code of Correction and Simple Police*, published in Paris in Year VII of the Revolution. I believe it is difficult to find a negative definition of the tasks of police before 1770, the year when there appeared at Göttingen a work by the German jurist Pütter, *Institutiones juris publici germanici*, in which it is stated: 'One calls police that part of the public power charged with averting future dangers which are to be feared by all in the internal affairs of a state.'[11] If, as I am suggesting, this idea of police as a simple *cura advertendi mala futura* (that is, concern to avert future ills, and also maintenance of order) is a comparatively recent one, what did 'police' mean previously? How was Beccaria able to speak of it in the terms we have just cited?

Duchesne, in his *Code of Police* of 1757,[12] which is presented as being a sort of abstract of De La Mare's great treatise, starts by saying that 'police has as its general object the public interest', but then finds himself a little embarrassed when he seeks to be more precise, and finishes up with this startling formulation: 'the objects which it embraces are in some sense indefinite'; but, he continues, 'they can be adequately grasped only by detailed examinaion'. To the formula defining nineteenth-century police as *cura advertendi mala futura*, one can, I think, counterpose another formula current in the eighteenth century and earlier, which speaks of police as *cura promovendi salutem* (concern to develop or promote happiness or the public good). But, over and above this definition, it would be worthwhile to follow Duchesne's advice and move on to a detailed, but rapid examination of what we might call the field of police intervention. This will be all the more useful for an understanding of the object of police, in that it leads us to consider something much more concrete than the preceding definitions, namely 'police regulations'. Because all this literature on police was fundamentally nothing but a great effort of reflection, instigation and systematization which accompanied the un-interrupted production since the end of the Middle Ages of laws and regulations of police – laws and regulations which had a very wide domain of intervention. It is enough to look at the table of contents of Duchesne's book, which has indeed as its subtitle 'An analysis of police regulations', to get some idea of what is involved:

1. Of religion
2. Of customs
3. Of health
4. Of foodstuffs
5. Of highways
6. Of tranquillity and public order
7. Of sciences and liberal arts
8. Of commerce
9. Of manufactures and mechanical arts
10. Of servants, domestics and nurses
11. Of the police of the poor

This was in France in 1757. But let us take the case of the German-speaking countries at the end of the Middle Ages: for example, the *Police Regulations of the City of Nuremberg* of the late Middle Ages, published in the last century by a German scholar called (irony of history) Baader.[13] Here the picture is nearly the same:

1. Of security
2. Of customs
3. Of commerce
4. Of trades
5. Of foodstuffs
6. Of health and cleanliness
7. Of building
8. Of fire
9. Of forests and hunting
10. Of beggars
11. Of Jews

Now, among these regulations there are some very strange ones: on the use of the familiar pronoun between parents and children; on the dimensions of saddles and horsecloths; on what should be eaten and drunk during a wedding-feast; on what should happen on the death of a woman who owns a seat in church; and so on. One might be inclined to say that what we have here is a sort of plethora of legislation largely concerned with matters of small importance. Actually I think there is something more than this.

If one tries to answer our question about the field of reality regulated by the police ordinances of territorial states, one finds in the texts of the period, as also in the books which later dealt with the problem, a canonical response: the 'good order of public matters' (*de la chose publique*). Now this response is liable to seem very vague, especially since at this period (from the fifteenth to the seventeenth centuries) the idea of an opposition between public and private spheres does not yet exist; that distinction is the end-product of a historical process whose effects become apparent only in the eighteenth century. The expression 'good order of public matters' can, I think, be more aptly understood here in terms of a different opposition, that between an administered society and what is called in German a *Ständegesellschaft*: that is to say, a society of orders or estates, in the sense that one speaks in France of a Third Estate. Putting it schematically, I would say that what police regulations regulate, or try to regulate, or purport to regulate, is everything which in the life of this society of three orders goes unregulated, everything which can be said, in the 'waning of the Middle Ages', to lack order or form. This is what the science of police is about: a great effort of formation of the social body, or more precisely an undertaking whose principal result will be something which we today call society or the social body, and which the eighteenth century called 'the good order of a population'.

One can picture the field of intervention of police regulations as like the vacant lots of a city, the formless provinces of a vast kingdom, a sort of no man's land comprising all those areas where the feudal world's traditional customs, established jurisdictions and clear relations of authority, subordination, protection and alliance cease to rule. Within the formless 'monster', as the police thinkers called the Holy Roman Empire, there are indeed still islands of order and transparency; not everything in the ancient society of orders and estates requires regulating; but does not what escapes it cry out for intervention?

This no man's land is beginning to be perceived as an open space traversed by men and things. Squares, markets, roads, bridges, rivers: these are the critical points in the territory which police will mark out and control. The prescriptions or regulations of police are instruments of this work of formation, but at the same time they are also products of a sort of spontaneous creation of law, or rather of a demand for order which outreaches law and encroaches on domains never previously occupied, where hitherto neither power, order nor authority had thought to hold sway. One could perhaps adapt here the formula of Roman law, *res nullius primi occupandi* (property held by no one falls to the first occupier), and say *potestas nullius primi occupandi*: power held by no one falls to the first occupier. Not that power is installing itself here in what was previously a total void, but rather it installs itself where there was a void of power and where a demand for power can be generated.

But power of whom, over whom, by what means? That indeed is the crucial question for this type of analysis, if one wants to avoid making power into another myth, building empty genealogies of power which would be of no more use than the genealogies of capital we spoke of at the beginning.

We will put forward this hypothesis, then. The power whose existence is attested by these parallel series of documents, the regulations of police and the vast literature which accompanied them (a recent bibliography listed, for German-speaking areas alone within the period between 1600 and 1800, no fewer than 3,215 titles under the heading 'science of police in the strict sense'),[14] is exercised by administration or, better, government, over that new reality (about which a little more must be said in a moment) which began at this period to be called 'population'. I say 'administration' or 'government', and not 'bureaucracy', because one is dealing here not with a class or a group, but with a web or ensemble of functions which together constitute the proper form, or 'good police' (as the phrase went), of the social body. (Cf. on this notion the lecture by Michel Foucault in Chapter 4.)

One can get an idea of what we find emerging with this literature from a text which is partly a political project, and partly a kind of utopia. It is all the more remarkable a document when one considers the fact that it was written at the beginning of the seventeenth century by Georg Obrecht, a high official of the city of Strasburg who was also Rector of its university. The text is the fourth of five little treatises which the author entitled 'The five political secrets', in which, as its title indicates, a certain police order is discussed.[15]

I think it is important to note here that Obrecht is the first writer to speak no longer in the political language of prince and people, but instead in that of population and *Obrigkeit*, a term which means authority but also public power or government. If one thinks of Machiavelli and his *Prince*, one can see how great is the distance which suddenly separates Obrecht's conception from that which I believe was characteristic of the Renaissance: the idea of the state as the dominion or property of the prince; the framework of political thought, at one domestic and patri-archal, in which the problem of power is posed from above. Obrecht is only one early exemplar of a language and a set of preoccupations which are constantly to be met with in German-speaking areas, especially after the Thirty Years War. The problem which he poses is that of the constitution of a science, equipped with adequate practical means, of augmenting the annual income of a state, at a time when one of the central problems in Europe was that of war and all that war implied in terms of armies, discipline, the need for a numerous population, and above all the relentless demand for money. And for Obrecht, as for all these authors, it is clear that the treasury cannot be steadily replenished if taxes and levies are not complemented by a set of measures designed for the development of wealth. But this is only the starting point for a project or political utopia which goes much further, and is elaborated in terms of the idea of police.

Obrecht enumerates three tasks of police. First, information, conceived as a sort of statistical table bearing on all the capacities and resources of population and territory; second, a set of measures to augment the wealth of the population and enrich the coffers of the state; third, public happiness. Obrecht has a formula which summarizes all this in a synthetic manner, composed of the two Latin words *census* and *censura*. By *census*, he means the obligation of each person to pay his taxes. By the word *censura* he refers to the task of the public powers to take in charge the people's lives, the life of each and all. 'The object of police is everything that has to do with maintaining and augmenting the happiness of its citizens, *omnium et singulorum* (of all and of each).' Thus, more than a century and a half later, Von Hohental in his *Liber de Politia*.[16]

Obrecht envisages, for the accomplishment of the tasks which he assigns to police or administration in his state of prosperity, elected functionaries – whom he calls *Deputaten* – whose function is to inspect and manage the population. Among the tasks of the Intendants, together with that of maintaining population data on an almost daily basis with registers of deaths, births, etc., there is one which is quite singular, that of obliging each person to render his or her life into discourse, in order that each person can then be advised how to lead a 'Christian life'. The task of intelligence, which every citizen must participate in for the security and happiness of the state – which here, once again, means the security and happiness of all and of each – is transformed into a great general and uninterrupted confession. I am not forcing the meaning of the text when I speak of 'obliging to render into discourse' one's life; I am not quoting Foucault's *History of Sexuality*, but Obrecht himself who literally says 'zu red setzen': to make a person speak and answer for his or her acts, as though testifying before a court.

If you want to be protected, assisted, taken charge of – if, in other words, you want happiness and well-being – we must know and you must pay: *census et censura*. This is the discourse that the form of government known as police, in the old sense of that word, has been addressing to us now for some centuries. Confession or rendering into discourse are certainly a necessary part of this formula, but, in the supreme interests of information, covert denunciation is also strongly commended by Obrecht and his Intendants. To the old royal slogan of *justitia et pax* (justice and peace), there is now added this new one, prosperity. The state of prosperity will be the rallying cry of all the discourses and practices affiliated to this form of power, the banner of the science of police, from

Obrecht to Seckendork and Von Justi. At each stage it will function on the dual levels of promise and blackmail.

Either happiness will be social or it will not exist. 'Without subordination and obedience, no society can be hoped for, and without society every evil is to be feared and scarcely any good can be hoped for': thus, at the beginning of the eighteenth century, the *abbé* Castel de Saint Pierre formulates the axiom of the state of prosperity.[17] If one looks at the text by Obrecht which I have just attempted to summarize, one can agree that:

> the difference between the ancient popular tribunal and the modern power of administration is this: whereas a tribunal performs its activity only when someone is involved in a legal action or trial, the *Deputaten* have a competence relating to the entirety of a population, including even women and children, though they are not juridical subjects. And whereas the courts sit in public, at fixed moments and in the sight of all, the *Deputaten* perform their task in silence, sitting without interruption, and have before them only solitary individuals.[18]

Isolated persons, individuals. This is what constitutes a population, that abstract concept which is none other than the object of police administration. Population: another relatively recent neologism, invented in Germany by Obrecht, and coming into standard use, in France, at least, only during the eighteenth century, thanks to the state of prosperity. Population and individuals, where previously, in the old social structure, there had been only groups, *Stände*, orders or estates, inviolable (juridically, at least) in their eternal hierarchy.

For Obrecht, then, the central tasks of police were information and happiness. This marks, so to speak, the ideal point of departure for a set of knowledges and practices which appear and develop in the seventeenth and eighteenth centuries, which bear on the social body as a population, and slowly constitute and fashion it. I am thinking for example of demography and statistics, which, as its derivation from the word *Staat* shows, is nothing else but the science of the state: statistics, born in Germany with Conring and Achenwall, which in England, with Petty and Davenant, came to be called 'political arithmetic'. In Germany, again – the Germany which Marxism has taught us to regard as backward and philosophical, and philosophical because backward – there appears in 1740 the great treatise of demography, *The Divine Order of the World in the Transformations of the Human Species, from Birth to Death and to Procreation*, by the *abbé* Süssmilch, whom Rümelin, writing at the end of the nineteenth century, called 'the founder of social biology'.[19]

'One thing alone is lacking to you, O great State, the knowledge of yourself, and the image of your strength.'[20] These words from Montchréstien's *Treatise of Political Economy* of 1615 express a demand to which statistics and demography will be the response. Moheau repeats in 1778: 'There can be no well-ordered political machine, nor enlightenment administration in a country where the state of population is unknown',[21] and he explains how useful this knowledge will be for war, for taxation, for commerce.

To be exercised, power needs to know: we are talking about knowledge, but also – and this is the other side of the picture – a force towards public happiness. Von Justi writes on this matter, on (one might almost say) the development of the forces of production:

> Another thing which contributes to the powers of a state is the industry and talents of the different members who compose it. It follows then that to maintain, augment and serve public happiness, one should oblige subjects to acquire the talents and kinds of knowledge necessary for the different employments to which they may be destined, and maintain among them the order and discipline which tend to the general good of society.[22]

Now, among all these knowledges, all these social sciences and new technologies bearing on population, that new territory in which relations of power become inscribed, population which, in contrast with the old society of three orders, now falls into subdivisions by age, sex and occupation, posing their different problems which require different sorts of intervention, a population which no longer merely lives and dies, but has a birth rate and a death rate – at the very heart, then, of this problem of population, there is a preoccupation which makes itself felt with growing force, that of health. To quote Moheau again: 'Man is at once the final term and the instrument of every kind of product; and, to consider him only as a being with a price, he is the most precious of a sovereign's treasures.' 'The city does not consist only of houses, gateways, public places; it is men who make up the city.' 'Kings and their Ministers are not the only ones who may draw knowledge from the table of population . . . The progress or loss of population present a host of truths from which Physics, Medicine and all the sciences which have for their object the health, conservation, protection or succour of humanity may profit.'[23]

The health of the population thus becomes a value, a new object of analysis and intervention. Petty has said so already, after having been a doctor in Cromwell's English army during the massacre of 600,000 Irish and the deportation of the survivors to the great concentration camp of a Northern province, and after having also very actively participated in the redistribution of Irish lands conquered by the revolution, which brought him a double benefit: a theoretical one, of being counted, by virtue of his 'Political anatomy of Ireland', the founder of economics; and a practical benefit, of being able to acquire for himself a good share of the conquered lands; after all this, William Petty declared, to the approbation of the

Royal Society, that each young Englishman who dies represented a net loss of £69 sterling. The fact that he only rated the loss of a young Irishman at £15, the same value as for negroes and slaves, may appear inconsistent.[24] But no matter, science deals only with principles, and the principle was there. Population is wealth, health is a value. A century later, a great campaign of medicalization was launched in Europe. I will not pursue its history here. My point here is only to indicate how medicalization came to connect, among all the other practices of police, with the great new body politic of population – an event which I believe can only be grasped by shifting one's perspective away from the terrain of genealogies of capital.

I asked the question about power: exercised by whom, over whom, by what means. I have tried to show in what sense I think it is possible to argue that it was exercised by 'government', through police, on population, that new object which a new form of power constitutes and within which that form of power takes its shape.

By what means? (And this, I believe, is the central problem around which this type of analysis will stand or fall). Well, I would say by means of a whole cluster of practices and knowledges which I have referred to at different points in this discussion under the general rubric of police: assistance, tutelage, medicalization (not to mention areas which have already been analyzed by others, such as the prison and its disciplinary mechanisms, sexuality, psychiatry and the family); practices and knowledges whose analysis we are variously trying to further, all the more because together they have woven that ever-tightening web which constitutes the social.

All of which leads me to say a few words on a problem fleetingly mentioned above: the problem of the state. If one rids oneself of the idea of the state as an apparatus or instance separate from the social body, the focus of all political struggle, which must be either democratized or destroyed once its veritable nature has been revealed, or which must be appropriated in order to take power: if one frees onself of this old idea, canvassed in the political theatre since Kant at least, one can perhaps recover another meaning of this word 'state', which was more or less that which it had in the seventeenth century for an author like Conring, the inventor of statistics, who considered the state to be the 'entire body of civil society'.[25] This would mean resituating the analysis of relations of power wholly within the interior of this social body. The state would then, in one aspect, signify a kind of viewpoint, created and developed little by little since the end of the Middle Ages, since the abandonment of, on the one hand, the symmetrical and complementary perspective of Christendom and the Empire, and, on the other, the perspectives of local powers and the society of three orders – as people began to speak in the name not of the bourgeoisie, but of society, nation or state. And, from another angle, the state would then signify not the site or source of power, the one great adversary to be smashed, but rather one instrument among others, and one modality of 'government'.

I realize how far this discussion has attempted at once too much and too little, talking about many things without concentrating on one clear, precise issue. But it seemed that it might be useful to suggest a few hypotheses, to try to sketch a few possible objects of analysis, to go behind the scenes and to wander a while in a landscape of investigation which others before me have opened up. But there is a final problem, a problem for me, which at once obliges me to continue and brings me to a halt. It can be put like this: if the theatre of our political reason is empty, I believe this is not just because the piece which has been, and is still being, played in it is laughable. I think it is much more because a ground has crumbled away beneath our feet, the ground upon which there emerged and developed the discourse and practice of what for a century at least has been known in Europe, and for us, as the 'left' – including the 'far' left. On what ground are we standing now? I do not think any of us really knows. What interests me much more than easy certainties, whether in the direction of rhetorical optimism or philosophical disarray, is the possibility that perhaps, here and there, we can make the experience we have of our present interact with the excursions that it can seem useful to us to make into the past: this possibility, and also the fact that all these fragments of research still have for me the flavour of an adventure.

NOTES

1. Piercy Ravenstone, *A Few Doubts as to the Correctness of Some Opinions Generally Entertained on the Subjects of Population and Political Economy*, London, 1821, pp. 292–4.
2. Adam Smith, *An Inquiry into the Nature and Causes of the Wealth of Nations*, 2 vols, ed. R. H. Campbell and A. S. Skinner, London, 1976, vol. 1, p. 48.
3. *Ibid.*; John Millar, *An Historical View of the English Government from the Settlement of the Saxons in Britain to the Revolution in 1688*, 4 vols, London, 1803; Adam Ferguson, *An Essay on the History of Civil Society*, Edinburgh, 1767.
4. Carl Wilhelm von Humboldt, *Ideen zu einem Versuch die Gränzen des Staats zu bestimmen*, Breslau, 1851, trans. J. Cailthard jun. as *The Sphere and Duties of Government*, London, 1854.
5. William Godwin, *Enquiry Concerning Political Justice and its Influence on General Virtue and Happiness*, London, 1793; Benjamin Henri Constant, *Cours politique constitutionelle*, Paris, 1836.
6. Humboldt, *Ideen*, chapter 3.
7. John Maynard Keynes, 'Economic possibilities for our grandchildren', in *Collected Writings*, London, 1972, vol. IX, p. 323.

8. Honore Antoine Frégier, *Histoire de l'administration de la Police de Paris depuis Philippe Auguste jusqu'aux Etats généraux de 1789*, 2 vols, Paris, 1850.

9. Joseph Alois Schumpeter, *History of Economic Analysis*, ed. E. B. Schumpeter, London, 1954, pp. 170–1; Johann Gottlob von Justi, *Die Grundfeste zu der Macht und Glückseligkeit der Staaten*, Leipzig, 1760–1; Joseph von Sonnenfels, *Grundsätze der Polizey, Handlung und Finanzwissenschaft*, Vienna, 1768–76.

10. Cesare Beccaria Bonesana, *Elementi di economia pubblica*, Milan, 1804, pp. 22–3; Avoue Sagnier, *Code correctionel et de simple police, on recueil des lois, édits, arrêts, règlements et ordonnances composant la legislation correctionelle et celle de simple police*, Paris, 1798/9.

11. J. S. Pütter, *Elementa juris publici germanici*, Göttingen, 1770.

12. M. Duchesne, *Code de la police, ou analyse des règlements de police*, Paris, 1757.

13. *Nürnberger Polizeiordnung aus dem XIII. bis XV. Jahrhundert*, Stuttgart, 1861.

14. Magdalene Humpers, *Bibliographie der Kameralwissenschaft*, Cologne, 1937.

15. Georg Obrecht, *Eine Sondere Policey Ordnung, und Constitution, durch welche ein jeder Magistratus, vermittels besonderen angestelten Deputaten, jederzeit in seiner Regierung, eine gewisse Nachrichtung haben mag*, Strasburg, 1608.

16. P. G. G. von Hohenthal, *Liber de Politia*, Lipstal, 1776.

17. Charles Castel de Saint Pierre, *Les Rêves d'un homme de bien qui peuvent être réalisés*, 2nd edn, Paris, 1775, p. 39.

18. H. Maier, *Die ältere deutsche Staats und Wervaltungslehre*, 1966, p. 155.

19. Johan Peter Süssmilch, *Die göttliche Ordnung in den Veränderungen des menschlichen Geschlechts aus der Geburt, dem Tode und der Fortpflanzung desselben erwiesen*, Berlin, 1741.

20. Antoine de Montchréstien, *L'Economie politique patronale. Traité de l'oeconomie politique, dédié en 1615 au roy*, Paris, 1889, p. 34.

21. M. Moheau, *Recherches et considérations sur le population de France*, Paris, 1778, p. 20.

22. Justi, *Grundsätze der Policey-Wissenschaft*, Göttingen, 1756, p. 16.

23. M.Moheau, *Recherches*, pp. 10–11, 16, 22.

24. A. Roncaglia, *Petty*, Milan, 1977.

25. Hermannus Conringius, *Notitia rerum publicarum 'integrum corpus' civilis societatis*, cited in John Vincennes, *Geschichte der Statistik*, Stuttgart, 1884, p. 63.

CHAPTER SIX

Peculiar interests: civil society and governing 'the system of natural liberty'

Graham Burchell

. . . every order of social relations (however constituted) is, if one wishes to *evaluate* it, to be examined in terms of the human type to which it, by way of external or internal (motivational) selection, provides the optimal chances of becoming the dominant type.[1]

Every man thus lives by exchanging, or becomes in some measure a merchant. . .[2]

1. The many, says Adam Ferguson, are often governed by one, or by a few who 'know how to conduct them'. When we are governed, when our behaviour is managed, directed or conducted by others, we do not become the passive objects of a physical determination. To govern individuals is to get them to act and to align their particular wills with ends imposed on them through constraining and facilitating models of possible actions. Government presupposes and requires the activity and freedom of the governed.[3] It is for the simple reason that individuals are active when governed by others that, as Paul Veyne says, there is a problem of subjectivity in politics.[4] What kind of subjectivity is involved, for example, when individuals obediently perform their assigned tasks and conduct themselves in prescribed ways? What kinds of reason do governments offer individuals for doing what they are told?

Veyne suggests that because individuals attach a value to their 'self-image' they are most deeply affected by political power when it impinges on this relation they have to themselves. They are most profoundly affected when the way they are governed requires them to alter how they see themselves as governed subjects. It is then, as Vaclav Havel puts it, when a 'line of conflict' is found to pass not just between distinct subjects but through the individual person, that individuals may be led to resist or even revolt.[5]

This view invites us to consider the relation between individuals and the political order from the perspective of the different processes whereby the former are objectified as certain kinds of subject through the ways they are targeted by political power. The affirmation (and refusal) of forms of subjective identity might then be examined as a function of

119

political power relations.[6] As Veyne has argued, governors and governed are not simple historical universals. Governed individuals may be identified by their governors as members of a flock to be led, as legal subjects with certain rights, as children to be corrected and educated, as part of a natural resource to be exploited, or as living beings who are part of a biological population to be managed.[7] In each case the subjective self-identity of governed individuals presupposed or required by the exercise of political power will be different.

The nature of the individual's relation to the political order has been and remains a central theme in liberal political thought. It is an essential element in modern returns to, or renewals and re-inventions of, supposedly classical liberal principles. In this context of contemporary liberal revivalism, Foucault's contribution to a genealogy of liberalism in terms of government and subjectivity is, I think, worth considering and deserves to be more widely known and discussed. I restrict myself to presenting here only certain selected aspects of his analysis of early liberal thought, amplified here and there with my own comments and illustrations.[8]

How, Foucault asks, through the operation of what practices of government and by reference to what kind of political reasoning, have we been led to recognize our self-identity as members of those somewhat indefinite global entities we call community, society, nation or state?[9]

2. I must observe, that all kinds of government, free and absolute, seem to have undergone, in modern times, a great change for the better, with regard both to foreign and domestic management. The *balance of power* is a secret in politics, fully known only to the present age; and I must add, that the internal POLICE of states has also received great improvements within the last century.[10]

The greatness of a state, and the happiness of its subjects, how independent soever they may be supposed in some respects, are commonly allowed to be inseparable with regard to commerce.[11]

A necessary condition for the possibility of classical Athenian democracy, according to Christian Meier, was that qualifying members valued, developed and interiorized an essentially political self-identity. Above all else they had to think, feel and affirm themselves as *citizens*.[12] Consequently, the *isonomia* of the Athenian *polis* involved a radical separation between the civic, political order and the domestic, social order. One's identity changed as one passed from the *oikos* to the *polis*. It was in and for the latter domain that one styled one's existence.[13]

This view that the fundamental meaning and value of one's identity is to be found in political citizenship, as a member of the political community participating in public life on an equal footing with one's co-citizens, has been an enduring theme in Western political thought. John Pocock, for example, has shown the critical role played in the early modern period by the 'civic humanist' re-interpretation of the classical model of citizenship in the *polis* or *respublica*.[14] He describes the complex course taken by the confrontation between this model of citizenship as the essential source of value for the personality and a new historical self-awareness of the political order as existing and having to survive and maintain itself within an indefinite, secular time of change and contingent circumstances which threaten the bases of civic virtue. It was, he says, against the neo-classical ideal of the republican citizen's civic virtue – 'the only secular virtue yet known to Western Man'[15] – that the problems involved in elaborating a new and self-consciously modern account of the bases of social and political personality, or identity, had to be and were initially formulated. Eighteenth-century political thought is seen as marked by a dilemma arising from the challenge posed to this ideal of the self-aware and self-defining citizen's (*civic*) virtue by what were identified as newly emergent, essentially historical and uncertain (*civil*) forms of the individual's private and professionalized subjectivity and conduct. With it becoming possible to acknowledge that the modern 'individual's relation to his *res publica* could not be simply civic or virtuous',[16] but in the absence of a readily available theory of political personality applicable to 'trading man', eighteenth-century political thought is described as being preoccupied with finding a way to rescue man from a kind of 'Faustian dissociation of sensibility',[17] from a split between civic and civil models of subjectivity.

The work of Pocock and others demonstrates the extent to which problems of social and political subjectivity were a fundamental and insistent concern for early modern and, particularly, for eighteenth-century political thought.[18] These studies are, I think, complemented in highly interesting ways by Foucault's treatment of the theme of government in the same period. The latter's point of departure is the development, in the early modern period, of a kind of political reason that, in contrast with the principles of classical Athenian *isonomia*, is fundamentally antinomic. Modern political reason has been shaped, he says, by the project (and problem) of combining, or of making a 'tricky adjustment' between, on the one hand, the state's exercise of power through the totalizing legal–political forms of its unity, and, on the other, its exercise of an individualizing form of power through a 'pastoral' *government* concerned with the concrete lives and conduct of individuals.[19]

Where Pocock sees the development of a 'Faustian dissociation of sensibility', Foucault identifies the development of modern Western political reason in the truly 'demonic' project of a *political* "governmentality" ', or state 'pastorship'.[20] Closely connected with the appearance of the idea of *raison d'état* in the sixteenth century, Foucault sees a political rationality taking shape which seeks to combine the legal-political form of the state's unity with what hitherto was its opposite – an individualizing, pastoral government. For the first time in the West, he suggests, one finds a project for governing the state in accordance with rational principles which involve a political concern with the details of individuals' lives and activities, and which takes as its object the concrete reality of states as they exist historically in a secular, non-eschatological time. For Foucault, the forms of our modern 'self-identity' must be referred to the rationality and practice of an *individualizing* art of government that has developed in Western states since the early modern period.

The distinctive character of Foucault's approach can be briefly and somewhat crudely indicated by setting one or two of its themes alongside complementary themes in Pocock. Both Foucault and Pocock refuse to see what the latter calls the 'privatization' of the individual as the inevitable effect of a nascent capitalist economy or as the expression of an anticipatory ideology of 'bourgeois' society. Both examine the different ways in which forms of individuality are thematized as a *problem* in eighteenth-century thought. Modern or 'liberal' conceptions of economic, social and political individuality are, they argue, the invented product of a lengthy and complex process of, above all, ethical and political questioning.

At the risk of oversimplification, the problem Pocock sees eighteenth-century political thought confronting might be expressed in the following way: how can and how must the social and political subjectivity of modern individuals be conceptualized when the civic humanist ideal of virtuous citizenship no longer applies, and when, moreover, the characteristic features of the modern bases of social and political personality are precisely those which the neo-classical model identifies as corrupting? In what Pocock calls the 'nervous classicism' of the eighteenth century, manifested in the constant use of Sparta, Athens and Rome as critical reference points, the civic humanist model functions as a kind of foil against which the divergence of contemporary reality from the necessary conditions for civic virtue are offset and attempts are made to construct an alternative ethico-political model.

The field of problems Foucault discusses can be described, equally summarily, as being concerned with what conception of individuals is possible and necessary when they are targeted by rationally reflected political techniques of government whose objective is simultaneously to augment and secure the 'greatness' of the state and the happiness of its subjects. Foucault focuses on the connections between ways in which individuals are politically objectified and political techniques for integrating concrete aspects of their lives and activities into the pursuit of the state's objectives.

Both authors discuss how commerce – that is, in the first instance, commerce between rival states – figures in eighteenth-century thought as essentially a *political* theme and problem. Pocock's account emphasizes the role of the civic humanist model of ethical personality in responses to what were perceived as the challenging and worrying effects of the development of states into rival trading nations. An important aspect of this, he suggests, is what was identified as an increasing 'specialization of the social function' associated with the growth of exchange relations between individuals – in the broad, cultural as well as economic sense – and between individuals and the state. Specialization was problematic because, Pocock says, it was seen as being incompatible with the unity of personality found only in the republican citizen's practice of civic virtue.[21]

According to Pocock, specialization is identified as a problem in connection with tendencies in the field of secular statecraft associated with the development of states into rival trading nations. Of particular importance in this respect is the emergence of a growing body of professional political administrators and, especially, the question of standing armies and the appearance of 'specialists in warfare'. A further, related development noted by Pocock in this area of statecraft is the late-seventeenth-century identification of 'national prosperity' as an 'intelligible field of study' for an art of political arithmetic which 'estimates every *individual's* contribution to the political good'.[22]

There is here an interesting point of contact with, but also divergence from, Foucault's account. The latter's analysis cuts in a different, but possibly complementary, direction. Whereas Pocock examines 'specialization' in terms of the problems it poses for an ethical model of *citizenship*, Foucault identifies what he calls a 'professionalization' of individuals who are the sovereign's *subjects*: that is to say, who are the targets of methods of government.[23]

The accent in Foucault's account is less on the perception of the problematic effects of state commercial rivalry on the ethico-political personality of citizens than on the role of commerce as an *instrument* of state policy which straddles and connects governmental techniques developed within the framework of *raison d'état*. He sees mercantilism as the first rationalized application of *raison d'état* in the form of state *policy*. Inter-state commerce functions here as the 'common instrument' of both internal, administrative techniques of *police* for enriching and strengthening the state, and an external, 'diplomatico-military' system for pursuing the same end within the framework of a balance of power between rival states competitively pursuing growth.[24] It is from this perspective that he discusses political arithmetic and the phenomenon of 'professional-ization'.

Political arithmetic, Foucault says, represents a type of political knowledge very different from a knowledge both of virtue and of the rules of justice. It is, so to speak, a form of the state's secular knowledge of itself and of rival states. It objectifies individuals and their activities as calculable component elements and forces contributing to the state's wealth and strength. Foucault sees political arithmetic as a political knowledge made possible by, and which functions as an instrument of, a form of power embodied in the administrative techniques of police which aim to maximize the differential contribution of these elements and forces by means of their intensive regulation and, increasingly, their 'disciplinary' formation. That is to say, Foucault identifies a process of individualization which is intelligible less in terms of the development of new social relations expressed in abstract and speculative representations of relations of exchange, credit and 'mobile property', than by reference to its positive promotion by a 'professionalizing' political technology: a government of individuals in terms of what could be called their marginal utility *vis-à-vis* the objective of strengthening the state by maximizing the appropriate and particular contributions of each and all.

Interestingly, both Foucault and Pocock accord less significance than some others have to political and civil jurisprudence in the elaboration of modern conceptions of social and political subjectivity. Here again their perspectives differ but in a possibly complementary way. Pocock notes that the natural law theory of political jurisprudence does not conceptualize the political order in terms of relations between equal citizens participating in the public life of the *polis* or *respublica*, but in terms of relations of authority and submission founded in a contractual exchange and transfer of rights. Moreover, civil jurisprudence conceives of property as something to which one has a right which is exchangeable. This, Pocock hypothesizes, would seem to incline jurists to be less hostile to 'mobile property' and commercial exchanges than were those who referred themselves to the civic humanist tradition. For the latter, landed property (in the model form of the *oikos*) possessed a privileged ethico-political meaning as the essential precondition for the virtuous citizen's autonomy. For both these reasons, then, the forms of social being associated with 'commercial society' would not seem to have posed a critical problem for the jurists.[25]

Now Foucault notes that the mercantilist formulation of *raison d'état* was articulated within, and remained subordinate to, the conceptual and institutional structures of sovereignty. It gave itself the objective of promoting the strength of the state and the happiness of its subjects without questioning the existing forms of state sovereignty. If jurists attempted to find ways of reconciling the theory of the contract with developing forms of the art of government, none the less *governmental* reason continued to be thought of as *state* reason – that is to say, as a rationality for the exercise of sovereign power, as the sovereign's rationality – even though, at the same time, its targets, instruments and ends were not codifiable within the juridico-political thought in which problems of sovereignty were conceptualized. Political jurisprudence, then, would seem to have been not only unreconcilable with the civic humanist framework of thought, as Pocock suggests, but also, as Foucault claims, implicated in the promotion and political instrumentalization of the very activities identified in this framework as corrupting political life and personality (even if, as Foucault goes on to argue, it was also an obstacle to the autonomous development of an art of government).

These overly schematic comments are not intended to suggest either that Pocock and Foucault offer competing accounts of the same phenomena or that their different approaches can be immediately superimposed on each other. Rather, their respective analyses follow distinct lines of investigation which might, perhaps, prove to be complementary in a more complete picture. I have wanted only to indicate through this rapid juxtaposition of elements of their different perspectives that early modern problematizations of social and political subjectivity might fruitfully be analyzed in connection with the development of a governmental rationality for the exercise of power by the state and of the attempt to combine this with the unifying legal–political forms of sovereignty.

3. How, according to Foucault, does liberalism modify the terms of this problematic of political governmentality, and what new figure of social and political subjectivity does it introduce?

Liberal politics is often described as seeking to set limits to state or governmental activities. This is sometimes expressed negatively in terms of curtailing excessive state power by appealing to the imprescriptible rights of individuals. However, Foucault notes that the jurists of the eighteenth century neither attempted to nor succeeded in elaborating a positive liberal art of *government*. They were concerned less with the development of an autonomous art of government than with finding ways of codifying government within the conceptual and institutional structures of sovereignty. As he says in Chapter 4, the specific and autonomous development of governmental reason was blocked in the seventeenth and eighteenth centuries to the extent that the mercantilist elaboration of *raison d'état* remained trapped within the unquestioned juridical framework of sovereignty on the one hand, and the family–household model of oeconomy on the other. It was, he says, through the specific ways in which phenomena of *population* were reconfigured as a political problem that a renewed development of governmental thought became possible. Foucault identifies the political problematization of population as a fundamental condition of possibility for that epistemological and practical conversion of governmental thought that takes place in the late eighteenth century, as a result of which limits are set to the capacity of governmental reason and will by the specific *naturalness* and *opacity* of the domains to be governed.

The critical principle of *laissez-faire*, introduced by the Physiocrats or *économistes*, is directed against a particular way of governing and is premissed on an objectification of what is to be governed as a specific, naturally self-regulating domain. Methods of governing through exhaustive and detailed regulation are criticized as presupposing the capacity of the sovereign's or state's rational will to dictate to reality. Against the assumption that reality is modifiable at will, the Physiocrats identify the object-domain of government as possessing a naturalness of immanent, self-regulatory mechanisms and processes which make the sovereign's despotic imposition of regulations both futile and harmful. Not only is the attempt to govern reality in this way unnecessary, since reality contains intrinsic mechanisms of its own self-regulation, but it is harmful because it is likely to produce effects other than those desired.

What Foucault sees as emerging from this type of criticism of the 'folly' of administrative despotism is a recasting of governmental tasks through their referral to the naturalness of processes of population and wealth. Population in the eighteenth century is identified increasingly as both a specific and relative reality. It is no longer conceived of as a set of elements and forces contributing to the state's greater wealth, strength and glory, or as the sum of useful individuals to be put to work in accordance with the regulatory decrees of the sovereign's rational will. Nor is it a simple collection of legal subjects. Least of all, perhaps, is it an ethical community of equal citizens. Population comes to be seen through the grid of politically or administratively identified regularities in the natural phenomena and processes affecting relations between individual living beings coexisting within a general system of living beings, or 'species', and what increasingly is seen as a kind of vital environment.[26] At the same time, population is also objectified relatively to economic factors, or to the elements of wealth, to the extent that it is possible to identify regularities in the effects of natural and artificially modifiable variables of the former on those of the latter.

The specification of phenomena of population as a political problem of government is, Foucault suggests, an important condition for making possible a political isolation of economic processes. Both the family and economic processes are disengaged from the essential connections they have with each other within the model of oeconomy.[27] Increasingly the family is politically objectified outside of this model as an instrumentalizable, ethico-natural system within the nexus of relations constituting a population.[28] At the same time economic processes are separated out and their natural mechanics resituated within a complex set of relations to population as the subject of elements of wealth.

The principle of *laissez-faire*, then, is premised on a type of objectification of population and wealth which constitutes an epistemological precondition for the possible specification of new, practicable techniques of management. It is a principle for governing in accordance with the grain of things, and presupposes a specification of the objects of government in such a way that the regulations they need are, in a sense, self-indicated and limited to the end of securing the conditions for an optimal, but natural and self-regulating functioning.[29]

The Physiocrats formulate the notion of *laissez-faire* in relation to processes the fundamental mechanism of which involves the unrestricted pursuit of individual *interests* which spontaneously converge in the production of the general or public interest. Government by *laissez-faire* is a government of interests, a government which works through and with interests, both those of individuals and, increasingly, those attributed to the population itself.[30] It is a government which depends upon the conduct of *individuals* who are parts of a population and subjects of particular, personal interests. That is to say, the individual subject of interest is at once the object or target of government and, so to speak, its 'partner'.

This individual living being, the subject of particular interests, represents a new figure of social and political subjectivity, the prototype of 'economic man', who will become the correlate and instrument of a new art of government.

4. the governors have nothing to support them but opinion. It is therefore, on opinion only that government is founded.[31]

Every man's interest is peculiar to himself, and the aversions and desires, which result from it, cannot be supposed to affect others in a like degree.[32]

David Hume's philosophy is eminently practical: that is to say, political. His doctrine of the passional and imaginative principles of human nature provide the basis for a theory of empirical subjectivity and practical principles for a kind of social rationalization of *individual* conduct and its integration into artifically contrived social wholes or 'schemes'. Hume, like other thinkers of the 'Scottish Enlightenment', can certainly be seen to be grappling with the problems of a modernity identified in the terms established by the 'civic humanist' tradition. But, as Duncan Forbes has shown, his thought also critically engages with the jurisprudential tradition of natural law.[33] It seems to me at least arguable that elements of his thought, particularly as presented in his political essays, can also be situated within a framework of problems determined by principles of *raison d'état*. The possibility of reading Hume through these different (but not necessarily incompatible) grids may be due to his attempt to mark out the distinctiveness of his 'new scene of thought' by constituting the ways in which problems of modern political life are formulated in these different areas as a set or field of obstacles to be overcome. In any case, his thought makes, I think, an essential contribution both to the elaboration of an alternative to the 'civic humanist' ideal and, at the same time, to the possibility of thinking government outside the framework of jurisprudential conceptions of sovereignty. The nature of this dual contribution can be indicated roughly by a brief look at the themes of *opinion* and *interest* in his work.

Pocock identifies the late-seventeenth-century 'financial revolution' in England, and the associated development of relations of *credit*, as giving rise to the disturbing image of a fictive world of relations between individuals, and between individuals and the state, governed by the fancy-directed passions of man. Credit had become a central element in political relations in the concrete form of speculation in the future stability of the political order itself. But also, with its connotations of reputation and trust, of uncertainty and probabilistic calculations concerning the future, credit was, Pocock says, associated with forms of subjectivity prey to unrealistic, fiction-fed passions of hope and fear which contrasted starkly with the idea of the self-possessed, virtuous citizen. Pocock suggests that these disturbing features of the emergent world of credit constitute an important dimension in the preoccupation of eighteenth-century political thought with the conflict between reason and the passions, and that a significant strand in the attempt to find a way of rendering the latter governable consisted in the conversion of credit into a regularized opinion which would give grounds for reasonable expectations of the predictability of others' conduct and so provide a basis for an ethic of sociability.[34]

For the eighteenth century, opinion is simultaneously an epistemological and a political concept.[35] Opinion belongs to the realm of probabilities and the 'measures of evidence on which life and action strictly depend'.[36] At the same time, it is the epistemological insecurity of opinion, its susceptibility to imagination-directed 'unruly passions', that makes it an immediately political notion. Moreover, by the middle of the eighteenth century, opinion was a tangible political reality in the form of lively debates on the issues of the day taking place in a political press and the growing number of clubs, coffee-houses, journals and books.[37] A political culture of opinion, existing independently of government, had taken shape. 'Conversation' is the term Hume uses to describe the form ideally taken by the 'commerce' of this world of opinion, the appropriate cultural form of exchanges between individuals of the 'middling rank' immersed in 'common life'. An essential aspect of Hume's practical philosophy is the attempt to establish principles for moderating this political culture of opinion, to find ways of correcting and stabilizing it, and to fashion rules for conducting exchanges so that opinion can function as the settled currency of a secure, 'conversible' and sociable world.

As an essayist, Hume describes himself as an 'Ambassador from the Dominions of Learning to those of Conversation' and sets himself the task of fashioning the materials provided by 'Conversation and common life' into the articles of a 'Commerce' between the interdependent realms of the 'learned' and the 'conversible'.[38] It is in this role that he addresses himself to the world of opinion on which, as he says, governments depend for their security. Philosophy, occupying the world of learning, is made servant to the task of methodizing and correcting the 'reflections of common life'.[39] Hume's sceptical philosophy simultaneously seeks to correct the pretensions of abstract reasoning and to provide reason with a practical, instrumental role in individual and collective life.

Humean scepticism with regard to the claims of abstract reasoning furnishes principles for a tactics of correcting 'dogmatical' opinions and prejudice, of introducing a balance of evidence into our beliefs, and of probabilizing our imagined certainties so as to check the impatient passion with which we act on them.[40] The principal targets of Hume's critical scepticism here are 'enthusiasm' and 'faction', the enemies of conversibility, which often are linked to the uncorrected assertion of one of the two forms of opinion on which governments are founded: opinion of principle or *right* (to property and to power).[41]

Hume is famous for saying that reasoning is and ought to be no more than the obedient servant or slave of the passions. He limits reason to the instrumental role of identifying the objects and calculating the means for satisfying our passions.[42] Hume situates the existence, exercise and development of reason in the midst of, and as the instrument of, the practical conduct of 'common life':

> Laws, order, police, discipline; these can never be carried to any degree of perfection, before human reason has refined itself by exercise, and by an application to more vulgar arts, at least, of commerce and manufacture. Can we expect, that a government will be well modelled by a people, who know not how to make a spinning wheel, or to employ a loom to advantage?[43]

This subordinate, instrumental role of reason as the servant of man's passional activity is brought out most clearly in connection with the other form of opinion distinguished by Hume: opinion of *interest* ('the sense of the general advantage which is reaped from government'). It is, he says, the prevalence of opinion of interest which 'gives great security to any government'.[44]

Albert Hirschman describes how, during the eighteenth century, the 'passion of interest' or 'interested affection' is gradually singled out as a privileged means of solving the problem of how to make the potentially disruptive passions of man governable.[45] Interest, he suggests, is increasingly seen as a kind of control mechanism *vis-à-vis* the other passions. Hirschman's account shows how this role assigned to interest is associated with defences of the regularizing, calming, refining or, in short, civilizing benefits of 'commerce'. This separation out of interest as a fundamental and irreducible modality of man's passional nature goes together with a tendency for it to be identified as essentially 'economic'.

For Foucault, this isolation of interest-motivated choice and conduct represents a profound transformation in Western theories of subjectivity with critical consequences for how the individual's relation to the political order is thought.[46] The theory of an empirical subject of interest is seen by him as having significant implications for understanding the relations between 'interest' and 'right' – Hume's two forms of opinion – and constitutes a key element in what makes possible a renewal of governmental reason outside the frameworks of both *raison d'état* and the problems of sovereignty.

The individual subject of interests 'peculiar to himself' is, for Hume, a subject of choices motivated by, and directly expressing, ultimate non-rational or 'felt' preferences. As such, interests are irreducible in that they are not the product of reasoning or transcendent moral principles but the expression of passions with an 'original existence'.[47] Passions, volitions and actions are 'original facts and realities, compleat in themselves' which cannot be true or false, conformable or contrary to reason.[48] As the irreducible expression of felt preferences, interests are, unlike rights, non-transferable. Reasoning is incapable of 'disputing the preference with any passion',[49] and nothing can oblige one to exchange what happens to be, as 'a matter of fact', one's immediately felt, present preference, for some other preference.[50]

Interest, then, functions as the principle of a personal choice which is unconditionally subjective or private. As Foucault puts it, it makes the individual an isolated atom of preference-motivated choice and action. It is an immediately and absolutely subjective form of the individual will essentially different from the juridical form of will posited in contract theories of sovereignty.

Ernst Cassirer notes the implicit challenge to every transcendental system of ethics or obligation once it is recognized that no such obligation can 'presume to annul or to alter fundamentally the empirical nature of man. This nature will continue to appear and it will be stronger than any obligation.' [51] As Duncan Forbes says, Hume's *Treatise* gives us a 'political philosophy in which there is no mention of God'.[52] In Foucault's terms, Hume's version of the social contract is one in which all transcendence is radically excluded. Natural law versions of the social contract may attempt to reconcile interest and right by making the former the empirical principle of the latter, so that the individual *initially* contracts out of calculations of interest. But having contracted, the individual is found to be under a higher obligation, transcendent in relation to peculiar interests: he or she is now obliged as a different, legal kind of subject. Hume rejects this and claims that interest can never be superseded and must remain the ultimate basis for continued submission to the terms of the contract.[53]

For Hume, individuals will accept the obligation to submit to government only for so long as they calculate that their interest in doing so continues: that is, for so long as they continue to see their interests being served by the 'security' that the artifice of justice and the enforcement of its rules by civil magistrates provide.[54] Hume does allow for a second, distinct but equally invented 'moral obligation' of obedience to the laws of political society. But ultimately this second obligation depends upon the first 'natural obligation of interest' and does not establish any transcendence in relation to it. Interest always remains without ever being subsumed under the later obligation: there can be no civil obligation of obedience to law without a prior 'natural obligation of interest' irreducible to legal obligation and permanently outstripping it.

What Hume's theory introduces is a form of subjective will which is different in kind from, and irreducible to, a juridical form of will. Each is expressed in a different logic of action. The juridical form of will is actualized in an exchange, surrender and transfer of natural rights by which the individual becomes a legal subject who, whilst retaining certain rights, is at the same time made subject *to* a system of rights superimposed on these. In becoming legal subjects, individuals accept a limitation of their natural rights and assume a form of subjective will transcending their pre-contractual status.

The subject of interest's will is expressed in a completely different way. Interests can never be exchanged, surrendered or transferred. Individuals are never required to relinquish their interests, but only to 'adjust' them to each other so that they 'concur in some system of conduct and behaviour' – *the better to satisfy them*.[55] As Deleuze notes, Hume's is a political philosophy of the institution rather than of law.[56]

Rules of justice, according to Hume, are invented and 'artificial'. They are 'natural' also, but precisely in the sense that contriving artificial means for exerting his passions is a common characteristic of man as an 'inventive species'.[57] The rules of justice are the 'offspring' of vigilant and inventive passions, 'a more artful and more contriv'd way of satisfying them'.[58] Justice is a means to an end and does not establish a form of legal subjectivity which supersedes the empirical subjectivity which discovers or contrives it. Deleuze remarks that Hume's account of justice and government reverses the poles of positive and negative in juridical conceptions of the constitution of political society. Grotius, for example, defines justice negatively as what is not unjust, and injustice as what is contrary to the rational–juridical order of political society.[59] In a sense, what is positive is outside society, in nature and the natural rights possessed prior to the constitution of political society. Right is what remains after determining the prohibitions on which political society is founded. In contrast, Hume's is a philosophy of invention and institutional artifice, of 'oblique and indirect' means for the satisfaction of our passions.[60] By contrivance and artifice, interests are not so much protected as *directed* and provided with positive means for their pursuit and satisfaction. Rather than being limited, they are multiplied and diversified in a spontaneous, combinatory scheme in which they converge to the advantage of the public. What is outside society is negative in the sense that outside society human nature itself cannot even exist.[61]

According to Foucault, this theory of an empirical subject of interest brings to the fore the figure of a form of subjectivity which is the starting point for the elaboration of a dynamics or 'mechanics' of interests. He situates this new figure of subjectivity in the domain created at the intersection of the theory of the empirical subject of interest and analyses of economic processes.

5. How, in this astonishing variety of labours and products, of needs and resources; in this alarming complication of interests, which connects the subsistence and well-being of an isolated individual with the whole system of society; which makes him dependent upon all the accidents of nature and every political event; which extends in a way to the entirety of his capacity to experience either enjoyment or privation; how, in this apparent chaos, do we nonetheless see, by a general law of the moral world, the efforts of each serving the well-being of all, and, despite the external clash of opposed interests, the common interest requiring that each should be able to understand their own interest and can freely pursue it?[62]

In the Physiocrats' and Adam Smith's analyses of the mechanics of exchange, not only must the free pursuit of 'self-interested commerce' be given the greatest possible scope, but individuals must pursue their particular interests as far as possible since this will increase the interests of all other individuals. The pursuit of private interests by each individual operates according to a mechanics which spontaneously multiplies the possible objects and means of satisfying interests, and which results in a spontaneous co-ordination of the will of each with the wills of all other economic subjects.

Hume notes that the irreducible peculiarity of subjective preferences to the individual who has them, and the particularity of his or her circumstances in relation to the world, make the action resulting from the individual's calculations an isolated, particular event.[63] This theme of the atomic particularity and localized conditions of interest-motivated choice is frequently taken up (as both a positive and negative phenomenon) by late-eighteenth-century writers and is an important element in the development of a model of economic rationality as a rationality of *individuals*. In the game of private interests, isolated individuals are situated within an indefinite field of immanence in which their action is conditioned by an entire series of accidents and events which escape their knowledge and will. Equally, their action unknowingly and unintentionally contributes to all the interests comprising the public good. In their 'local situation' [64] individuals are found in what Foucault describes as a doubly involuntary world of dependence and productivity.[65] On one side, the individual's actions depend on an indefinite and involuntary world of natural accidents and the actions of others. And, superimposed on this, the individual's actions involuntarily contribute to the world of an indefinite collection of interests making up the interest of society.

Far from this situation disqualifying the rationality of individual subjects of interest, it is what founds it. In their local situation individuals calculate and thereby connect themselves to other subjects similarly adjusting themselves to each other. In the 'scheme of actions' that results from the actions of isolated subjects of interest, the economic positivity and rationality of each individual's calculated actions – the production of 'an end which was no part of his intention' [66] – is possible *only* if the ultimate conditions and effects of the individual's actions escape his or anyone's knowledge and will. This, says Foucault, is the meaning of Smith's 'invisible hand': the identification of economic men with subjects of interest situated within a system of dependence and productivity which escapes their knowledge and will, but which constitutes the conditions for the economic rationality of their actions.

Foucault emphasizes less the providential touch of Smith's hand than the invisibility of its operations. In Smith's famous doctrine, economic egoism is beneficial because attempts to direct the individual's actions on the basis of the collective good are harmful, leading only to the imposition of 'impertinent obstructions'.[67] Since the collective good is in principle incalculable, no one *should* seek to totalize economic processes because no one *can*. No sovereign, no 'single person, . . . council or senate' can 'safely be trusted' with authority over the pursuit of private interest,[68] because there is 'no human knowledge or wisdom' sufficient for performing the duty 'of superintending the industry of private people, and of directing it towards the employments most suitable to the interest of the society'.[69]

The removal of restrictions on the mechanism of the pursuit of private interests goes together, then, with the epistemological and practical disqualification of sovereignty over economic processes. It is the opacity of economic processes, the necessary invisibility of a non-totalizable multiplicity of essentially atomic points of calculation and action, that founds the rationality of economic agents as individual subjects of interest: *only* the isolated subject of interest is rational, only the individual is in a position to know his or her own interest and be able to calculate how best to pursue it.[70] As a formula for the economic subject's dependence and productivity, the 'invisible hand' designates the localized conditions of an economic rationality which is the rationality of essentially isolated individuals whose particular actions converge with those of others on condition that they are not totalized.

If, as the Physiocrats say, the self-regulating naturalness of population and economic processes sets limits to the sovereign's capacity to direct things at will, and if, as Smith says, the opacity of the totality of economic exchanges disqualifies the sovereign's capacity either to know or to direct them, if in short economic processes appear to be in some sense 'off limits' to government, what then becomes the appropriate domain for governmental action?

6.   Mankind, in following the present sense of their minds, in striving to remove inconveniences, or to gain apparent and contiguous advantages, arrive at ends which even their imagination could not anticipate, and pass on, like other animals, in the track of their nature, without perceiving its end . . . He who first ranged himself under a leader, did not perceive, that he was setting the example of a permanent subordination . . . Like the winds, that come we know not whence, and blow withersoever they list, the forms of society are derived from an obscure and distant origin; they arise long before the date of philosophy, not from the speculations of men . . . nations stumble upon establishments, which are indeed the result of human action, but not the execution of any human design.[71]

Adam Ferguson's *An Essay on the History of Civil Society* offers us a 'natural history' of man as a 'particular species of animal'.[72] This turns out to be a history of mankind 'taken in groups, as they have always subsisted'.[73] Human nature is social–historical. Civil society, or simply society, is not founded by an original contract involving the exchange, transfer and surrender of natural rights, but is always–already there, the natural–historical form of human species life. Society is 'as old as the individual',[74] and if:

we are asked, therefore, Where the state of nature is to be found? we may answer, It is here; and it matters not whether we are understood to speak in the island of Great Britain, at the Cape of Good Hope, or the Straits of Magellan.[75]

Like Hume's, Ferguson's man is 'destined from the first age of his being to invent and contrive'.[76] Both primitive cottage and palace are equally distant from any mythical state of nature and are in that sense *equally* 'unnatural': that is, natural to man as an inventive species. With Ferguson, we find a human nature both historicized and, in a sense, relativized: man is placed in a perspective which will become that of anthropology.

Ferguson's man in civil society is animated by what Adam Smith calls both 'social' and 'unsocial passions', with 'selfish' passions in 'a sort of middle place between them'.[77] He has a 'mixed disposition to friendship or enmity', 'union' and 'dissension', 'war' and 'amity', 'affection' and 'fear'. Most of all he is, like Humean man, 'partial' in that he is bound to others by localized forms of both cohesive and divisive partisanship which mutually nourish each other: the 'disinterested passions' of love and hatred go together, the divisive hatred of enemies promoting the cohesive love of friends.[78]

Ferguson does not establish the dynamics of civil society on a foundation of egoistic, economic interests alone. Rather, economic interests arise, find their place and operate within a spontaneously unifying framework of 'disinterested' interests or, as Foucault puts it, of the (non-egoistic) interests of the (economically) interested.[79] There is a tension in Ferguson's work between these two kinds of 'interest' and their respective modes of action. Both are spontaneously cohesive *and* divisive, both produce a productive synthesis of human action *and* set person against person. But egoistic, economic interests function differently from the 'disinterested passions' in so far as the latter, even when divisive, produce *localized* unities and allegiances, whereas the former tend to sever social bonds whilst, at the same time, creating other, abstract and non-localized relations. It is in a 'commercial state', Ferguson says:

> where men may be supposed to have experienced, in its full extent, the interest which individuals have in the preservation of their country . . . that man is sometimes found a detached and solitary being . . . The mighty engine which we suppose to have formed society only tends to set its members at variance or to continue their intercourse after the bonds of affection are broken.[80]

There is, as it were, an inevitable quotient of deterritorialization in the activity of subjects of economic interest. The abstract, isolated economic ego, the 'merchant' that, as Smith puts it, every man 'becomes in some measure', is 'not necessarily the citizen of any particular country. It is in a great measure indifferent to him from what place he carries on his trade.'[81] Partial, localized, communitarian and spontaneously generated social bonds, animated by disinterested interests, form a milieu in which non-localized, economic interests introduce a fissiparous tendency at the same time as they provide the basis for new, Humean schemes which adjust and combine the interested actions of isolated individuals.

If egoistic, economic interest is relativized in Ferguson, so too is the juridical codification of political power. Ferguson, in common with John Millar, Adam Smith and others,[82] does not seek either the origin or the essential nature of political power in a pact or contract which establishes a legal right to authority and a corresponding obligation to submission. Civil society spontaneously generates forms of 'casual subordination' which are distinct from (and may be opposed to) the 'formal establishment' of power: 'we move with the crowd before we have determined the rule by which its will is collected. We follow a leader, before we have settled the ground of his pretensions, or adjusted the form of his election.'[83] Or, as Millar puts the same point: 'A school-boy, superior to his companions in courage and feats of activity, becomes often a leader of the school, and acquires a very despotic authority.'[84] Millar, in *The Origin of the Distinction of Ranks*, develops the point in greater detail than Ferguson, and in a particular direction, but the general principle is the same. As in Ferguson, a natural basis of power is found in differences in personal qualities and capacities – especially those which manifest themselves in times of war – and exists in the form of *authority*. Authority derives from natural or acquired differences in skill, knowledge and accomplishments made evident in the performance of necesary collective tasks which evoke the admiration, esteem and respect of others. It involves the capacity to influence others, to command their obedience in actions and gain their submission to one's views in counsel. On these, and on the associated or consequential bases of age, property and descent, it gives rise to 'ranks'. Authority, then, has a natural–social foundation, fulfils necessary functions and takes historically variable forms. Finally, the legal codification and restriction of authority comes after, and is a function of, spontaneously formed social relations of authority and subordination. There is in both Ferguson and Millar, in addition to the celebrated theme of the effects of commerce in promoting the division of labour in society, the idea of another, natural kind of division of labour in the domain of relations of power or authority. Power is seen as being as natural and necesssary to civil society as civil society, language, arms and feet are to man as a 'particular species of animal'.[85] The subordination of some to others exists from the start, and natural–social forms of human existence are the permanent matrix for the emergence and development of forms of political power and government.

Finally, this scheme of a society spontaneously bonding and dividing out the tasks of authority and subordination gives rise to the theme of an immanent dynamic of historical and political transformation engendered principally, but not exclusively, by the 'concurrence or opposition of interests'. This cohesive–divisive dynamic is both what generates social bonds and the principle of what tears them apart, transforms them and produces varied forms of government or 'modes of proceeding' suited to different nations and ages.[86] This stadial vision of the history of civil or 'natural' society is a recurrent theme in thinkers of the 'Scottish Englightenment'.

Already, as a consequence of the political problem of population, the objectification of a naturalness specific to man's spontaneously self-regulating forms of coexistence had begun to define a domain of possible analysis and intervention comprising the forms of sociality natural to man. It is in relation to this domain, which will be called civil society, society or nation, that Foucault sees a renewal of the problematic of government taking place.

> Men are tempted to labour, and to practise lucrative arts, by motives of interest. Secure to the workman the fruit of his labour, and give him the prospects of independence or freedom, the public has found a faithful minister in the acquisition of wealth . . . The statesman in this, as in the case of population itself, can do little more than avoid doing mischief . . . Commerce . . . is the branch in which men committed to the effects of their own experience are least apt to go wrong . . . If population be connected with national wealth, liberty and personal security is the great foundation of both: and if this foundation be laid in the state, nature has secured the increase and the industry of its members.[87]

Liberalism begins, Foucault says, with the recognition of the heterogeneity and incompatibility of the principles regulating the non-totalizable multiplicity of economic subjects of interest and those operating in the totalizing unity of legal–political sovereignty. Legal and economic forms of subjectivity are formally heterogeneous and integrated into their respective domains differently. Consequently, they involve different relations with the political order and appeal to distinct principles for limiting the exercise of political power. The legal subject of rights says to the sovereign: 'You must not do this, you do not have the right.' The economic subject of interest says: 'You must not do this because you do not and cannot know what you are doing.' The latter *disqualifies* governmental reason in the form of *raison d'état*. It disqualifies a government exercised according to the rationality of a would-be omniscient sovereign's will. Sovereign power is threatened with a kind of dethronement. It is confronted with the prospect of either a subtraction of the economic domain from the space of sovereignty or, as the

Physiocrats propose broadly speaking, a division of this space in two and the reduction of the sovereign to the status of passive functionary of an independent economic science.

In fact, Foucault argues, neither of these possibilities is taken up.[88] The problem to be resolved is that of how, in accordance with what rational principles, is political power to be exercised within a unified space of sovereignty inhabited by individuals acting in accordance with heterogeneous principles of subjectivity, by individuals who are both empirical subjects of interest and legal subjects of rights? By posing this problem in relation to civil society – that is, by identifying society as what has to be governed – an art of government can be defined which does not have to sacrifice its globality or specificity. It makes possible an art of government which has neither to withdraw from a sector of the unified domain of political sovereignty nor submit passively to the dictates of economic science. Ferguson's *Essay* describes a domain of unifying bonds and collective forms of life which are generated spontaneously at different levels and sites within civil society, and which are characterized by neither purely economic nor purely juridical relations. The problem of political power is thus expressed in terms of governmental tasks and objectives in relation to an already existing domain, an already *civil* society, which enframes both economic and legal subjectivity as partial but invariable elements within the dense complexity of an historically dynamic, socio-natural milieu.

Foucault suggests that it is by situating the egoism of economic interests within the network of social bonds created by associative (and dissociative) non-egoistic interests that economic man, the atomic element of rationality and liberty, can be objectified, and thereby rendered governable, as *also* natural–social man.

Liberal criticism of economic sovereignty is not developed as a critique of the global unity of political sovereignty. The unifying framework of legal–political sovereignty is not in itself challenged, but only the identity of governmental reason with a totalizing reason of the sovereign or state. Reformulating the objects, instruments and tasks of government by reference to civil society makes it both possible and necessary to reformulate also the problem of the relation between government and the legal unity of the state.

All rationalized forms of government may be said to involve a principle of cost-effectiveness. That is to say, all governments seek to maximize their effectiveness at minimum political and economic cost. What, according to Foucault, is distinctive about liberal political rationality is that it breaks the identity of maximum governmental effectiveness and maximizing government itself.[89] Liberalism registers an incompatibility between the optimal functioning of economic processes and the maximization of governmental regulation. It pegs the rationale for its activities, and the principle of their necessary self-limitation, to the naturally self-regulating processes of what must be governed. The objective of a liberal art of government becomes that of securing the conditions for the optimal and, as far as possible, autonomous functioning of economic processes within society or, as Foucault puts it, of enframing natural process in mechanisms of *security*.[90]

At the end of the eighteenth century, the terms liberty and security have become almost synonymous. At the heart of the processes whose self-regulation government must secure is the individual, the essential atomic element of its mechanics, whose freedom to pursue his or her private interests is absolutely necessary to these processes. Liberty is thus a *technical* requirement of governing the natural processes of social life and, particularly, those of self-interested exchanges. The security of laws and individual liberty presuppose each other. The government of interests must of necessity be government of a 'system of natural liberty'.[91] Liberty is not merely determined negatively as what is not prohibited by law or by reference to imprescriptible natural rights. It is positively required as the necessary correlate and instrument of a government whose task is to secure the optimal functioning of natural processes: liberalism requires a proper use of liberty. In this respect an essential and original feature of liberalism as a principle of governmental reason is that it pegs the rationality of government, of the exercise of political power, to the freedom and interested rationality of the governed themselves. It does not identify governmental reason with the rationality of the sovereign who, in turn, identifies himself or herself with the state. Rather, it finds the principle for limiting and rationalizing the exercise of political power in the operations of the freedom and rationality of those who are to be governed.

The liberal principle of security–liberty might be described as one which provides a formula for a mutual adjustment of the antinomic principles of law and order. Pegging government to the requirements of natural processes – and to the free pursuit of interests that these processes presuppose – provides a principle for rationalizing the state's legal regulation of economy and society. A 'government of laws not of men' is required less on the grounds of juridical conceptions of the contractual foundation of political society than by reference to the technical adequacy of juridical forms to the regulation appropriate to a liberal art of government. Legal regulation of state activities and governmental intervention through 'general and equal laws' exclude exceptional, particular and individual forms of intervention by the state. The rule of law excludes 'arbitrary' forms of state activity with no internal principle of limitation. Also, the participation of the governed, 'interested' subjects themselves in formulating laws in a legally constituted democratic or 'representative' parliamentary system constitutes the most effective system for providing a rational check on governmental activity within a unified framework of legal–political sovereignty.

As the correlate of a new way of governing, civil society can be seen as providing a basis for rationalizing the legal regulation of a self-limiting, economical or 'frugal' government index-linked to economic processes. However, Foucault argues that, just as liberalism was not the product of juridical thought, nor was it the spontaneous expression or ideology of an emerging reality of market relations or a logical derivation from political economy. Rather, he sees the system of economic exchanges as providing the liberal critique of governmental reason with a kind of privileged test-site for identifying and measuring the effects of too much government.[92] It is in this sense that liberalism presents itself as a rationality of economic government in the immediately connected senses of both a government orientated by the performance of the economy and a government which is economical or frugal.

The scheme of civil society situates the problem of exercising political power in relation to a natural domain in which power, in the form of spontaneously developed relations of authority and subordination, already exists in an internal, dynamic relation to the play of egoistic and non-egoistic interests.[93] Thus government can be thought of as a function of already existing social and economic relations in the form of relations of authority and subordination. To the extent that the objective of government is to provide the regulatory framework which will secure the more or less automatic functioning of civil society, the state's exercise of governmental power can be seen as in continuity with, or as grafted on to, society's immanent relations of power. It is in the name of society and its economic processes, in the name of their specific naturalness and immanent mechanisms of 'self-government' or self-regulation, that government by the state is both criticized and, so to speak, demanded. That is to say, government can be thought of as a function of a social demand for the order necessary for society and economy to function more or less on their own and as they should.

What Foucault's analysis brings out is the problematizing character of liberalism in relation to the existence of civil society as both the object and end of government. It is by reference to already existing society that the state's role and function has to be defined, and it is the natural, self-producing existence of this society that the state has to secure so that it functions to optimal effect. The attempt to attain this objective by enframing its natural processes with mechanisms of security places society in a complex and variable position both within and outside the state. It exists within the state's unifying framework of legal regulations yet, at the same time, is a natural reality which is, in essential respects, inaccessible to centralized political power.

Civil society is not, Foucault says, a kind of aboriginal reality that finally we are forced to recognize; it is not a natural given standing in opposition to the timeless essential nature of the state. Nor is it an ideological construct or something fabricated by the state. It is, he says, the correlate of a political technology of government. The distinction between civil society and the state is a form of 'schematism' for the exercise of political power.[94] Foucault describes civil society as in this sense a 'transactional reality' existing at the mutable interface of political power and everything which permanently outstrips its reach.[95] Its contours are thus inherently variable and open to constant modification, as is, correspondingly, the diagram of power relations which describes the form of its government.

For Foucault, the political objectification of civil society plays a central role in determining a relatively open-ended and experimental problem-space of *how* to govern: that is, of finding the appropriate *techniques* for a government oriented by a problematic of security. This 'transactional' domain at the frontier of political power and what 'naturally' eludes its grasp constitutes a space problematization, a fertile ground for experimental innovation in the development of political technologies of government.

This can be illustrated by the development, in the first half of the nineteenth century, of a hybrid space of government in which public law is coupled with forms of 'private' power and authority. That is to say, forms of power existing already within 'civil society' are both legally enframed and instrumentalized as techniques of government. Jacques Donzelot[96] and François Ewald[97] have described striking examples of this in their analyses of the early-nineteenth-century system of employer 'paternalism'. In the French case, the central state declares the determination of the specific regulatory and disciplinary requirements of different production processes to be beyond its legislative competence. The power and responsibility for determining the disciplinary order necessary for production is therefore best left to individual employers. The resultant system of employer tutelage might be described as a kind of private governmental order, legally sanctioned by the state, for integrating individuals into economic life. Within this order the technical organization of production is linked inextricably with the exercise of a disciplinary power often extending into the workers' domestic lives. The state is, as Adam Smith might have put it, 'discharged from . . . the duty of superintending the industry of private people'[98] but, as he may not have foreseen, with the result that responsibility for determining the detailed procedures for governing aspects of the 'system of natural liberty' falls to a certain category of individuals within the 'private' domain.

In a different area, Jeremy Bentham's coupling of the Panopticon's technical principle of central inspection with the administrative principle of contract management offers a model for executing the government's 'public security' function which, through private management, at the same time makes 'an economy for the state'.[99] Or again, one could cite John Stuart Mill's insistence on a fundamental distinction between the necessity for the state's legal enforcement of education, and its disqualification from responsibility for the actual content and conduct of education.[100]

One can see here how Foucault's analysis of governmental rationality connects up with the 'micro-physical' perspective of his analysis of an individualizing, disciplinary technology in *Discipline and Punish*.[101] Liberal principles for rationalizing the exercise of political power outline a framework for a possible art of government which depends upon and facilitates a proliferation of techniques for the disciplinary integration of individuals at critical points in the social order. They delineate a space for the possible formation of a tactically polymorphous political technology for governing the lives of individuals which aims to fashion the forms of conduct and performance appropriate to their productive insertion into (or exclusion from) the varied circuits of social life.

Much of Foucault's work focuses on the clusters of relations between 'institutional' and epistemological elements of practices through which, around the end of the eighteenth century, individuals are objectified as living beings who are parts of a population existing in a necessary relation to a natural–social environment. Through analyses of the practices in which particular aspects of the life and conduct of this individual living being have been problematized, he has described the development of possible fields of analysis by the human and social sciences and the associated development of individualizing political technologies. Foucault's analyses suggest that the political problematization of this network of relations constituted a privileged terrain for the elaboration of practical formulae for adjusting the operation of individualizing technologies to the requirements of a liberal government. It is in this area that natural–social man appears as *normal* man, the correlate and target of specific kinds of professional expertise which address the problems of integrating individuals into forms of social order and which answer to the demand for a governmental management of an individual–population–environment complex.[102] What might be called a natural–social demand for order, or for mechanisms to integrate individuals into appropriate schemes of behaviour and activity, is met by an expertise licensed by the state but formally independent of it: medicine, psychiatry, psychology, criminology, pedagogy and so on.

8. Foucault's analysis of liberalism is pitched at the level of its practice as a critical reflection on governmental reason. It is not an analysis of liberalism as a theoretical doctrine, a utopian dream, an ideology or a collection of particular governmental policies. Rather, liberalism is presented as a principle and method for rationalizing governmental practice, for a constant reflection on and criticism of what is. Its internal regulative principle is seen as the need to maintain a suspicious vigilance over government so as to check its permanent tendency to exceed its brief in relation to what determines both its necessity and limits – society. In the name of society, the state's interventions in particular areas of life are brought under critical scrutiny in terms of both their legitimacy (do they encroach on the *necessary* freedoms of individuals?) *and* the competence and cost-effectiveness of its methods (can the objectives be achieved without state intervention: that is, by members of society themselves?). It is in the name of society and of the capacity of its members to 'manage their own affairs' that government is both demanded and criticized. Government is demanded as a function of the security and order necessary for society's continued existence and for its capacity to develop according to its intrinsic, natural dynamic. But the state's competence and entitlement to govern is at the same time placed under strict critical supervision in the name of this same society.

I have attempted to show how this approach might help to make intelligible certain features of early liberalism as a form of governmental reason which programmes a practical realignment of the totalizing, legal–political form of the state's power with the practices of an individualizing, pastoral form of government. But these roughly sketched formulae of early liberalism do not amount to a definitive theorem of government (nor, of course, has all modern government been liberal in either inspiration or practice). The elements and relations characteristic of early liberal experiments in the art of government have not remained constant and unchanged. Early liberal political rationality provided methodological principles for an art of government and a schema for their application to particular *problems*. But this is not to say that the problems addressed could be solved without putting liberal rationality itself to the test. In this respect, Foucault notes that problems of governmental practice posed by phenomena specific to a set of living beings constituted as a population were the source of a fundamental challenge to liberalism. A 'biopolitical' rationalization of these problems of population – health, hygiene, birth and death rates, life expectancy, races, etc. – was not obviously possible within the framework of a liberal rationalization of government premised on the rights and necessary free initiative of *individuals*.[103] Certainly, it was in relation to these and other related problems that early forms of liberal governmentality were challenged and transformed in important ways (see Chapter 1).

Undoubtedly we live in a different world today, but a world, perhaps, in which a recognizably liberal form of questioning remains a constitutive element of contemporary political thought with, I want to suggest, an enduring effect on how problems of political identity are currently framed.

At the risk of considerable oversimplification, let us say very generally that the principles and procedures of government in our kind of democratic political order presuppose, either explicitly or implicity, some kind of more or less unified and unifying legal–political framework whereby governed individuals are integrated into the state. They presuppose a legal framework for determining the conditions and forms of governed individuals' membership of and possible activity within the unified state. But this on its own will not be sufficient a basis for government. Practical principles for the effective conduct of government additionally will presuppose some way of conceiving how these individuals with diverse social and economic forms of existence, individuals who are members of particular groups and 'communities', who are living beings, parts of a biological population, and who have different particular interests, needs, aptitudes and abilities, are to be integrated within various sectors of 'society'. The problem, then, that attempts to formulate practicable principles of government have to confront is how to establish a scheme in which these different modes of integrating the individual within society and its englobing political order can be co-ordinated. Foucault's analysis of early liberalism indicates the ways in which our political objectification as living beings who are part of a population, as members of society, as rational interest-motivated economic agents and so on, sought to render us *governable*.

But if this, however crudely, describes the terms of the problem of practical governmental reason, correspondingly it describes the conditions which have made possible contemporary forms of the politics of identity and citizenship. It also indicates conditions that have to be met by any viable model for political identity and citizenship. Foucault's analysis of liberalism brings into focus the kind of rational principles which have informed the shaping of an essential element of modern politics which is characterized by an oscillation between a suspicious fear and criticism of the state's impertinent interventions in detailed aspects of our lives, and an expectation that government will, and/or a demand that it should, respect our rights while taking responsibility for improvements in the conditions and quality of our individual lives, for sheltering us from insecurities and dangers, for providing the conditions and opportunities for individual advancement, for meeting our individual health needs, for protecting the local community and natural environment in which we live, and so on. In other words, our relation to political power has been shaped by what Foucault calls the 'governmentalization' of the state. That is to say, it is in the name of forms of existence which have been shaped by political technologies of *government* that we, as individuals and groups, make claims on or against the *state*. It is in the name of our governed existence as individual living beings, in the name of our health, of the development of our capabilities, of our membership of particular communities, of our ethnicity, of our gender, of our forms of insertion into social and economic life, of our age, of our environment, of particular risks we may face and so on, that we both revile and invoke the power of the state.

Neither classical nor contemporary liberal political thought succeeds in suppressing the antinomies of modern Western political reason. The impossibility of reconciling law and governmental order without subordinating the former to the latter remains. This is why Foucault declares himself sceptical with regard to both a politics confined to the affirmation of rights and a politics which reinvokes the (mythical) virtues of a civil society independent of and opposed to the state. Both propose a codification of the individual's relation to the state's power which, in important respects, avoids the problem of power at the level of government. There can be no *right* to health, Foucault notes.[104] Areas like the provision of health care, or of an education in accordance with individual 'needs and abilities', raise complex issues of power and decision making which cannot be settled in purely juridical terms. Similarly, whatever form of regulation or 'self-government' is proposed for an independent civil society, the exercise of power over individuals will remain an essential element and its alignment with the central power of the state will continue to be a problem.[105] This is not, of course, to suggest that either a politics of rights or a politics of collective, 'institutional' experiment has no value. But it is, perhaps, to suggest that any attempt to construct a politics of the relation of individuals and groups to political power has to confront problems of government which are specific and irreducible to, for example, questions of the legal codification of 'citizenship'. This means, among other things, that models of social and political self-identity – of our relation to ourselves as citizens and as concrete living individuals – must, at the same time, address the question not only of how we are to be governed by others, but also of how we ourselves are to be involved in the practices of governing others.

It is, perhaps, not surprising that there should be a 'return' to liberal themes in the contemporary politics of both the left and right, since we seem to be witnessing a significant mutation of liberal governmental rationality which aims to modify the relation of individuals to political power by seeking, in part, to get them to economize on their expectations of or demands on government. A change in the political objectification of ourselves as individual subjects accompanies current modifications in the relation between the state's centralized power and the techniques by which we are governed as concrete individuals.[106] A new figure of rational–'economic' subjectivity seems to have emerged as the proposed correlate-partner of this modern version of liberal governmental reason (see Chapter 1). As Veyne and Foucault suggest, it is when we are called upon to change our relation to government that we are also required to change our relation to ourselves, to change our subjective self-identity, and it is then that we become aware of the ways in which the political power of state impinges on our individual lives, that we *feel* it.[107]

NOTES

1. Max Weber, cited in W. Hennis, *Max Weber, Essays in Reconstruction*, London, 1988, p. 59.
2. Adam Smith, *An Inquiry into the Nature and Cause of the Wealth of Nations*, Oxford, 1976, p. 37.
3. Adam Ferguson, *An Essay on the History of Civil Society*, Edinburgh, 1986, p. 187. On the question of power presupposing the freedom and activity of those over whom it is wielded, see Michel Foucault, 'The subject and power', *Critical Inquiry*, vol. 8, Summer 1982; and Foucault's pseudonymous autobiographical essay, Maurice Florence, '(Auto)biography, Michel Foucault 1926–1984', *History of the Present*, vol. 4, 1988.
4. Paul Veyne, 'L'individu atteint au coeur par la puissance publique', in *Sur l'individu*, Paris, 1987.
5. Vaclav Havel, 'The power of the powerless', in Vaclav Havel *et al., The Power of the Powerless*, ed. John Keane, London, 1985, p. 37.
6. For one of the clearest general statements of Foucault's perspective of government and subjectivity, see '(Auto)biography'.
7. Paul Veyne, 'Foucault révolutionne l'histoire', in Veyne, *Comment on écrit l'histoire*, Paris, 1979.
8. The source for much of the following presentation is the series of lectures given by Foucault at the Collège de France in 1978 and 1979. The introductory lectures for each year's course have been published in the form of cassette recordings, *De la Gouvernementalité*, Paris, 1989. Transcripts of the rest of the lectures have not yet been published, but cassette recordings can be consulted at the Bibiothèque du Saulchoir, Paris. Foucault's own course summaries have been published as Michel Foucault, *Résumé des cours, 1970–1982*, Paris, 1989.
9. Foucault, 'The political technology of individuals', in L. H. Martin, H. Gutman and P. H. Hutton, eds., *Technologies of the Self*, London, 1988, p. 146.
10. David Hume, 'Of civil liberty', in *Essays Moral, Political, and Literary*, ed. E. F. Miller, Indianapolis, 1987, p. 93.
11. Hume, 'Of Commerce', in *Essays*, p. 255.

12. Christian Meier, *La politique et la grâce*, Paris, 1987.
13. Meier's essay examines the possibility of a political anthropology of the ancient Greek idea of beauty. His analysis of grace as a political virtue complements at many points Foucault's analysis of the elaboration in ancient Greece of 'arts of existence' and the connection between techniques of governing oneself and governing others. See Foucault, *The Use of Pleasure*, Harmondsworth, 1986.
14. J. G. A. Pocock, *The Machiavellian Moment*, Princeton, 1975.
15. *Ibid.*, p. 431.
16. *Ibid.*, p. 436.
17. J. G. A. Pocock, *Virtue, Commerce, and History*, Cambridge, 1985, p. 69.
18. See, for example, Albert Hirschman, *The Passions and the Interests*, Princeton, 1977; Gerhard Oestreich, *Neostoicism and the Early Modern State*, Cambridge, 1982; Norbert Elias, *The Civilizing Process*, Oxford, 1978; Elias, *The Court Society*, Oxford, 1982; and I. Hont and M. Ignatieff, eds., *Wealth and Virtue*, Cambridge, 1983.
19. 'Politics and reason', in Foucault, *Politics, Philosophy, Culture: Interviews and other writings 1977–1984*, London, 1988, p. 67.
20. *Ibid.*, p. 71; *Résumé des cours*, p. 101.
21. *Machiavellian Moment*, p. 499; *Virtue, Commerce, and History*, p. 110.
22. *Machiavellian Moment*, p. 425, emphasis added.
23. Foucault, lecture 29 March 1978.
24. Foucault, 'Sécurité, territoire et population', in *Résumé des cours*, and Collège de France lecture, 5 April 1978. See also Denis Meuret, 'A political genealogy of political economy', *Economy and Society*, vol. 17, no. 2, May 1988.
25. Cf. Pocock, 'The mobility of property and the rise of eighteenth-century sociology', in *Virtue, Commerce, and History*, and 'Cambridge paradigms and Scotch philosophers', in Hont and Ignatieff, eds, *Wealth and Virtue*.
26. Foucault notes that mercantilism privileges a wealth–population connection at the same time as 'police' techniques effectuate a politico-administrative *découpage* of population and the phenomena of life in the eighteenth century. It is, he says, through the particular ways in which the phenomena of population are identified as politically problematic that the mercantilist view of population and wealth is eventually questioned and transformed. He has written in a number of places on the emergence in the eighteenth century of a specific 'biopolitical' dimension of government. See, for example, 'The politics of health in the eighteenth century', in Foucault, *Power/Knowledge*, ed. Colin Gordon, Brighton, 1980; *The History of Sexuality, I: An Introduction*; and also *The Birth of the Clinic*, London, 1973, especially chapters 2 and 3.
27. For the structure of political oeconomic thought see K. Tribe, *Land, Labour and Economic Discourse*, London, 1978.
28. Foucault notes that the family plays a key role in the emerging politics of health and in the late-eighteenth-century problematization of forms of assistance. See *Birth of the Clinic* and *Histoire de la folie à l'âge classique*, Paris, 1972.
29. For a valuable comment on this kind of objectification of reality as manageable by virtue of its intrinsic self-regulatory mechanisms, see Colin Gordon's 'Afterword' to Foucault, *Power/Knowledge*, pp. 248–50.
30. Population acquires interests of its own due to the decisive shift in the focus

of economic analysis from circulation to production, which makes population the *subject* of the elements of wealth rather than a sum total of elements and forces calculated as components of the state's wealth.

31. Hume, 'Of the first principles of government', in *Essays*, p. 32.
32. Hume, *Enquiries concerning Human Understanding and concerning the Principles of Morals*, Oxford, 1975, p. 228.
33. Duncan Forbes, *Hume's Philosophical Politics*, Cambridge, 1985.
34. *Machiavellian Moment*, pp. 450ff., and *Virtue, Commerce, and History*, chapter 6.
35. For the epistemological aspects of opinion and the transformation of the medieval notion of *opinio* into the modern concept of opinion, see Ian Hacking, *The Emergence of Probability*, Cambridge, 1975.
36. Hume, 'An abstract of a book lately published, entituled, a treatise of human nature, &c.', in *A Treatise of Human Nature*, Oxford, 1978, p. 647.
37. See Nicholas Phillipson, *Hume*, London, 1989.
38. 'Of essay-writing', in *Essays*, pp. 533–7.
39. *Enquiries*, p. 162.
40. *Ibid.*, p. 161.
41. 'Of the first principles of government', in *Essays* p. 33.
42. *Treatise*, pp. 415 and 459.
43. 'Of refinement in the arts', in *Essays*, p. 273.
44. 'Of the first principles of government' in *Essays* p. 33.
45. A. O. Hirschman, *The Passions and the Interests*, Princeton, 1977.
46. Foucault, lecture 28 March 1979.
47. *Treatise*, p. 415.
48. *Ibid.*, p. 458.
49. *Ibid.*, p. 415.
50. *Ibid.*, p. 416.
51. Ernst Cassirer, *The Philosophy of the Enlightenment*, Princeton, 1951, p. 246.
52. *Hume's Philosophical Politics*, p. 65.
53. *Treatise*, pp. 550–3. See also, 'Of the original contract' and 'Of passive obedience', in *Essays*.
54. *Treatise*, p. 553.
55. *Ibid.*, p. 529.
56. 'The institution is not a limitation like the law but, on the contrary, a model of actions, a genuine enterprise, an invented system of positive means, a positive invention of indirect means.' Gilles Deleuze, *Empirisme et subjectivité*, Paris, 1973, p. 35.
57. *Treatise*, p. 484.
58. *Ibid.*, p. 526.
59. Grotius, *The Law of War and Peace*.
60. *Treatise*, p. 497.
61. *Enquiries*, p. 206.
62. Condorcet, *Esquisse d'un Tableau Historique des Progrès de l'Esprit Humain*, Paris, 1971, p. 209.
63. *Treatise*, p. 531.
64. Smith, *Wealth of Nations*, pp. 456 and 531.
65. Foucault, lecture 28 March 1979.
66. *Wealth of Nations*, p. 456.
67. *Ibid.*, p. 540.
68. *Ibid.*, p. 456.
69. *Ibid.*, p. 687.

70. Of course, as Hume and Smith both recognize, individuals may be mistaken about whether particular objects will satisfy their interests and about whether a chosen course of action is in fact the best for achieving their interests. Hence the need for education and other supplementary means for meeting what Condorcet sees as a requirement, namely that individuals, as individuals, *should* be able to understand where their interest lies.

71. Ferguson, *History of Civil Society*, p. 122.

72. *Ibid.*, p. 2.

73. *Ibid.*, p. 4.

74. *Ibid.*, p. 6.

75. *Ibid.*, p. 8.

76. *Ibid.*, p. 6.

77. Adam Smith, *The Theory of Moral Sentiments*, Oxford, 1976, p. 74.

78. 'Our attachment to one division, or to one sect, seems often to derive much of its force from an animosity conceived to an opposite one: and this animosity in its turn, as often arises from a zeal in behalf of the side we espouse, and from a desire to vindicate the rights of our party.' *History of Civil Society*, p. 16. See also pp. 3 and 15.

79. Foucault, lecture 4 April 1979.

80. *History of Civil Society*, p. 19.

81. *Wealth of Nations*, p. 426.

82. John Millar, *The Origin of the Distinction of Ranks*, reprinted in William C. Lehmann, *John Millar of Glasgow 1735–1801*, Cambridge, 1960. Smith develops the theme in Book V of *Wealth of Nations*. See also Pocock on Josiah Tucker, in *Virtue, Commerce, and History*, chapter 9.

83. *History of Civil Society*, p. 133.

84. John Millar, 'The principles of law and government', in *John Millar of Glasgow*, p. 348.

85. *History of Civil Society*, pp. 63, 84 and 100.

86. *Ibid.*, pp. 62 and 134.

87. *Ibid.*, pp. 143–4.

88. Foucault, lecture 4 April 1979.

89. Foucault, 'Naissance de la biopolitique', in *Résumé des cours*.

90. Foucault, lecture 5 April 1978.

91. Smith, *Wealth of Nations*, p. 687.

92. Foucault, *Résumé des cours*, p. 114.

93. See *History of Civil Society*, pp. 98–100 and 133.

94. *Résumé des cours*, p. 113.

95. Foucault, lecture 4 April 1979.

96. Jacques Donzelot, *L'invention du social*, Paris, 1984; and the translation of a chapter from this, 'The promotion of the social', *Economy and Society*, vol. 17, no. 3, August 1988.

97. François Ewald, *L'Etat providence*, Paris, 1986.

98. *Wealth of Nations*, p. 687.

99. Bentham cited by Elie Halévy in *The Growth of Philosophical Radicalism*, London, 1972, p. 85.

100. 'The objections which are urged with reason against State education do not apply to the enforcement of education by the State, but to the State's taking upon itself to direct that education; which is a totally different thing.' John Stuart Mill, 'On liberty', in Mill, *Utilitarianism, Liberty, Representative Government*, London, 1972, p. 161.

101. Foucault, *Discipline and Punish*, London, 1977.
102. These themes were already developed at some length in the unfortunately still untranslated sections of Foucault's *Histoire de la folie à l'agê classique*, as was the question of aligning natural–social, normal man with legal man. See Colin Gordon, '*Histoire de la folie*: an unknown book by Michel Foucault', *History of the Human Sciences*, vol. 3, no. 1. They are taken up more directly in *History of Sexuality, I*.
103. Foucault, *Résumé des cours*, pp. 109–10.
104. Foucault, 'Social security', in *Politics Philosophy, Culture*, p. 170.
105. *Ibid.,* pp. 167–8.
106. One might speak here, perhaps, of a new and quite different programme for a 'privatization' of the pastoral.
107. 'Social security', p. 163.

CHAPTER SEVEN

Social economy and the government of poverty

Giovanna Procacci

Assisting the poor is a means of government, a potent way of containing the most difficult section of the population and improving all other sections.[1]

We are accustomed to think of the end of the eighteenth century and the beginning of the nineteenth as the moment of historic emergence of a new discourse, political economy, a discourse destined to teach us much about the nature of our society. One of the singularities of this discourse's fortunes has been the fact that, all through the nineteenth century and even down to the present day, it has remained positioned at the *centre* of our history, the privileged terrain for domination and resistance alike, the arena for all the conflicts of which our societies are bearers.

But what if we were to relinquish for a moment this certainty which has so regularly governed our historical vision of the economy? What if, instead of accepting this postulate of centrality as an incontestable pre-given of all analysis, we were to begin by posing the question of how this centrality is constructed, and what purposes it serves.

This, after all, is the essential contribution genealogical analysis has had to offer: the impulse to see every object represented to us as irreducible, every truth as irrefutable, as the end-product of a series of retraceable operations, and accordingly to search out the dynamics of the process which constituted them. *Power is brought into play as an analytical principle.* Returning to history no longer means retracing the vicissitudes of certain already given objects, but exploring lines of convergence and derivation through which certain specific configurations are shaped, under conditions where alternative historical possibilities confront one another.

A genealogy of political economy undertaken in this spirit must of necessity call into question the centrality attributed to its object, and this questioning leads to a number of important clues. There is, for instance, the obscurantism of the centralist thesis. The official history of economic thought has singled out its classical texts and themes in such a way as to disqualify a whole area of production labelled as 'vulgar economics', relegating it to the margins of that history, as representative of the

151

inevitably lethargic, tentative, botched qualities of its accompanying intellectual environment. To differentiate between 'noble' material, which matches the profile of *our* truth concerning political economy, and 'vulgar' material, whose divergent by-ways can be legitimately disregarded, was a convenient procedure for a historiography which already has its cast of characters – with the mode of production officiating as the structural element of society, the principal site of conflict and criterion for identifying historical protagonists – and for which nothing more is required than to set them in motion in order duly to arrive at an appropriate moral. But if what is required of history is not to revalidate that which is already known, but to offer us new clues about ourselves, then it no longer makes sense to let ourselves be put off by distaste for the 'vulgar'.

What is proposed here is an attempt to look again at this material which the history of economic thought has relegated to oblivion, and to gather the new clues which such a re-reading can offer us concerning political economy and its relation to the process of formation of modern society. And this attempt arises out of an initial *uncertainty*, an uncertainty which has come to be widely shared and which has forced us to rethink the fabric of our social being. We have rediscovered in turn the insane, the beggars, the paupers, the criminals, the women and children, the heretics, those real micropopulations which the historiography of the working-class movement claims to reduce to sociological categories; and through these rediscoveries new light has been thrown on both them and us. We are the heirs of their vagrancy, their insanitary slums, their illegalities, as of all the sociotechnical inventiveness that has been at once demanded and produced by the need for their socialization; for, as Karl Polanyi writes, 'social and not technological invention was the principal intellectual source of the industrial revolution'.[2] And this social inventiveness was an omnipresent force, applying itself to every hotbed of variant social existence, through the converging action of a zealous multiplicity of novel or renovated techniques.

But this does not mean replacing the cult of a central myth of origin with the new myth of a uniquely creative marginality. That would, in any case, be a misconceived way of posing the problem. Each element in this history can equally well be said to have been central – or marginal. What we are aiming at here is to outflank these massive declamatory categories which can be employed only for the reciting of epics, in order instead to seek to rediscover the materiality of the lines of formation and transformation of the social domain. This is a materiality which is composed not of macroscopic relations of domination and submission, but of a multiplicity of social islands dealt with at a local level, a plurality of diverse modes of behaviour needing to be combated, encouraged or promoted; in this sense, labour itself figures as a technological apparatus productive of specific patterns of sociality, alongside such techniques as mutual benefit societies, schemes for compensating industrial accidents, hygiene and psychiatry. And, to the extent that political economy forms an integral component of this universe of invention, it requires to be examined in terms not of an opposition between truth and ideological mystification, but of the 'transformation of society' (Polanyi) which it made possible. It needs to be regarded not as an imperious instance which subordinates society to its demands, but as a set of special technologies which opened up new social spaces; and what is needed is to trace the vicissitudes to which these new techniques gave rise, the displacements they effected, the strategies they promoted and those which they made obsolete.

The 'vulgar' material to be re-read here is that which goes under the name of *Sozialpolitik* in Germany and *économie sociale* in France – as also in Italy. In this chapter, only the French aspect will be examined: a discursive field which is heterogeneous in respect of the positions occupied by its authors, the sources of their inspiration and the proposals they put forward; but homogeneous in its strategic location midway between public and private life, and in its preoccupations.

The discursive reference-point for social economy is the critical discourse which appears within classical political economy, with Malthus in Britain and Sismondi in France. We will not enter here into an extensive summary or a detailed analysis of this relationship, but only note the problematic issues which were taken up by social economy for use as instruments to make it autonomous of classical political economy. Social economy was a critical discourse in the sense that it took its start from that same discovery of society as something that exists positively, and not only as a result of laws, something that has its own rules and functioning, that discovery which with the Physiocrats became an essential doctrine of political economy; but here this discovery was turned round and used against political economy itself. This championing of the social against the economic drew its central arguments from the analysis of the question of *pauperism*.

Pauperism in this context denotes at once the critical element of the socioeconomic order which economics takes as its end, society's answering riposte to economics, and the line of economic penetration into the evasive substance of the social. The political significance of discourse on poverty, for Malthus and Sismondi, as for social economy (whose whole theoretical and practical identity it defines) throughout the first half of the nineteenth century, resides in this double meaning of poverty, as both the limit to economic discourse and the key to economic conquest of a new continent. On the one hand, it allows the refinement of the instruments of political economy through analysis of crises and mechanisms of systemic breakdown and dysfunction (this analysis, however, makes little significant progress within economics before the end of the nineteenth century, nor indeed any decisive advance prior to Keynes' revival of social economy); on the other hand, it permits the instruments of 'economic' government to be mediated by a more varied and flexible set of tools, which provide access to a whole series of social situations which political economy alone was incapable of handling. Though it undoubtedly derives from the philanthropic spirit of the eighteenth century, social economy elaborates its problematic of poverty around some themes which connect in an extraordinarily modern way the techniques of a philanthropy which gradually breaks away from older charitable perspectives, with the problems of the new social order implanted by industrialism. The new philanthropy associated with social economy works through specific methods which effect a linkage between political economy and population otherwise than through the medium of labour.

This is not to say that the problem of poverty had been absent from the conceptual horizons of the first classical economists. Political economy, which was constructed as a discourse on the increase of wealth, never evaded the problem of poverty: 'In the highest stage of social prosperity, the great mass of the citizens will most probably possess few other resources than their daily labour, and consequently will always be near to indigence.'[3] One thinks of the considerations on poverty in Adam Smith's *Draft of the Wealth of Nations*, and on the 'subsistence wage' in Ricardo. But poverty here appears as the counterpart to abundance, in the sense that it serves as the backcloth against which the discourse on wealth is developed, and also as a reservoir continually tapped for its energies, motives and propulsive forces. Poverty is the counterpart to wealth in as much as it is the territory of unfulfilled needs, or of needs not yet invented; a territory that extends indefinitely, the symbol of a market without limits:

> The desire of food is limited in every man by the narrow capacity of the human stomach; but . . . what is over and above satisfying the limited desire is given for the amusement of those desires which cannot be satisfied, but seem to be altogether endless.[4]

As an element set in counterpoint with wealth, poverty in itself has no independent meaning: as theoretico-practical support for the prospect of increasing abundance, poverty's vocation is to make possible its realization. No wonder then that, caught between this 'economic' reading which treats it as a fact of nature impossible to control by direct intervention ('What can the law do relative to subsistence? Nothing directly . . . The force of physical sanction being sufficient, the employment of the political sanction would be superfluous')[5] and a regime of administration which amounted to simple policing, the theme of poverty found no other utilization: classical political economy did not discover the utility of a *politics of poverty*. And its interventions in the legislation governing the poor in Britain (Poor Law Amendment Act, 1834) never looked beyond the aims of protecting the labour market, unburdening the taxpayer and generalizing wage labour as a means of subsistence. Poverty, for this discourse, is not an administrable datum. And when Ricardo pronounces against all poor laws,[6] he does not do so in order to replace them with a different perspective of management. Poverty must simply be eliminated; even if in reality, as we have seen, it is an integral part of the discourse on wealth.

This contradiction is made explicit by Malthus. His famous example of the Irish[7] serves to show how poverty is not the external limit of the economy, but rather its internal limit: contrary to the 'law of trade outlets' (*loi des débouchés*) which was being elaborated by Say, James Mill and Ricardo. Malthus's Irish peasant stands witness to the futility of producing goods with which to invade a new market if there has been no previous concern there to 'create the consumer', that other product which is of such particular and primary importance. The poor Irishman who lives on potatoes and dresses in rags appears as the extreme version of the consumer in need of management; stubbornly indifferent to the lures of well-being, indolent in regard to that fundamental activity for the economic system, the perpetual expansion of 'needs', he represents in caricature the threat lurking on the rosy horizons of production, personifying the mechanism of crises of underconsumption. If it is true that penury is the critical social point of anchorage for the economic system founded on wealth, not its ideological justification but the technical condition of possibility of its intervention, then the Irish peasant embodies at once the danger of 'subversion' (the refusal to make the passage from penury to comfort, which is not a moral but a technico-social transition) and the privileged subject of political economy in so far as he is the ideal model for the expansion of needs.

Having made his entrance as a fully fledged participant on the stage of the economy, the 'pauper' is destined also to become a new scientific object. But for this to be possible, economic science will have to be redefined, and this will be the constant preoccupation of Sismondi. In his polemic against Ricardian political economy, Sismondi's tones revert almost to those of the eighteenth century: political economy as the 'science of government', inasmuch as it assumes 'happiness' as its end. But this revival of the late-eighteenth-century theme of the state of prosperity – which had, for example, been a key theme of the German Cameralistic 'science of police' – now happens in a changed context, that defined by political economy; within it, happiness becomes the technical means for resolving a new problem, that of reconciling the social groups which the economic project brings together in the growth of wealth, but which are incapable by themselves of giving up their antagonisms. Given this new way of construing the social problem in terms of technical innovations of political economy, such as the productive role of property, the contract-form as an extension of market mechanisms for labour relations, the division of labour, etc., Sismondi's purpose is to make clear the problem's economic significance: it is the system of wealth itself which is endangered. He addresses himself to the economists, to make them appreciate how important the management of the social problem is for the future of their own project; he does not yet imagine that this problem could form the origin of another science, and in this sense his conception of political economy remains akin to Adam Smith's. But the problem he identifies is a new one: the eighteenth century had thought of 'happiness' as a global project, the end of society which political power had the task of realizing for it; whereas 'happiness' now appears as part of an articulated project which brings into relation distinct sectors of the population and takes control of their reciprocal connections. The problem of equilibrium, which remains central to Sismondi's strictly economic preoccupation[8] and leads to his development of a theory of the crisis of general overproduction that challenges the hypothesis of an automatic adjustment achieved through the workings of the market, is in its most general sense rooted in the problem of *social* equilibrium.

The new problem which surfaces with Malthus and Sismondi is that of the management of population; and though they see the problem as one for political economy, the response in fact comes from elsewhere: the problem will be taken up by a disparate band of administrators, economists, philanthropists, doctors and others, giving rise to a discourse which, compared with classical political economy and its successors, functions on a different and intermediate level, that of *savoir*.

The term *savoir* is used here to designate a type of discourse which has a crucial position in the discursive universe: a *savoir* acts as an 'exchanger' (*échangeur*) mediating between the analytico-programmatic levels of the 'sciences' and the exigencies of direct social intervention – whether this intervention is imaginary or real matters little in this context. Whereas a 'science' begins with the invention of an object of analysis, an epistemological operation based on abstraction from the real, as the starting point from which it develops its own 'project of reality', a *savoir* relocates the object thus scientifically delineated within a field of relationships in which the instruments of the scientific project are forced into contact with all the rigidity, inertia and opacity which the real displays in its concrete functioning. And it is precisely in this sense that a *savoir* can more explicitly assume the viewpoint of power, if we interpret this last as an exercise in relating elements external to one another and a principle for deciphering such a network of connections. Reinserted within this 'field', the object of *savoir* is no longer pre-eminently a scientific object, but instead first and foremost an object upon which intervention is possible. It is in this play of reshaping and recomposing that science and *savoir* – not one against the other, but in mutual support – render discourse into at once an instrument capable of creating new objects and a source of new and complex configurations.

Such a *savoir* is what goes under the name of *social economy*. It was to make its own, and henceforth take for granted, the distinctive position relative to political economy which had been adopted by Malthus and Sismondi. As Buret put it, economy had been political because, for the Physiocrats and Smith, what was required was a science of administration; subsequently it had come to limit its object of analysis ever more narrowly, to the point of reducing it to production in the strictest sense and defining itself as the science of wealth: 'The theory of wealth neither can nor should constitute an independent science because the facts on which it rests are connected indissolubly to facts of a moral and political order, which determine its meaning and its value.' [9] Along with the Physiocratic 'table of wealth', wrote Buret, the '*tableau* of poverty' must become an object for economic analysis.

Political economy and social economy, however constantly articulated one on another, from now on have distinct existences. This distinctness arises from the recognition of a specific object of analysis of social economy: 'These relations between moral facts, or institutions, and industrial facts or the growth of labour, are what is most important in the study of social economy.' Its true object will thus be 'knowledge of all the means of order and harmony which found and maintain this public prosperity, for which wealth is one of the resources, but is ultimately only one of the elements'; the problem is then that of treating 'moral well-being, or order, and material well-being, or comfort, as insepar-able'.[10]

What is involved here is, in Jacques Donzelot's phrase,[11] a 'systematic grafting of morality on to economics', the technico-discursive instrument that makes possible the conquest of pauperism and the invention of a *politics of poverty*. 'Morality' does not stand here for ideology, or for strategy; one should not be misled into thinking that the social economists are pedantic moralists, gripped by nostalgia for the past. 'Morality' signifies a discursive mediation which allows a whole range of technologies to be brought to bear on the social as *behaviour*: 'The behaviours of a people are its morality; the task therefore is to give them nothing but good ones.' [12] The moral element is *order*, that order which liberal society discovers as a vital need: 'Between freedom and order, there is no opposition, the second is in fact a condition of the first.' [13] And order faces a series of adversities/adversaries, which the first half of the nineteenth century terms 'the poor'. Morality is the discourse which describes them, one which is still remote from the statistical–mathematical discourses which at the end of the nineteenth century make possible the disaggregation of the notion of 'the poor' and the creation of new agglomerations, in accordance with new criteria; morality is also the discourse which unites them, inserting itself in continuity with the older discourse of charitable assistance. But in the space opened up between these two moments, this grafting of morality on to economics will make possible the elaboration of a whole set of technical instruments of intervention.

'We must find a remedy for the scourge of pauperism, or else prepare for the convulsion of the world.' [14] If the '*tableau* of poverty' is recognized as defining an urgent political problem, what does 'pauperism' signify in this discourse? What does this category designate, and what are its purposes?

> This floating population of the great cities . . . which industry attracts and is unable to regularly employ . . . is an object of serious attention and disquiet for both thinkers and governments. And it is among its ranks that pauperism is recruited, that dangerous enemy of our civilisation.[15]

> Pauperism is the class of men injured by society who consequently rebel against it.[16]

> Pauperism is that kind of indigence which becomes by its extension and intensity a sort of scourge, a permanent nuisance to society.[17]

Pauperism is thus poverty intensified to the level of *social danger*: the spectre of the mob; a collective, essentially urban phenomenon. It is a composite (and thereby all the more dangerous) population which 'encircles' the social order from within, from its tenements, its industrial agglomerations. It is a magma in which are fused all the dangers which beset the social order, shifting along unpredictable, untraceable channels of transmission and aggregation. It is insubordinate, hidden from the scrutinizing gaze of any governing instance. The definition of pauperism, as we have seen, does not work essentially through economic categories; rather than a certain level of poverty, images of pauperism put the stress principally on feelings of fluidity and indefiniteness, on the impression, at once massive and vague, conveyed by the city crowd, accounting for all its menacing character.

This enables us to understand the distinction which social economy draws between pauperism and poverty, and how discourse on the elimination of the former can go hand in hand with discourse on the conservation of the latter: 'When pauperism has been conquered, only the poor will remain, that is a certain sum of accidental poverty.'[18] Why does poverty itself, as the effect of social inequality, the existence in society of rich and poor, not become the object of attack for this discourse? Why is it not assumed under the same category as pauperism? Because the elimination of social inequality is not the purpose of discourse on pauperism. On this, all the social economists concur with the position of Sismondi: 'It is not in fact equality of conditions but happiness in all conditions which should be the legislator's aim.'[19] Inequality is never taken as being a target for attack, but as a 'natural', irrefutably given fact of industrial society:

> Poverty . . . derives from inequality of conditions . . . It is humanly impossible to destroy inequality. There will always therefore be rich and poor. But in a well-governed state, poverty must not degenerate into indigence . . . It is in the interests of the rich as much as of the poor that this should be so.[20]

Compared with poverty, then, pauperism appears immediately as 'unnatural' as well as antisocial, a deformity which insinuates itself into that natural order which the discourse of political economy, the discourse on wealth, purported to establish. As the natural ground for the development of wealth, the inexhaustible source of the extension of needs, the technical working principle of political economy's social project, poverty was nevertheless marginalized by it as a topic, being considered a fundamental yet un-analyzable, unadministrable given. Alien in the concreteness of its existence to the planned order of social nature, poverty only figured as a counterpoint, a candidate for negation. In these terms, the 'poor' could figure in the scenario only as virtuous exemplars of renunciation of pauperism and adhesion to the values of well-being. These model personages were evoked from time to time in the literature as the 'respectable' or 'independent' poor; the same thinking accompanied the British economists' objections to the Poor Laws as giving legal status to poverty, and their criticism of public assistance which recognizes rights to poverty or rights of poverty.

But alongside this discourse which ratifies the wealth–poverty relationship and excludes pauperism from the picture, social economy is involved in formulating a different scenario, where pauperism is perceived as anti-social in the sense of being a 'hyper-natural', rudely primitive mode of life. On the basis of an analysis of the instinctive antisocial tendencies of the individual, society comes to be presented as inevitable restraint: freedom and equality, innate tendencies which can find expression in their pure state only in 'savage' society, and there encounter only natural limits and obstacles, are unavoidably frustrated and repressed in civilized society: 'Civilized man constantly restrains himself, every day and every hour, because he *may not.*' Furthermore, 'In civilized society, faculties unequal at the moment of birth tend to become constantly more so.' [21] Thus, if it is true that humanity is spontaneously social, this means that it tends instinctively towards an uncivilized society based on natural appetites; but instinct does not impel humanity towards civil society: not only does it fail to provide a natural basis for cohesion, but humanity is set against itself, and revealed as its own enemy 'in those social classes where poverty, ignorance and isolation have diminished the influence of associative ideas'.[22] The task of governing poverty will be not to suppress these innate tendencies, in so far as they provide the favourable terrain for social development – so far, that is, as they are useful and necessary to the project of wealth – but to channel them so that they 'aspire to find their satisfaction through the means permitted them by the social regime'.[23] Restraint and guidance, in apposite proportions, thus become the basis of administrative action to harness the alien force of pauperism, which political economy – and its discourse of natural order – could only exclude as extraneous. It is a discourse in two registers, each one reinforcing the other; and if it is the 'unnaturalness' of society which is used to found the possibility of a government of pauperism, the innovative significance of this discourse cannot be missed, despite the old-fashioned language in which part of it is formulated. Moreover, if it is true that, when Cherbuliez analyzes what could enable people to be persuaded to accept a reduction of their freedom for the sake of civilization, his answer is 'the influence of religious ideas', it is also true that, in order to illustrate what he means by this influence, he cites the entry in Bayle's *Dictionnaire historique* on Brazil: 'Even if we were also to instil in them only enough Christianity so that they feel the need to go around dressed, this would be of great benefit to English manufacture.'[24]

But then, if it is not poverty which discourse on pauperism takes as its object of attack, if it is not towards the disappearance of the poor – the indispensable support of the existence of the rich – that this discourse is directed, what is its purpose? Its objective is the elimination not of inequality, but of *difference.* And here 'moral' language finds its exact meaning. By the term 'difference' I want to underline that the essential significance of the term 'pauperism' consists in indicating a series of *different forms of conduct*, namely those which are not amenable to the project of socialization which is being elaborated: 'Indigence is a set of physical and moral habits.' [25]

Pauperism is mobility: against the need for territorial sedentarization, for fixed concentrations of population, it personifies the residue of a more fluid, elusive sociality, impossible either to control or to utilize: vagabondage, order's itinerant nightmare, becomes the archetype of disorder and the antisocial: 'The vagabond, the original type of all the forces of evil, is found wherever illegal or criminal activities go on: he is their born artisan.' [26] Mobility also means *promiscuity:* indecipherable couplings, difficult to use as cohesive supports for the social fabric; spontaneous solidarities which elude 'legal' or 'contractual' definition, evading any attempt to orient them towards the goals of the social project. Concubinage, connivance, neighbourhood or trade solidarities: our authors seem unable to find sufficiently powerful images for the mass of threats and dangers constituted by the poor quarters, constantly liable to pour out and invade the entire city with their pollutions.

Pauperism is independence: the refusal of organic ties of subordination, as of all other restraints implemented through contractual exchange, illustrates the difficulty of using need as the structuring element of a new social cohesion, spanning and uniting all ranks of the population in a hierarchically constituted chain. The 'shameless' poor, who keep alive traditional types of alliance system and refuse to relinquish control of the organization of their survival, remain an impenetrable zone of the social fabric. The economic critique which reproaches public assistance for maintaining islands of dependence in a society organized around the 'free' disposal of one's self, is actually an attack on those existing social ties that are seen as obsolete, and obsolete precisely because of the specific way in which they mediate dependence: forming people into a bloc, resisting the 'free' circulation of individuals in the network of the labour market, neglecting the consideration which the satisfaction of needs is entitled to claim. Moreover, the fact that the poor on relief do as they wish with the money allowed them, and liberally dispose of what is theirs, is also only too well illustrated by the ample descriptions of licentiousness, drunkenness and improvidence which characterize this section of the population. Another characteristic feature is the play on the opposition between manufacture and piecework: the disregard for the criterion of earnings levels, the tenacity with which the poor defend their independence, is what marks them as falling under the category of pauperism; the discontinuity of their conduct leads the authors of investigations into the conditions of the working class in the first half of the nineteenth century to assert that, when they have free disposal of their own time, they devote only half of it to productive activity, while in general spending the other half in 'disgusting orgies'.[27]

Independent, masters of their own time, the poor are also the masters of their future: *pauperism is improvidence and frugality:*

We can affirm, as a general proposition, that workers think little of tomorrow, especially in the cities; the more they earn, the more they spend . . . work, but enjoy: this seems to be the motto of most of them, with the exception of those in the country.[28]

The habit of living with the present as the only certainty and the refusal to be blackmailed by the future ill accords with the 'abstinence' which Cherbuliez characterized as the peculiar trait of civilized man. The whole discourse on savings – which during the same period political economy is identifying as the principle device of capital accumulation – with its promised mirage of economic independence attainable through accession to small property, encounters a technical obstacle here; and thus the introduction of the savings bank, beside creating easily disposable capital, will have the function of a technology of abstinence, diffusing among the popular masses that 'spirit of economy which is highly unfavourable to everyday disorder'.[29] It is also the frugality of the poor which poses a problem: the poor represent a refusal of the expansion of 'needs', an insensibility to their inexhaustible solicitations, to the never fully slackened mainspring of well-being. Malthus's celebrated Irish peasant, faced with the marvels of English manufacture, remained indifferent, incapable of 'recognizing' his need and hence of accepting a further reduction of his freedom in order to procure the wherewithal for something more than his potatoes and his rags.

Pauperism is ignorance and insubordination, and the fact that the two qualities are connected is beyond doubt for the social economists: 'Nature has made man, education makes the citizen; pay more teachers and there will be less need for policemen, and if there were more colleges there would be fewer prisons.'[30] The ignorance spoken of here certainly includes that technical backwardness which hinders the organization of labour (cf. the projects for schools of arts and crafts); but much more disturbing on the whole is that kind of ignorance which 'deserves to occupy the foremost place among the causes of indigence, since it leads to idleness, immorality, uncleanliness, improvidence, as well as to many diseases and infirmities', namely 'ignorance of duty and its usefulness'.[31] And it is exactly this ignorance of their duties, of the necessity of these duties, which makes for the insubordination of the impoverished masses, which thrusts them on to the streets, which inspires the arrogance of their demands: it is this ignorance which lies at the origin of their challenge to political power, which they consider responsible for their fate, and of their belief in political struggle as a possible instrument for transforming their situation.[32]

To say that pauperism *is* these modes of conduct may lead to a misunderstanding: it is not a question here of determining the concrete 'reality' of the existence of the poor, and still less of eulogizing the mode of social being they express. It is not their 'real' existence which is being analyzed here, because in this discursive context pauperism is a *pretext:* a political laboratory for an intellectual experiment designed to isolate certain social bacteria (themselves not necessarily unique to pauperism) and to make possible the invention of techniques adequate to deal with such bacterial action (although the techniques in question are not designed for this purpose alone). The homogeneous consistency of the category of pauperism, used without any concern to break it down into a distinct conception of the various micropopulations it brackets together, indicates its fictitious character: what is really designated by the term is, as we noted earlier, the ensemble of adversities/adversaries which confront the project of social order.

Neither is it intended here to counterpose the social world of 'the poor' to the social world of the industrial order, to oppose the positivity of the first to the negativity of the second, as if the poor constituted a political riposte to that order. Every social transformation is accompanied by inevitable frictions at a localized, capillary level: what I am interested in analyzing here is the precise site where these frictions occur, and what this site tells us about the transformation which is taking place. Not for the sake of nostalgia for what we have lost by the invention of government of the poor; rather out of curiosity about the effects that this 'historic' confrontation induced, the special inflections it gave to the social fabric. Not to regret the insanitary quarters in which the poor were housed, or the forms of alliance which were preserved in them, not to vindicate poverty against wealth; but to reach down to the underside of our own present, in whose origins discourse on poverty proves to have had at least as much importance as discourse on wealth, and to assemble as many clues as possible to the nature of the social order which the conjunction of these two discourses inspired.

The problem of indigence and assistance was perceived from the end of the *ancien régime* and throughout the Revolutionary period in the context of the economists' discovery of the intrinsic bond between labour and wealth.[33] In the light of this discovery, it seemed that the problem could be resolved at a stroke by removing all obstacles to the free access of labour to the market, thereby integrating the population of the indigent into the productive cycle: labour, the inexhaustible source of wealth, which in turn is the inexhaustible source of labour, represents the magic key to social organization. For the nineteenth century, such faith in the miracles of labour was no longer possible. Far from succeeding in absorbing all forms of poverty to the point of eliminating them, labour itself created new ones; and, as if this were not enough, it posed on another level a whole new order of problems: 'Labour is an element of moralization; but it is also, or at least is liable to become, through abuse of the resources it procures, an element of disorder.'[34] Labour is inadequate as a general principle of order and incapable even of solving all those problems which its own order creates: the zones of unemployment, heavy concentrations of people and capital with the promiscuities they foster, the inequalities aggravated by its hierarchical organization, the intimate contacts it sets up between wealth and poverty, the irreducible role it assigns to the latter in the development of the former. What the invention of a politics of poverty signifies here is not the generalization of the order of labour, the recuperation of unproductive zones by the production cycle, but, on the contrary, the valorization of those zones as supports for a different mode of administering the social from the one that techniques linked to the category of 'labour' make possible. Thus one finds that the discourse on pauperism covers a diversity of social populations, those which work and those which remain outside the organization of production, the rebellious and the contented, those who apply for relief and those who maintain themselves through a traditional alliance system, and so on. The poor are the site where the problems we have noted can be clarified, their symptoms grouped together. As a field of analysis, it is basically extraneous to the world of the factory; the factory is not its destined goal or terminus. Poverty constitutes a development area for techniques designed to structure an organic social order which, whatever the concrete localization of the human subjects it deals with, is able to bring under its management those zones of social life which have hitherto remained formless. What is involved is the constituting of a different subject from the productive subject: a subject 'aware of its duties', a civil and political subject, one might say; it is not poverty as the stigma of *inequality* that is combated, but pauperism understood as a cluster of behaviours, a carrier of *difference*.

What are the weapons of this combat? There is a whole rich and coordinated arsenal, which we can only briefly survey here.

Statistics, first of all, serves as the technique of decipherment enabling the chaos of pauperism to be disentangled. The savings bank and the providential society, instruments of that education in abstinence and exploitation of the future to blackmail the present which we have already mentioned. The insurance system. The mutual aid societies, the worker's *livret* (pass-book), workshop regulations, the organization of bonuses, and particularly the construction of a 'labour aristocracy' as a means of mediation and persuasion enabling hierarchy to extend down to the lowest and most turbulent levels: the use of overseers, the inclusion of workers in the *Conseils des Prud' hommes* (arbitration councils), foremen. The paternalistic regime of quasi-familial relations between boss and workers, extended to take a hand in the moral education of the worker and his family and the organization of free time on Sundays. An organization of social assistance, articulating public and private spheres, which made possible the rationalization of the range of existing benevolent activities and (most importantly) of their strategic advantages: assistance becomes in this context a sacrament of moralization, control and dissuasion, far exceeding the capabilities of the old logic of alms. The pivot of this new guise of benevolent activity is the 'visitor of the poor',[35] the true forerunner of social work, the instrument at once of the capillary distribution of 'household relief' and of that 'study of character' which was beginning to be considered indispensable for good social administration. A figure with a great future.

Another group of techniques place their emphasis on hygiene: rules for public hygiene in cities, 'police of dwellings', rules of hygiene in the workplace, hygiene in marriage and procreation (of Malthusian fame): hygiene for these authors is a grid for reading social relations, a system which serves at once to canalize them and to invent new paths of circulation that are more 'orderly' and more decipherable. There are, in addition, innovations of hygienist provenance such as workers' housing schemes (mining towns, for example) and agricultural colonies, which directly involve the displacement and reconstitution of groups, and therefore a whole system of social relations invented *ex novo*.

Yet another essential element is the reinforcement of the family, utilized simultaneously as a means of stabilizing individuals and breaking down the old systems of kinship, but also as a polymorphous social instrument whose different members can be played off in turn against each other.[36]

Education, through a whole constellation of specific functions, constitutes another important technological nexus: the need for free elementary schools and kindergartens, for internal discipline and for a staff trained in surveillance (and hence for training schools, like the Écoles Normales), the role of gymnastics and recreation, the shortening of holidays, etc. Also illuminating, in certain respects, is the discussion of the syllabus, in particular regarding the necessity of introducing elementary notions of political economy from the primary classes on: 'this would be the best possible corrective for the flights of imagination set off by the study of letters',[37] and, above all, 'the inestimable value of time, the miraculous scope of progressive saving, the absolute necessity for prudence in conjugal unions, are rudimentary truths of which the populace are profoundly ignorant'.[38] The teaching of political economy allows popular insubordination to be combated in a more effective way than with the instruments hitherto adopted, 'the penal code and the bayonet',[39] since its effect is to spread the fundamental notions of participation in the social order and to develop the spirit of association as a vehicle of disciplinary and disciplined organization of the masses.

We see political economy reappearing here, this time as a technical instrument adopted by social economy in response to a precise problem: the ignorance of duties which was one, and not the least serious, of the dangers discerned in pauperism. This is an interesting convergence, one which enables us in the first place to recognize how the destined object of these educative techniques is not the child alone: if it is true that school is conceived as a counter to the street with its pleasures, its mobility, its promiscuity, it is also true that this discourse aims at reaching other sectors of the population, whose mode of conduct is assimilated to that of childhood:

> Institutions are impotent against poverty, but they can attenuate it; the means is not alms, humiliating for the recipient and repugnant to the man of feeling, but to prepare the populace from infancy to have good habits and to practise them in later life.[40]

Infantilization of the poor and valorization of childhood as a vehicle for socialization: the two operations go together as technical supports for an immense enterprise of permanent educability.

Political economy also permits a connection to be made with another discourse. Ignorant of their duties, the poor must certainly be educated, but they must also, above all, be implicated in the order into which they are to be integrated: 'Men in general respect most the institutions in which they participate';[41] 'An institution is not stable unless sanctioned by public opinion.'[42] Therefore, alongside the perspective of tutelage provided by infantilization, another is opened up here, that of the constitution of the politically responsible subject, capable of entry into the machinery of political representation. This indicates a completely different aspect of technical intervention, centred on the two key notions of *participation* and *association*. Participation in property (a technique for the enlargement of the middle classes) as an instrument for implication in the defence of order; participation at the intermediate levels of hierarchical power as an instrument for co-option in decisions; participation in political activity through associative forms as an instrument to defuse conflict in the political field; and in a more general sense, association as a vehicle for structured and structuring ties which allow the progress of subjects from a merely individual level to that of joint interests which reproduce on a reduced scale the relations of discipline and authority.

Poverty, politically defined, constitutes for the first half of the nineteenth century the surface of emergence of the social problem; but between this first appearance and the moment when it becomes a field of real and systematic intervention (the 'social laws' at the end of the century) and when political economy is redefined in terms of the conjunction with the social question which Malthus and Sismondi had proposed, a whole series of transformations are operated. Pauperism is decomposed into new constellations, and it will no longer be around the wealth–poverty opposition that the conceptual instruments of social economy will assume concrete shape: employment and unemployment will become the new analytic couplet. To understand how this passage is effected and what gradually makes the earlier opposition inadequate remains a central problem in reconstructing the lines of transformation and constitution of the social, that special object of *savoir* and government. In the meantime, what interested me here was to try to see how the discourse of political economy was unable to function outside of the wealth–poverty coupling, and how social economy's conquest of political economy's foil, of the open terrain of poverty, became the productive conquest of a new object and of a whole technology destined to outlast the discourse which initiated it. If the theme of poverty accompanied, in antiphon, the celebration of the miracles of industrialism, then the governing of poverty permitted the realization of a new and different strategy: parallel with the utilization of need as support for a social project for the indefinite expansion of wealth, there is a strategy to disconnect need from this programme, in which it was liable to act as a principle of subversion, in order to utilize it instead as an instrument of social integration.

NOTES

1. Firmin Marbeau, *Du paupérisme en France et des moyens d'y rémédier au principes d'économie charitable*, Paris, 1847.
2. Karl Polanyi, *The Great Transformation*, cited from the Italian translation, Einaudi, 1974, p. 151.
3. Jeremy Bentham, 'Principles of the Civil Code', in *The Works of Jeremy Bentham*, ed. J. Bowring, Edinburgh, 1843, vol. 1, p. 314. Cf. also the considerations on poverty in the Draft of Adam Smith, *The Wealth of Nations*, and on 'subsistence wages' in Ricardo.
4. Smith, *An Inquiry into the Nature and Causes of the Wealth of Nations*, ed. R. H. Campbell and A. S. Skinner, 2 vols, London, 1976, vol. 1, p. 181.
5. Bentham, 'Principles of the Civil Code', p. 303.
6. David Ricardo, 'The principles of political economy and taxation', in *The Works and Correspondence of David Ricardo*, ed. P. Sraffa, Cambridge, 1951–73, vol. 1, p. 108.
7. *Principle of Political Economy*, Book 1, chapter 1, section IV.
8. Cf. Henryk Grossman, *Simonde de Sismondi et ses théories économiques*, Varjaviae, 1924.

9. Antoine Buret, *De la misère des classes laborieuses en Angleterre et en France*, Paris, 1840, Introduction.
10. 'De l'enseignement de l'économie politique', *Revue mensuelle d'économie politique*, vol. 2, 1833.
11. Jacques Donzelot, *The Policing of Families*, London, 1979.
12. Louis Villermé, *Tableau de l'état physique et moral des ouvriers*, Paris, 1840, vol. 2, p. 48.
13. Charles Dunoyer, *De l'industrie et de la morale dans leur rapports avec la liberté*, 1825, p. 47.
14. Buret, *De la misère des classes laborieuses*, p. 74.
15. *Ibid.*, p. 69.
16. De La Farelle, *Du progrès social au profit des classes populaires non indigentes*, 1847, p. 7.
17. Antoine Cherbuliez, *Précis de la science économique et de ses principales applications*, Paris, 1826, vol. 2, p. 305.
18. Cherbuliez; *Étude sur les causes de la misère*, Paris, 1853, p. 121.
19. Jean Simonde de Sismondi, *Nouveaux principes d'économie politique*, Paris, 1819, vol. 1, p. 11.
20. Firmin Marbeau, *Du paupérisme*, p. 20
21. Cherbuliez, *Étude sur les causes de la misère*, pp. 13–14.
22. *Ibid.*, p. 15.
23. *Ibid.*, p. 24.
24. *Ibid.*, p. 25.
25. Cherbuliez, *Précis de la science économique*, vol. 2, p. 305.
26. Honore Frégier, *Des classes dangéreuses de la population dans les grandes villes*, Paris, 1840, vol. 1, p. 50.
27. Villermé, *Tableau*, vol. 2, p. 66.
28. *Ibid.*, vol. 2, p. 34.
29. François Dupin, *Progrès moreaux de la population parisienne depuis établissement de la Caisse d'Épargne*, Paris, 1842, p. 8.
30. Marbeau, *Politique des intérêts*, Paris, 1834, p. 136.
31. Marbeau, *Du paupérisme*, pp. 33–4.
32. Cf. Jérome Blanqui, *Des classes ouvrières en France pendant l'année 1848*, Paris, 1849.
33. Cf. Robert Castel, *L'ordre psychiatrique*, Paris, 1977, chapter 3.
34. Frégier, *Des classes dangéreuses*, p. 276.
35. Joseph de Gérando, *Le Visiteur du pauvre*, Paris, 1820. Translated into English as *The Visitor of the Poor; designed to aid in the formation of Provident Societies*, London, 1833.
36. Donzelot, *The Policing of Families*, chapter 3.
37. Michel Chevalier, *De l'instruction secondaire*, Paris, 1843.
38. De La Farelle, *De la nécessité de fonder en France l'enseignement de l'économie politique*, 1846.
39. *Ibid.*
40. Villermé, *Tableau*, vol. 2, p. 147.
41. Alexandre de Laborde, *De l'esprit d'association dans tout les intérêts de la communauté*, Paris, 1821, vol. 1, p. 16.
42. *Le Censeur européen*, vol. VII, p. 296.

CHAPTER EIGHT

The mobilization of society

Jacques Donzelot

Evaluating the interest of neo-social-democratic approaches to the crisis of the welfare state and comparing the relative strengths of neo-social democracy and neo-liberalism seems to me to be a problematic venture, because of the way both these discourses present themselves as at once diagnosis and cure. From whichever end one tackles the problem, one has little chance of being able to develop arguments motivating a clear standpoint on the matter, since one finds oneself obliged to depend on either arbitrary opinion or the arbitration of experts.

The only way I can see out of this impasse is to resituate this debate in its most general meaningful context, that of the *governability of democracy*. This means the following:

1. Asking what it was in democracies that the welfare state provided a solution to. This is not at all the same thing as proposing a general history of the growth of states which merges the specific problem of the state into the problem of development. The point is to ask to what extent the formula of the welfare state was specifically constructed by democracies, in France as a solution to the problem of actualizing the Republic.
2. Studying to what extent this solution is now in a state of crisis with respect to its political function. Only by knowing what the welfare state was a solution to, and how, will it be possible to determine how far and why it now stands in an impasse.
3. Situating discourses like neo-social democracy in relation to this problematic of the governability of the Republic.

WHAT IS THE WELFARE STATE A SOLUTION TO?

1. The expression 'welfare state' (*État-providence*) began to be used in the second half of the nineteenth century to designate a type of response, positive or negative depending on one's point of view, to the question of the role and place of the state in a democratic society.

If there is an answer, then there must have been a problem. Now in fact the question of the state had hardly been posed in France during the first part of the nineteenth century. What people talked about was despotism, which was contrasted with natural right, as in the eighteenth century. Taking cognizance of the novel problems of industry, natural right is enlarged to include the right for workers of free association, so that it will provide an end to mercantile as well as political oppression. Benjamin Constant analyzes the Terror, but he sees it as the effect of an inverse form of despotism rather than as a problem engendered by the state. Guizot is more interested in the problem of government than that of the state: he writes works on methods of government and opposition, in which the few remarks he makes on the state refer to its usefulness for building prisons in order to make room for free play in the government of private interests and passions. Proudhon talks about the state, but only in the same way as he talks about the Church or any other symbol of authority, in order by denouncing them to make room for his own federalist schemes.

Only after the Second Republic does a whole literature spring up which is specifically concerned with the state. In 1853 Tocqueville's *L'ancien régime et la Révolution* demonstrates the growth of the state both under the ancien régime and after the Revolution, its development having been accelerated by the Revolution itself, and thus sets down the first pointers of the subsequent theme of decentralization. In *The Eighteenth Brumaire of Louis Napoleon Bonaparte*, Marx uses the example of the failures of the Second Republic to analyze the role and nature of the state in class relations, showing how it can be at once an obstacle to revolution and an instrument of it. Dupont-White takes up Hegel's theses on the state's emancipatory function for the individual, in a book on the state and the individual published in 1852 which had a great impact among the republican opposition to the Second Empire.

Thus the problem of the state first emerges in France with the 1848 revolution. It arose out of the fracturing of the generic theme of right which until then had served as a rallying point for the supporters of the republican ideal, and enabled the Republic to have no enemies on its left. The proclamation of rights had been expected to put an end to despotism and install a reign of harmony. Every right proclaimed meant a privilege suppressed, and thus a return to natural order. Thus the political sovereignty of all men through universal (male) suffrage was proclaimed along with what seemed to be the natural correlate of this right, the means of making it effective: the right to work. This proclamation was in February 1848. In June of the same year there broke out the most savage civil war France had known since the Wars of Religion. The conflict was between those who expected the state to decree measures in accordance with the proclamation of the right to work, and to intervene to ensure that society conformed to this right, and those who expected from the Republic a reduction of state intervention in society, which they regarded as a continuation of the old despotism. So there is a fracturing of the theme of right, as two thoroughly antagonistic views of the function of right in the Republic emerge in regard to the issue of the right to work and the rights of property. And it is through this split, by virtue of the contradictory implications for society that are derived from it, that the question of the state, its nature and role surges into prominence.

The founders of the Third Republic come once again to be faced with this problem, the non-resolution of which had led to the downfall of their predecessors. They seek to solve it by means of two operations which may be seen as constitutive of the welfare state:

(a) The establishment of a distinction between solidarity and sovereignty.
(b) The substitution of the homogeneous language of statistics for the contradictory language of rights.

2. The problem of the state for progressive republicans amounts to this: how can the state exert a corrective influence on society to counter the revolutionary threat fuelled by the perceived contrast between the proclaimed sovereignty of citizens at the ballot box and their subjugation in the factories, without exposing the state to denunciation of this intervention as leading to the negation of civil liberties and the indefinite expansion of the state? How can the republican state lay down for itself a consistent line of intervention that runs between the revolutionary summons to act as the instance for reorganizing society, and the combined liberal–traditionalist animosity to any state infringement of the prerogatives of civil society?

The problem is an insoluble one within the classical terms of right, in so far as these entail that all argument is founded on the sovereignty of the individual:

(a) If right resides solely in the individual, the individual can always repudiate and paralyze the intervention of the state.
(b) If the state is the embodiment of the general will, the active synthesis of individual sovereignties and powers, there is nothing left to oppose it, and nothing can contest it.

The state has therefore to be cut loose from this infernal circle of the metaphysics of sovereignty, and, to achieve this, a different basis must be found for it.

The solution was found in the notion of solidarity, a notion which is conceived as distinct from that of sovereignty, which henceforth is used solely as the principle of election of those who govern, and not as the principle of action by the state.

It is Emile Durkheim who develops this concept, one which becomes immensely influential around the turn of the century, to the extent even of providing the theme of a doctrine of the state, Leon Bourgeois' *solidarisme*. Durkheim sees the concept of solidarity as encapsulating a general law of social development. The original basis of social organization is a solidarity based on the similarity of its members' situations, which gives rise to a sentiment of common identity. Durkheim calls this 'mechanical solidarity'. This mechanical solidarity gradually comes to be replaced, although never completely eliminated, by an organic solidarity which at once reinforces and overlays the unity which arises from similarities with the interdependence created by the increasing division of labour and the resulting tendency for people to identify themselves as individuals.

Thus formulated, the concept of solidarity simply expresses the rationality of the organizing practices of society brought into operation at the outset of the Third Republic. The idea of a solidarity based on similarity would seem to correspond closely to the criteria which decided the question of trade union legislation. It was important to allow the establishment of a social bond that would prevent a situation where isolated individuals came up against the state as their sole interlocutor; but the form of organization chosen for this purpose must not be allowed to engender a society within a society, a state within the state, on the model of the revolutionary clubs which had amply demonstrated their capacity to undermine the Republic through their pretensions to embody the general will. Similarities of social and professional conditions provided an acceptable criterion for the organization of sociality, while leaving political sovereignty to take the conscience of the individual as its point of reference.

As for the notion of organic solidarity, this accords equally well with the new forms of intervention by the state into the family, through compulsory schooling, legislation on the protection of minors and on divorce. The problem was to find a criterion which would justify breaking into this sphere of natural association, hitherto always deemed by liberals and traditionalists to take precedence over the state by virtue of its prior existence. The concept of organic solidarity justified this intervention by allowing the principle of the interdependence of the individuals composing society to override the state of dependence in which they were placed inside the framework of so-called natural associations. Thus it is in the name of social solidarity that the state is entitled to intervene in associations like the family or the enterprise.

This concept of solidarity, with the rationalization that sociologists, especially Durkheim, gave it, was used to redefine the juridical context of state intervention, its justification and its limits. The notions of public service (Léon Duguit) and institution (Maurice Haureou) are developed wholly out of this concept of solidarity. These notions make it possible to specify the scope of state intervention: when it is entitled to encroach on the prerogatives of citizens, and when citizens are justified in challenging it. The state can act in the name of social solidarity, in accordance with the existing conditions of social advancement and the measures which these necessitate, but it cannot go further.

It is in the name of social solidarity that the republican state develops its social legislation and, subsequently, its economic intervention. The concept of solidarity makes it possible to arrive at a situation where the state itself is no longer at stake in social relations, but stands outside them and becomes their guarantor of progress.

3. This concept of solidarity serves to define not only the framework but also the specific mode of state intervention, one which affects the forms of the social bond rather than the structure of society itself. The aim is not the recognition of the right to work and its application, with all that that would entail, but the development of forms of solidarity in society which take account of the greater risks faced by certain of its members, risks to which they were also in a position to expose society as a whole. Problems regarding work were in this context no longer a matter of distributive justice but one of restorative justice. They led to the creation of rights which exist not as absolutes but rather as a function of specific recognized facts and empirical contingencies. This was not a matter of seeking to undermine the rights of property, but (once again) of taking account of the fact that not all individuals have the same opportunity to satisfy their wants, and of putting into effect measures of social solidarity to reduce this inequality. The homogeneous language of statistics provided a pragmatic interactive medium for relations between social forces, in place of the antagonisms generated by the contradictory language of rights.

4. The foundations of the welfare state lie in the two operations outlined above which make it possible to understand its origin and its aim.

The principle of the welfare state, the state which stands outside society and whose function is to guarantee society's progress, turns on a strategy of dispelling hostilities between liberals and communists, traditionalists and revolutionaries.

Its aim, or rather its mode of legitimation, consists in tracing out, within the perspectives of regulatory state intervention, the prospect of a realization of the republican ideal secure from the stresses which beset its beginnings. By breaking down antagonistic attitudes, it aims at the gradual realization of a consensus society, which will satisfy the demands of democracy as much as those of socialism:

(a) By enlarging opportunities, by the social promotion of the individual, it acts as a force for emancipation, and creates freedom.

(b) By reducing risks, by the promotion of the social and the corresponding limitation of the irrationalities of the economic, it acts as a force for socialization, and creates collective security.

TO WHAT EXTENT IS THE WELFARE STATE IN CRISIS?

Any discussion of the crisis of the welfare state involves examining to what extent the two operations which are constitutive of it have ceased to fulfil their function.

It is clear that both of the two movements which in France have come to reformulate the question of the forms of government of society, 1960s reformism and ultra-leftism, call into question in their different ways the sharing of roles between state and society which corresponds to the distinction between solidarity and sovereignty.

1. The reformism of the 1960s represents ideas which had been worked out and discussed in debating groups like the Club Jean Moulin and Citoyen 60; these activities were continued during the 1960s by the Échanges et Projets clubs, and gave rise to a whole literature about the state, one of whose best-known products, entitled *Nationalizing the State*, was published in 1968. This title gives some indication of what this movement was attacking: that extrinsic position of the state *vis-à-vis* society which the concept of solidarity had served to found. The position is criticized for having encouraged a quasi-autarchic development of the state, an entity (to use Jacques Delors' words) bloated by its expansionary logic and made impotent by its separation from society. Evolving in the refuge of its exteriority, the state has shifted away from its role as a simple external guarantor of the progress of society towards that of a manager directly responsible for society's destiny. And by slowly appropriating the mechanisms of society's evolution, by capturing the powers of decision, it has more or less wrecked the effective sovereignty of society. Hence the emergence of the phenomenon of depoliticization.

The loss of civil feeling induced by the state's overbearing position is used to explain the difficulties now encountered by the state in accomplishing the progress which society expects of it. The reformist thinkers criticize, for example, the attitude of the 'social partners' (management and labour) which consists of holding back whenever something has to be decided, leaving the state to take the decision, so as the better to be able to repudiate it afterwards. In other words, the pursuit of progress itself is put at risk by the classic role of the state.

2. What the left denounces, on the other hand, is precisely the reality of progress as effected under the auspices of the state and the technocrats. The real effects of progress on everyday life, what it changes, not always for the better, what it does not change, life itself, the way changes are carried out over people's heads: all these things provide the specific material of the leftist discourse. It is, furthermore, a discourse which occupies a peculiar place: that left empty by political organizations and trade unions which now speak the same progressive language as the state, a quantitative language which leaves little or no room for the everyday life of the citizen. It is a discourse which stresses its disaffection from the classic forms in which sovereignty is exercised, and articulates the demand for its reappropriation, highlighting themes such as *spontaneity* and *workers' control*.

In other words, leftism puts forward a line which denounces the process of progress as carried out by the state, on the grounds that this corresponds to a usurpation of the sovereignty which properly belongs to society.

3. It is easy to see how the implications of these two lines of contestation undermine the whole conception of the social.

The (reformist) critique of the exteriority of the state, its inflated role and the loss of civic sense this induces, focuses attention on the system of expectations which this situation sets up and which underlies the inflation of social expenditure: the *benefit function* of the state, linked to the growing discrepancy between social security expenditure and the gross national product, and the *statutory function* of its cyclical intervention, which prejudices the requirements of the labour market.

The (leftist) critique of the technocratic nature of the state's social intervention amounts to a denunciation of the reductive and coercive nature of the social *per se*: against the unitary language of the social order, it asserts the specificity of different categories and situations; against the statistical nature of the social, it focuses on the damaging effects of selection, exclusion and coercion that this entails. In short, the unitary language of statistics is challenged by the language of difference and autonomy.

4. It is now perhaps easier to see why the welfare state is in crisis.

(a) The distinction between solidarity and sovereignty should have made it possible to determine the respective positions of state and society, to put a proper distance between the state and society's conflicts, setting the state to keep a watchful eye on society's progress, which was expected eventually to fulfil the republican ideal by making the solidarity organized by the state coincide with the sovereignty acknowledged to inhere in society.

What is actually happening seems in some ways like the reverse of this. As a result of its keeping its distance from society, the state is bound to have greater and greater difficulty in bringing about solidarity. At the same time, society seems to lose any real sense of its own sovereignty.

(b) Social intervention by the state was a way of conjoining two lines of development which between them had been expected to lead to the realization of social harmony through the social promotion of the individual and the promotion of the social, through the simultaneous enhancement of freedom and security.

Here, too, what seems to be happening is the reverse of this. Satisfaction of the need for security obeys its own inflationary logic, by creating the expectation that the state will take responsibility for all problems. At the same time, freedom starts to work against a state which has emptied it of all substance by its control over the course of events. And, far from complementing each other to make a harmonious society, these two tendencies gave rise to a spectacular conflict in 1968, where a freedom wrested from the weight of tradition was pitted against a security interpreted as renunciation of the perspective of revolution.

WHAT ROLE IS THERE FOR THE STATE NOW?

Three points can now be made about what is at issue in the present situation.

1. The first refers to the context of the debate between neo-social democracy and neo-liberalism: the general burgeoning of proposals designed to solve the crisis of governmentality which set in during the 1960s.

Put schematically, the problem is this: given that the state has changed from a guarantor of progress to a manager of destiny, charged with providing a form of security whose cost weighs ever more heavily on the economy, while being faced with a citizenry whose liberty has been widened by the decline of traditional forms of authority which the state itself has helped to displace, and yet been emptied of content by the state's monopoly of the levers of change – what is the state to do?

Should it – as neo-liberalism proposes – cut back on its security function, so as to enforce a more responsible interpretation of civic freedom? Or – as the neo-social democrats argue – should it draw on the spontaneous resources of this social freedom, in order gradually to transfer to it some of the state's current security mission?

This debate corresponds to a substitution of the theme of change for that of progress. No longer is there the same faith in the effects of time which enables the real convergence of solidarity with sovereignty to be postponed into the future. Instead, the objective – whichever of the two routes one chooses – is to force the two terms together, to make them coincide in the present: which implies the invention of a new relation of society to time.

The very fact that this debate has arisen signals the breakdown of social democracy's utopian perspective. The social-democratic project contained the implicit promise of a society which would be both democratic and socialist, thanks to the combination of emancipation of individuals and the gradual triumph of the social over the economic. It is this dream which is doomed by the crisis of the welfare state, the stalemate between a form of security which reinforces the role of the state and a freedom which repudiates that role.

The frustration of its utopian hopes does not, however, mean that the *strategy* of social democracy has failed. The essence of that strategy was to establish a line of development for society between tradition and revolution, liberalism and communism. The moment at which people began to speak of the crisis of the welfare state happened also to be the point at which the political weight of social democracy's two main enemies fell away to nothing. In a paradoxical way, the events of May 1968 in France were a concrete expression of the triumph of this middle way, with a social revolt running out of the control of, and even turning against, the Communist Party, a movement that disposed of the hypothesis of revolution at the same time as it liquidated the debt of tradition.

The very nature of the debate between neo-social democracy and neo-liberalism crowns this strategic triumph, since their opposition is no longer mobilized around any confrontation that crucially threatens the structure of society, but around the choice of the best way of utilizing conflicts to make society more dynamic (cf. for example, the arguments between the neo-liberal Michel Crozier and the neo-social democrat Alain Touraine). This is therefore a debate conducted on the terrain of social democracy: it has to do with the forms to be taken by the social bond, not with the structure of society itself.

2. 'Does it make sense to speak of a crisis of the social, as though the current debate meant that the counters of history had been wound back to zero?' Would it not be more accurate to speak of a crisis in the growth of the social, since the debate is only about alternative modalities of the

social bond, not about that opposition between differing ideals of the social order which the social-democratic strategy had undertaken to exorcise?

It is no doubt true that the current debate signals the end of that whole conception of the social order which was obsessed with the need to avert dangers of conflict, dangers whose only possible source it supposed to lie in the continuance of oppression imposed by tradition or of poverty imposed by underdevelopment – a point of view directly inherited from the Enlightenment.

Yet does not this farewell to the old conception of the social at the same time create room for a new one, based to some extent on an opposite set of principles: making use of conflicts instead of trying to eliminate them, applying a newly realistic awareness of conflicting needs and interests by disseminating among social partners and individual citizens new procedures for the acceptance and sharing of responsibilities (permanent retraining, self-management, decentralization)? Moreover, this new conception modifies the previous regime of the social only to maintain its basic orientation. Just as before, it strives to set aside the barriers that have been set up between individual and society, society and state. It intensifies the process of socialization through the permanent retraining system which sets an apparatus for the collective mediation of fulfilment and satisfaction in the place of legalized state protection of the individual. The same holds true of decentralization, where this operates as a pluralization of the centre, enabling the problems of the state to rebound back on to society, so that society is implicated in the task of resolving them, where previously the state was expected to hand down an answer for society's needs. What, in other words, seems to be taking place under the auspices of this crisis is a continuation of that hybridization of the private and the public, the state and the civil – which has been the very principle of the social for the past century and more.

3. If one is going to talk about crises at all, would it not be more apt to speak of a crisis of politics, rather than a crisis of the social? Our political parties developed out of antagonisms which followed from the fracturing of the republican theme which we discussed above. At their outset they were fuelled by ideologies each of which served to rationalize a different and conflicting understanding of right. For the political parties, the thematic of progress had the great merit of providing them at once with the basic minimum of consensus necessary to allow an alternation of power, and with a sufficient basis for their differences, thanks to the ambiguities inherent in the idea of progress and, even more so, in the idea of the social. One could be in favour of progress in so far as one saw it as providing suitable rewards for capitalism and smoothing its onward path.

One could also be in favour of progress in so far as it paved the way to socialism. In the former case, one invoked the authority of tradition as a force tempering the advance of progress. In the latter, one valorized the prospect and the threat of revolution, a goal defined by the order of the future, not by that of the past.

But when the social ceases to function as the thematic medium of transactions between antagonistic forces, and instead becomes the actual dimension within which such transactions have to be conducted; when the social comes to signify the mobilization of society in its entirety, rather than the sphere of state solicitude for society; what then becomes of politics as a zone of relations between forces? What can its basis be? One can suggest that politics will be driven into either a deficient or an excessive mode of existence.

The deficient mode is illustrated by Giscard's presidency, with its complete abandonment of any attempt to base authority on the representation of an order of society, the jettisoning of traditional foundations. Giscard's is a power which wants no authorization except that of reality itself, with its external, changeable and unpredictable constraints. Here the individual is left facing a nameless constellation, stripped of all transcendent qualities, and thus led to opt for itself, to take itself as the only real value, reorganizing no transcendence beyond itself.

The excessive mode of politics is manifested in Mitterrand's successful election campaign, in the form of a discourse which purports to fill the void created under Giscard, yet which can do so only in a way that distorts or violates the principle of mobilizing the concrete institutions of society. Hence the current spectacle of governmental oscillation or indecision between ideological trills and attempts to redistribute decision making; between decree and generalized negotiation.

CHAPTER NINE

How should we do the history of statistics?
Ian Hacking

1. STATISTICS AND THE HUMAN SCIENCES

Statistics is not a human science, but its influence on those sciences has been immense. I do not have in mind the fact that it is a tool of the sociologists, for it is used in many other fields as well – agriculture, meteorology, and sometimes even physics. I am concerned with something more fundamental than methodology. Statistics has helped determine the form of laws about society and the character of social facts. It has engendered concepts and classifications within the human sciences. Moreover the collection of statistics has created, at the least, a great bureaucratic machinery. It may think of itself as providing only information, but it is itself part of the technology of power in a modern state.

1.1 The form of laws

Different schools of sociology assign different roles to statistics. In the early 1830s August Comte wanted to give the name of 'social mechanics' or 'social physics' to his new science. But at about the same time the Belgian astronomer Adolphe Quetelet took the very same name for a new statistical science of mankind. Comte always resisted this, and coined the name 'sociology' just to get away from probabilities.[1] But Quetelet was a great propagandist. He organized the world statistical congresses and was even instrumental in starting the statistical section of the British Association in 1833. He became the grand old man of a new 'science'. Today we see that Quetelet triumphed over Comte: an enormously

A colloquium with the general title, 'Comment et pourquoi faire l'histoire des sciences humaines?' was held at Nanterre, Université de Paris X, 30 May – 1 June 1980. This is the translation of one of the numerous papers invited for discussion. It was intended to provide enough factual background to address some of the methodological questions suggested by the title of the conference. Naturally there are many important ways of doing the history of statistics that do not even overlap with the project suggested below.

influential body of modern sociological thought takes for granted that social laws will be cast in a statistical form.

1.2 The character of statistical facts

It was long thought to be possible that statistical laws are epiphenomena deriving from non-statistical facts at the level of individuals. By the 1890s, Durkheim had the opposite idea, urging that social laws act from above on individuals, with the same inexorable power as the law of gravity. This opinion had philosophical roots. Durkheim was well versed in the debates about emergent laws in science, laws that come into being at a certain stage of evolution. Durkheim's innovation was to found his argument on the sheer regularity and stability of quantitative social facts about statistics and crime. One name for statistics, especially in France, had been 'moral science': the science of deviancy, of criminals, court convictions, suicides, prostitution, divorce. There had been an earlier practice, also called 'moral science'. That was an a priori science of good reason, founded upon Lockeist theory of ideas. It was institutionalized as the second class of the Academy, and was abolished by Napoleon in 1803. The second class was re-established in 1834, but by then 'moral science' meant something completely different.[2] It was above all the science that studied, empirically and *en masse*, immoral behaviour. By the time that Durkheim wrote, moral science had flourished for sixty years. The great founder of modern numerical psychology, William Wundt, could say even by 1862 that statisticians had demonstrated that there are laws of love just as for all other human phenomena. In 1891, even before Durkheim's *Suicide*, Walter F. Willcox published his doctoral thesis *The Divorce Problem*[3] noting that divorce and suicide rates are correlated social indicators. During his enormously long career, Willcox (1861–1964) was to play almost as dominant a role in American statistical sociology and the census as Quetelet had once done. From the time of Quetelet to that of Willcox social facts simply became facts that are statistical in character.

1.3 Concepts and classifications

Many of the modern categories by which we think about people and their activities were put in place by an attempt to collect numerical data. The idea of recidivism, for example, appears when the quantitative study of crimes began in the 1820s. Thanks to medical statistics a canonical list of causes of death was established during the nineteenth century. It is perpetuated to this day. The classification demanded by the World Health Organization is based on that devised for the (England and Wales) Registrar General's office, run by William Farr. In most parts of the world it has long been illegal to die of anything except causes on the official list – although the list of causes is regularly revised. It is illegal, for example, to die of old age.[4] As for the censuses: Article 1, §2 of the American constitution decrees that there shall be a census every ten years. At first that was only to determine the boundaries of electoral districts, and only four questions were asked. In 1870, 156 questions were asked; in 1880, the number was 13,010. More important, perhaps, were the changing categories. New kinds of people came to be counted, and the categories of the census, and of other bureaucracies such as the Factory Inspectorate in England and Wales, created (or so I would urge) the official form of the class structure of industrial societies.[5] In addition to new kinds of people, there are also statistical meta-concepts of which the most notable is 'normalcy'. It is no accident that Durkheim conceived that he was providing a general theory to distinguish normal from pathological states of society. In the same final decade of the nineteenth century, Karl Pearson, a founding father of biometrics, eugenics and Anglo-American statistical theory, called the Gaussian distribution the normal curve.

1.4 Bureaucratic power

It is a well-known thesis of Michel Foucault that a new kind of power emerges in the nineteenth century. In one form it is a strategic development of medicine and law. More generally he sees it as part of what he calls biopolitics. There is a certain preoccupation with bodies. The disciplines of the body that he describes in his work on the prison and on sexuality form 'an entire micro-power concerned with the body', and match up with 'comprehensive measures, statistical assessments and interventions' which are aimed at the body politic, the social body. One need not subscribe fully to this model to see that statistics of populations and of deviancy form an integral part of the industrial state. Such a politics is directly involved in capital formation through social assurance; there is what Daniel Defert calls a *technologie assurentiel* which has to do with providing a stable social order.[6] He notes that of the two chief French funds for industrial assurance, one provided the capital for home investments while the other gave us Indo-China.

It is certainly not true that most applications of the new statistical knowledge were evil. One may suspect the ideology of the great Victorian social reformers and still grant that their great fight for sanitation, backed by statistical enquiries, was the most important single amelioration of the epoch. Without it most of you would not exist, for your great-great . . . -grandparents would never have lived to puberty. Statistical data do have a certain superficial neutrality between ideologies. No one used the facts collected by the factory inspectors more vigorously than Marx. Yet even Marx did not perceive how statistical bureaucracy would change the state. It is a glib but true generalization that proletarian revolutions have never occurred in any state whose assurantial technology was working properly. Conversely, wherever after any even partial industrialization it has failed, a revolution, either to left or to right, has occurred.

2. MY OWN CONCERNS FOR A HISTORY OF STATISTICS

I am not a historian but a philosopher with a strong after-taste of positivism. I differ from my colleagues who practise analytic philosophy chiefly over the question of history. I was trained to do 'conceptual analysis' as an undergraduate, and I still do that. However I believe that the organization of our concepts, and the philosophical difficulties that arise from them, sometimes have to do with their historical origins. When there is a radical transformation of ideas, whether by evolution or by an abrupt mutation, I think that whatever made the transformation possible leaves its mark upon subsequent reasoning. I toy with the idea that many of what we call philosophical problems are a byproduct of dim 'memories' of our conceptual past. There is a long post-Hegelian tradition according to which a philosophical problem arises because of some unnoticed feature of our thought. In English philosophy that tradition tried to fix on ahistorical facts about ordinary language. I guess instead that conceptual incoherence which creates philosophical perplexity is a historical incoherence between prior conditions that made a concept possible, and the concept made possible by those prior conditions. Many of the fundamental problems about probability, chance and determinism may be of this sort.

I do not believe that exposing the historical ground of a problem make it go away. I am concerned with explanation, not therapy. This is an unusual motivation for historical studies, and the result is hardly history at all. It is a use of the past for understanding some of the incoherence in present ideas. It cannot aim at exhausting the historical material, but rather at producing an hypothesis about the relationship between concepts in their historical sites. Such an enquiry may not be very different from George Canguilhem's early studies. Among the many respects in which he is a good model is his deliberate limiting of questions. A philosopher is in danger of trying to survey too much. Canguilhem shows how to fix on a definite question, say the issue of the normal and the pathological in nineteenth-century medicine. One is then led into all sorts of crannies of intellectual history, but instead of rambling on one is drawn back to the core from which one began. For my purposes I choose the following family of questions.

2.1 Indeterminism

At the end of the eighteenth century the great physicist Laplace set the tone with a classic statement of determinism.[7] Even the smallest of events happen necessarily, determined by the past and by the great laws of nature. Laplace's own conception of society was set by predecessors like Turgot or Condorcet who speak of 'physical necessity' or of 'physical laws of nature' in the study of economics or society. Yet by the end of the century the American philosopher C. S. Peirce could maintain that we live in a universe of chance,[8] and Durkheim was telling us that there are irreducible statistical laws of society. I think that such events mark a fundamental transition of our categories of causality. It culminates in a metaphysical revolution. Although there had been Lucretius with his swerving atoms, physical determinism has long been the entrenched view of students of nature. What events produced what we may call the *erosion of determinism*?

2.2 The laws of chance

Laplace believed that probability is subjective, relative in part to our knowledge and in part to our ignorance of underlying causes. In 1800 there were some laws of a statistical nature, like the laws of mortality, but these were thought to be superficial, a summary of the facts. The reality of death was produced by individual causes, and that reality had nothing to do with probability. By the end of the century those very causes of death were described as probabilistic in nature. Although determinism had been eroded, it was not by creating some new place for freedom, indeed we might say that the central fact is the *taming of chance*; where in 1800 chance had been nothing real, at the end of the century it was something 'real' precisely because one had found the form of laws that were to govern chance.

2.3 The enthusiasm for figures

In 1832 Charles Babbage, often called the inventor of the computing machine, published a pamphlet urging the publication of books of numerical constants.[9] The learned societies of Paris, Berlin and London were to take turns, every two years, in producing a list of the numbers known to mankind. Babbage had twenty kinds of numbers to be listed. They begin with familiar enough material, astronomy, atomic weights, specific heats and so forth. They quickly pass to the number of feet of oak a man can saw in an hour, the volume of air needed to keep a person alive for an hour, the productive powers of men, horses, camels and steam engines compared, the relative weights of the bones of various species, the relative frequency of occurrence of letters in various languages. Most of the numbers that were to be published were new, only a decade or so old. Between 1820 and 1840 there was an exponential increase in the number of numbers that was being published. The enthusiasm for numbers became almost universal. Nor was this avalanche limited to the human sciences. T. S. Kuhn suggests that there was a hidden transformation in the physical sciences, at exactly the same time.[10] One may develop Kuhn's insight in an obvious way. Galilean science had once said that the world was written in mathematical language, but geometry and algebra furnished the model. Only in the nineteenth century did empirical numbers assume their paramount role. It had finally become a task of the natural scientist to measure.

Despite Comte's hostility to numbers, positivism soon took for granted that positive facts were measured by numbers. Even when one reads a conservative sociologist such as Frederic Le Play who inveighs against number-crunchers of the statistical sort, one finds nothing much except numbers in his great book on European workers.[11] In the first edition of 1855 we have the budgets of the extended family ranging from semi-nomadic shepherds in the Urals to carpenters in Sheffield. Each family is recorded by about 500 numbers, how much was spent on shoes, or milk, school fees, cabbages and cauliflowers, the cost of candles. At the end of the century no one could dissent from the saying of the physicist Lord Kelvin, 'that when you can measure what you are speaking about, you know something about it; when you cannot measure it . . . your knowledge is of a meagre and unsatisfactory kind'.[12]

3. WHAT PERIOD OF TIME IS IMPORTANT?

1820 to 1900 suits me. By 1905 it was recognized that for example the fundamental law of radioactive decay is a chance process, and people were even using Monte Carlo simulation in the study of biological problems. Chance had been tamed. But, of course, any periodization is suspect. How ignore 1900–36, which ends with John von Neumann's professed proof that the quantum mechanics then current is formally inconsistent with any underlying deterministic 'hidden variables'? Then, on the other side, how can one neglect the origins of political economy, and the work of Helvetius, Say, Smith, Bentham, Malthus or Ricardo? It was Condorcet, dead in the Terror of 1794, who got Laplace going on the probability of social matters, and who was the spiritual grandfather of Comte and Quetelet alike.

The answer is that one must choose a problem. For me, as philosopher, it is indeterminism and the taming of chance. I am interested in the growth of the possibility that real chance exists and is part of the underlying structure of the world. This possibility was confirmed only with the advent of microphysics, but it was recognized as a possibility in 1900 as it had never been in 1800. My hypothesis is that events after Laplace, and after Ricardo, make the doctrines of Peirce and Durkheim viable.

Is this to be a sharp break? Should one look for a rupture between a determinist world of 1860, say, and an indeterminist one in 1880? I do not think that kind of analysis is right here. I am not intrinsically opposed to it, and urge something of the sort, two centuries earlier, in my book *The Emergence of Probability*. But the erosion of determinism did not happen suddenly. It was rather an almost systematic interaction of a great many events, some famous, some unnoticed. Most of the events were produced by people with clear views of what they were doing, and no thought at all for indeterminism. Chapter by chapter in the course of the story that should be told, one will find a fairly steady decrease in metaphysical determinism, but no one took any notice of it. Here is a sketch of some of these events.

(a) At the start of the nineteenth century, there was the idea that in human affairs one would find economic laws; laws of mortality and so forth. These laws were thought of as unequivocal and uniform. If there were irregularities they were produced by perturbing causes (and the metaphor of perturbation was taken from the theory of planetary motions). In those early days the model of human science was Newtonian.

(b) There was the theory of probability which had been cast into a definitive form by Laplace. Its probabilities were not real facts in nature but represented our ignorance of true causes.

(c) The avalanche of numbers after 1820 revealed an astonishing regularity in statistics of crime, suicide, workers' sickness, epidemics, biological facts. Mathematicians attempted an analysis of such phenomena. The great applied mathematician S. D. Poisson invented the term 'law of large numbers' in 1835 as the name of a mathematical fact, that irregularities in mass phenomena would fade out if enough data were collected.[13] Although the term 'law of large numbers' is standard in probability mathematics, Poisson's first usage was in connection with the analysis of jury trials.

(d) Meanwhile Quetelet, in addition to his propagandist work for statistics, and his fundamental role in preparing the Belgian census of 1840, which was to stand as an international model, had convinced the world that Gauss' bell-shaped 'law of errors' was precisely the type of law for the distribution of human, social and biological traits.

(e) There was a great debate about statistical determinism. Philosophers in our days have thought that indeterminism could provide room for free will. In 1860 the feeling was quite the opposite. If the suicide rate for an *arrondissement* of Paris is precisely predictable – and the breakdown into suicide by carbon monoxide, drowning etc., is equally foreseen – how then were the people who committed suicide free to refrain from that mortal sin? It was as if statistical laws had to act on some of the individuals in that district, and thus human freedom itself was challenged. These debates took many forms, and include the then immensely popular 1857 *History of Civilization in England* by Henry Buckle. He held that it was proved by statistics that human actions are governed by laws that are as fixed as those occurring in the world of physics.

(f) The social reformers thought that one could reorganize the 'boundary conditions' under which a population was governed by statistical laws, so that by self-consciousness one could come to affect Buckle's story of inevitable historical development. Characteristically, however, it was the facts of deviancy, poverty, and *les misérables* which would be changed by the wise intervention of lower-level bureaucrats. *Les misérables*, incidentally, is not only Hugo's title, echoing Eugène Sue; it is also a standard topic for the world statistical congresses. In 1860 William Farr introduced one of these great meetings by saying that statistics did not exclude free will, because although statistical laws determined the course of a population, we ('We', not they) could change the boundary conditions and so change the laws under which the population would evolve. The most powerful critique of such statistical utilitarianism, with specific satire on freedom of choice, is found in Dickens' *Hard Times* of 1854.

(g) After 1860 James Clerk Maxwell in Britain and Ludwig Bolzmann in Germany developed statistical mechanics, one of the great new ideas of physics, which in the setting of thermodynamics provided the first account of irreversible change within theoretical physics. But far from being avowedly indeterministic, Bolzmann thought one could understand the stability of molecules in large numbers precisely in terms of Poisson-style laws of large numbers. Maxwell however, was well aware of Quetelet's investigations of the Gaussian error curve for human populations, and of related derivations that had occurred in British publications.

(h) Darwinism played its part, but it was only after the groundswell of social Darwinism that influential readers began to give a probabilistic interpretation to Darwin's work.

(i) Darwin's cousin, Francis Galton, began to explain biological facts, and the phenomena of human heredity, by deducing them from the normal or Gaussian distribution. Thus what he called regression towards mediocrity (what we call regression towards the mean) was prompted by questions about traits of notable European families, and led to our modern conception of the correlation coefficient. When we use a statistical law not only to predict and organize phenomena but also to explain them, chance is well on the way to being tamed. Yet Galton himself may have had a curiously deterministic attitude to the normal curve: 'the law . . . which reigns with serenity and in complete self effacement amidst the wildest confusion . . . the supreme law of Unreason'.[14]

(j) The erosion of determinism occurs systematically in topic after topic. Gustav Fechner, who with Wundt is the great founder of experimental psychology, employed the normal law of error to explain why his experimental subjects misjudged, for example, relative weights, but he insisted on an absolutely deterministic law of transmission from a stimulus on the body to a sensation experienced by the mind.[15] His derivation of the so-called Weber–Fechner law is probabilistic in character, but at all the essential points of interaction between body and mind no probability could, for him, conceivably enter. That was in 1860. In 1879 Ebbinghaus would commence the study of short-term memory using probability curves. His generation could begin to regard these as embodying intrinsic probabilities rather than merely extrinsic random error. As chance was tamed, the probability in these theories acquired a completely new significance.

In short, almost no domain of human enquiry is left untouched by the events that I call the avalanche of numbers, the erosion of determinism and the taming of chance. Some which we now think of as obvious but minor were once of cardinal importance. Epidemiology is an instance. For half a century after the great cholera epidemic of 1832, Europeans were obsessed by fears of epidemic disease, but as the fears declined, so the very notion of an epidemic passed from a deterministic scourge to a probabilistic contagion, and much able, although localized, probability reasoning was connected with this. Those who prefer a large canvas can relate the development of economic theory in terms of the introduction of chance mechanisms into causal processes.

After countless stories like (a)–(j), it was not surprising that Durkheim, surveying fifty French books about suicide statistics, could think that probabilistic social laws have their own reality. It was natural for Emile Boutroux to argue for the contingency of the laws of nature.[16]

C. S. Peirce was only a concluding link in a chain of philosophical thought that had begun to teach that we live in a universe of chance.

4. PARADOXES

There are a couple of instructive paradoxes here. After the avalanche of numbers, the incessant counting of social and biological facts, and the almost insanely precise measures of physical quantities, produced too many numbers to leave the Galilean and Newtonian world intact. Everyone had once thought that the Newtonian laws were altogether exact, give or take this or that 'perturbation'. Such a claim is entirely credible in a qualitative universe where one does not in fact count or measure very much. But in a quantitative universe, exactness became impossible, 'deviation from the mean' became the 'norm'. Indeterminism was about to arrive.

I found a second paradox in Ernst Cassirer, who opened my eyes to a whole range of oddities. He says that for Laplace, determinism was only a metaphor that helped him to explain that probabilities represent our ignorance rather than any objective reality. Cassirer says the modern idea of determinism is first found in a famous speech by Emil Du Bois-Reymond in 1872.[17]

Cassirer put his finger on something important although the story is complex. The word 'determinism' entered German about 1789 for an idea somewhat different from any present notion, but it does not get used regularly in French or English until the 1860s, when it is the rage for, among other things, posing questions of the free will. This date is consonant with Cassirer's observation, especially when we find that it was not Du Bois-Reymond in 1872, but Charles Renouvier in 1859, who is the first to begin to take Laplace's classic statement in the modern way.[18] The old problem of free will had chiefly been the question of whether a person with given motives and states of mind can then choose freely, or whether choice is predetermined by mental state. But Du Bois-Reymond had, in 1847, been one of a small but influential group in Berlin that had proclaimed that the mind must be understood solely in physical terms, chemistry and electricity. As a grand old man in 1872, he asks how to find a place for either consciousness or free will in such a scheme, given the Laplacian picture of complete physical determinism. For Laplace, who might well have been Cartesian, the necessary determination of the movement of particles need not call in question the choices of the mind, but they did for Du Bois-Reymond. Thus Laplace was indeed a determinist, but his determinism was seen to create a whole family of new problems only at the moment when determinism itself was eroded.

This is a common pattern in the history of thought: an idea becomes sharply formulated, and even named (as 'determinism'), at exactly the moment that it is being put under pressure. A vast array of new and slightly mad debates about statistical determinism in the 1860s confirms the hunch that that was a time of pressure.[19]

5. IS THIS A HISTORY OF DISCOURSE?

Historians of science distinguish internal and external history. External history is a matter of politics, economics, the funding of institutes, the circulation of journals, and all the social circumstances that are exterior to knowledge itself. Internal history is the history of individual items of knowledge, conjectures, experiments, refutations, perhaps. We have no good account of the relationship between external and internal history. One might hope for some sort of Foucaultian archaeology, which would treat an anonymous discourse. That would be a theory of what is said, regardless of who said it. Or should we take quite the opposite tack, and study this or that initiator or agent, who quite knowingly brought about this or that event?

5.1 External history

The avalanche of numbers is at least in part the result of industrialization and the influx of people from the country to the town. Many of the thought patterns for the new counting must have been set up in the Napoleonic era. We can hardly imagine that those extraordinary armies got about without a great echelon of quartermasters keeping track of how much of what was needed to feed, arm and equip scattered units all over Europe, Egypt and the East. There was almost always a perfectly good self-conscious reason for the vast majority of new countings. For example, assurance and annuities were of no importance for the peasant or agricultural worker. But when the extended village family was destroyed by the town, new forms of security were needed for daily labourers. We can often trace quite exactly how this produced new numberings.

In Britain, for example, there arose hundreds of friendly societies to provide workers with assurance against sickness or death. Although mortality tables had long been known, there were actuarial difficulties everywhere. The poor died younger than the rich, but to what extent? No information about sickness was to be had. Between 1825 and 1827 Select Committees of the House of Commons addressed themselves to the

191

question.[20] What are the statistical laws of sickness? Every notable statistician in Britain testified. The chief actuary for the national debt asserted there could not be such a law. Parisian authorities were consulted; they pleaded ignorance, with regret. In fact in 1824 there was one piece of data, due to the efforts of the Highland Society (which was chiefly an effective instrument of agricultural reform).[21] Few believed it. Yet a decade later a host of workers had found out specific laws of sickness for trades, regions and so forth. William Farr could assert that every disease has its own mathematical law of development. In short, during the period of the avalanche of numbers there was a problem for the friendly societies, of how to set premiums. It was solved in a decade by people who well knew what they were doing.

Statistics is an applied science. Naturally we find plenty of fine examples of such external history in which men and women of the world have practical problems to solve, and which they address in an intelligent way. Despite that, we have to notice something of a different order. There arose a certain style of solving practical problems by the collection of data. Nobody argued for this style; they merely found themselves practising it. One can often illustrate the emergence of a new style of reasoning by mentioning its extremes. Their very madness makes one begin to doubt that the practical people were merely pursuing an obvious and unproblematic form of enquiry.

(a) There was a sheer fetishism for numbers. A. M. Guerry was a French lawyer whose statistical reflections on crime and suicide are of great interest.[22] By 1832 he had unsystematically developed what we now call the rank-ordering method of testing statistical hypotheses. But we also find him amassing 85,564 individual case reports on suicides, each report with a guess at the motives. Between 1832 and 1864 he analyzed 21,132 cases of persons accused of attempted or successful murder, and broke them down into 4,478 classes of motives. This fetishism for numbers is something more than a handy external history of people solving practical problems.

(b) Guerry devised a series of classifications of suicides that now seem to us almost crazy, yet a good many of them became part of what the police were required to put into the formal reports. When the avalanche of numbers began, classifications multiplied because this was the form of this new kind of discourse. Even though any single new classification usually had a straightforward motivation that can be reported by the external historian, the very fact of the classifications and of the counting was internal to a new practice. We still lack a methodology for describing the emergence of a new way of talking and doing.

I do not know how to provide an honest analysis of this complex of issues. One ought to be faithful to details of politics, commerce and diseases, and yet at the same time recognize that politics, commerce and disease did not of themselves demand that everything in the social realm should be a question of counting.

5.2 Anonymous discourse

Nothing is more anonymous than the bureaucracy of the statisticians. All the same the founders of the science – Quetelet, Villermé, Farr, Lexis, Galton, Edgeworth or whomever we choose – imposed their personal character. Farr ran the Registrar General's office in London between 1839 and 1879. The official statistics of England and Wales served as a model for the world, and it was Farr, the man, who made it so. Quetelet's Belgian census quite clearly bears the imprint of the man, Quetelet. We still live in the shadows of these men. Our governments classify us, lodge us, tax us according to the systems that they began, and by law we shall die of the causes enumerated in Farr's nosology. Ought we to employ the model of Foucault's archaeology, and speak of an organization of statistical *connaissances* of the sort produced by Farr or Quetelet, and at the same time postulate a *savoir* of countings that is the ground for the possibility of particular *connaissances*?

6. POWER, PHILOSOPHY AND PHILANTHROPY

To some extent the difficulties I find are to be found in a historical approach to any of the human sciences. I shall conclude with something peculiar to my subject, although it has some relation to Foucault's medico-legal researches. His history of the penitentiary begins with Jeremy Bentham's Panopticon. The penal programmes of the Benthamites are part of a larger vision of sanitary reform and philanthropic effort by the utilitarians. Every physical change had moral intent. (Even late in the century routine advertisements for cheap water closets emphasize their benefits to the morality of the workman's family and the resulting stability of the social order.) I would like a term less English than 'utilitarian'. French hygienic reformers after Villermé are not utilitarians in the strict sense of the word, but their language and their activities are the same as the great English sanitary utilitarian, Edwin Chadwick. It is all part of a transnational industrial philosophy that marks the very beginning of statistics. One candidate for the first *'oeuvre'* of statistics was *The Statistical Survey of Scotland*, a twenty-one volume collection, 1791–9. The ministers of the Church of Scotland respond to detailed questionnaires about the state of their parishes. By the word 'statistical' Sinclair tells us that he means 'an inquiry directed at the conditions of life of a country, in order to establish the quantum of happiness of the inhabitants'. Neither Sinclair nor the Calvinist ministers of the Church of Scotland were Benthamites, but they were all part of a game that would establish a 'calculus of felicity'.

Perhaps the general name of this phenomenon could be one I have already mentioned, 'moral science'. That was a more common name for the science of immorality in France than in Germany or Britain, but it was also, for example, the name given in 1858 to the new faculty at Cambridge which would combine economics, philosophy and psychology. (By 1969 all the sciences had long formed their own departments or faculties and only philosophy was left, so the term 'moral science' was finally dropped). The fundamental principle of the original moral sciences was the Benthamite one: the greatest happiness to the greatest number. It was necessary to count men and women and to measure not so much their happiness as their unhappiness: their morality, their criminality, their prostitution, their divorces, their hygiene, their rate of conviction in the courts. With the advent of laws of statistics one would find the laws of love, or if not that, at least the regularities about deviancy. The erosion of determinism and the taming of chance by statistics does not introduce a new liberty. The argument that indeterminism creates a place for free will is a hollow mockery. The bureaucracy of statistics imposes not just by creating administrative rulings but by determining classifications within which people must think of themselves and of the actions that are open to them. The hallmark of indeterminism is that cliché, information and control. The less the determinism, the more the possibilities for constraint. The time when all this began was well expressed by our friend Guerry – the above-mentioned lawyer who personally collected 85,564 suicides: 'L'importance de la statistique, comme instrument de surveillance et de contrôle, dans les diverses branches des services publiques, ne pouvait échapper au coup d'oeil de Napoleon 1er.'[23]

NOTES

1. The most convenient source of references for work by Quetelet, and his relationship to Comte, is still J. Lottin, *Quetelet, statisticien et sociologue*, Louvain/Paris, 1912.
2. This distinction between the two kinds of moral science, with special emphasis on enlightenment 'moral science', is well described in Lorraine Daston's 1979 doctoral thesis at Harvard: 'The reasonable calculus: classical probability theory 1650–1840'.
3. Walter, F. Willcox, 'The divorce problem: a study in statistics'. *Studies in History and Economics and Public Law*, vol. 1, pp. 1–74, 1891.

4. I owe this observation to Anne Fagot's remarkable draft dissertation of 1978. 'L'explication causale de la mort'. An English translation is in preparation for Reidel.

5. This theme is elaborated in my 'Biopower and the avalanche of numbers', to be published in a volume of papers, edited by Mark Poster, from a conference on Foucault entitled 'Knowledge, Power, History', which took place at the University of Southern California in October 1981.

6. No theoretical exposition of this idea is yet available. D. Defert, J. Donzelot, F. Ewald, G. Maillet, C. Mevel, *Socialization du risque et pouvoir dans l'enterprise*, Ministère du Travail, 1977; Arpad Ajtony, Stephane Callens, Daniel Defert, François Ewald, Gerard Maillet, *Assurance-Prevovance-Sécurité: Formation historique des techniques de gestion sociale dans les sociétés industrielles*, Ministère du Travail et de la participation, 1979.

7. P. S. de Laplace, *A Philosophical Essay on Probabilities*, trans. Truscott and Emory, New York/Dover, 1951. This was the basis for lectures in 1795 and served as the introduction for Laplace's major work on probability, the *Théorie Analytique des Probabilités*.

8. C. S. Peirce, 'The doctrine of necessity' 1892, reprinted in, for example, Charles S. Peirce, *Selected Writings*, ed. P. Wiener, New York/Dover, 1966.

9. C. Babbage, 'On the advantage of a collection of numbers to be intitled the constants of nature and art', *Edinburgh Journal of Science*, N.S. vol. 12, 1832.

10. T. S. Kuhn, 'The function of measurement in modern physical science', in *The Essential Tension*, Chicago, 1977.

11. F. Le Play, *Les Oeuvriers européens étude sur les travaux, la vie domestique, et la condition morale des population ouvrières de l'Europe*, Paris, 1855.

12. Sir William Thomson (Lord Kelvin), 'Electrical units of measurement', in *Popular Lectures and Addresses*, London, 1889, vol. 1, p. 73.

13. S. D. Poisson, *Recherches sur la probabilité des jugements en matière criminelle et en matière civile*, Paris, 1837. The phrase 'law of large numbers' was introduced in public lectures two years earlier.

14. F. Galton, *Natural Inheritance*, London, 1889, p. 66.

15. G. T. Fechner, *Elemente der Psychophysik*, Berlin, 1860, 2 vols. (*Elements of Psychophysics*, vol. 1 only, trans. Adler, New York, 1966). See esp. vol. II, pp. 430–2.

16. Emile Bourtroux, *De la contingence des lois de nature*, Paris, 1875.

17. Ernst Cassirer, *Indeterminism and Modern Physics*, Chicago, 1961; Emil Du Bois-Reymond, '*Ueber die Grenzen des Naturerkennens*', in Bois-Reyden, *Reden*, Leibzig, 1885.

18. Charles Renouvier, 'L'homme: la raison, la passion, la liberté, la certitude, la probabilité morale', in Renouvier, *Essais de critique générale*, Paris, 1859.

19. See my 'Nineteenth century cracks in the concept of determinism', forthcoming in the *Journal for the History of Ideas*.

20. *Report of the Select Committee to Consider the Laws Respecting Friendly Societies*, 5 July 1825.

21. *Report on Friendly or Benefit Societies, exhibiting the law of sickness to be deduced from returns by Friendly Societies in different parts of Scotland, drawn up by a committee of the Highland Society of Scotland*, Edinburgh, 1824.

22. André-Marie Guerry, *Essai sur la statistique morale de la France*, Paris, 1833; *Statistique morale de l'Angleterre comparée avec la statistique morale de la France*, Paris, 1864.

23. *Ibid.*, p. 3.

CHAPTER TEN

Insurance and risk

François Ewald

The term 'insurance' is an equivocal one. It can designate, in the first place, the *institutions* of insurance, whatever their objective or social form may be. Private and nationalized companies, social security schemes, mutualist societies, companies run on a premium basis, insurance against accidental death, fire, civil liability: there are a multiplicity of such institutional types, which specialists have set out to classify in various ways, distinguishing between insurances of persons and property, mutualist and premium systems, social and private insurances. Each insurance institution differs from the others in its purposes, its clientele, its legal basis.

This plurality suggests a question. Why do such different activities come to be thus grouped together under a common rubric? What do they have in common? Actually, the term 'insurance' denotes not just these institutions but also a factor which gives a unity to their diversity, enables an institution to be identified as an insurance institution and signals to us what an institution has to be to be an insurance institution. In this second meaning, insurance designates not so much a concept as an *abstract technology*. Using the vocabulary of the nineteenth-century actuaries, economists and publicists, we can say that the technology of insurance is an art of 'combinations'. Not that insurance is itself a combination, but it is something which, on the basis of a technology of risk, makes possible a range of insurance combinations shaped to suit their assigned function and intended utility-effect. Considered as a technology, insurance is an art of combining various elements of economic and social reality according to a set of specific rules. From these different combinations, there derive the different sorts of insurance institution.

But the term must also be understood in a third sense. What in fact is the relationship between the abstract technology of insurance and the multiple insurance institutions we contract or affiliate with? One might say that the institutions are the applications of the technology, which would suggest that insurance institutions are all fundamentally alike, apart from their difference of purpose and mode of management. But this is not so. Insurance institutions are not repetitions of a single formula applied to different objects: marine insurance is different from terrestrial insurance, social insurance institutions are not just nationalized insurance companies. Insurance institutions are not *the* application of a technology of risk; they are always just *one* of its possible applications. This indeed is something that the term 'combination' helps to make clear: insurance institutions never actualize more than one among various possible combinations. So that, between the abstract technology and the institutional actualizations, we need to find room for a third term, which we will call here the insurance *form*. Where the elaboration of the abstract technology is the work of the actuary, and the creation of the institution that of the entrepreneur, one might say that the aim of the sociologist, historian or political analyst should be to ascertain why at a given moment insurance institutions take one particular shape rather than another, and utilize the technique of risk in one way rather than in another. This variability of form, which cannot be deduced from the principles of either technology or institutions, relates to the economic, moral, political, juridical, in short to the social conditions which provide insurance with its market, the market for security. These conditions are not just constraints; they can offer an opportunity, a footing for new enterprises and policies. The particular form insurance technology takes in a given institution at a given moment depends on an *insurantial imaginary*: that is to say, on the ways in which, in a given social context, profitable, useful and necessary uses can be found for insurance technology. Thus, the birth of social insurance at the end of the nineteenth century needs, for example, to be analyzed as a realization of a new form of insurance, linked to the development of an insurantial imaginary which in this case is also a political imaginary.

So one has an insurance technology which takes a certain form in certain institutions, thanks to the contribution of a certain imaginary. The way these categories – technology, institution, form, imaginary – articulate together is a problem of logical description which of course does not correspond to the real historic process by which maritime and terrestrial insurances were constituted. Insurance technology and actuarial science did not fall from the mathematical skies to incarnate themselves in institutions. They were built up gradually out of multiple practices which they reflected and rationalized, practices of which they were more effects than causes, and it would be wrong to imagine that they have now assumed a definite shape. Existing in economic, moral and political conjunctures which continually alter, the practice of insurance is always reshaping its techniques.

Insurance can be defined as a technology of risk. In fact, the term 'risk' which one finds being used nowadays apropos of everything has no precise meaning other than as a category of this technology. Risk is a neologism of insurance, said to derive from the Italian word *risco* which meant 'that which cuts', hence 'reef' and consequently 'risk to cargo on the high seas'. Say's *Dictionary of Political Economy* states that 'the whole theory of insurance rests on the fundamental notion of risk'.[1] The notion of risk is likewise central to the juridical definition of insurance: 'risk is the fundamental element of insurance, since it is the very object of this type of contract'. Risk constitutes an essential element of insurance; the fundamental element, even, for Picard and Besson who add: 'this notion of risk is specific in its origin to the law and science of insurance, and differs markedly from the notion of risk utilised in civil law and everyday speech'.[2] So what is this thing called risk?

In everyday language the term 'risk' is understood as a synonym for danger or peril, for some unhappy event which may happen to someone; it designates an objective threat. In insurance the term designates neither an event nor a general kind of event occurring in reality (the unfortunate kind), but a specific mode of treatment of certain events capable of happening to a group of individuals – or, more exactly, to values or capitals possessed or represented by a collectivity of individuals: that is to say, a population. Nothing is a risk in itself; there is no risk in reality. But on the other hand, anything *can* be a risk; it all depends on how one analyzes the danger, considers the event. As Kant might have put it, the category of risk is a category of the understanding; it cannot be given in sensibility or intuition. As a technology of risk, insurance is first and foremost a schema of rationality, a way of breaking down, rearranging, ordering certain elements of reality. The expression 'taking risks', used to characterize the spirit of enterprise, derives from the application of this type of calculus to economic and financial affairs.

Rather than with the notions of danger and peril, the notion of risk goes together with those of chance, hazard, probability, eventuality or randomness on the one hand, and those of loss or damage on the other – the two series coming together in the notion of accident. One insures against accident, against the probability of loss of some good. Insurance, through the category of risk, objectifies every event as an accident. Insurance's general model is the game of chance: a risk, an accident comes up like a roulette number, a card pulled out of the pack. With insurance, gaming becomes a symbol of the world.

Insurance is not initially a practice of compensation or reparation. It is the practice of a certain type of rationality: one formalized by the calculus of probabilities. This is why one never insures oneself except against risks, and why the latter can include such different things as death, an accident, hailstorms, a disease, a birth, military conscription, bankruptcy and litigation. Today it is hard to imagine all the things which insurers have managed to invent as classes of risk – always, it should be said, with profitable results. The insurer's activity is not just a matter of passively registering the existence of risks, and then offering guarantees against them. He 'produces risks', he makes risks appear where each person had hitherto felt obliged to submit resignedly to the blows of fortune. It is characteristic of insurance that it constitutes a certain type of objectivity, giving certain familiar events a kind of reality which alters their nature. By objectivizing certain events as risks, insurance can invert their meanings: it can make what was previously an obstacle into a possibility. Insurance assigns a new mode of existence to previously dreaded events; it creates value:

> Insurance is eminently creative where, completing the interrupted work snatched by death from the hands of the family man, it instantly realizes the capital which was to have been the fruit of savings; it is eminently creative when it gives the aged man with inadequate resources the pension needed to sustain his declining years.[3]

Insurance is the practice of a type of rationality potentially capable of transforming the life of individuals and that of a population.

Thus there is not a special domain of certain kinds of thing specially suited for being insured. Everything can be a risk, in so far as the type of event it falls under can be treated according to the principles of insurance technology. For certain thinkers, 'insurance is called upon to extend indefinitely the field of guarantees it affords against risk and to attain the form of an "integral" insurance. Here, in fact, it tends to the character of an indefinite, unlimited guarantee.' Doubtless there are technical limits to insurance, doubtless risks can only be insured when they are sufficiently separable and dispersed, and when the value of the risk is not in excess of the insurer's capacities; but it is striking nevertheless how something which at one time seemed impossible to insure later becomes possible thanks to the progress of insurance technology, via coassurance or reinsurance operations. The technique of reinsurance in particular, with its special kind of alchemy, shows very well what a risk can be from the insurance point of view: an abstract quantity that can be divided at will, one part of which an insurer can hand over to a reinsurer in Munich or Zurich, who will balance them up with risks of a similar kind but located on the other side of the world. What can there be in common between that singular event which each person individually fears, and this other singular object, the risk, manipulated by the chain of its insurers?

Insurance is one of those practices linked to what Pascal called the 'geometry of hazard' or 'algebra of chances' and is today called the calculus of probabilities. Thus it is a sister activity, along with demography, econometrics and opinion polls, of Quetelet's *social physics*. Like this, it is an application of probability calculus to statistics. Social physics had introduced a series of decentrings into the way one considered people, things and their relationships; it proposed a mode of thinking completely foreign to the moral, moralizing mode which underpinned and was supposed to validate the juridical notion and practice of responsibility, and yet it did this without entering into conflict with juridical practice. While sociology brought to light many other factors of social regularity in addition to law (*droit*), and while it no longer conceded to law more than a regional function among the mechanisms of social regulation, it did not contest the domain that *was* assigned to law. The discovery of the constancy of criminal tendencies and the regularity of criminality itself as a social fact had no immediate incidence on the way the law was able and obliged to judge infractions and deal with actual criminals. The sociological discovery of the regularity of criminality did not lead to the deduction that it was inadequate to treat the criminal juridically in terms of responsibility. No doubt it affected the philosophical foundations of law and its pretensions as the great regulatory instance in society; it did not affect it in its practice. But the same is no longer true in the case of the development of insurance: insurance is a practice situated at the same level as legal right, which, as a law of responsibility, has for its object the reparation and indemnification of damages. Insurance and law are two practices of responsibility which operate quite heterogeneous categories, regimes, economies; as such, they are mutually exclusive in their claims to totality. This is the famous controversy over risk and fault which for nearly two centuries now has fuelled debate about civil responsibility. Sociology contested the juridical theory of responsibility in its philosophy, but left it in peace in its practice; insurance directly challenges this practice. Sociology and insurance – this is what gives them their historical importance – carry the seeds of a new theory and practice of legal right. And they do so not politically, not through their envisaging new objectives of social equality, but through what they are *in themselves*, in terms of their special kind of technological rationality. Insurance and the law of responsibility are two techniques which bear on the same object. As technologies they are independent of the political policies which will utilize them. It would be wrong to say that in the nineteenth century the liberals were partisans of juridical responsibility while the socialists were defenders of insurance. Both sides had their respective policies for the use of these two technologies. The same political positions can become partisans and take on the colours of one or other of them.

Risk in the meaning of insurance has three great characteristics: it is calculable, it is collective, and it is a capital.

1. *Risk is calculable.* This is the essential point, whereby insurance is radically distinct from a bet or a lottery. For an event to be a risk, it must

be possible to evaluate its probability. Insurance has a dual basis: the statistical table which establishes the regularity of certain events, and the calculus of probabilities applied to that statistic, which yields an evaluation of the chances of that class of event actually occurring.[4]

In the juridical logic of responsibility, the judge takes as the point of departure the reality of the accident or the damage, so as to infer the existence of its cause in a fault of conduct. The judge supposes that there would have been no accident without a fault. The insurer's calculation is based on the objective probability of an accident, regardless of the action of will: no matter whether it results from someone or other's fault, or whether it could have been averted, the fact is that, regardless of the good or ill will of people, regardless of what they might or might not have been able to do, accidents occur at a particular, specific rate. Juridical reason springs from a moral vision of the world: the judge supposes that if a certain individual had not behaved as he or she actually did, the accident would not have happened; that if people conducted themselves as they ought, the world would be in harmony. The insurer's attitude, on the contrary, is wholly one of registering a fact: small matter what would have happened if . . ., the fact is that there is such and such a number of industrial or traffic accidents annually, that whatever the wishes may be that one cares to voice, the figures repeat themselves with overwhelming regularity.

This is what emerged in the mid-nineteenth century from the first industrial statistics, those for the mines:

> taking a large number of workers in the same occupation, one finds a constant level of accidents year by year. It follows from this that accidents, just when they may seem to be due to pure chance, are governed by a mysterious law.[5]

This constancy strikingly manifests the objective nature of risk. Regardless of the size of a workforce or the turnover of its recruits, a given mine or factory will show a consistent percentage of injuries and deaths. When put in the context of a population, the accident which taken on its own seems both random and avoidable (given a little prudence) can be treated as predictable and calculable. One can predict that during the next year there will be a certain number of accidents, the only unknown being who will have an accident, who will draw one of existence's unlucky numbers. All of which means not that accidents are unavoidable, or that they are works of a destined fate; but that the juridical perception of them in terms of fault and responsibility is not the only possible one, or perhaps the one which is the most pertinent and effective.

2. *Risk is collective.* Whereas an accident, as damage, misfortune and

suffering, is always individual, striking at one and not another, a risk of accident affects a population. Strictly speaking there is no such thing as an individual risk; otherwise insurance would be no more than a wager. Risk only becomes something calculable when it is spread over a population. The work of the insurer is, precisely, to constitute that population by selecting and dividing risks. Insurance can only cover groups; it works by socializing risks. It makes each person a part of the whole. Risk itself only exists as an entity, a certainty, in the whole, so that each person insured represents only a fraction of it. Insurance's characteristic operation is the constitution of mutualities: conscious ones, in the case of the mutualist associations; unconscious ones, in the case of the premium companies.

Under the regime of juridical responsibility, the accident isolates its victim and its author. It distinguishes them, singularizes them, isolates them, because within this system the accident can only ever be an exception, something which disturbs an order conceived in itself as harmonious. The accident is due to some individual fault, imprudence or negligence; it cannot be a rule. Moral thought uses accident as a principle of distinction; an accident is a unique affair between individual protagonists. Insurance, on the other hand, functions through a quite different mode of individualization. A risk is first of all a characteristic of the population it concerns. No one can claim to evade it, to differ from the others like someone who escapes an accident. When legislation makes a form of insurance compulsory, it acknowledges the mythical character of the principle of juridical goodwill. Each person's conduct, however immaculate and irreproachable it may actually be, harbours within itself a risk to others which may be minuscule but nevertheless exists. No will is absolutely good; even the 'good father of his family' traditionally cited as a yardstick of rectitude in judicial evaluations of conduct can have characteristic weaknesses which put others in danger. The idea of risk assumes that all the individuals who compose a population are on the same footing: each person is a factor of risk, each person is exposed to risk. But this does not mean that everyone causes or suffers the same degrees of risk. The risk defines the whole, but each individual is distinguished by the probability of risk which falls to his or her share. Insurance individualizes, it defines each person as a risk, but the individuality it confers no longer correlates with an abstract, invariant norm such as that of the responsible juridical subject: it is an individuality relative to that of other members of the insured population, an average sociological individuality.

The mutualities created by insurance have special characteristics: they are abstract mutualities, unlike the qualitative mutualities of the family, the corporation, the union, the commune. One 'belongs' to the latter kinds of mutuality to the extent that one respects their particular duties, hierarchies, orderings. The family has its rules, the trade union its internal regulations. These mutualities place one, moralize one, educate one, form one's conscience. Insurance mutualities are different: they leave the person free. Insurance provides a form of association which combines a maximum of socialization with a maximum of individualization. It allows people to enjoy the advantages of association while still leaving them free to exist as individuals. It seems to reconcile those two antagonists, society-socialization and individual liberty. This, as we will see, is what makes for its political success.

3. *Risk, lastly, is a capital.* What is insured is not the injury that is actually lived, suffered and resented by the person it happens to, but a capital against whose loss the insurer offers a guarantee. The lived injury is irreparable: afterwards can never be the same as before. One does not replace a father or mother, any more than one relaces an impairment of one's bodily integrity. Considered as suffering, all of this is beyond price, and yet it is the nature of insurance to offer financial compensation for it. Insurance, the risk-treatment of injury works through a dualization of the lived and the indemnified. One and the same event acquires a dual status: on the one hand, a happening with the uniqueness of the irreparable; on the other, an indemnifiable risk. Hence it is a major problem here to know how to establish a relation between the unique event and its financial compensation. To the extent that things have a monetary value, their insurance admits of such a relationship being satisfactorily determined. But how can one fix the cost of a body, a hand, an arm, a leg? There is no possible common measure for the indemnity paid out by the insurer and the loss which is suffered. The indemnity will necessarily be arbitrary in relation to the injury. But this does not mean that it will be unjust, or that it will not be subject to a rule. Unlike legal damages, which are required to match the full extent of an injury, insurance compensation payments are defined by a contractually agreed tariff. Tables or scales of compensation rates are fixed in advance so as to define the 'price of the body' in all possible eventualities, and the indemnity entitlement for every form of injury. One can always argue that life and health are things beyond price. But the practice of life, health and accident insurance constantly attests that everything can have a price, that all of us have a price and that this price is not the same for all:

> Man first thought of insuring his shipping against the risks of navigation. Then he insured his houses, his harvests, and his goods of all kinds against risk of fire. Then, as the idea of capital, and consequently also that of insurable interest, gradually emerged in a clear form out of the confused notions that previously obscured them, man understood that he himself was a capital which death could prematurely destroy, that in himself he embodied an insurable interest. He then devised life insurance, insurance that is to say

against the premature destruction of human capital. Next he realized that if human capital can be destroyed, it can also be condemned to disuse through illness, infirmity and old age, and so he devised accident, sickness and pension insurance. Insurance against the unemployment or premature destruction of human capital is the true popular form of insurance.[6]

This dualization of the injury as lived by the victim and the fixed indemnity paid out by the insurer (either a private company or a social security) gives rise to pitiable speculations, arguments, demands and misunderstandings between insurer and insured. For the insured, the guaranteed level of indemnity will never be enough to equal the suffering undergone, the loss endured. And the fact that bodily damage can thus be transformed into a cash price may lead an insured person to speculate on his or her pain, injury, disease or death, so as to extract the maximum profit from them. Before industrial accidents came to be covered by social insurance, employees had to take legal action against their employers. No doubt this was an unjust and unequal combat for the worker to have to fight, but it did make the struggle for compensation of an injury into a struggle against the power of the boss, a struggle for recognition of individual dignity. The worker had to enforce a public recognition that the employer was 'wrong'. With the coming of accident insurance, this combat changes its character: it becomes a matter for the worker of getting as much money as possible out of his or her disablement. The place of the judge is taken over here by the expert, who assigns a person's insurantial identity, allocates a placement in a table of categories where the individual is 'objectively' located by the criteria it applies.

From these three characteristics of risk as 'the actual value of a possible damage in a determined unit of time', one can deduce a definition of insurance as: 'the commpensation of effects of chance through mutuality organised according to the laws of statistics':

> Insurance does not, as has been mistakenly said, eliminate chance, but it fixes its scope; it does not abolish loss, but ensures that loss, by being shared, is not felt. Insurance is the mechanism through which this sharing is operated. It modifies the incidence of loss, diverting it from the individual to the community. It substitutes a relation of extension for a relation of intensity.[7]

This might be taken as a canonical definition, except that it fails to bring out what is, perhaps, the essential element of insurance combinations considered from the social and juridical angle: the element of *justice*. Insurance is not just an operation which provides at a minimum premium for compensation through mutuality of losses that fall on one person or another. To define its scope so narrowly would hardly be enough to differentiate insurance from the equivalent roles of corporations and guilds. What distinguishes insurance is not just that it spreads the burden of individual injuries over a group, but that it enables this to be done no longer in the name of help or charity but according to a principle of justice, a rule of right:

> Insurance is nothing but the application to human affairs of the rule in games of chance by which one determines the outcome for players who want to withdraw before chance has decided between them, and recover disposal over the common fund created by their play. For equity to be strictly respected, each of them should get back on his stake a share proportional to the chances he would have had of winning.[8]

This 'proportional share' is what defines the notion of risk used in insurance. Liberal thought held that the attribution by nature of goods and ills is, in itself, just. Chance has to be allowed free play. It is up to each individual to provide against this state of things, freely and voluntarily. It followed from this approach that judicial decisions on accident compensation had to be linked to investigation of the cause of injury: it had to be ascertained whether a damage was due to natural causes, or to some person who should bear its cost. The problem was one of putting things back in order. Insurance proposes a quite different idea of justice: the idea of cause is replaced by the idea of a distributive sharing of a collective burden, to which each member's contribution can be fixed according to a rule. The idea of risk is not an instrument for identifying the cause of an injury, but a rule by which to distribute its weight. Insurance offers a justice which appeals no longer to nature but to the group, a social rule of justice which the group is to some extent free to specify, and which makes naturally evident the injustice of social inequalities. As Proudhon explained:

> The savings bank, mutuality and life assurance are excellent things for those who enjoy a certain comfort and wish to safeguard it, but they remain quite fruitless, not to say inaccessible, for the poorer classes. Security is a commodity bought like any other: and as its rate of tariff falls in proportion not with the misery of the buyer but with the magnitude of the amount he insures, insurance proves itself a new privilege for the rich and a cruel irony for the poor.

But, conversely, to the extent that one does seek to extend its benefits to the greatest number, the idea of insurance 'naturally' implies the idea of social redistribution.

Insurance, then, is the practice of a certain type of rationality. It has no special field of operations; rather than being defined in terms of its objects, it is a kind of ubiquitous form. It provides a general principle for the objectification of things, people and their relations.

Insurance possesses several distinct dimensions of technique. In the first place, it is an economic and financial technique. This indeed was how it came into being as an effect of the Church's prohibition on interest, since

interest no longer came under the ban when it was made the remuneration of a risk. Terrestrial forms of insurance derive from the methods
of state loans, either in the speculative form of tontines, or in the already
rationalistic method applied by Johann de Witt to life-pensions.

Secondly, insurance is a moral technology. To calculate a risk is to
master time, to discipline the future. To conduct one's life in the manner
of an enterprise indeed begins in the eighteenth century to be a definition
of a morality whose cardinal virtue is providence. To provide for the
future does not just mean not living from day to day and arming oneself
against ill fortune, but also mathematizing one's commitments. Above all,
it means no longer resigning oneself to the decrees of providence and the
blows of fate, but instead transforming one's relationships with nature,
the world and God so that, even in misfortune, one retains responsibility
for one's affairs by possessing the means to repair its effects.

Thirdly, insurance is a technique of reparation and indemnification of
damages. It is a mode of administering justice which competes with that
of legal right. It maintains a type of justice under which the damage
suffered by one is borne by all, and individual responsibility is made
collective and social. Whereas the principle of right concentrated on
preserving the 'natural' allocation of advantages and burdens, insurance
conceives justice according to a conception of sharing for which it
undertakes to fix equitable rules.

The combination of these different dimensions make insurance a
political technology. It is a technology of social forces mobilized and utilized
in a very specific way: 'Insurance creates a new grouping of human
interests. Men are no longer juxtaposed alongside one another in society.
Reciprocal penetration of souls and interests establishes a close solidarity
among them. Insurance contributes substantially towards the solidariza-
tion of interests.'[9] It constitutes a mode of association which allows its
participants to agree on the rule of justice they will subscribe to.
Insurance makes it possible to dream of a contractual justice where an
order established by conventions will take the place of natural order: the
ideal of a society where each member's share in social advantages and
burdens will be fixed by a social contract which is no longer just a
political myth, but something wholly real. Insurance makes it possible to
envisage a solution to the problem of poverty and working-class
insecurity. Thanks to insurance, by a minimal contribution which can be
afforded, the worker can safeguard against the ills that continually
threaten: 'Among the normal costs to be covered by wages, one should
not hesitate to include the cost of insurance, because without insurance
everything is uncertain for the worker: the present lacks confidence, the
future hope and consolation'.[10] The worker, according to Brentano,
should contract six kinds of insurance: (1) a life insurance on behalf of his

children; (2) a pension insurance for old age; (3) an insurance for the purpose of paying for a decent funeral; (4) an insurance against possible infirmity; (5) a sickness insurance; (6) an insurance against unemployment due to shortage of work, this last being also an insurance that the premiums of all the other insurances can be regularly paid.

Insurance, finally, liberates man from fear:

> One of the first and most salutory effects of insurance is to eliminate from human affairs the fear that paralyses all activity and numbs the soul. Seneca says somewhere *Rex est qui metuit nihil*: he who fears nothing is a king. Delivered from fear, man is king of creation; he can dare to venture; the ocean itself obeys him, and he entrusts his fortune to it.[11]

Insurance allows enterprise, and hence multiplies wealth. As a liberator of action, insurance is seen as comparable with religion:

> A remedy so potent that the emancipation of action by insurance can only be compared with that effected in another domain by religion . . . This global sense of security produced already by our fragmentary existing forms of insurance, and still more by its integral forms yet to come, is like a transposition on to the earthly plane of the religious faith that inspires the believer.[12]

One should not underestimate the importance of the epistemological transformation which produces what might be called the *philosophy of risk*. This mutation attests to a sort of conversion process in mental attitudes towards not only justice and responsibility, but also time, causality, destiny, desert and providence. All man's relations with himself or herself, with others and with the world are overturned. With insurance and its philosophy, one enters a universe where the ills that befall us lose their old providential meaning: a world without God, a laicized world where 'society' becomes the general arbiter answerable for the causes of our destiny.

From a juridical point of view, the new politics of insurance security works through a new strategy of rights. This is, in particular, the beginning of labour law (*droit du travail*). The strategy has the characteristic of making it the categorical imperative of every benefit system (public or private, operated by employers or by workers) that it must always be in a position to keep its promises. Workers who pay a subscription must be sure that they will get back what they have subscribed for (a sickness benefit, an old-age retirement pension, an indemnity in case of accident, etc.) Insurance technology needs to permeate all of the existing provident institutions, enabling them to rationalize their functions and really to offer the security they are supposed to promise. There are two key factors here, both of them pioneered by the insurance companies. One is a mathematical form, the *technique* of probabilistic calculation which ensures the certainty of the institutions' operations, disciplining the future and ensuring that their combinations are more than a mere lottery. The other is the juridical form of the insurance *contract*. The person who pays a premium *acquires a right of indemnity*; the company he or she contracts with has obligations towards that person which are juridical as well as moral. Insurance allows security to be simultaneously contractualized, legalized and juridicalized.

By the end of the nineteenth century, no one is any longer in doubt that provident institutions must conform to the rationality of insurance, so that every type of benefit organization, whatever its nominal structure, becomes an insurance institution *de facto*. Insurance now really signifies not so much a particular, distinctive type of institution as a form, an organizing schema of management and rationality capable of being realized in any and every kind of provident institution.

It is the imperative of *guaranteed* security in workers' insurance that leads to the debate over state insurance. For it is not enough that the legislator merely confer rights on workers; it must also be ensured that these rights are actually guaranteed. And who better than the state can guarantee the stability of insurance institutions? Behind this problem of guarantees there lies another, profounder one, namely the problem of the permanence of insurance institutions. Since they are supposed to be providing security, these need to have a quasi-infinite longevity. With insurance one comes to experience a sort of dilation of timescales, stretched out to span not just one generation or lifetime but several, and thus positing the survival of society for an indefinite future.

One moves from a limited conception of time bound to the life of individuals, to a social time measured against the life of society, actualizing the Comtian conception of progress which founds the idea of *solidarity* as formulated in the political theory of *solidarisme*. In guaranteeing security, the state is equally guaranteeing itself its own existence, maintenance, permanence. Social insurance is also an insurance against revolutions.

The development of insurance is accompanied by a transformation of social morals, a transformation of an individual's relation to himself or herself, to his or her future, and to society. Social insurance gives concrete form to the laicized morality sought for by the French Republic and articulated by *solidarisme*. Where Kant could speak of 'the starry heavens above me and the moral law within me', in future people will speak only of society: the society to which I am joined in solidarity by history, carrying the weight of my inheritance and my share of responsibility for the future, and by contemporaneity, since I participate in society's ills and owe a debt to my fellows for the advantages society procures me. The development of insurance at the end of the nineteenth century is paralleled by what one might call the birth of a *sociopolitics*: that is to say, a political philosophy which no longer seeks to found or legitimize 'society', to find for it a directing principle outside itself, in the dawn of its creation (a state of nature, a social contract, a natural law), but instead makes 'society', enclosed (so to speak) in itself, along with the laws of its history and sociology, into a permanent principle of political self-justification. The legislators of the French Revolution believed they were legislating for man, defining and guaranteeing his natural, human, eternal rights; henceforth, right will be 'social', legislation 'social', politics 'social'; 'society' becomes its own principle and end, cause and consequence, and man no longer finds salvation or identity except by recognizing himself as a social being, a being who is made and unmade, alienated, constrained, repressed or saved by 'society'.

At the end of the nineteenth century, insurance is thus not only one of the ways the provident person can guard against certain risks. The technology of risk, in its different epistemological, economic, moral, juridical and political dimensions becomes the principle of a new political and social economy. Insurance becomes *social*, not just in the sense that new kinds of risk become insurable, but because European societies come to analyze themselves and their problems in terms of the generalized technology of risk. Insurance, at the end of the nineteenth century, signifies at once an ensemble of institutions and the diagram with which industrial societies conceive their principle of organization, functioning and regulation. Societies envisage themselves as a vast system of insurance, and by overtly adopting insurance's forms they suppose that they are thus conforming to their own nature.

NOTES

1. L. Say, *Nouveau Dictionnaire d'Économie Politique*, Paris, 1896; article 'Assurance', T. I, p. 94.
2. Picard and Besson, *Traité general des assurances terrestres en droit français*, T. I, Paris, 1976, p. 35.
3. Chauffon, *Les Assurances leur passé, leur présent, leur avenir*, Paris, 1884, T. I, p. 309.
4. In fact the practice of insurance precedes the constitution of the statistics which at a later date enable practice to be rationalized.
5. O. Keller, *Premier Congrès International des Accidents du Travail* (Paris, 1889), T. I, p. 269.
6. Chauffon, *Les Assurances*, p. 228.
7. *Ibid.*, p. 216.
8. E. Reboul, *Assurances sur la Vie* (Paris, 1863), p. 44.
9. Chauffon, *Les Assurances*, p. 303.
10. *Ibid.*, p. 230.
11. *Ibid.*, p. 296.
12. F. Gros, *L'Assurance, son sens Historique et Social* (Paris, 1920), p. 108.

CHAPTER ELEVEN

'Popular life' and insurance technology
Daniel Defert

INSURANCE TECHNOLOGY

Histories of social policy have a tendency to lay stress on episodes of political conflict and the enactment of legislation which punctuates or temporarily puts an end to such conflicts. But in doing so they do not always find it necessary to decide whether the solutions arrived at were really in accord with the goals of the popular struggles and demands which led up to them. Social history is in fact traversed by a number of other, more covert issues, whose genealogy is not without its surprises.

Such is the case with the history of industrial accident insurance. The state of affairs in which financial compensation for an industrial accident is automatic, unquestioned and guaranteed by a system of insurance may seem like a people's victory when compared with the situation of the poor in the nineteenth century. Yet the fact is that in France the workers' movement only gradually came to give its endorsement to this solution, eventually embracing a piece of legislation originally passed without its support. For the history of insurance in industrial society begins with the invention of a technique for managing a population and creating funds for compensation damages, an emerging technology of risk which was originally devised by financiers, before later becoming a paradigm of social solutions to all cases of non-labour: first that of industrial accidents, then sickness and old age, and finally unemployment. This reparatory technology for coping with the chances and uncertainties of industrial labour came, as it was developed into the social insurance system, to play a significant role in transforming the management of industrial capitalist societies, a part which seems not to have been accorded as much study and attention as, for example, the history of banking. This discussion draws on the findings of a group research project on the formation of the insurance apparatus, considered as a schema of social rationality and social management.[1]

The industrial accident occupies a strategic position in the emplacement of what was to become social insurance. What we today call social insurance was originally established in France by nationalizing the industrial accident departments of the private insurance companies. But this did not come about as a result of working-class struggle. Instead, industrial accident insurance was initially framed within the logic of life assurance, a practice which the finance companies had previously been unable to implant on a popular level. It was through its investment of human life that the technique of insurance, after having a century earlier conquered the shipping market, prospected its decisive advances and achieved the status of a general principle for providing bourgeois solutions to proletarian problems. The first crucial threshold within this story was the passage from the old technique of life annuities to its contrary, life insurance. This radical change brought together for the first time the following basic features:

1. A way to manage populations which conceives them as homogeneous series, established in purely scientific terms rather than by way of empirical modes of solidarity such as a trade, a family or a neighbourhood.
2. A method of finance based not, as hitherto, on speculation on the death of individuals, but on speculation on the medically supervised prolongation of life.
3. The first real economic rationalization of what later came to be termed human capital: though one should note that here the subject of human capital was the rentier, not the owner of labour-power.
4. A new channel for the concentration of capital.
5. A new set of rules for supervising the behaviour of individuals: a system of extra-judicial rules grounded not in traditional moral or social imperatives, but in technical modes of knowledge.

Our project also set out to reconstruct a second line of development of insurance as a managerial principle: the demutualization of the workers' movement. Social insurance had the effect of completely marginalizing the old territories of working-class solidarity, and of reorganizing them around a novel set of political notions.

The nineteenth century rethought the question of assistance to the poor in terms of liberal social philosophy, just at the moment when the new social system was multiplying the number of the poor. Charity gives way to providence. Each person is held responsible for his or her own fate; saving is seen as a matter of will-power. The misery of the labouring poor is treated as the consequence of improvidence: that is to say, of a moral attitude inadequate to the worker's conditions of existence, an attitude which one's main priority must be to correct through education.

Some employers took the view that the wage relation cannot wholly free the employer from all further obligation to the worker: a surplus to the wage must be provided, a supplement consisting of educational institutions, improved housing, medical care, gardens, savings banks, shops, etc. – the institutions of paternalism. For the strict liberal, on the other hand, the condition of the labourer should be left to the workings of common law: paternalism has the injurious effect of interfering with those workings by creating a system of private, local institutions. But neither of these two schools of thought envisages a particular branch of law relating to labour. Paternalism broadens the responsibilities of the employer, but it does not confer any new rights on the worker, only liberalities. Common law operates here only through the general form of contracts for the hire of labour, which in turn falls under the regime of legal contracts in general. The new solutions proposed by insurance meant a shift away from both of these viewpoints which created the possibility of an industrial branch of law. But the employers' insurantial solutions were at the same time a way of outsmarting the emerging modes of working-class organization: strike funds, community chests, associative movements whose juridical structure had not been provided for in the Napoleonic Civil Code.

We were dealing with a double process: the slow reconstitution of forms of working-class association, from the First Empire to the 1848 revolution, followed by the demutualization of the workers' movement, beginning with the Second Empire in 1852. Even if the mutualist organizations are still numerous right to the end of the nineteenth century, their way of working and the kind of political and cultural solidarity which they foster is by that time no longer substantially different from that of the insurance companies. Meanwhile, a new juridical and ideological framework of collective association is constructed, its main instalments being the recognition in 1848 of the right of association, the company and union laws of 1863–7, and the generalization of unions' rights, enacted in 1901. The conceptual design of this new construct seems to have been provided by Saint-Simonism.

The strategy of insurance runs right through the heart of this effort of dissociation and reconstitution of the social fabric. The triumph of insurance resulted from its technical and financial superiority over both workers' mutualism and philanthropic paternalism. But the great difference is that the insured do not constitute a social community among themselves. The framework of sociability in industrial societies is displaced. It would be interesting to make a comparison between those countries where the workers' movement retained control of its mutualist organizations, and those where the movement was demutualized.

A third line of forces whose effects we sought to retrace was the transformation of industry's liberal juridical framework as defined by the Civil Code, with the emergence of insurance providing compensation without assignment of responsibility. Law is the framework for the redress of damages; yet, with the establishment during the 1870s of compensatory insurance for the injured worker, and civil liability insurance for employer responsibility in industrial accidents, the scope of judicial actions for damages is bypassed. Compensation becomes unconditional and contractual, no longer based on the notion of one party's responsibility. Transacted between the employee and the insurance company, it assumes the existence of a calculated *professional risk* which is specific to each branch of industrial activity, a statistical datum which it may be technically possible to alter but which lies outside the sphere of individual will on which civil law is based. The universe of fault, whether employer's negligence or employee's imprudence, in which the courts undertook to decide and assign liability, gives way to a new universe of 'professional risk' deemed inherent in the normal work process, where compensation as of right is available to *all* injured workers. Enterprise, profit and professional risk all now become juridical notions. This historic change came about out of the possibilities opened up by systems of commercial compensatory insurance. As these developed, two alternative procedures came to cohabit in industry: penal damages, obtainable, albeit with difficulty, through legal action by the injured worker against the employer; and guaranteed compensation by an insurance company, where the outcome is certain but the amount paid out is less. But, even before the issue is definitively concluded by the law of 1898,[2] these two alternative systems are already guaranteed by a single system of compensation: workers' injury insurance and employers' liability insurance. These two juridically distinct insurances are funded by contributions deducted by the employer from wages, being thus computed as a part of costs of production which ultimately fall on the consumer. Society becomes the ultimate general referent of damages claims. This new regime of compensation works directly against the principle of civil responsibility, establishing on the one hand a fault-less responsibility and on the other the compensation of injury by a collectivity which lacks the traditional means of surveillance. This 'metamorphosis' of civil law leads to the crystallization of new conceptions of equity. All accidental injury entails a social demand for compensation: the social body is the general debtor for individual compensations.

These transformations are formalized by the creation of labour law (*droit du travail*). Initially elaborated through private ventures, insurance develops into a true *political technology* in the course of the debates in European parliaments which fashion it into an instrument of social policy. Until then it had simply been a lucrative form of commercial activity, yet already it had introduced new constraints into the enterprise, and put new pressures on the medical profession to limit the scale of insurance companies' damages liabilities. Hence one has a new policy of social insurance accompanied by new political ideologies like *solidarisme*, and international congresses for the study and harmonization of the effects of these legislations on the costs of production and the level of productivity. And meanwhile, alongside and articulated on to this new juridical framework, there emerges a new, statistical mode of management of populations: an establishment of series of data, a determination of thresholds, medians and margins. Populations in their entirety and with all their random variations are thus available for indefinite analysis: each new risk identified has a new cost associated with it. Each new measure of protection makes visible a new form of insurable insecurity. A general economic ordering of the future becomes possible: security can be an inexhaustible market, or alternatively an impulse towards a motive for ever more interventionist political action.

In its form as a *generalizable technology* for rationalizing societies, insurance is like a diagram, a figure of social organization which far transcends the choice which some thinkers are currently putting to us between the alternatives of privatization and nationalization of security systems. People all too often seem to have a false picture of insurance, as a function of community self-regulation antagonistic to the costly bur-eaucratic centralism of state institutions. In fact insurance's potential for nationalization was always there, even though it was created entirely within the force-field of liberalism which broke through the collective solidarities and territorializations obstructing the free circulation of skills, commodities and capitals – obstacles which had themselves previously been given a positive theorization by the juridico-regulatory doctrine known in the seventeenth and eighteenth centuries as *police*. What police had monitored and supervised, insurance technology de-controlled.

HUMAN LIFE: LABOUR POWER OR CAPITAL?

One of the most widely shared ideas underlying the writing of history today is an analysis of the development of collective modes of consumption (health, hygiene, education) as part of an increasing appropriation, operating through the intermediary action of the state, of labour power by capital. When the facts are looked at more closely, however, other perspectives suggest themselves. The copious writings of the nineteenth-century hygienists whom Marx and Engels used as an essential source on working-class conditions were continually sounding the alarm at indus-try's wastage of labour power, with physical exhaustion often setting in even in childhood, and miners in particular broken in health long before the age of twenty-five which was supposed to mark the peak of manly vigour and the acme of productivity. Here the problem of the conservation of (human) energy was already being posed. But the prolongation of workers' lives was a matter of concern not so much for industrialists as for doctors, philanthropists, state inspectors and military men appalled by the findings of recruitment assessment boards. These latter groups transcribed the question of working-class conditions into the vocabulary of hygiene. But they were not the spokespeople of triumphant industrial thinking. It was not, in fact, the problem of industrial productivity which acted as the surface of emergence of human longevity as a factor in economic calculation. Rather the origin for this preoccupation lies in the world of finance, where for some time calculation had already been practised whose object was the lives of the rich or, more precisely, of the *rentier* class; this is where techniques were first elaborated which made it possible for the late nineteenth century to take an economic interest in 'popular life', to use the insurance companies' term. Life insurance, the historic matrix of employees' insurance, has to be understood first of all as the inversion of an older practice, the life annuity. Life annuities were for a long period in France the favoured mode of royal borrowing on account of the adage that 'life annuities have an infallible extinction'. The practice of 'donations on condition of a life pension' was officially represented as an unsecured gift, with no mention of repayment or interest: this meant that it avoided the prohibitions attaching to usury. Computed usually for an expected duration of twenty years, a life annuity might on occasion run for up to sixty years. For the traditional life annuity had these two features: it differentiated the recipient of the annuity from the person whose life was taken as its term of reference (known as the 'head' of the annuity); but there was no variation in the annuity's implicit rate of interest according to the initial age of its 'head'. Nothing, however, better guaranteed a *rentier* the lifelong security of his pension than the state of being himself both 'head' and beneficiary. This was consequently the most common arrangement. But it could also happen that an elderly aunt might take out a life annuity from the Treasury on the head of her young nephew, who would then privately arrange to assign a pension, higher but of shorter expected duration, to his aunt for her lifetime. Here one already had a rudimentary form of reinsurance. Hope of life, and of death, became a prime factor in these family financial calculations.

From the standpoint of public borrowing, things were less simple. When the state's credit was well established, it was possible for it to reduce its indebtedness by specifying graduated levels of interest for different age groups: during Louis XIV's period of greatest success, for example, the rate was 7 per cent for younger and 14 per cent for older heads. But when the credibility of the state's finances declined, it was forced to offer a uniformly high rate in order to replenish its coffers. One can follow the fluctuations of Louis XIV's credit by looking at when he was in a position to discriminate between age groups when issuing life annuities.

The study and classification of life expectancies thus entered into financial calculations by way of a dual economic preoccupation: the prospect of a debt's liquidation by the death of the creditor, and the need to control the rate of an annuity depending on its probable duration. The value of such knowledge here was simply one of cutting one's costs.

At every date of maturation of such an annuity, the *rentier* had to attest to the continued life of his 'head'. This was one reason for choosing as one's 'head' a near relative over whom one could keep up regular vigilance. During the years between 1750 and 1780, however, Genevan bankers devised a variant of the life annuity, in which one can identify all the basic elements of the life assurance invented in England during those same years by Dodson, Simpson and Price. This was the famous formula of the 'Genevan heads'.

1. A Genevan banker concentrates all the life annuities he issues on to a restricted group of heads chosen by him from among the Genevan population as having the highest probable life expectancy, assessed on the basis of genealogical data, current health, the differential mortality of age groups, sex and material situation – all this having been established by Tronchin, the most famous doctor in Geneva, and his students.

2. On the basis of these empirical and scientific considerations, the banker draws up uniform lists of heads having similar life expectancy. He charges himself with the supervision of these 'Genevan heads': health examinations, vaccination (smallpox inoculation is beginning just at this time), travel and removal of domicile, and death certification.

3. The banker consolidates his annuities into a set of identical contracts, equal in number to his chosen heads, so that risks to their lives is spread evenly over all the annuities; thus each death will reduce the capital by $1/x$.

   The best known of these contracts was that for the 'heads and lives of 30 young spinsters of Geneva', whose health bulletins, published in the gazettes of Europe, acquired an importance equal to those of princes.[3]

4. The banker now subdivides this homogeneous mass of annuities into fractions available to private investors; being all of equal value, these fractions become negotiable securities, unlike the old life annuities which were totally heterogeneous in real value, and hence non-negotiable.

5. The private *rentier* now has no connection with the Treasury, but deals only with the banker. Rather than setting his hopes on the longevity of

a head belonging to his own family, the *rentier* now invests in the statistical certainty of an optimum probable lifespan.

These protracted historical preliminaries can help us to situate a crucial moment of transformation. First of all, the state speculates on the death of its creditor. Then the Genevan banker, acting as an entrepreneur between the Treasury and the *rentier*, speculates on the longevity of his heads, while taking steps to guarantee that longevity according to criteria established by a series of expert knowledges. For death as the happy stroke of fortune which liquidates a debt, he substitutes a plenitude of life determined by sex, age, hygiene, genealogy and family environment. In other words, he substitutes for the lottery of death a measurable capital of life. From speculation on death we move to a kind of practice in which the first rationalization can be discerned of what we now call 'human capital', a capital understood however as a patrimony of life, not a life as labour power. In this transformation of speculation on death into financial rationalization of human capital, I would suggest that the essential theoretical condition is provided for the emergence of life insurance as the matrix of our modern systems of providence. The life annuity ceases to signify a family lottery or an expedient of state; from a non-negotiable asset it changes into a movable capital. This new form of financial rationality scientifically incorporates into itself the question of chances of mortality, and puts surveillance of those chances under the joint control of a banker and of a medical adviser who functions in this situation as an economic expert. The banker constitutes and manages an abstract group of individuals united by criteria which break with the natural forms of sociability.

THE LIFE OF THE RICH

We undertook a survey of this new way of managing human life as capital by studying the unpublished archives of the oldest French life assurance company, the *Compagnie d'Assurances sur la Vie des Hommes*.[4] After the restoration of the Bourbon monarchy in 1814–15, returning *émigrés* brought back with them the English technique of life assurance. The founder of the first French life assurance company was a legitimist, Monsieur de Gourcuff. His company, modelled on the British Equitable, offered three kinds of insurance, one of which was based on death, the other on the *prolongation of life*. The former was an assurance for life by which, in return for a payment either outright or in ~nnual instalments, the company pays an agreed capital at the decease of the insured person (or that of a specified head) to his or her heirs. The second method was a temporary assurance: if death occurs within a given number of years the company pays, otherwise it pays nothing. The third was a deferred assurance: at a specified moment a capital sum is paid out provided the insured person is still living.

For each form of insurance and each age group, the rates of payment are determined in accordance with the general table of mortalities in France, drawn up by the state actuary. As it is the better off who insure themselves, however, their life expectancy is higher than the average, and the insurance company gains accordingly. As an asset that can be bequeathed to one's heirs, an assurance obeys the rules of family inheritance under the Civil Code; it readily fits in with the juridical problematic of patrimony. The company excludes from its provisions death by war and its repercussions, by execution, by suicide, on sea voyages outside Europe, during very early childhood and very old age, and in case of failure to vaccinate against smallpox. The target population for insurance is precisely that population which conforms to the general laws of mortality; it is the true, regular plenitude of biological life that here becomes the object of observation. Yet even what falls outside this model can become the object of a specific form of insurance by adding a supplement to the premium. You aren't inoculated for smallpox? A supplement. You travel? A classification of countries is drawn up according to their dangerousness, to fix your additional premium. And so on.

The overall effect of this is to open up a population to indefinite analysis into more and more finely detailed sub-classes of risk. Insuring a population means classifying it, subdividing it in line with a scale of degrees of risk and with an analysis of behaviours, thresholds, marginal categories which are first excluded, then treated as special sub-classes while excluding still more marginal groups, and so on. The method allows an indefinitely generalizable economic treatment of behaviours in terms of their dangerousness.

Whereas with mutualist or philanthropic forms of solidarity, where respectively one's fellow workers or one's philanthropic employer exercise their surveillance of individual expenditure, frauds and extra-vagances, in short of the morality of the population concerned, with this managerial method of insurance one simply has a hierarchy of kinds of danger, classified according to their cost. In short, one finds here the beginnings of a liberal mode of managing society and its risks.

ACCIDENT INSURANCE

Here we drew on the archives of the oldest French accident insurance company, the Sécurité Générale,[5] which was licensed by a special decree on 14 November 1865 and inaugurated on 2 December of that year, backed by the Crédit Industriel et Commercial.

> By a series of studies, M. Besnier de la Pontonerie has demonstrated that the quantity and proportionality of accidents conform to mathematical laws; that, by carefully comparing these facts one could determine both the scale of social liabilities and the tariffs appropriate for different categories of insurance. The dispositions drawn up in our statutes are the summation of these calculations.[6]

The company had modelled itself to begin with on a prosperous English company which dealt in railway accident insurance issues through premium tickets sold at railway stations. In France, however, the railway companies refused to countenance the association of the words 'railway' and 'accident'. (A similar debate later arose with the spread of air travel.) The company was consequently led to offer at its outset terms for collective insurance policies taken out either by the heads of industrial enterprises or by mutual and provident societies. One has here a simple form of reinsurance grafted on to the mutualist and paternalist networks previously established to cover against industrial accidents but curbed by the 1852 legislation which imposed reorganization and registration on these existing associative media, emptying them of ideological content evocative of the revolution of 1848. The history of the treatment in France of industrial accidents in terms of 'coverage of professional risk' has two stages: first of all that of the unexpected problems encountered in the implanting of travel insurance; and then afterwards an unexpected confrontation with state competition.

For it was by no means an obvious idea for nineteenth-century workers to take out individual insurance policies. Insurance was a practice for the propertied rather than for the small saver; in brief, a matter for the bourgeoisie. Yet Britain, and then the United States, did succeed from the 1850s on in developing a flourishing branch of the life assurance business aimed at attracting the savings of the 'laborious classes'. The point during the Second Empire in France when popular life assurance took off was at a time when wage levels had just been raised by 30 per cent. All the same, one should not exaggerate the size of the popular investment resources then available. J. Bouvier has shown that at the beginning of the twentieth century two-thirds of deaths in major French cities left no fortune whatever.[7] Popular savings could not have been the decisive target of the companies' skilled techniques of capital centralization. The banking system, created during the same years as the accident insurance companies (the Crédit Lyonnais began to set up its network in 1863, as soon the law on limited liability companies was passed), hunted for investment capital for the railways, but it dealt in shares, the bourgeois form of savings. The ingenious pursuit of working-class insurance premiums cannot therefore be analyzed wholly in terms of this process of capital centralization, although it cannot be understood either outside of the legal–financial context inaugurated between 1863 and 1868, where a policy is practised not just to regulate the quantity of money in circulation but to alter its composition. If it was not an obvious idea for a worker to pay a premium to an accident insurance company, it was not an obvious idea either for a company actively to canvass for such premiums, especially when one considers the extreme insecurity of proletarian employment and housing in the nineteenth century. The cost of collecting the premium would have wiped out its value. Even the Americans abandoned the attempt. There was, moreover, another argument to dissuade the worker from insuring: the levels of indemnity offered by the companies were far below those that could be secured through the courts under Article 1382 of the Civil Code.[8] This was a crucial aspect of the question, for worker and employee as also for the insurer and the state.

'Popular life' insurance covered three kinds of accidental injury:

1. Fatal accidents, which were rare but expensive.
2. Permanent disablements, which carried a right to a pension for life, a principle strongly endorsed by public opinion and serving as a good publicity argument for insurance. Since, however, the average age of such injured pensioners was only forty years, the companies were unable to make a profit on their operation and were continually being forced to try to reduce the costs of these pensions, either by buying themselves out for a lump sum equivalent in value to a more short-lived annuity, or by rehabilitating the handicapped.
3. Recoverable injuries, which entitled the injured to short-term indemnities, accounting for one-third of the operation's total turn-over. The companies themselves liked to represent these payments as unemployment indemnities and thus as serving a global social function in combating pauperism. The average duration of such disablements was made an object of constant statistical supervision and medical vigilance intended to keep down durations and costs.

These three categories together form the essence of the popular insurance market.

The doctors were soon put under commercial pressure to help cut the costs of these risks. Many of the modern medical corps' ethical and professional positions emerged out of their resistance to the insurance companies. The idea of reducing costs and risks by rationalizing not only the treatment of injuries but also the actual organization of the labour process developed only later, when competition with the state led companies to offer insurance direct to the employers. Only in 1876 do we begin to find recorded in the papers of the Sécurité Générale recriminations about 'the inattention and imprudence of workers', 'failure to observe factory rules' and 'the dangerous nature of the work undertaken, particularly the work on the Paris fortifications', the latter having led to many accidents during 1875. Subsequent cost-cutting zeal was directed mainly not at medical practice but at the point of origin of the industrial accident. Broadly one can say that the driving force towards new technical investment in and supervision of the labour process was not the shortage or high cost of *labour power* but rather the existence of systems of compensation, engendered by a strategy of financial profit, which makes the *worker's life* a valuable commodity which it pays to save.

It is this link-up with the financial machinery of compensation that confers value on the worker's life, not the value of his or her life that necessitates the financial connection.

COMPETITION WITH THE STATE

On 2 January 1864 Jules Favre challenged the government over the deplorable situation of employees injured at work: 'Workers had no alternatives except recourse to their employers' generosity or to legal action.' For the government, Rouher replied that:

> the law had provided for accidents by making owners responsible for acts of imprudence and breaches of regulations. All I can say on behalf of the government and with the approval of this legislature is that, if we knew any effective means of relieving these cruel ills, we would urgently examine them and gladly put them into practice.

To this the Minister of Public Instruction added that 'if an institution offered itself which could give workers the daily sustenance they are deprived of when an accident stops the work their family depends on, this would mark a fresh conquest made by civilization'.[9]

This exchange occurred at a time when the statutes of the Sécurité Générale had already been drawn up and submitted to the government for its approval. As the company remarked, 'Here we have already achieved the required goal by offering workers a form of benefit no longer drawn from the resources of others but created by the workers themselves out of the product of their own labour.' Napoleon III's government desired, however, to manifest its particular sympathy for the masses and for the sufferings inflicted on the working class by industrial accidents, whose gravity was attested by the severity of the damages imposed by the courts on employers in such cases. Consequently, it did not propose to leave in the hands of private finance the implementation of the solution which the latter had explained to the government. The Sécurité Générale recorded its mortification:

> Finding ourselves at one with the government in a shared purpose, it was natural that we should unite with it in joint action. Relations were consequently established between our board and the government; the company's statutes and the prospectus of its initial activities were drawn up under these auspices. We received unequivocal indications of the government's sympathetic co-operation . . . Considering ourselves therefore as being regarded by the government as an associate, and prompted in this direction by the government itself, we came to devise an arrangement which would enable the government to make use of our operation to benefit the workers it sought to help; in view of this, we placed no restrictions on the provision of documentation requested from us. Nothing led us to expect to find the government itself competing against us. Hence it was something of a surprise when the government announced last June that it proposed establishing a fund to deal with precisely the ills which it was our company's goal to remedy. The *Moniteur* of 31 July 1866 informed us that a decree had been drafted by the Council of State to establish an Industrial Invalids' Fund to be administered by the government with an endowment of four million francs raised by a 1% levy on all public works, and with a minimal rate of contributions by the workers themselves.
>
> We will not enter into discussion of the principle of this combination. As a political doctrine it raises questions of great gravity:
>
> 1. How far is the state entitled to intervene in, and in some sense to substitute itself for, individual action and providence?
> 2. How far is it justified in raising from the public fortune a fund destined to cater for the needs of a particular group, forming a relation of solidarity between itself and certain classes of its citizens, to the detriment of others?
>
> Our board's duty is not to discuss doctrines but to avert the harmful consequences of the government's measure. We have made representations to the Emperor about this unexpected competition of the state with us, setting itself up as an insurer at the expense of a company established, as we were led to understand, with its own approval.[10]

The board of the Sécurité Générale was right to identify two points of doctrine involved in the first social insurance legislation enacted in France. In the first place, the state, by taking over the role played by individual providence, breaks with the liberal conception of the state as merely a guarantor of order. In its substance it is now no longer the will of all (even though Louis Napoleon had recognized the universal suffrage as the basis of his legitimacy), but the will of the state itself as a particular agent. Secondly, the instrument for the execution of that will is taken from the public fortune. The operation amounts to a twofold redistribution of incomes. A tax is levied on the state's market for public works, guaranteeing the main finance for the Industrial Invalids' Fund;

but these public works have themselves a dual purpose, providing both an economic infrastructure and a measure of full employment. A subsidized form of employment serves in addition to finance a state unemployment benefit. Napoleon III was undoubtedly influenced here by the idea of the social welfare state as conceived by the Saint-Simonians and the German socialists, particularly Rodbertus. One needs to remember that nineteenth-century state socialism was a philosophy of law and the state much more than a socialism in the way we understand the term today. The model for the security which Napoleon III offers the workers is that of the soldier whom the state provides for, houses and takes care of in old age. The Industrial Invalids' Fund makes use of the new technique of insurance in order to extend to the worker the kind of benefits provided through the recently opened military hospices at Vincennes and Vesinay.

The insurance company's way of responding to this challenge was thoroughly liberal in spirit: it competed against the state by offering new kinds of service:

> The government's venture was so prejudicial to us that we thought the company might be forced into liquidation. We wondered whether the state would not be bound in its own interests to prefer the concerted system we had jointly planned. Eventually we made an offer to take on at fixed rates all insurance transactions specified by the state, up to a maximum of one million clients. No response being forthcoming, the Sécurité Générale resolved to redouble its own efforts.
>
> We regarded it as a *point d'honneur* to prove that the basic principles of our operation were sound, just, conceived in a spirit of sympathy with the working classes, and beneficial to them. These fresh efforts of ours might serve as the best possible critique of the system established in opposition to us. Our goal was to make the benefits of insurance available for every type of risk. We thought it appropriate to offer proposals to mutual benefit societies, seamen's benefit funds and firemen's companies for an advantageous association with our company. From the company's outset we had envisaged offering the mutual societies a reinsurance policy for accidents, leaving the mutualist society to deal with the costs of illness and consequent incapacitation.[11]

The Minister of the Interior responded to the proposal for reinsurance of mutual benefit societies as follows:

> Because of its ability to renounce all hope of gain, and even to expose itself to certain losses for the sake of the public interest, only the state is in a position to offer the mutual societies sufficiently generous and advantageous terms; the committee set up to establish the best means for realizing the conception formulated in the Emperor's letter of 31 July 1866 is about to submit for his approval a plan to create simultaneously an Industrial Invalids' Fund and a Fund for Assurance in Case of Decease.[12]

Replying to the government, the company affirmed the superiority of commercial principles of operation, and it was in the context of this claim that advances were made in the insurance of professional risks that arose neither directly from state legislation nor from industrial speculation, but from a situation of politico-financial competition. Some time previously, the state had established certain forms of protection first for miners and then for war invalids. The Sécurité Générale set out, with the help of officials at the Sea Ministry, to compete with the state by offering more and better accident insurance for seamen. Its scheme amounted to a combined travel and industrial accident insurance, with a novel added feature: automatic insurance for a whole ship's crew, incorporated into its contract of employment. A few years later the company restricted its offer of cover to a maximum of ten seamen in any one crew. Nevertheless, the linking of a collective contract of insurance to the recruitment of seamen by a shipping company which itself only entered into individual employment contracts deserves note as a forerunner of later collective industrial agreements. Indeed it seems to us that it was within the context of the new juridical problems posed by the extension of insurance to industrial accidents that the future principles of labour law came to be thought out.

Its competition with the state influenced every detail of the Sécurité Générale's activities. It suspended publication of its statistical reports in order to deprive the administration of their use; it resorted to the practice of 'pantouflage',[13] hiring as its new Director in 1896 Auguste Pouget, a long-serving legal expert in a major ministerial department. And it used every possible method of publicity.

The company's progress had been momentarily braked by employers' anticipations of a forthcoming government insurance scheme, and its operation as yet still remained unremunerative, but the most valuable sector of its business was still its collective industrial contracts. Its competitive efforts were applied to a 'conscious and reasoned study of the acceptance and classification of risks' – in other words, to the acceptance of ever more types of risk, and the reduction as far as possible of the rates of compensation paid out. But cutting compensation for industrial accidents meant playing into the hands of the state fund. Workers who were dissatisfied with its scale of indemnities were liable to opt for a lawsuit against their employer, levels of penal damages awards being much higher. Consequently, in order to keep down its payments without loss of clientele, the only solution was to provide insurance cover for the employers against whom the dissatisfied workers were liable to take legal action.

The employers had long had their own mutual systems, but the amounts these raised to cover compensation payments were less than those which could be raised through the much more extensive network of an insurance scheme. The Sécurité Générale's best prospect for holding out against state competition was to recruit the employers as clients, insuring them for a new kind of risk: employer liability. The Second Empire policy of alliance with the working class made it difficult for the government to offer insurance for employers. The company began doing this in an indirect fashion:

> The Sécurité Générale certainly aims to secure a profit for its investors. But the aim of its constitution is also a philanthropic one. Its low tariffs and its system of cover for major disasters are in accord with this conception. Nevertheless, there is a need to preserve a just equilibrium between these two elements of our undertaking. Until now indemnity levels have been too high in relation to premiums, disasters too frequent, disaster victims too demanding, and death benefits treated as an asset inheritable without limit on degree of kinship.[14]

To reduce its costs so as to stay in competition with the state, and at least to retain its existing industrial clientele, the Sécurité Générale offered to link together two industrial insurances: compensation insurance for workers and liability insurance for employers. And it was the existence of this new form of compensation, linked *de facto* into a system of collective accident cover, that provided the key to the codification of industrial jurisprudence, paving the way for the new provisions of the 1898 law on industrial accidents.

The first year's operation of the state insurance fund secured as many contracts as the Sécurité Générale procured in one week: 597. The company's great competitive advantage lay in its ability to reduce its level of compensation payments to employees without having to fear an increase in lawsuits against the employers, since henceforth the company itself provided legal representation for the employer in court actions where the employee had turned down its insurance indemnity.

In 1865 when its statutes were laid down, Article 1 merely specified that 'the company has as its object insurance against bodily accidents to which the insured fall victim', and Article 12 'extends these conditions to collective insurance policies taken out by the heads of industrial undertakings or by mutual aid and provident societies'. On 22 August 1871 the board redefines its vocation in the following terms: 'As you know, the Sécurité Générale's aim is to insure the working class against industrial accidents, to provide for the care of the injured, and to offer widows and dependants of accident victims the consolation of an indemnity.'[15] Having offered the employers cover from a special fund against damages that their employees were liable to demand through the courts in cases when they judged the insurance company's own indemnities inadequate, and having offered employers its legal representation, which led to the transfer of the lawsuit from the locality of the enterprise to that of the insurance company's head office, and all of this in return for the collection of workers' premiums by the employer as a deduction from wages made at the point of payment, the Sécurité Générale now felt able to propose itself as the insurer of the working class.

Thus the company took over the function of previous traditional forms of mutualist, paternalist and juridical compensation. The court, as the public arena of industrial conflicts over accidents and their compensation, now yields its function to the technique of insurance. The company's efforts to keep its costs down lead to procedures for the medical inspection of injuries, supervised convalescence and rehabilitation; before long, it extends its surveillance to the dangerousness of working conditions.

THE DEMUTUALIZATION OF THE WORKERS' MOVEMENT

On 14 June 1791 the National Assembly promulgated one of the great laws of the French Revolution, the Le Chapelier Law prohibiting the formation of workers' combinations, which the Assembly saw as dangerous recrudescences of the old trades corporations of the *ancien régime*. The law provided for an immediate, face-to-face relationship between the state and the individual, conducted in a social space evacuated of intermediate collective forms of solidarity. This collective void was spanned, over the period down to the 1871 Commune, by a subterranean battle to establish new forms of industrial association, the different competing models of which were key issues in the class struggles of the time. No sooner had the old feudal orders been abolished than contemporaries became aware of a pullulating multiplicity of new clubs. Friends of man, philanthropists, associationists, mutualists, stockholders, co-operators, phalanstery-dwellers, socialists, communists: such were the self-designations of the political agents of the nineteenth century. All these schemes of socialization have been measured in retrospect against the yardstick of organizations of our own day, as though they had been no more than stumbling prototypes of the workers' party or the welfare state. But it was only by thrusting aside these different, antagonistic associative tactics that the specific form of serialized solidarity characteristic of insurance was able to establish itself.

There had been an initial popular welcome for the National Assembly's measures against the old corporative order, which were understood as aiming to put an end to aristocratic power. Wage-earners liked having the right to find employment where they pleased. But with the increasing threat of unemployment under the Directory, the pre-Revolutionary *compagnonnages* were reconstituted, together with mutual societies. Economic freedom now became for the wage-earner, as the historian Georges

Lefebvre aptly put it, a symbol of the others.[16] It is difficult to establish
the precise importance of the *compagnonnages* in nineteenth-century
society, where small employers and fellow craftsmen were all still linked
by close economic ties. In any case, there were built up on the
foundations of the old trade crafts the mutual benefit funds which from
around 1834 became the nerve-centres of the new political groups which
sought not so much a change at the political level as a total remaking of
society. The workers' mutualist associations developed into resistance
groups with their interior zones of partial communism, a co-operative
network within the capitalist economy which sought its victory not
through a capture of power but through economico-social superiority in
competition with the capitalist organization of labour – superiority of
workers' organization of units of production, superiority in its system of
distribution and consumption, and ultimately the superiority of workers'
banks. Down to the 1871 Commune, which itself symbolized the old
communal idea of social organization through trades guilds which had
inspired labourers' and craftsmen's struggles from 1789 to 1848, none of
these programmes envisaged a centralized political leadership of the
working class. The basic unit of these organizations was more the
neighbourhood than the factory. Working-class mutualism constituted
the precise point of interchange between traditional tactics of financial
solidarity and the elaboration of new systems of sociability. The
newspaper *L'Atelier* wrote:

> the mutual societies covering against sickness and shortage of work are only
> palliatives. We will transform them into provident associations. In future,
> these associations will assure the worker of a paid retirement, something
> which is as much the labourer's right as the soldier's, since all have equally
> given their service to the *patrie*. Gradually we will see the reduction of the
> exploitation of man by man. We will achieve this by establishing workers'
> industrial associations, a principle already defined but not yet developed in a
> popular form.

The tactic of insurance succeeded in imposing its solutions on this
sector, which the British companies called 'Popular life', only after two
struggles had been fought out: one between workers' mutual institutions
and employers' philanthropic paternalism; the other between the
employers' institutions, which soon took over the mutualist formula, and
the financiers' insurance companies. Bourgeois projects for mutual
societies were already springing up in the eighteenth century. In 1805 the
intensely paternalistic Société de Bienfaisance adopted the mutualist
approach, and was soon followed by the Société de Philanthropie de
Paris, which had been founded in 1786 and was the true ancestor of later
social medicine services. The Société de Bienfaisance de Marseille
followed suit in 1808. In 1821 a Council of Benevolent Societies was set

up to co-ordinate these groups. A Higher Commission for Encourage-
ment and Providence continued the promotion of mutual organizations
until 1852. Parallel with these bodies were the more strictly working-
class mutual associations, which supported strikes and were banned in
1834. The working-class newspaper *L'Atelier* warned against philanthropy
'which arrogates to itself a right that it does not possess: patronage'. In
1848 working-class mutualism often underwent a Proudhonist transformation:

> If the only basis of workers' association is production, inequality will
> reappear. If it is founded on consumption, the worker will be subjected to
> the consumer. The ideal principle is one of reciprocity, a system of insurance
> that will cover the whole of life: then, we would all mutually serve each
> other.

After mutualism comes the passage to socialism. After 1852 the mutual
societies became politically suspect and were subjected to administrative
registration and surveillance. Unauthorized associations were auto-
matically treated as clandestine.

In 1849, after the closure of the national workshops, the Constituent
Assembly voted a loan of three million francs to mutualist associations.
But the credits were only made available to joint employer–worker
associations; the loan acted as a disguised subsidy to distressed employers'
associations. Credits were refused to associations representing the whole
of a particular trade. Whereas the 1848 revolution had seen the meeting
of a Chambre du Travail which put itself forward as the arbitration board
(Conseil de Prudhommes) of the mutualist associations, and planned the
creation of a mutualist People's Bank, by 1852 the few public loans that
were made were being allocated to employers' groups in financial
difficulty. It was then that the first state insurance schemes came to be
formulated. 'Mutuality had left the working class': with this terse
formula, H. Hatzfeld aptly summarizes fifty years of social and political
history.[17]

While the employers were reconquering working-class mutualism, the
insurance companies were waging war on the mutualist system in its
entirety. Before the Revolution of 1789 there had, for example, existed
funds set up by the clergy for aid to victims of fires. At the start of the
Empire, these funds, now laicized, were reconstituted under the name of
Department Funds, modelled on the format of the benevolent associations. After the Restoration the indemnified returning *émigrés*, landowners
and bankers set up a hundred or more mutual fire associations. At the
same time, however, two subsidiaries of the large banks, the Nouvelle
Royale and the Phenix, began competing with the mutuals by establishing
a branch of insurance of fire risks, modelled on maritime insurance. This

rivalry has a double interest for us: on the one hand, it opens up new channels for attracting local reserves of capital to Paris, the location of these new companies' head offices; on the other, one sees insurance breaking down the disciplines of mutualism.

Mutualist practice worked by paying out disaster indemnities at the end of each year's operations, when their total number and cost had been ascertained and computed. This might result in either a surcharge on premiums or a reduction in standard compensation levels. This situation gave rise to a mutual surveillance by all members of such an association of the conduct of individuals and the nature of their indemnity claims, including their statements about the origin and extent of fires. The insurance company, on the other hand, offered a fixed premium and immediate payment of indemnities. This was a considerable advantage which ensured the victory of the insurance technique in this field. It displaced the internal collective discipline of mutualist surveillance in favour of the elaborate calculations of the probabilities expert. A quite different system of information and verification is established. There are denunciations of the immorality of insurance: will it not act as a motive driving people to crime? The theme has remained to this day a staple one for thriller-writers. The supreme audacity was that, whereas the mutual fire associations insured only fixed assets open to verification by the common gaze, the insurance company covered goods whose value and composition were unknown or unspecified. In 1848 the true forms of mutualist solidarity were already being abandoned, in the camp of capital as well as in that of labour. People looked to insurance and to the state which insurance was seeking to recruit: insurance was an instrument of serialized, centralized management, equally adaptable for use by banking or the state as by centralized trade unionism. The mutual institutions which flourished at the end of the nineteenth century had in fact adopted the techniques of insurance.

The mutual associations were quickly accused by employers of distorting the labour market by funding workers' collective resistance to wage cuts. Rather than this kind of mutualism, they favoured the format of provident associations whose funds, exclusively earmarked for relief of sickness, infirmity and old age, were kept under the control of the employer who, on that condition, was also prepared to contribute. Honorary members would then be brought in to help administer the funds; different trades would be mingled together among the beneficiaries of a common fund. So it was that 'benevolence' made its advances. Struggles for workers' control of their solidarity funds were far more frequent than struggles for security against industrial accidents. This context of struggles over efforts to impose certain forms of financial solidarity that would also be particular forms of sociability is what helps to account for the form and success of the insurance technique, which, thanks to its superior financial capabilities, marginalized the political questions that had been linked to workers' association.

The provident regime of insurance had the following characteristics:

1. Unlike workers' mutualism, insurance does not link its associated participants horizontally with one another, but links each client individually and serially to a central management. Its entire juridical frameworks consists in the contract between the individual client and the company manager.
2. the insurance company's reserves are not at the disposal of the insured. (This was also one of the *raisons d'être* of the savings bank.) For the labourer to work regularly, he has to be induced not to consume the whole of his pay (the feast of Saint Monday was actually liable to prolong itself over several days of the week). But in order for the inculcation of the savings habit not to provide the worker with a means of forming a strike fund, the worker must be deprived of free disposal of these savings. Insurance funds were tied by contract to the purpose of providing precisely specified forms of indemnity, their level fixed in advance by a scale of compensation.
3. Providence against those defined risks is made the sole purpose of this mode of saving.
4. Only the client's subscription ensures the provident cover: it therefore implies regular work, ordered time, disciplined consumption, individual responsibility. The system dispenses with the need for the benevolence of the wealthy or the participation of the state.
5. The political issues which had remained visible in the struggle between workers' mutualism and paternalist philanthropic societies fade away with the coming of a technical solution based on an arithmetical knowledge: tables of probability, regulated indemnities, defined risks and compensations.
6. The insurance system does not as a rule address itself to particular social classes, but to populations defined by age, sex, professional danger and the nature of risks. These risks can themselves cut across different classes. Instead of opposing capital to labour, insurance provides cover for both alike.
7. The social factors which might have demanded interventionist political solutions are thus deterritorialized; all that remains is a multi-directional, class-collaborative technique resting on a probabilistic apparatus of expertise inaccessible to the non-specialist.
8. Between the alternatives of arbitrary private benevolent patronage and obligatory state responsibility, insurance offers a space of regulated freedom. In this sense it offers a gain for the rich who insure

their life and goods, and a gain for the peasant who can insure his harvest and so, by mastering the effects of chance, hope to rise to the status of a freeholder. For the less fortunate, however, insurance is long able only to offer insurance of their health, hence achieving the *tour de force* of driving them to work and save in order to insure against the loss of a health they do not even possess.

In the issue for 2 December 1852 of *Le Paquebot*, a shipping newspaper, one reads that:

> The insurance companies have distinguished themselves in their dealings with us by a solidity of principle and regularity of operation which have made them into veritable public institutions. French law moreover subjects their existence to such strict conditions that the public is able to look to them for guarantees such as are perhaps to be found in no other country.[18]

Insurance as a public institution: during these years there emerged the thinkers who we might call the 'statists' of insurance, armed with widely differing tactics and springing from hostile camps: some are exponents of state socialism, like Louis Blanc in France and Lassalle in Germany; others envisage a policy of state guarantees or state penetration into a zone where it may gain both profits and a new social image.

In the years after 1848, when the fire and agrarian insurance businesses were making profits, the idea of nationalized insurance suggested itself initially as a new economic resource for the state. The idea was continually being raised in the French parliament, invariably in the company of proposed state monopolies for tobacco and alcohol as well as for insurance. It offered the attraction of a source of state revenue free of the black traditional reputation of predatory state taxation, and evoking contrary positive images of redistribution, security and health. This would be a modern state of security, guaranteeing the citizen against old age and misfortune, redistributing resources, where security comes now to signify not the old military notion which referred to the occupation of a territory, but that modern idea which enfolds in itself the lives of each and all. Under the auspices of insurance, an immense opportunity opened up for the state to introduce itself as an intimate, regular presence in the existence of its citizens. The socialists, Napoleon III, Bismarck and Gladstone all appreciated the implications.

NOTES

1. D. Defert, J. Donzelot, F. Ewald, G. Maillet, C. Mevel, 'Socialisation du risque et pouvoir dans l'entreprise', Dactylogramme (Paris, Ministère du Travail, 1977); A. Ajtony, S. Callens, D. Defert, F. Ewald, G. Maillet, 'Assurance-Prévoyance-Sécurité: Formation historique des techniques de

gestion dans les sociétés industrielles', Dactylogramme (Paris, Ministère du Travail, 1979).

2. 'Loi sur la Responsabilité des Accidents dont les ouvriers sont victimes dans l'Exercice de leur Travail'. This law, debated from 1880 to 1898, marks the passage from fault to professional risk.

3. H. Luthy, *La Banque Protestante en France de la Révocation de l'Édit de Nantes à la Révolution* (Paris, S.E.V.P.E.N., 1959).

4. Archives Nationales. Archives Manuscrites de la Compagnie d'Assurance sur la Vie des Hommes. Microfilms 47 AQ sq 1818–1966.

5. Archives Nationales. Manuscrits de la Sécurité Générale, 117 AQ 16.

6. Archives Nationales. Manuscrits de la Sécurité Générale, 117 AQ 16.

7. J. Bouvier, *Un Siècle de Banque française* (Paris, Hachette, 1973).

8. Code Civil, article 1382 définissant la responsabilité délictuelle.

9. Archives Nationales. Manuscrits de la Sécurité Générale, 117 AQ 16.

10. *Ibid.*

11. *Ibid.*

12. *Ibid.*

13. 'Pantouflage' is a term of administrative slang, and refers to the acceptance by senior state functionaries of private sector employment where they are able to make use of their previous connections.

14. Archives Nationales. Manuscrits de la Sécurité Générale, 117 AQ 16.

15. *Ibid.*

16. G. Lefebvre, *La Révolution Française* (Paris, PUF, 1930).

17. H. Hatzfield, *Du Paupérisme à la Sécurité Sociale* (Paris, Armand Colin, 1971).

18. *Le Paquebot*, journal de la Marine (Décembre 1852).

CHAPTER TWELVE

Criminology: the birth of a special knowledge

Pasquale Pasquino

In Chapter 111 of *The Man Without Qualities*, Robert Musil records the 'sensational conversion' to 'the social school of thought' of Ulrich's father, an elderly jurist and member of a committee 'set up by the Ministry of Justice for the purpose of bringing the criminal code up to date', whose theoretical U-turn led to his being denounced by some of his colleagues as a 'materialist' and a 'Prussian'.

What had our lawyer's ideas been prior to this moment, and what did they now become? This is the question which I would like to take as my (in some respects arbitrary) starting point for a discussion of the transformation of penal law towards the end of the nineteenth century.

The epithet 'Prussian', 'maliciously' employed to discredit the old jurist's change of theoretical viewpoint, was at that time a code-word in Kakania (Musil's name for the Austro-Hungarian monarchy) for how not to conduct oneself; but in the vocabulary of his fellow jurists the word no doubt also had a more precise signification, referring to the *Jungdeutsche Kriminalistenschüle* (Young German School of Criminal Psychologists), whose leading figure, von Liszt, had taken up the Chair in Penal Law at Berlin in 1899.

Our commentary on Musil might well begin with Liszt's inaugural lecture at Berlin.[1] But this was itself only a moment of synthesis within a more protracted process, a purely juridical recodification of a wider debate which had shaken the theoretical foundations of law and was beginning to transform the perspectives of jurisprudence throughout the European continent, from Russia to Holland and Italy, namely the debate concerning criminal anthropology. In order to reconstruct this debate, we need instead to begin at the southernmost point of this juridical Europe, at Naples, where fifteen years earlier in 1885 Enrico Ferri had delivered a university lecture on 'The positivist school of criminology'.[2]

This chapter was written as a paper for a seminar on transformations in law during the late nineteenth century, organized at the Collège de France in 1979 by Michel Foucault. I would especially like to thank Professor Paul Veyne of the Collège de France and Professor Antonio Negri of the University of Padua, imprisoned since April 1979 owing to a scandalous prosecution, whose intelligence and learning greatly helped me to find my bearings in an unfamiliar field of research. The chapter was translated by Colin Gordon.

This lecture will provide us with an exegesis of the 'sensational' character of the conversion of a jurist who, at the beginning of Musil's Chapter 111, was still of the opinion that 'so far as jurists are concerned, there are no semi-insane people' it also throws light on the following passage:

> The social view tells us that the criminally 'degenerate' person cannot at all be considered from a moral aspect, but only according to the degree in which he is dangerous to society as a whole. What follows from this is that the more dangerous he is the more he is responsible for his actions. And what follows again from this, with compelling logic, is that the criminals who are apparently least guilty, that is to say, those who are insane or of defective morality, who by virtue of their nature are least susceptible to the corrective influence of punishment, must be threatened with the harshest penalties.[3]

Since, as Musil puts it 'it is difficult to do justice to justice in brief',[4] I must ask the reader to excuse me if the following account is a little too rapid and perhaps obscure on some points.

We turn, then, to Naples in 1885. At the outset of his lecture, Ferri (a personage, or rather a career, about whose exemplary significance it will be necessary to say a few words in a moment) states with a reformer's ardour all the major theses of the social school of law. And he formulates them by means of contrast drawn on a number of crucial points with the then prevailing doctrines of the classical school of legal theory.

A person who commits a crime, says Ferri, is a criminal:[5] that is to say, a person whose psychic and moral constitution is not normal. There is no point in searching for the motive of his or her act: the reason for the crime is, precisely, the person's criminality. In a sense these few peremptory words mark the registering of a new object of penal science and practice: *homo criminalis*, a new figure engendered outside the sphere of classical penal thought, but which in the course of the nineteenth century gradually advances to its forefront. In order to show that we have to do here with more than a mere fantasy of Ferri's criminological brain,[6] let us cite here just one testimony to the seriousness with which this new object-personage was viewed. At the International Penitentiary Conference of 1925 in London, its President, Ruggles Brise, declared in his opening speech:

> In every civilized country, it has been increasingly recognized that the person of the criminal must enter into the concept of law in as much as this concerns the degree of responsibility and the extent and form of punishment, and that consequently it is necessary to undertake the pathological and psychological [and – he might have added – sociological] study of criminals.[7]

But why should we suppose that this 'criminal' is a novel personage – a view which may well appear paradoxical given that our penal theory was not invented at the end of the last century? The reason is that in fact the whole classical theory of penal law, whether in Italy with Beccaria, in

England with Bentham or in Germany with Anselm Feuerbach, in fact posited and assumed the existence of a figure quite different from *homo criminalis*, namely *homo penalis*.

In classical theory, penal justice is constructed around a triangle formed by law, crime and punishment. The relations between these three terms are defined in three canonical formulae: *nulla poena sine lege; nulla poena sine crimine; nullum crimen sine poena legale*: no punishment except on the basis of existing law – an act is punishable only if it violates the law; no punishment without a crime – the existence of a criminal act must be proved; and lastly, a crime consists simply in an infraction defined by law.[8]

Let us briefly note the fact that classical penal justice emerged within a double historical movement of a much more general order: on the one hand, the fixing of limits to arbitrary royal power – one should bear in mind here the important phenomenon, often passed over in silence by historians of 'society', of the great juridical codifications, notably the one carried out, prior to the Napoleonic Codes, by the *Preussisches Allgemeine Landrecht* of 1794, and, parallel to the promulgation of codes, the disappearance of the special decrees and ordinances issued by monarchs, police, parliaments and other administrative instances; and on the other hand, the movement for the defence of law, the affirmation of the duty of one and all to respect the contract which founds civil society. This tendency is exemplified in the writings of Anselm Feuerbach, known as the father of German penal jurisprudence. In his *Lehrbuch des gemeinen in Deutschland gültigen peinlichen Recht* (*Manual of German Penal Law*), he writes, at the beginning of section 8:

> Civil society [*die bürgerliche Gesellschaft*] is founded through the union of the wills and powers of individuals which guarantees the liberties of each in respect to others. A civil society organized by submission to a general will and to a constitution: this is what is meant by a state. Its [the state's] end is the maintenance of a state of legality [*rechtliche Zustand*], that is to say the coexistence of men in accordance with laws.[9]

This, then, in brief, is the double movement within which the classical theory of penal law takes shape.

What interests us here about this triangle of law, crime and punishment is the absence of the figure of the criminal. What occupies its place is the postulate of a 'free will' as establishing the subjective basis of the power to punish. Now by its very nature this free will is precisely the faculty which is common to all (i.e. to every juridical subject). As such, it is not the object of a special form of knowledge. Anyone can commit a crime: *homo penalis* is not a separate species, but a function. What serves to explain the actions of *homo penalis* is not criminology but rather a 'general anthropology' (in the now anachronistic sense of a general theory of the human subject) – the same theory, in essence, as that which explains the behaviour of *homo economicus*. This free and hence responsible will thus completes the circle of classical penal theory without it being necessary to presuppose any special corresponding mode of knowledge apart from the utilitarianism of a 'calculus of the goods and evils of this life'.[10]

Within the classical regime of penal theory, it will no doubt be said of a man who commits a crime, or rather he himself will say '*video meliora proboque, deteriora sequor*' ('I see and approve the better, I follow the worse' – Ovid). *Homo penalis* is nothing more or less than the citizen, the man of the contract. *Homo penalis* exists as a potentiality in each of us, but is actualized only through such violations of the law as any person may commit simply as the outcome of an erroneous calculation. Now it is precisely this 'rationality' of the old penal order which Ferri, along with many others, will call in question. The discourse of the 'social' or 'positive' school of legal theory is organized around two main poles: the criminal and society. Without being eliminated, the themes of law, crime and punishment recede to a secondary level of importance. Very schematically, we can say that *homo penalis* is joined here by a new subject, *homo criminalis*, which constitutes a veritable new species, a separate race of people whose acts are not results of a false calculation (where imprisonment would be a consequence somewhat akin to bankruptcy), but manifestations of an evil nature. If crime amounts in classical law to a sort of accident of the mind, a confusion of representations, the new legal theory will regard the criminal as an excrement of the social body, at once a residue of archaic stages in the evolution of the species and a waste-product of social organization. Ferri says, again in his Naples lecture, that the criminal is naturally a savage, and socially an abnormal.

In order to render these dry formulae a little more intelligible, let us consider the social school's analysis and interrogation of one of the two main apparatuses making up the classical penal order, the one which the German jurists termed *Abschreckung*: intimidation, dissuasion, also known as intervention '*ad deterrendum*'. (Concerning the other main apparatus, the prison, I need only refer the reader to Michel Foucault's *Discipline and Punish*.[11]

> Penal laws are the motives which experience shows us to be capable of containing or annihilating the impulses which passions impart to the wills of men.

> Thus penal laws, by displaying terrifying objects to men whom they suppose to be capable of fear, present them with suitable motives to influence their will.[12]

These two quotations, drawn not from juridical texts but direct from Holbach's *System of Nature*, illustrate how the juridical utterances of the classical age of law emerge as elements within that discursive practice which I have termed 'general anthropology'. Of course, the apparatus of intimidation presented here by Holbach in its most general form is not new in itself. Hobbes and Pufendorf, among many others, had already written about it; and, after all, the institution of the *supplice*, public judicial torture and execution served a function of intimidation. But what is new and specific to the eighteenth-century reformers is the idea that intimidation, as prescribed by a system in which punishments are graded and modulated in accordance with the diverse forms of crime, coupled not with the exemplary yet discontinuous terror of the *supplice*, but with the mild yet inexorable and integral efficacy of justice,[13] will necessarily exert a pressure on human wills such that the force of the passions can be arrested at the point where contract and law fix the bounds of each person's liberty in relation to that of others. Promote the happiness or interest of each, says utilitarianism, but within the limits of the law. In other words, intimidation is no longer the threat of a *sovereign power* against whoever may dare to ignore or defy it, but rather has for its basis and instrument *law*, that discreet yet uninterrupted threat which acts through the medium of representations on that particular form of mental representation which forms the 'calculus of the goods and evils of this life'.

Here is what Bentham has to say on this question in his *Théorie des peines et des récompenses*:

> Each individual conducts himself, albeit unknowingly, according to a well- or ill-made calculus of pleasures and pains. Should he foresee that a pain will be the consequence of an act which pleases him, this idea will act with a certain force so as to divert him from that action. If the total value of the pain appears greater to him than the total value of the pleasure, the repulsive force will be the greater; the act will not occur.[14]

Two of Bentham's further remarks on this question seem to me to throw light on the punitive rationality of the classical theory. The first occurs in a chapter entitled 'Fortification of the impression made by punishments on the imagination':

> If an abridged edition of the penal code were to be published, illustrated with woodcuts showing the specific penalty laid down for each kind of crime, this would act as an imposing commentary, a sensible image of the law. Each person would then be led to think to himself: this is what I must suffer if I should break this law.[15]

Bentham accordingly rejects as 'ineffective' 'those penalties which can produce no effect on the will and consequently cannot serve to prevent similar acts'.[16]

The second remark I wish to cite concerns the Panopticon, and is of interest here because it shows how the apparatus of the prison itself assumes a signification within the framework of the apparatus of *Abschreckung*:

> The penal scene is located in the neighbourhood of a metropolis, the place which contains assembled the greatest number of men, including those who most need to have displayed before their eyes the punishment of crime. The appearance of the building, the singularity of its form, the walls and moats that surround it, the guard at its gates, all of this serves to reinforce the idea of malefactors confined and punished: the ease of admission could not fail to attract a great number of visitors . . . What a most striking spectacle for the most numerous class of spectators! What a theme for conversations, allusions, domestic lessons, useful stories! . . . And yet the real penalty is less great than the apparent one . . . The punishments being visible, the imagination exaggerates them.[17]

An imaginary theatre of punishments. Anselm Feuerbach is restating the same principle in the more abstract language of Kant's *Critique of Pure Reason*, when he writes in a paragraph of his manual dealing with 'psychological constraint'.

> All breaches of law have their psychological source in sensible nature, in so far as the faculty of desire in man is stirred by pleasure either during the committal of the offence or from the moment of the desire to commit it. This sensible impulsion can be annulled by the fact that each man knows his criminal act will ineluctably lead to an evil greater than that of the loss of pleasure occasioned by the non-satisfaction of the impulse to perform the act.[18]

So much by way of a reconstruction, at any rate with respect to one quite important point, of the theoretical background and juridical *credo* of Ulrich's father, prior to his conversion. We will now try and explain the nature of the conversion itself.

From the 1870s and 1880s, the essential elements of the old penal rationality began to be definitively overturned. Ferri (to confine ourselves to him – but examples could be multiplied endlessly) argues as follows. Beccaria's theory of punishment as an instrument *ad deterrendum* counterweighting the interest in the committing of crimes is false, both theoretically and practically: practically, because the statistics of crimes and criminals simply continue to rise; theoretically, because the criminal does not think like a normal and honest person such as Beccaria – indeed, we may say that he or she does not think at all. The criminal cannot be a *homo penalis* because he is not a Man.

What then is to be done, given the impotence of punishments and the rising number of crimes? For Ferri, the answer consists fundamentally not so much in intimidation as in the elimination of the very sources of crime. One must pass from *Abschreckung* to *Unschädlichmachung*, from deterrence to neutralization. The new penal theory will be concerned far less with dissuading the citizen from law breaking than with rendering the criminal incapable of harm. The problem which thus comes to be posed is that of the origin or aetiology of crime.

The question of free will had long been the grand showpiece theme of debate among jurists, since, as we saw above, it was free will which functioned in classical theory as the subjective foundation of the right to punish. This debate, traversed by arguments of exquisite subtlety and linked from an early date to the alienists' speculations on insanity, went on throughout the nineteenth century. The first authoritative general work on the subject, Vaillant's *De libera voluntate ad delictum necessaria*, was published at Amsterdam in 1837. Enrico Ferri likewise began his university career in 1878 with a thesis on 'The theory of the imputability and negation of free will'.[19] Here he initially summarizes his position by citing a work on determinism by Fouillée where it is stated that:

> without venturing upon metaphysical considerations, we may justify punishment from a human viewpoint. And this purely social justification has no need to ascend to the absolute truth of things, for it derives from social relations as they exist in fact.[20]

Much more than the problematic of free will, the issue here is that of the very basis of the right to punish. In this perspective, it is society, not law or sovereignty, which is seen as being attacked or endangered by crime, or rather by the criminal. The question is whether it is law which is primordial for society – in the sense of being the immediate expression of the will of every subject – or whether law is no more than the secondary and variable codification of the rules of social functioning.

We must pause on this point, since it leads on to the theme of 'social defence' which becomes the slogan of the new penal theory. It is in the writings of the Belgian jurist Prins – who, with Liszt and von Hamel, was to head the International Union of Penal Law at the turn of the century – that one finds the most explicit statement of this theme. But first it should be noted that the problematic, and even the expression 'social defence', are not in themselves new. Soon after 1830, the Italian jurist Carmignani had published an important book entitled *Theory of the Laws of Social Security*. Already he argues here for the replacement of the notions of crime and punishment hitherto assumed as fundamental in penal theory by the new concepts of 'social offence' and 'social defence'.[21] Feuerbach himself says that the *raison d'être* of punishments is the necessity to avert the dangers which menace social life.[22] But since words are not things, or at any rate not practices, we need to examine the question more closely. For Prins, as for Liszt and Ferri, 'social defence' is much more than a verbal formula. It is the keystone of the new penal rationality, whose central elements seem to me to be the following.

1. First, Imputability. The question of the subjective foundation of the right to punish, even if it never disappears from the codes, recedes little by little into the background: 'this "I" [the free will of the subject] is a mystery, and one cannot found the right to punish on a mystery':[23] the axis of responsibility is no longer, as for Kant and the classical legal theorists, reason and its good or bad calculations, but conformity or nonconformity with respect to social life.

2. Second, Social defence. If the idea of social defence is not new, why are we speaking here of a transformation in the order of penal theory? To answer this question, we need first of all to ask in turn, for each successive stage of penal theory, what the 'society' is which it is sought to defend, and what exactly is meant in each case by the notion of 'defence'.

Let us take the latter point first. Intimidation does not vanish from its place among the elements of the penal apparatus. But it remains no more than an element, and a minor one at that. The social school continues to recognize its value, but only as a means of dealing with what are termed 'occasional delinquents' (in Liszt's term, *Augenblicksverbrecher*). Now this occasional delinquent is only the residue of *homo penalis*: his actions are evil and dangerous, but not his inherent nature. But the true criminal is quite another matter. The defence of society against the criminal will involve what we termed above his or her 'neutralization'. We should add that, between the two extremes of residual intimidation for occasional delinquents and neutralization (tending towards physical liquidation) for hardened criminals (Liszt's *unverbesserliche Verbrecher*), there opens up a vast domain of intervention for what the International Union of Penal Law will term social hygiene, designed to act as a preventive clean-up of the social breeding grounds of crime.

This new theory of right is thus centred not on crime considered as a purely anthropological or mental fact, but on the rebellious hordes of the criminal, understood as a social phenomenon. There is a strange paradox here: if it is claimed that criminality is a phenomenon with a social aetiology, how is it possible to say that the criminal has an asocial nature? In reality it is Darwinism which supplies the solution of the paradox. Within the same social organism there can coexist different stages of the evolution of the species; in this sense, society is a mixture of different natures. At the very heart of social evolution and by virtue of that process itself, one can recognize as archaic residues those individuals and groups which, unable to keep up with the proper pace of evolution and left behind by it, endanger by their existence the proper functioning of the whole.

Thus we can begin to see that the society whose defence is in question here is something quite different from Feuerbach's *bürgerliche Gesellschaft*, in which and for which the state of right acts as the guarantor of law, and where society and law are one and the same, or rather where law – the contract – founds society. By prescribing the limits of sovereign power, law operates a sort of symbolic zeroizing of unequal privileges: in real terms, it will function as the act of recognition and formalization of the great and little machines of *assujettissement* (subjection/subjectification) which come in late-eighteenth-century Europe to combine into a relatively unified continuum.

Now the new 'society' conceived of by late-nineteenth-century jurists and criminologists is, or so we may suggest, the outcome of the failure of the old liberal programme of *laissez-faire* and the rule of law. Ever since the Physiocrats, liberalism as an effective governmental rationality had proved impossible to realize, and it was to remain so for the remainder of the nineteenth century at least. The demarcation of the zones of legitimate state interference, the division between its *agenda* and its *non-agenda*, had never been satisfactorily established; the policy encapsulated in Quesnay's advice to the king that 'to govern, one should do nothing', turned out to be a difficult and ultimately quite untenable course. Nineteenth-century political strategies were dominated by a 'reforming' current, seeking and finding, not without conflicts and vacillations, the difficult middle path between 'doing nothing' and 'doing too much'. The strength of this current had lain in its capacity to define for governmental activity a space and a legitimation in relation to the different newly emerging social and economic forces. But in the process, the project of a society built out of individual subjects had aborted. The natural society which was supposed to emerge through *laissez-faire* had failed to materialize. The machines of *assujettissement* had begun to malfunction to the extent of its being said, with Renan, that 'nature is unjustice itself'.[24] And without a good nature, no government in law is possible.

What then is to serve as the new founding principle? Not subjects or law, but society itself, considered as a complex of conflicts and interests. A society which is not nature but community, *Gemeinschaft, Volksgemeinschaft*. Let us now return to the specific problem of penal law. Liszt writes in his treatise that the law exists to defend vital interests. Law breaking is defined in these terms as:

> the defective state, demonstrated by the act committed, of the social mentality necessary for life in community . . . my object is to designate the material content of infraction which is not created by law but presents itself to law, and which is thus definable only outside and beyond law. But above the law there exists only society itself, organized in the state. Hence it is here that the principle of infraction is to be sought.[25]

Here, then, society emerges as the only meaningful basis for the right to punish, laws being nothing but the changeable mode of codification of society's vital interests. And all the more so because society is regarded no longer as natural but as historical. The theoretical basis on which it will be possible to speak of society will no longer be that of law, but that of a 'historical sociology'. Hence the great role played by the reactivation and development of a whole anthropological knowledge (this time in the modern sense of the term) which will call in question the idea of natural freedom. There will no longer be the possibility of founding society on legal right, since each society that arises in historical space and time produces its own form of legal right, just as it produces its mythology, its culture and, along with everything else, its criminals and its means of defence against them. For the new penal order, society will thus not only be the source of the right to punish but also the immediate source of all right, of all laws, and also of criminality.

Marx, Spencer, Darwin: for Ferri these three names represent, as it were, the epistemological preconditions – to speak in a language other than his – of a criminal sociology. But Ferri often also cites a fourth name, the rather less well-known one of the French psychiatrist B. Morel. There is insufficient space here to discuss this important figure, whose name is closely linked to the theory of degeneracy: one should consult the pages Robert Castel devotes to him in *L'Ordre psychiatrique*.[26] I will limit myself to the assertion (which would still need to be demonstrated) that without Morel's theory of instinctive acts, the formation of this special *savoir* of criminology would have been far less readily accomplished.[27]

3. Finally, as the third of the main components of the new penal rationality, we have the figure of the criminal. It too does not just emerge one fine day out of nowhere into the landscape of law. It has diverse ancestors, and a convoluted prehistory. To retrace this would involve the reconstruction of the history of another special knowledge, that of legal medicine. In the eighteenth century Gayot de Pitival had already published a collection in several volumes of remarkable legal cases, accompanied by observations of every kind.[28] About a century later, Anselm Feuerbach in Germany does the same thing in his *Darstellung merkwürdiger Criminalrechtsfälle*.[29] But the crowd of characters represented in this forensic literature lacks the coherent identity which it will afterwards assume. Neither species nor race, the ancestor of *homo criminalis* we encounter here is a monster, alien to nature and society alike. It has yet to become the object of a knowledge; at best, it is classified in such bestiaries as the works of Pitival and Feuerbach as a curiosity or accident, not of spirit but of nature. Later in the nineteenth century, the monster becomes madman and is transposed from the bestiary to the asylum; it comes to figure in all the pamphlets which psychiatrists and jurists started to produce in the wake of the great cases of monstrous or motiveless crime which break out in France in the 1820s.[30] At the

conclusion of a struggle like that between angel and devil over the soul of the dying, doctors and judges finally arrived at an understanding. The doctors were to be accredited as the experts in questions of insanity, while the judges found themselves rescued by the alienists from the legal dilemmas which had threatened to cripple the apparatus of justice.[31] No doubt the character of Moosbrugger in *The Man Without Qualities* is the last, imaginary representative of this lineage of monsters.

But at this point the criminal *per se* is no longer an especially disquieting figure – except perhaps where he kills a king or prime minister, or turns anarchist. He becomes an exhibit – as witness the museum of criminology which Lombroso established in a suite of rooms in Turin:[32] a docile animal which has lost even the privilege of terror. The figure of the monster had inspired fear because it was itself impervious to fear. Prins simply says this of criminals:

> Is it admissable that society should be incapable of dealing with its waste-products as industry does with its? We too can cut down the overheads of social administration, recycle society's residues and endeavour to keep the loss of strength to a minimum. Even an inferior organism can prove useful provided one succeeds in adapting it to an inferior function.[33]

The essential point is that the genealogical precursors of the criminal include other figures besides that of the monster, personages the nineteenth century had already learned to live with, from incorrigible children to perverts, from homosexuals to prostitutes (whose physiological characteristics were tabulated at an early date by Parent-Duchâtelet)[34] and the common poor, the 'dangerous classes' which social economists never ceased to evoke following Sismondi's discovery of the ills of industrialism.

It is around this figure of *homo criminalis* that penal theory will construct its special *savoir*. It is obliged to do so, because a general regime of knowledge of man in the manner of Bentham had either ceased to be, or had yet to become, possible (according to the latter point of view, what remained lacking was works such as those of von Mises). And this special anthropology will assume, or so I have been rapidly trying to indicate, a place alongside that of sociology, the general knowledge of societies. Rusche and Kirchheimer rightly say in their book *Punishment and Social Structure* that for criminologists of the late nineteenth century 'the science of crime was essentially a science of society'.[35]

Throughout this discussion we have been following the argument set out in Ferri's Naples lecture. Who was Ferri? An academic and jurist, a pupil of Lombroso, Ferri was undoubtedly the most active and best-known member of the Italian legal school. He had a singular political career. He joined the Socialist Party as a young progressive in the 1880s, and played an important role as a leader of its left or 'maximalist' wing (to which Mussolini also later adhered), becoming editor of the party newpaper *Avanti* from 1900 to 1905. After the coming of fascism he became a convert to the regime and died in 1929 a senator of the kingdom. In 1919 he was nominated president of the Royal Commission for the Reform of the Penal Code; in 1921 he published a 'Project for a Penal Code'[36] which became the basis not only for the fascist Rocco Code in Italy but also for the codes of other counties including Cuba and the Soviet Union.

From the pre-fascist Italy of Ferri and Prampolini, and the Italian Socialist Party's 'confusion of tongues and monstrous accents',[37] let us turn to the University of Berlin and Professor von Liszt's inaugural lecture on the object and method of the penal sciences. In this lecture Liszt enumerates three tasks of the penal sciences, tasks which I will very rapidly summarize:

1. The first task is to establish a pedagogy providing future practical criminologists with the knowledge necessary to carry out their duties. On this point he remarks that knowledge of the rules of law and justice is not enough. For example, a judge cannot simply confine himself to imposing a prescribed penalty for a specified crime: he will need to adjust the punishment to fit not so much the offence as the criminal subject who has committed it (see his important discussion here of 'variable sentences').
2. The second task is to explain the socio-psychological causes of crime and thereby demonstrate that punishment is nothing but the specific reaction of society to anti-social acts. Law merely serves to regulate this 'reaction'. This seems to me to be a fundamental formulation of the notion of social defence.
3. The third task goes beyond the field of penal theory and practice as thus defined; it consists in calling on the legislator in the name of the struggle against crime to launch an attack on the very roots of criminality. This is what is termed, in contrast with the generalized strategy of prevention based on *Abschreckung*, specialized prevention, or social hygiene.[38]

If, then, classical penal theory derived the juridical apparatus calculated to maintain and reaffirm order, by way of the algebra of a general anthropology which knows no other person but man, from law as the constitution of liberty and eternal social order, one can perhaps say that the penal theory which established itself in the late nineteenth century proceeds from the premise of society as source of life and right to deduce the activity of society as a self-defending subject, via a special anthropology which is at once a symptomatology, a pathology and a therapeutic for a social body prone to all the disorders induced by subjects who are unreliable (*infidi*) because inadequately subjected/subjectified, and therefore always dangerous.

If one recalls the remark by Prins cited above, one can see two distinct lines of development which emerge at this point. One of these leads towards a policy of neutralization: one can reflect here on Ferri's proposal to send hardened criminals to reclaim the marshes of Latium, where they would perish of malaria, thereby at once ridding society of them for good and procuring it an economic gain.[39] This suggestion was indeed put into effect during the fascist era. The other perspective, which might be called that of a principle of economy and which is more explicitly stated by Prins, consists in the minimization of the cost of administering social disorders. But clearly this point, where constraints of space oblige us to break off this history of penal regimes, does not mark their ultimate stage of development.

To conclude, a word on the nature of this discussion. I would like briefly to address a problem which has already been posed in regard to this kind of analysis and might be formulated thus: what kind of a history have I been trying to sketch out here? What is it meant to be a history of? Let us say first of all that we are not dealing with the history of law or juridical theories properly speaking – to do so it would have been necessary to analyze, in the case of Germany for example, not only the work of Liszt but a whole theoretical debate involving such authors as Binding, Birkmeyer and others. Even less have I been attempting an overall history of jurisprudence: the point is too obvious to need labouring.

What I have been trying to do, albeit in a manifestly tentative and precarious fashion, is a history of punitive rationalities and their transformations. As I am convinced that there is no single, solid plane of consistency for all historical events, no immovable, nameable fundament of the tree of historical life, and that the real is not the immediately given, I would understand by 'rationalities' that which makes possible for us an intelligibility of practices, an intelligibility which at once traverses and is incorporated in these practices. In other words, the kind of research being attempted here might be taken as posing for history, and in the present instance for the history of law, the same question which Kant posed for 'reason', a question which might issue in a mapping of chronologically distinct rationalities and practices that renders visible at once their modes of functioning, their surfaces of emergence and their 'limits'. The old Marxist transformation-problem would thereby come to reoccupy the focal point of this 'critique' – the latter term being understood in its Kantian sense. But this undertaking would surely also aim to elicit, in the face of the present and of history, something other than either a posture of denunciation or the euphoria of world-historical expectancy. What it would rather be necessary to demonstrate would be the incessant attenuation of historical forms, to reduce (if I may put it thus) history to history. The political benefit which I would hope might be drawn from this enterprise would be to regain contact, via this detour, with present actuality: that is to say, with the possible.[40] To be able to do this it will be necessary to silence all that clamorous past which never ceases to din in our ears.

The past and history would then belong to us in the way the landscape belongs to the 'coastwise voyager' in Thomas Mann's *Joseph and his Brothers*, 'who finds no end to his journey, for behind each headland of clayey dune he conquers, fresh headlands and new distances lure him on'.[41]

NOTES

1. F. von Liszt, 'Die Aufgaben und die Methode der Strafrechtswissenschaft', inaugural lecture in Penal Law at the University of Berlin, 27 October 1899, in *Strafrechtliche Aufsätze und Vorträge*, Berlin, 1905, vol. II pp. 284–98. French edition, Paris, 1902.
2. E. Ferri, 'La scuola criminale positiva', lecture at the University of Naples, 1885.
3. Robert Musil, *The Man without Qualities*, trans. Eithne Wilkins and Ernst Kaiser, London, 1968, vol. 2 chapter 111, p. 285.
4. *Ibid.*, p. 283.
5. This stunning truism recurs almost a century later in R. Merle and A. Vitu, *Traité de droit criminel*, 2nd edn. Paris, 1978, p. 28: 'the delinquent is a human being who commits crimes' (*sic*).
6. This was the view held for instance by Benedetto Croce, who wrote in his *Logica*, 'For every little idea which stirs in a professor's brain, we see a new science born; we have thus been blessed with sociologies, social psychologies . . . criminologies, sciences of comparative literature and so forth, each endowed with its own special methodology' (p. 249).
7. Quoted by E. Ferri, 'Le congres penitentiaire international de Londres', *Revue Internationale de Droit Pénal*, 1 January 1926.
8. I believe these formulae first appear in Anselm Feuerbach, *Lehrbuch des gemeinen in Deutschland gültigen Rechts*, 1801. In the 13th edition used here, they occur at para. 20, p. 41. Cf. the article on this question by S. Glaser cited by Hayek, 'Nullum crimen sine lege', *Legislation and International Law*, 3rd Series, vol. XXIV.
9. Feuerbach, *Lehrbuch*, p. 36.
10. C. Beccaria, *Dei delitti e delle pene*, 1764.
11. See also M. Ignatieff, *A Just Measure of Pain*, London, 1978.
12. Holbach, *Système de la Nature*, vol. 1, ch. 12, pp. 191 and 197, quoted by K. Binding, *Die Normen und ihre Ubertretung*, Leipzig, 1877, vol. II, p. 25.
13. Cf. M. Foucault, *Discipline and Punish*, London, 1979, pp. 92f., 101–3.

14. Jeremy Bentham, *Théorie des peines et des récompenses*, ed. Dumont, London, 1811, pp. 12–13.
15. Bentham, *Traités de legislation civile et pénale*, 3 vols., Paris, 1802. vol. III, pp. 75–6.
16. *Ibid.* vol. II, p. 381.
17. Bentham, *Théorie des peines*, p. 203.
18. Feuerback, *Lehrbuch*, para. 13, p. 38.
19. Ferri, *La teoria dell 'imputibilitá e la negazione del libero arbitrio*, Firenze, 1878.
20. A. Fouillé, *La liberté et le déterminisme*, Paris, 1872, vol. II, para. 3, p. 26, cited in Ferri, *La teoria*, p. 7.
21. G. Carmignani, *Teoria delle leggi sulla sircurezza sociale*, 4 vols, Pisa, 1831–2, vol. I, p. 21.
22. Feuerbach, *Lehrbuch*, para. 103, p. 203.
23. A. Prins, *La Défense sociale et la transformation du droit pénal*, 1910, p. 10. See also the same author's previous book: *Criminalité et répression*, Brussels, 1886.
24. Renan's words appear as the epigraph to E. de Laveleye and H. Spencer, *L'Etat et l'individu ou darwinisme social et christianisme*, Florence, 1885.
25. F. von Liszt, *Lehrbuch des deutschen Strafrechts*. Cited here from the French edition. *Traité du droit pénal allemand*, Paris, 1911, pp. 94 and 232–3 note 2; cf. also Prins, *Criminalité et répression*, p. 22.
26. Robert Castel, *L'Ordre psychiatrique*, vol. 1: *L'age d'or de l'aliénisme*, Paris, 1976, pp. 276ff.
27. To illustrate this point, a quotation from Morel's *Traité de la médicine légale des aliénes*, Paris, 1866, pp. ii–iii and iv. 'To suppose that from a juridical or medical point of view a treatise of this kind concerns only the inmates of our asylums, or indeed only those whose palpable insanity is generally recognized by public opinion, would be to misunderstand its aim and scope. Experience teaches us that, over and above madness in the strict sense as described in books and observed in lunatic asylums, madness as it is generally understood in the world, there occur a mass of human actions which by their strangeness, their exceptionally dangerous character, and so to speak their authors' instinctive and reasoned perversity, arouse great perplexity in the minds of judges . . . What use to us are the more or less vague definitions of madness, the theories on the degree of criminal responsibility of lunatics and the medico-legal consequences of partial deliria? It is sufficient if we can observe and prove that madness is a disease, a *corporis affectus*, as the masters of antiquity taught; that there is not just one madness, but diverse varieties of this condition; that the lunatic is not an ideal, unique, abstract type . . . but that there are diverse categories of lunatics.[2]
28. Gayot de Pitival, *Causes célèbres et intéressantes avec les jugements qui les ont décidés*, Paris, 1734–43.
29. Feuerbach, *Merkwürdige Kriminalrechtsfalle*, 2 vols, Giessen, 1808–11.
30. Cf. *I, Pierre Rivière . . .*, ed. M. Foucault, London, 1978.
31. Cf. Castel, 'Doctors and Judges', in *ibid*.
32. On Lombroso's museum, see F. Colombo's book *La scienza infelice*, remarkable especially for its photographic documentation.
33. Prins, *La Défense sociale*, p. 162.
34. Parent-Duchâtelet, *De la prostitution dans la ville de Paris considérée sous le rapport de l'hygiène publique, de la morale et de l'administration*, 2 vols, Paris, 1836, especially chapter 3.

35. Rusche and Kirchheimer, *Punishment and Social Structure*, New York, 1939.
36. E. Ferri, *Relazione sul progetto preliminare di codice penale italiano*, Book I, Roma, 1921, edn in four languages: Italian, French, English and German.
37. Dante, *Inferno*, trans. J. Ciardi, New York, 1954, p. 25.
38. Cf. note 1 above, *passim*.
39. Ferri, 'La scuola criminale positiva', pp. 57–8.
40. 'The possible' is meant here in the sense in which Musil writes in *The Man Without Qualities:* 'If there is such a thing as a sense of reality, there must also be a sense of possibility' (vol. 1, chapter 4, title); I am also thinking especially of the following passage: 'The possible, however, covers not only the dreams of nervously sensitive persons, but also the not yet manifested intentions of God. A possible experience or a possible truth does not equate to real experience of real truth minus the value 'real'; but, at least in the opinion of its devotees, a fiery, soaring quality, a constructive will, a conscious utopianism that does not shrink from reality but treats it, on the contrary, as a mission and an invention' *Ibid.*, p. 48.
41. Thomas Mann, *Joseph and His Brothers*, Part I: The Tales of Jacob, Harmondsworth, 1978, p. 3. I owe this quotation, among many other things, to my friend E. Galzenati.

CHAPTER THIRTEEN

Pleasure in work

Jacques Donzelot

INTRODUCTION

The last ten years have seen the emergence in France of a new discourse about work, one that might be termed the search for 'pleasure *in* work', to distinguish it from that slogan of infamous memory, 'joy *through* work'. The theme of this new discourse is not, as was the case with its fascist predecessor, a mere ideology, a representation concocted by a state apparatus to serve and celebrate the ends of productivity. Instead, it is the outcome of a series of reforms and experiments conceived in response to a malaise caused by the pursuit of productivity, designed to induce a range of local improvements in the regime of work, the sum of which would amount to a global change in the relationship between the members of our society and that regime. To continue our contrast with fascism, one can say that these measures are intended to make work come to be perceived not just as a matter of pure constraint but as a good in itself: as a means towards self-realization rather than as an opportunity for self-transcendence.

No doubt these reforms and experiments must seem of minor scope if compared with the objective of transforming the actual structures of production. Flexible hours, job enrichment, self-managed work-teams, continued retraining (*formation permanente*): none of these innovations can be regarded as serious attempts to modify the capitalist regime. And in fact their ambition is not to transform the organization of production, but to change the relation of individuals to their productive work. But the latter aim, it will be said, is impossible without the attainment of the former one; capitalism's already long history enables us to judge the effectiveness of such reveries as the pursuit of workers' happiness within a logic which knows only one motive: to increase profit and productivity. It must however be recognized, without seeking to pre-judge their final

This chapter first appeared as an article in J. Carpenter, R. Castel, J. Donzelot, J. M. Lacrosse, A. Lovell and G. Procacci, *Résistances à la médecine et démultiplication du concept du santé*, CORDES/Commisariat Général du Plan, Paris, 1980.

outcome, that while these initiatives often originally emanated from modernizing circles among management, they are now beginning to be taken up by the state; and their recognition of the primacy of productivity has been sufficiently evident for it to have been possible to replace France's previous governmental Agency for the Increase of Productivity by an Agency for the Development of Continued Training (ADEP) and an Agency for the Improvement of Working Conditions (ANACT).

By the practices they promote, both these new agencies aim to modify the relation of individuals to their work, but they approach the problem from different directions. In a sense, ADEP and all the continued training institutions address this problem from an indirect and external point of view, their main concern being with the psychological ties that the individual himself establishes with his work. They seek to break down the *statutory* perception the worker has of this link, the idea that work defines the individual and stamps his place on him like a destiny, robbing him of his identity if he loses his job and making any change in the place or content of his work into a potential threat to him. The new approach involves putting the accent instead on the individual's autonomy, his capacity to adapt. It invites him to become 'an agent of change in a world of change'. Instead of defining the individual by the work he is assigned to, it regards productive activity as the site of deployment of his personal skills. Whereas the individual's freedom hitherto basically meant the possibility of either accepting or refusing his assigned status, it is now seen as meaning the possibility of permanently redeploying one's capacities according to the satisfaction one obtains in one's work, one's greater or lesser involvement in it, and its capacity thoroughly to fulfil one's potentialities. Hence the success in the field of 'continued retraining' of the whole 'new psychological culture' (dynamization groups, human potential groups, etc.) discussed elsewhere by Robert Castel.[1]

The Agency for the Improvement of Working Conditions aims on the other hand to modify work from within, by transforming its content. Previously the theoreticians of business studies, like the 'public relations' school of thought, and also (though in a different perspective) the trade unions with their demands in terms of wages, hours and job creation, had only concerned themselves with the environment and context of work. One side wanted measures designed, in the name of economic calculation, to improve psychological adaptation to work; the other wanted measures socially to reward work, in the name of a social domain conceived precisely as the site of compensation for every kind of human lack engendered or necessitated by the world of work. But either way work itself still acts as a reality-principle, an absolute datum presiding over this division between economic and social domains. The goal of the proponents of ANACT is to erode as far as possible this quality of massive givenness, to soften work by the introduction of flexible hours, to enrich it by restructuring jobs, breaking down the self-evidentness, the sense of fatedness attaching to work, annulling the arbitrary division between the economic and the social. By thus restoring a degree of fluidity to its content, it becomes possible to modify the social relations work imposes, through the introduction of self-managing work-teams and worker participation in the simultaneously economic and social decisions implicit in such a reorganization of production. The relation between work and the social at last becomes open to change. While work had hitherto been seen as serving the satisfaction of needs, these needs had themselves been multiplied by the frustrations inherent in work, thereby paradoxically accentuating the need not to work. The new discourses claim to transform this problem by making work itself the territory of the social, the privileged space for the satisfaction of social need.

How significant are these challenges to the status of work and the working subject? To what extent are they merely superficial effects of a deeper crisis, palliatory measures to ease a deeper set of transformations? Should we say that this new discourse on pleasure in work is just a byproduct of the crisis currently besetting the concept of health, and the boom in new psychological techniques; or should we say on the contrary that it marks a point where these tendencies begin to assume real meaning and effect? But we can hardly attempt to answer these questions without adding another one: where do the components of this discourse come from? What underlying reasons determined their formation?

We need first of all to ascertain how far back in time the configuration of work and working subject extends which the present initiatives are seeking to efface. How old is the status-oriented definition of the worker's position? What causes gave rise to this autonomized vision of work as a process obeying its own logic and exerting its constraining force regardless of other social relations?

From contract to status

During the first three-quarters of the nineteenth century, the place of the worker in production was formulated simply in terms of dependence or autonomy. From the moment he enters the factory gate, the freedom which presides over the contract of employment is transformed into a process of subjection. The conditions of industrial work are determined there by the boss alone, through his exclusive prerogative over the systems of regulations, rewards and penalties he uses to organize the life of his business. The worker's relation to production is thus a relation to domination; and this domination becomes the target of attack for the main nineteenth-century working-class demand, that of the right to self-organization and free association, this being in the workers' view the only way to re-establish in the actual business of working the freedom of contract which the 1789 Revolution had originally accorded them. The force of this demand was all the greater because its conception of work was still linked to ideas of technical skill, personal competence and craft pride. Towards the end of the nineteenth century, however, two parallel changes occur: the progressive reduction of this craft element in work, and the achievement of workers' rights – rights which protect their conditions of work and reduce the arbitrary power of bosses in their employment of a deskilled workforce. It is as though the one change were the condition for the other, as though the gradual professional deskilling of the worker gave rise to his juridical requalification. If work was to lose its qualifying value in terms of skill, the source of qualification henceforth came to reside in the workers' rights this had made possible.

So the worker regains his autonomy, his status as a subject, only through the rights which protect a workforce which can no longer lay claim to autonomy through its mastery of its occupation. We know how anarcho-syndicalism marked the final flowering of the idea of the worker as master of his work and hence as the subject of the production process, at the very moment when the foundations were being laid of protective industrial legislation endowing the worker with rights and guarantees which limit the use of his labour power, transposing his autonomy from the register of work itself to that of its limitation and guaranteed reward. Moreover, this industrial legislation establishes strictly speaking not so much rights for the worker as protection for his wages. The legal provisions dealing with industrial accidents, and subsequently also with retirement and unemployment, amount to the principle of maintaining a wage in the various situations where the worker is unable to work – not to a right attributed to the worker in the performance of his job. No doubt the worker becomes, through union action and collective agreements, not only a beneficiary but also a creator of rights, since industrial agreements come to have force for whole categories of the employed and not just for particular contracting parties (employers and unions). All the same, this juridical activity in the defence and conquest of rights does not change the contract of employment in its nature, but only regulates its conditions. In a word, what it does is to enlarge the sphere of the *statutory* at the expense of that of the *contractual* in the definition of the contract of employment. To the extent that the contract symbolizes a domination, every measure favourable to the worker's status functions as a resistance to this domination, even and above all when this resistance serves only to accentuate the worker's disengagement from the productive process, even when it sanctions and organizes the worker's moral separation from his work.

The autonomization of work is the effect of this double process, the dequalification of work and the juridical requalification of the worker. This is, as we know, the consequence of Taylorism. But Taylor was not just the man who emphasized and exploited the technical division of labour to the extent of making the worker a mere component in a mechanical production process. He was also the man who recognized and exploited the reduction in bosses' authority consequent on the conferment of protective rights on workers and unions. Taylor says that all the tension that exists between employer and workers comes from the particular form taken by the boss's authority, using factory regulations at once to cut wages by the imposition of fines and to raise productivity by the enforcement of military discipline. It is not surprising that in return workers exploit the new safety regulations to slow down the rate of production. If, on the other hand, instead of relying on this surfeit of discipline one set out to calculate the optimum conditions of adaptation of man to machine, taking proper account of safety margins instead of resorting to fraud to bypass them, discipline could be made to subsist in the machine itself, rather than behind the worker's back. Autonomized and freed from the bonds of authoritarian organization, work would become able to deliver higher productivity, and wages would remain as the single and sole object for union negotiations.

Schematic though this may be as a summary of what took place, and however much less idyllic the actual applications of Taylorism in France may have been, it remains true that they gave rise after the First World War to the pact between employers and unions, which Leon Jouhaux expressed in roughly these terms: yes to increases in productivity, if you improve safety at work, if you create social insurance, and (above all) if you increase wages.

The human factor

This process of autonomization enabled work to be made the object of a new science designed to serve the simultaneous increase of safety and productivity. In France this new science emerges during the 1920s, with the short-lived *Revue de la science du travail*, and then in 1933 with the journal *Travail humain* which is still being published today. It takes as its objective the 'knowledge of man with a view to the judicious utilization of his activity', and seeks to recruit the collaboration of physiological and psychological sciences:

so as to be able, by means of various indices, coefficients and evaluations of different organic functions, to characterize and differentiate individuals according to their aptitudes, and thus determine the optimum functioning conditions for this motor which is infinitely more complex than all others, the human motor.

The journal's two founders are J. M. Laby, a psychologist with the Paris Transport Authority (RATP) and the doctor H. Leugnier, a disciple of Emile Toulouse. What Toulouse, the founder of the League for Mental Health, had proposed to apply to the population of the abnormal, namely a vast enterprise of detection, selection and prophylaxis, Leugnier proposes to extend to the 'normal, working population'. Human biometrics is to be applied to serve the purposes of selection, adaptation and vocational guidance. How can individuals be oriented towards the function they are most suited for? The problem itself is seen as a self-evident one, since 'workers' happiness depends on making this science of adaptation as precise as possible'. Job aptitude tests are developed first for the most demanding occupations such as those of aircraft pilots and engine drivers, and then gradually extended to cover every skilled job category. How are the optimum conditions to be determined for the use of an individual's powers at a precise task, avoiding excessive fatigue which can be as harmful to productivity as it is to safety? This question of fatigue which so much preoccupies the biometricians is made the object of investigations as simple-minded in their methods as they are serenely confident in their positivistic expectations. One learns for example that the optimum rate of exployment of a worker's labour to turn a crank positioned 1 metre above ground level, with a radius of 40 centimetres and moving a weight of 13 kilograms, is one of twenty-four to twenty-six rotations per minute. A lower figure is uninteresting in terms of productivity, a higher one is harmful to safety. However, notwithstanding the introduction of precautions in personal selection and the application of these expert calculations, the level of industrial accidents continues to rise. A third problem consequently emerges: how can one incorporate into both personnel selection and the work process additional criteria which will serve to reduce the accident rate? And so an effort is made, whose persistence is as admirable as it is futile, to detect beforehand individuals predisposed to cause accidents – since there must be *some* specific, concealed factor to account for both the increase in industrial accidents and the frequency of their repetition (a person who has had one accident is likely to have further ones). And if it is not possible to diagnose the accident-prone with certainty, those individuals who display one or more of the indicative traits can at least be directed into less dangerous jobs. This kind of factorial research is characteristic of the whole of this science. Its explicit project is the treatment of the 'human factor', considered as an element of production: the most complex element, no doubt, but nevertheless one which can be dealt with as such.

In the early part of the twentieth century we thus see the birth of two discourses which divide between them the problem of work, one of them *juridical*, the other *medico-psychological*: two discourses which institute the separation between the *worker* as *subject of rights* and *work* as *object of a science* for which the worker is only a factor; two discourses which organize the partition of production into two relatively distinct entities, the social and the economic. The *social* stands on the side of the *attribution of rights*, of resistance to the logic of production. It sets up the *status* of the worker against the contract which enslaves him to productivity, the solidarity of the employed against the profits of the employer, satisfaction through wages and leisure against the frustration of work. The *economic* stands on the side of the *distribution of forces* for the sake of *productivity*, the rationalization of jobs in the name of profit, the intensification of work in the interest of increased production. From the 1920s on, this new bipolarity governs the definition of sociopolitical issues relating to the organization of production, relegating to a secondary level of importance the older generic discourses on production, political economy and its critic Marxism. The reshaping of the inter-war political landscape can be seen as predicated on the system of relations it is possible to establish between these two new entities. At this time, the dominant perception of these two lines of transformation was as twin figures of progress. To enhance solidarity on the one hand and rationality on the other – did this not amount precisely to the reduction, by two different yet converging methods, of the egotistical role of profit and its irrational consequences which had so ravaged nineteenth-century society? All that is required is to guide the two processes so that from the first one can draw the benefits of the second – so that 'the social wins out over the economic', in Albert Thomas' formula. It will thus become possible to realize an industrial democracy – that hope born in the nineteenth century when the inadequacy of political democracy to deal with the 'social question' became evident. This point of view is shared at this time on a European scale by socialist and social-democrat parties, as well as by the ILO.

For the nascent communist parties, on the other hand, these two new entities signify not the elements of a harmony to be arrived at through the predominance of one term over the other, the growth of solidarity being made the goal of productivity; rather, they are the terms of a contradiction which can only tend to reinforce and intensify the opposition of capital and labour. Industrial rationality is, and (in the capitalist context) can only be, the instrument of profit, a supreme exacerbation of its logic. It brings the total Taylorized proletarianization of all workers; and the alienation this engenders, the worker's sense of his foreignness to the production process, provides its ultimate demonstration. The exercise and extension of workers' rights are consequently of value only in so far as they can thwart this logic, inscribing their contradiction within it. The aim is not to subordinate the economic to the social, but to destroy the economic by mobilizing the social – since it is precisely the latter's status as an end which is at stake.

Corporatism and after

It was against the threat posed by this strategy that all the neo-corporatisms of the inter-war period were directed. Their proponents ranged from right-wing socialists, inspired by Proudhon and Saint-Simon, like Hyacinthe Dubreuil and Maxime Leroy, to the avowed fascists, including on the way neo-socialists like Marcel Déat and H. de Man, the 'new right' of the period (A. Daudieu and the 'ordre nouveau' group), and the version of *spiritualisme* propounded in the journal *Esprit* and the theories of François Perroux.

It is not intended here to lump all these neo-corporatist tendencies together with respect to the extent of their resulting totalitarianism, yet one cannot avoid noticing the considerable resemblance of their initial analyses. They all see the basic evil as lying in the divorce of the worker from his work, a moral rupture which precipitates the demoralization of society. By bringing the worker's interests to bear exclusively on wage levels, this divorce is seen as leading to a process of desocialization and a reinforcement of individualism. Since individual satisfactions are now to be sought only outside of work, pressure is created to extend the sphere of private leisure, pushing up wages to the level necessary to support it. The worker thereby loses his singularity as a producer and becomes merged into an anonymous mass of atomized individuals, whose isolated state lays them open to political manipulation by those who put the blame on the productive system as prime cause of their dissatisfaction. Thus we find a double denunciation in these discourses of the 'American model' which creates this kind of individualism, and the communist model which exploits its consequences, the one following on from the other in a fatal causal chain which it is now seen as necessary to bring to a stop.

All these neo-corporatist thinkers basically propose the same remedy, albeit with endless variations in its proportions and dosages. Since the whole drama follows from the divorce between the worker and work, social rights and industrial rationality, the social and the economic, and since there is little hope to be found in the prospect of their spontaneous harmonization in some distant future, given the likely exploitation of the

258

intervening timespan by a strategy which sets the one element against the other and aggravates their division in order to provoke a final explosion, would it not be better to set about achieving the necessary *rapprochement* at once, to aim at an immediate reconciliation of worker and work? How is this to be done? By imbricating the worker's statutory claims in the demand for a renovated command structure in the enterprise, making possible the re-creation of a community of labour where each individual understands his place in the enterprise, and the enterprise itself attains the status of an institution seen as serving a common idea which transcends the individual – employer and employee alike.

This discourse on 'joy through work' is not a Nazi monopoly. It is equally the product of all these other neo-socialist and neo-traditionalist groups which come during the same period to pose the problem of work. Apart from their common disdain for intellectuals, their hatred of their bourgeois individualism which makes them ignorant of the meaning and beauty of human effort, these neo-corporatist formulae also share with fascism and Nazism the two basic operations which constitute the theme of 'joy through work'. The first of these is the projection on to the new techniques of work of the values of the medieval corporation. New technology, it argues, is not evil in itself, since it serves to organize and discipline effort; the evil lies in the values that have become associated with it and provide the basis for the Marxist analysis of proletarianization. A struggle is therefore called for to vindicate the glory of effort, to bring into being a new 'chivalry of labour' (Hyacinthe Dubreuil, 1941). The second basic operation consists in the reintegration of rights acquired or conquered by workers into the internal functional context of the enterprise, securing their commitment to exercise these rights in a participatory spirit, getting them to assume responsibility themselves for the risks and benefits of the enterprise instead of practising the irresponsibility encouraged by the wage system. Thus the organic unity of the enterprise will be restored and the nation brought together around its effective corporate elements – the business, the community, the region, the family; and so, finally, the movement will be dammed up that threatens to uproot the nation and turn society into a sum of individuals moved by the sole principle of unrestricted pleasure and purposeless enjoyment.

If the theme of separation between worker and work plays this part during the inter-war years in the fabrication of the sociopolitical issues which prepare the Second World War, what corresponding consequences can be seen to follow from this war? How far does it modify the problem posed by this fundamental division?

Two factors characterize the situation of post-war parliamentary democracies, especially of one such as France: the imprint of the fascist experience, and the virtuality of communism. The one acts as a censorship, the other as a threat and a challenge.

The fascist experience carries with it into shared disrepute the themes of nationalism, coporatism and military glorification of effort in work. Against the ideal of the nation, there is now expounded the idea of society. Nationalism bound individuals into corporate entities, mobilized their forces towards the sole aims of might and warfare, operated a ruthless selection among them according to their utility, and practised a 'final solution' for the inadequate. All of this is now rejected. Society, on the contrary, owes it to itself to mobilize whatever can serve to advance the satisfaction of its members, to remove the barriers which limit their interchange, to include rather than exclude. The result is that, while the concern with productivity is retained in the interest of satisfying society's needs, this concern is henceforth linked to the urgent question of its social cost and the need to take care of those whom it eliminates a priori (the unemployable), damages (accidents, illnesses) or discourages (absenteeism, unemployment) – and to bear the costs of this care. Fascist nationalism had made a speciality of the 'final solution' for the inadequate. Victorious democratic society has as its duty both to assist them and to ensure that this assistance does not degrade its recipients but treats them as full citizens. Where the science of work in its initial phase had serenely applied itself to an ever more exact demarcation of aptitudes and inaptitudes, sculpting the living flesh of labour power to obtain optimal efficiency in the *corps productif*, the disciplines which succeed it after the war regard this line of demarcation with misgiving, since they have a foot on either side of it; the double mission with which they are now entrusted inclines them as far as possible to erase it rather than redraw it. And while their predecessors were able to rely on a self-evident definition of health as optimal capacity for work, this very concept of health is now cast under suspicion.

The need for the parliamentary democracies to distance themselves from whatever might directly or indirectly evoke the memory of fascism is all the stronger where it was in these same democracies that fascism and Nazism had emerged in the first place – a fact which the communists do not neglect to cite in their denunciation of merely formal democracy, counterposing the real freedoms of socialist democracies to the illusory character of formal freedoms in parliamentary democracies, and ascribing to these formal limitations these societies' capacity to create the poverty and unemployment which led to fascism. This state of affairs gives rise to the imperative need, forcibly asserted at the end of the war, to join to the declaration of the rights of man the declaration of his social rights, guaranteeing all members of Western societies protection against the material need which illness, accident, old age and unemployment embody in its most sensitive forms. Throughout Europe and notably in France, Sir William Beveridge's report on this question served to inspire the organization of social security. True, guarantees of this kind had already been established in France by the social insurance laws of 1898 and 1930; but they had existed only in restricted forms, providing only for particular categories of worker and acting within the framework of private law, the public authorities intervening only to encourage or enforce this insurantial element in contracts drawn up between particular parties. The objective now was to generalize this protection to cover all members of society and to give it a state administrative organization. This is what has sometimes been called the birth of the 'providential State', and the term is wholly apposite in so far as the operation was made possible by Keynes' 'miraculous' discovery that the attribution of this role to the state was not only a moral duty but an economic remedy. In the inter-war period the social–economic bipolarity had appeared to admit of no possible resolution other than the hegemony of one term over the other or their regressive fusion. A way was now found successfully to articulate them, endowing the disjunction which establishes both terms with its own functional utility. The allocation of state subsidies entailed by the recognition of social rights can serve to stimulate the economy and so, by reducing unemployment, reduce the need for these same rights. How is the level of welfare subventions to be determined? The answer runs that this depends on the conjuncture and becomes chiefly a matter of political choice between those who blame the inadequacies of one factor for the excesses of the other and those who assert the opposite point of view, debate on the question of the economic cost of the social sphere comes to occupy the forefront of political argument.

The social cost of productivity on the one hand, the economic cost of the social on the other: if one retraces the transformations operated since the Liberation on these two lines of preoccupation, a cumulative modification can be seen to take effect in both the status of the worker and that of work. At the point of convergence of these two tendencies, it will be possible for us to locate the site of emergence of the new discourse on 'pleasure in work'.

THE SOCIAL COST OF PRODUCTIVITY

Before the war, the (physiological and psychological) science of work had dealt only with the healthy person, concentrating on the detection of his aptitudes and their utilization in such a way as to achieve his optimal adaptation to his work. Psychiatry's concern had been inversely limited to the detection and treatment of sick or abnormal persons. The principle of demarcation between the sick and the healthy had been provided here by work. The self-evident character of this distinction came to evaporate after the war under the influence of a further new discipline, the psychopathology of work, itself the product of an encounter between industrial doctors and psychologists on the one side and psychiatrists and ergotherapists on the other.

This encounter arose out of the war itself and the appetite for reform which followed it. During its years of embattled isolation, Britain had found itself obliged to mobilize its total productive resources and to succeed at putting to work men and women whom a short while earlier it would have been judged inappropriate or dangerous to employ in production. At a stroke, the previously instituted frontier of entry to the world of work came to appear an altogether relative affair, while at the same time the use of techniques of rehabilitation and reintegration came to seem a more profitable policy than the simple recourse to invalidity payments which had previously prevailed. Elsewhere, the reforming spirit abroad in psychiatric circles in the immediate post-war period led to a new accent being given to the possibilities of resocializing the mentally ill, and to the effectiveness of ergotherapy in readapting them to working life. The coming together of these psychiatrists with doctors working in industry prompted the perception which inaugurates the psychopathology of work: if the frontier between aptitude and inaptitude can be made so relative, and if work can (as some say) make people ill, and yet (as others say) can also heal, should it not be concluded that work in itself is neither a good nor an evil, and that its effect on the individual depends on its meaningfulness for the worker and the circumstances by which this is determined: the framework of relationships in which the worker is placed which define work for him as either meaningful or meaningless and thus make it the bearer either of health or of illness?

And so, without repudiating the task of detecting aptitudes, the psychopathology of work connects it with a second register of concepts where emphasis is placed on the subject's response to work, the way his behaviour can reflect its lack of perceived meaning (conceived in such terms as compensation, overcompensation and decompensation). The objectives assigned to this new science by the public authorities were the prevention of those phenomena which the positivistic pre-war science of aptitudes had proved unable to deal with on its own (industrial accidents, absenteeism, alcoholism), together with the treatment and rehabilitation of the handicapped. This new mission was inaugurated in France in the 1950s through the co-operation of the school of psychopathology of work at ELAN with doctors such as Claude Weil, Sivadou and Amiel. Collaborating with ergotherapists, ergonomists and industrial doctors, this current prompted a series of two decades of reforms in the treatment of the handicapped, the prevention of industrial accidents and the combating of absenteeism, with each reform tending in its own way to break down the existing distinction between the normal and the pathological in the world of work.

The impact of the psychopathology of work on the treatment of the handicapped can be summed up as a formula for enlarging the field of application of the notion 'handicap', discrediting the rival concepts of 'invalidity' and 'maladjustment' (*inadaptation*) and establishing on the terrain thus vacated a space of uninterrupted traffic extending from the most 'gratuitous' forms of therapeutic occupation to fully productive and profitable work. A law passed in 1957 officially replaced the term 'invalidity' by that of 'handicap', at the same time encouraging businesses (with the help of financial incentives) to employ a certain percentage of handicapped labour. The term 'invalidity' is rejected here precisely because of its incompatibility with a policy of readaptation. 'Invalidity' is mutilating, derogatory, negative; it connotes an irreversible loss, whereas 'handicap' leaves intact the idea of a functional objective, drawing attention to intervening difficulties only in order to help in their compensation by mobilizing the subject's innate capacity, when aided by a favourable environment, to discover compensatory powers of his own when work is offered to him as a goal – that orientation towards an end which acts as the crucial factor in the fulfilment of working man: the end in question being here, precisely, the overcoming of his handicap.

Universal handicap

With the further law passed in 1975 (called the law 'in favour of the handicapped'), it is the turn for the notion of 'maladjustment' to be declared obsolete on the grounds of its imprecision and ineffectiveness. A handicap admits of clear definition in relation to a job requiring specific aptitudes. The notion of maladjustment, in contrast, is defined in relation to society. But is this not to use too general a criterion, making society into too exacting, too exclusive rather than inclusive an instance? Is not the socially maladjusted person actually the person who rejects unsatisfactory social conditions, conditions that is to say which effectively handicap his possibilities for normal socialization? Why not instead broaden the notion of handicap from its initial restrictive meaning as a diminution of working capacity, into that of a general concept covering those factors which inhibit an individual's insertion into society? And this in a sense is what the 1975 law does, by grouping all these disruptive physical and mental factors together in a single theory of '*deficits*', for which a varied repertory of available solutions can be employed.

This policy of readaptation, because it prioritizes insertion over selection – or rather, because it sets out to add to the machinery of selection an additional mechanism serving to compensate selection's effect as exclusion – leads to a rethinking of the zones of treatment for what had hitherto been a population excluded from work, reorganizing them into a graded series of modes of intervention and establishing a continuous, progressive terrain for the management of relations between man and work.

Thus it becomes possible to progress, depending on the results the individual attains, from the compartment of purely therapeutic work (gymnastics, kynaestherapy, body training and group activities) to the semi-therapeutic sector of light domestic labour whose only real purpose is to act as a basis for sociotherapy; then on to organized activities, the creation of artistic or craft objects suitable for commercial sale; after which, thanks to this motivating experience, there is the step to the industrial training sector and habituation (or rehabituation) to normal rates and hours of work. This prepares the way for the assessment phase and appropriate job placement, leading to the final stage, productive work in either a sheltered workshop or a 'real' factory. The role of the doctor as manager of handicap ceases here at the factory gate; at most, he enters there only to help arrange certain jobs reserved for the severely handicapped. And yet – in the light of his own desire and calling, and in order to fulfil the other component of the mission entrusted him, namely to prevent such handicaps from occurring – ought he not also to take on the task of designing and arranging *all* job positions, so that the 'mildly handicapped' individuals who make up a large proportion of the working population will be able to perform their tasks without experiencing unnecessary difficulty and strain? For is not the way this notion of handicap is currently understood still too closely dependent on a corresponding notion of normality? What is the significance of the fact that hardly any women aged over thirty can be found working on production lines, and very few French workers aged over forty?[2] Could one not say that such data point to a handicap experienced by these groups in relation to such work?

The present, doubtless highly provisional outcome of this process is that a strangely circular quality is becoming apparent in the mechanisms it produces. For if we are invited on the one hand to 'give a hearing to the handicapped person who defines himself not just by a lack but by a difference that can enrich us, an appeal, a mode of being which can uplift us',[3] conversely the lack of enthusiasm manifested for the more disagreeable forms of manual labour is itself coming to be designated as the manifestation of a latent handicap to which we need likewise to pay attention. Given there is already a 'therapy for the normal', would it not be possible to conceive of an extension of techniques of care to the non-handicapped?

The prevention of industrial accidents offers another example of this erasure of the frontier between the normal and the pathological, and the consequent tendency towards intervention in the organization of work. At the Liberation, the first programmes of accident prevention were still marked by the man–machine distinction inherited from Taylorism. That is to say, they are geared on the one hand to the rectification of a human situation by identifying in advance those individuals who seem pre-disposed to cause accidents and, on the other, to progressive improvements to machinery through the addition of protective screens or other such devices. The overall principle in classifying the cause of accidents is the identification of a specific responsible factor, deducing preventive techniques accordingly. Safety thus constitutes a discipline independent in its conception both of the content of the work process itself and of the previous training of workers who fail to observe necessary safety procedures.

This conception of safety begins to change in the late 1950s, as a result of collaboration between doctors and ergonomists who put forward a joint theory of man–machine systems where the foregoing dichotomy between technique and psychology, machine and human factor is elimi-nated, giving way to globalized conception of productive operations (Ambredane and Faverge; Montmollin). Here it is no longer the deficiency of a man or a machine that needs to be identified, nor is there a responsibility to be imputed to the one or the other. Rather, what has to be detected is the process of degradation of a functioning system in order that this can be arrested before an accident ensues. The whole sequence of the productive process needs to be rethought so that these dysfunctions can be averted. At their origin stands the occurrence of some incident attributable not in any precise sense to man or machine alone but only to an inadequate conjunction of the two; this incident provokes an amplify-ing series of disruptive effects on other links in the chain of production which ends by provoking an accident. Beneath the apparent causes, beneath the non-observance of safety regulations, there lies a complex situation involving poor communication and lack of precision in com-mand and execution, deficiencies of organization which need to be dealt with if accidents are to be prevented.

This conception of accidents involved a change in the whole of preventive thinking; above all, instead of the assignment of direct responsibility (with all the sociopolitical repercussions this latter notion entails), it meant enlisting the co-operation of all the agents of production towards the discovery of an accident-process. And at this point it came to be realized that workers' disposition to respect safety mechanisms was in exact proportion to their degree of work satisfaction. Their involvement in the collective pursuit of safety worked properly only when workers had a sense of their own competence being duly recognized, of good relations with and among their supervisors, and of actually being allowed the possibility to reflect on the operation of their work. Thus it was found to be impossible to expect a qualitative shift of thresholds in accident prevention without at the same time initiating measures towards a revalorization of work and working relationships.

Similar conclusions soon came to be drawn regarding the question of absenteeism. In the 1960s employers continued attempting to combat absenteeism by treating it as a straightforward matter of laziness, to be dealt with by the same methods that Taylor had prescribed for raising productivity, namely the introduction of bonuses – in this case, a 'health bonus' which was basically only a variant kind of bonus for assiduity. But this tactic continued to treat as sacrosanct the distinction between sickness and non-sickness and the connection between health and work. During the 1970s two causes brought about the overthrow of this certainty, or what remained of it. First there was the emergence of what Rousselet called the 'work allergy', especially marked among younger workers in the early 1970s. This passive refusal to work, the diminished role accorded by individuals to work in the organization of their life, the fact of work becoming for many just a means of procuring oneself extra cash and maintaining one's benefit entitlement without becoming exposed to special investigations or compulsory retraining measures; all this gave absenteeism the quality of a collective attitude, against which it became necessary to elaborate a strategic position.

A law passed in 1975 provided for the extension of monthly wage payment to all wage-earners. This law affected the status of large numbers of workers, especially in the northern region of France. It introduced an important change in social insurance for wage-earners: whereas sick-pay had previously been fixed at 50 per cent of normal wages, paid by the Social Security, a second 50 per cent now had to be paid by the employer. This led to an organized reaction by employers when the implementation of the law was followed by a sudden growth in sick leave. Recourse was had to 'medical militias' such as the Securex Company, which hired doctors to make 'counter-visits' to workers on sick leave, thereby cutting the level of 'abuse'. This practice, scandalous enough in the way it set two different groups of doctors at loggerheads, thus casting suspicion on the credentials of their profession, served at least to provoke a debate whose major casualty was the notion of sickness in the domain of work. For what can the meaning be here of the distinction between sickness and non-sickness if, given the same pathological symptoms, some people go to work and others do not? If one chooses to speak of absenteeism for the one group, would it not be equally reasonable to speak of 'presenteeism' in the case of the others? And, as *social* reactions, how can either be evaluated in terms of health? How far is it possible to decide as to the seriousness or otherwise of a worker's assessment of his own state of health when he tells the doctor he feels too tired or unwell to go to work, if the non-acceptance of his discourse is followed within a short span of time by the occurrence of an industrial accident? And if women workers, and mothers in particular, practise a form of absenteeism with no consistent corresponding medical symptom, would it not be better to combat absenteeism by providing crèches and day-care centres, rather than by means of medical repression?

The uncertainty which weighs on the notion of sickness here thus converges with the embarrassment caused by the problem of 'work allergy'. If medical criteria no longer suffice to deal with attitudes to work by policing the boundary line between those who are obliged to work and those who must be allowed to rest; if what ultimately seems to be the crucial factor in inclination to work is the existence of a positive meaning in work for the worker, then the enhancement of this attractive element, the enrichment of jobs and work relationships, now comes to look like the best available remedy for absenteeism.

Beyond Taylorism

Reintegration of the handicapped, prevention of accidents, exorcism of absenteeism: these objectives lead the psychopathology of work, in developing the solutions it comes to propose, to construct the framework of a social pathology of the enterprise. Recently retracing the history of this discipline, Sivaudon drew from it the following contemporary lesson:

> The real problem now is no longer one of prevention and rehabilitation, but one of understanding the factors which determine the actual purpose of work. Work is accepted just in so far as it has meaning for the worker. When this meaning is a positive one, the worker is able to accomplish his personal self-development; when it is unfavourable, it sets off mechanisms of defence and resistance; if these mechanisms are unable to operate, it puts at risk the mental health of the individual and the productivity of the enterprise.

Thus the accident rate in an enterprise and the level of absenteeism become indicators of the enterprise's own social and economic health, since they enter into the measurement of its productive capacity. The institution of 'social audits' takes account of this analysis. A recent law requires businesses to draw up a social audit whose principal components are the levels of wage differential between different job categories and between men and women; the length of working hours and level of absenteeism; rates of accidents and industrial diseases; and the scale of effort devoted to worker training and job enrichment. Here, in this organized balance sheet where the social cost of productivity is set against the efforts of an enterprise to reduce this cost, the psychopathology of work comes into contact with another line of transformation of the world of work, arising out of the enterprise itself and developments in managerial techniques.

There are in fact two different lines involved here: the first of these is public, financed by the state; its point of departure is in the administration of the enterprise's 'social wastage' (*déchets*), the problem of its cost to society. It gives the highest priority to the question of safety, and hence comes (by way of a problematic akin to that of existential psychoanalysis) to encounter the problem of the meaningfulness of work; where it poses the problem of productivity this is in relation to the effects, the logical consequences of the safety problem. The second line of discussion emerges inside the private sector and is financed by business; its point of departure relates to problems concerning the internal functioning of the enterprise and the objectives of optimizing conditions and reducing costs so as to raise productivity; where it concerns itself with the status of the industrial worker, this is to the extent that the worker is prone to forms of behaviour which deviate from the purposes of the enterprise. It handles this latter question on the basis of a behavioural/behaviourist problematic; it raises the question of safety, but does so within the context of a preoccupation with increasing productivity.

The history of this latter series of discussions is relatively well known, so we need only briefly summarize its succeeding stages here as these arrive one by one from America with the introduction into business of the science of management. First, in the early 1950s, the technique of public relations puts forward an interpretation of functional disturbances in the enterprise as simply effects of a lack of human communication, capable of being remedied by the inculcation from above of an art of human relations and good contacts. This is followed by the school of social systems, which points out the relative lack of success of this first perspective, seeing its cause in the failure of this art of communication to recognize the different and sometimes antagonistic ways in which different social agents perceive their environment. The way to reduce dysfunctionings in the enterprise is consequently argued to lie in a system of communication which recognizes the ineluctable nature of these differences of perception, and proceeds on that basis to conduct a search for compromise solutions. But this remains still a matter of communication, a concern that is with changing the *ambiance*, the atmosphere of social relations of production, rather than acting directly on the relations themselves. The latest arrival among these schools of management, that of sociotechnical systems, starts out from a critique of this notion of 'atmosphere'. It sees 'atmosphere' as like a kind of drug which has to be prescribed in ever increasing doses in order to achieve ever smaller effects and benefits. If one wants to bring about a change in relations to work, it argues, this will not be achieved by the provision of extra incentives to work, but by transforming work itself, placing the worker in a position where he can arrive by himself at the satisfaction of his basic needs. For what is the need which makes itself everywhere felt, once the most elementary of needs have been satisfied, if not the need for self-organization, *societal* need? By developing autonomous work-teams which manage their own division of labour, rhythms of work and consequent levels of remuneration, the enterprise can put an end once and for all to the distorted relationship between worker and work which has been the bane of efficient management of production.

Between the social audit introduced by the psychopathology of work with a view to cutting the social cost of productivity, and the 'societal need' defined by the new schools of business management, it is possible to see the perfect adequation of a *diagnosis* and a *remedy*, the instauration of a new-found totality and the promise of utopia finally made real . . . However, the effect of the application of these two notions is (evidently) not the suppression of the imperative of productivity *per se* but – and this is none the less very important – a change in the *status* of this demand. The Taylorist conception of productivity involved the reduction of a man to a factor of production, and the reduction as far as possible of the place occupied by this factor. But this absolutism of productivity had led both to resistance within the enterprise, and to injurious social side-effects which imposed a heavy cost on the collectivity as a whole. The introduction of the social audit and of 'societal need' does not enable either of these consequences to be eliminated. But what it does provide is a set of terms which make it possible to measure with negotiable precision the cost and degree of acceptability of the socially harmful side-effects on the one hand, and the reduction of resistances engendered in the enterprise on the other. Thanks to these two new notions, productivity can become a phenomenon capable of being negotiated by the enterprise with the other two 'social partners' involved: the representatives of the collectivity, who intervene on account of production's injurious ecological and sociological effects, and are in a position to weigh up these effects against the corresponding cost of compensatory subsidies or tax rebates; and the representatives of the workforce, who wield the threat of various methods for restricting production, and with whom the enterprise can assess the feasibility of formulae for pay increases against the calculated cost to it of such action. The novelty of this conception of productivity resides entirely in its ability to include the human factor in its calculations, instead of excluding it as much as possible, as was the case with Taylorism. 'Pleasure in work' means the capacity attributed to each individual – or rather, the injunction issued to each individual – to negotiate the measure of meaning he wishes to give to his life, and the share of destruction that society is prepared to tolerate on his behalf, against the necessity of maintaining productivity in a world where economic competition becomes ever more bitter.

THE ECONOMIC COST OF THE SOCIAL

The foundation of the French social security system in 1945 was based on two essential principles. The first was the suppression of previous restrictions on the payment of social benefits, the centralized management of all benefits through a single organization, enabling all welfare guarantees thus to be predicated on the notion of a single 'social risk'. Provision for a particular need is no longer to be confined within the old individual, contractual framework of the insurance schemes created in the 1930s, but is to become (or is intended to become) an equal right for all. This right is no longer to be linked directly and individually to the world of work; it is to be linked to the collectivity, its object being in the first instance to maintain the individual's capacity for subsequent employment. The second great principle is that state management of these benefits is intended to make them into an effective tool for a policy of social progress, within the framework of a general policy for the maintenance of economic equilibrium. The state organization of contributions and benefits is designed to make possible a social redistribution of wealth leading to greater equality of incomes and, above all, to an improved relationship between savings and consumption.

Less than ten years had elapsed before his scheme began to show signs of delapidation, and active opposition arose to this conception of the providential state. In 1963 the report on the Budget by the Finance Committee of the National Assembly pointed to an alarming deficit in the social security fund. And, even more significantly, at the time of the preparation the following year of the fifth national Five-Year Economic Plan, a forecast of the social security position in 1970 indicated a likely growth in expenditure twice as rapid as that of the gross domestic product. So the system established at the Liberation, rather than harmonizing as intended the relations between the economic and the social, appeared to be disrupting them by allowing an uncontrolled rate of increase in the consumption of social benefits. A system which had been meant to simplify economic and social policy making proved to have an inflationary logic of its own which steadily disconnected it from the real state of production.

Consideration of the causes of this phenomenon led to renewed questioning of the two basic principles of social security. Social security supposed to organize the social redistribution of wealth. But why expect it to succeed in this where taxation itself had failed? The development of special compensation schemes had enabled demographically favoured socio-professional groups to provide themselves with a protective regime vastly superior to that enjoyed by others (certain growing industries as against other declining ones; management in particular, and industry in general, as against craft and rural occupations). And, if the state does not want these disparities to become too flagrant, it is obliged to add its own compensatory provisions, thus further contributing to the inflation of social expenditure. Social security had been intended to administer insurance of needs on the basis of a unitary concept of social risk. Yet was this not what was making a concerted social policy impossible to execute? Social expenditure falls into three main categories: sickness insurance, family benefits, industrial accidents. The separate assessment of expenditure under each of these headings resulted in the necessity of drawing on the resources of one sector in order to make good, as far as was possible, the deficit of another. For example the massive growth of sickness insurance expenditure obliged inroads to be made into funds earmarked for family benefits. Accounting policy rapidly comes to take the place of general policy, thus preventing, for example, the formation of any coherent social policy for the family. What with the workings of external social disparities which lead to inflated expenditure, and the workings of internal accounting disparities which obstruct the formation of policy, social security comes to look like an uncontrollable process which at once throws everything into a position of dependence on the state, and prevents the state from being able to apply any kind of coherent doctrine to it.

What is to be done? Should one abandon the general system of social protection, limiting the role of the state to an assistance scheme reserved for the least favoured, and leaving the collectivity to deal autonomously with its own problems? Or should one instead launch a vigorous new social policy which widens the recognition of needs so as for example to make possible a workable social policy for women, developing family schemes and new community facilities, and a policy for the aged which is not just an automatic function of the work they have done, but relates to the context they live in, the different needs they represent? These differing lines of argument in the debates of the 1960s in fact pose a challenge to a common target: the juridical conception of need, and the statutory conception of the subject which this entails, the position it assigns to the subject as simultaneously a beneficiary and a claimant. The price paid by society for this strictly statutory position of the subject is its inability to draw on the subject's own autonomous resources, or to mobilize the subject's sense of collective responsibility.

Now while there can (arguably) be no serious question in a democracy of going back on rights which have once been recognized, the reflections fuelled by this crisis of social security did play a large role in fostering the new neo-liberal philosophy of successive governments whose political decisions consistently tended to inflect the juridical and rights-oriented character of social policy towards the twin themes of individual autonomy and collective responsibility. This political shift gives rise to new policies for employment and health.

The crisis provoked during the 1960s by the question of social security involved two key factors: the widening gap between production and social expenditure, and the inflation in sickness insurance costs. The former disparity was all the more blatant because, while the state actually had the responsibility for administering the entirety of benefit distributions, it had no effective hold on the labour market, 90 per cent of which was operated outside its own services. And the labour market was working badly. Business, now operating in the context of the EEC and intensive restructuring of industry, complained of a shortage of manpower, especially in skilled categories, while the unions at the same time were pointing to the signs of rising unemployment. What were the real needs here that had to be met? To raise unemployment benefits and assistance, or to adapt the labour force to this transformation of industry? Where did the basic evil lie, if not in the subject's statutory rigidity, the attitude of preferring a position already gained to a desirable transformation, of preferring even unemployment to a job not strictly in accord with the subject's status and rights? The establishment of continued retraining schemes follows from this perception, and from a resolve to break down the growing separation between the domain of social benefits and that of production, combating the costly heritage of a restrictively statutory conception of the subject by appealing to the adaptive autonomy of the individual.

The other major element of the crisis was the inflation of expenditure on sickness insurance. This was by far the heaviest form of welfare cost, the one which unbalanced all the rest. But while the level of this expenditure indicates an irreversible recognition in our societies of the value of health, and while its overall cost cannot in principle be cut, it was – the argument ran – at least feasible, and even necessary, to treat health as a matter of concerted policy. Options and priorities could be brought to bear which would, at least in the matter of prevention, take account of the costs of sickness to the economy as a whole. To combat the irresponsibility of the subject, health campaigns are to be addressed to the whole population, accompanied by selective programmes of action aimed at particular social groups defined in terms of the greater pathological risk they present and the cost they impose on the collectivity.

Perpetual training

Continued retraining (*formation permanente*), instituted in 1971 by Jacques Delors, at that time a policy adviser to the premier Jacques Chaban-Delmas under President Pompidou proposes a co-ordinated response to two separate pressures: the public authorities' demand to reduce the costly burden imposed by the social subject's posture as a claimant, and the employers' aim of transforming workforce attitudes to the enterprise in view of the constantly growing role of technology in production costs.

The first of these requirements is perfectly expressed in the inaugural declaration made by B. Schwartz in 1971:

> The objective of *Formation Permanente* is to make every person capable of becoming an agent of change, capable that is of an improved understanding of the technical, cultural and social world that surrounds him, and of acting upon and changing the structures within which he lives. It aims to give everyone an awareness of his power as an active being; it aims to make people autonomous, capable that is of grasping their situation and understanding their environment, of influencing it and understanding the mutual interplay of society's evolution and their own, of becoming able to react to evolution and mutation in society.

In other words, it is a question of changing people's attitudes to change, in order also to change their attitudes to society and public power. And to do this, one needs to give people both the means and the inclination to adopt an active attitude in this process of change, rather than passively submitting to it while at the same time demanding compensations from the public power, which are necessary only in consequence of this incapacity for change. *Formation permanente* must therefore literally be a continuous process of retraining, from the cradle to the grave, designed to provide the individual with a feeling of autonomy in relation to work, and at work. It has to break down the split within the subject between a world of work, which is disagreeable but confers an identity and rights, and that other world external to work, which is protected by the law and yet has no real value in itself, serving merely as a costly and futile compensation. For example, the state of retirement, with its ambiguous character as at once reward and decline, as the object simultaneously of demands aimed at enlarging its importance and duration, and of the psychological attitudes of rejection to which old age is exposed: there is a possible theme here which *formation permanente* can address, with a view to altering the paradoxical situation where society is obliged to support a still able-bodied worker for whom active life has become unbearable. Continued retraining will make it possible to see life itself as a continuous progression, in which 'each age group has its own values to be respected, expressed, promoted and lived'. Retirement might come in such a context to be lived not as the recollection of a sacrificed lifetime and the prospect of an existence condemned to end in death, but 'a living image of the future, enabling younger age groups to see the effects of our social logic. Retirement, the laboratory of the future'.[4]

To understand the second set of demands, those posed by the employers, the most pertinent documents to read are the reports produced by the employers' own organizations, and by the OECD, during the 1960s. Here we learn how the balance between technology and manpower is beginning to shift in favour of technology, while at the same time this new and more expensive technology has a steadily shortening working life and the rate of machine obsolescence is rapidly rising. This opens up the prospect of new staffing policies adapted to the steady rise in the cost of labour, coupled with the necessity of adapting workforce attitudes to technological progress, making workers psychologically capable of accepting permanent change in the level and content of industrial skills.

A new juridical formula was invented for the creation of *formation permanente* which enabled these respective public and industrial aspirations to be brought together within a single organizationsl schema. This involves giving every worker the right to undergo – within certain time limits, of course – some form of retraining. A right: yet was it not a major element in the demands we have been outlining precisely to limit the role of rights? However, the right to continued retraining actually has the peculiarity of not being assignable to either of the two major juridical categories namely those of private and public law. If the force and importance of juridical institutions naturally resides in the distinction between that which belongs to the sphere of the individual's private freedom and that which belongs to the sphere of action of the public power, we may say that the establishment of permanent retraining constitutes a local instance of a manifest process of mutation of law over the past thirty years, towards the breaking down of this distinction between private and public, and thus also towards the decline of the legal element in the government of social relations. For while permanent retraining is a right bestowed on the individual, it is actually a right defined in such a way that it can only be given effect via social mediation: that is, through the agreement of the social partners to employ the services of some training agency approved by the public authorities. The formula thus enforces a conciliation of the two major motives which had inspired the birth of *formation permanente*.

In concrete terms, the two parties to the decision, employers and unions, invested quite different hopes in the possibility of continued retraining. For the unions, the principal interest lay in being able to open up access for workers to higher education, enabling them to benefit from this culture which had previously been reserved for an elite. But the university was too remote from the industrial world and too reluctant to take on this role; moreover, the employers themselves blocked this line of development. They preferred instead to use the private training institutions set up since the early 1950s for the purpose of recycling managerial personnel and disseminating managerial techniques. But these psycho-sociological techniques, geared to the functions of supervisory staffs, were too obviously allied to the interests of employers to be acceptable to the unions. Both universities and managerial training institutions did in fact come to play a part in *formation permanente*, but one which was limited by their propensity to satisfy only one or other of the partners. Instead the major beneficiaries of the continued retraining law, those who were able to satisfy the demand for joint consent and meet its inherent objectives, were the exponents of what Robert Castel has called the 'new psychological culture':[5] body-language gurus, human potential experts, transactional analysis, etc. It was of small consequence whether such imported techniques were invented *ad hoc*, or adapted to suit their new clientele. What counted was that they fulfilled the law's intentions by accepting the market logic it set up, simultaneously satisfying the two requirements which the law had decreed to be compatible. The content of these discourses, their wide variety and even greater versatility, can be entirely accounted for in terms of the kind of new 'loophole' or angle of vision which the law opens up, which can be summarized as follows: how is it possible to fabricate an object which at once has a seductive look answering to people's actual desires (since there is no obligation for anyone to take it up), is capable of being regarded as relevant and realistic (since we are concerned with the world of production), and can be made plausible in terms of commercial logic (since it is exposed to conditions of market competition)? In a situation of this kind, the quality of the product lies not so much in its intrinsic content as in its capacity to replicate the requirements stated above and reconcile them within a single package. The packaging itself can, and indeed must, be varied, in order for the product not to be reducible to a content whose meagreness would reveal it as mere discourse. What is actually at issue is the production of something altogether different from a discourse – a transformation, a point of coalescence of the position of the subject and the order of social relations of production. It does not signify the mechanical subordination of the one to the other, but rather the act of placing both terms on one and the same footing of truth. At first glance one would be tempted to see these products as bastardized offshoots of Marxism or psychoanalysis, and indeed they themselves are not averse to references in these directions. But this is not the important point; or rather, what one really has is the exact opposite. Psychoanalysis had said: there is a truth in each one of us, emergent in childhood, repressed in memory, a truth of which our own singular histories are at once the product and the secret. Marxism had said: there are forces that bear us, forces stronger than the strongest of us, and it is their truth which we have to decipher beneath the appearances of social relations. But what the new technicians say, or rather what they deploy as their own new certainty, is that no truth inheres either in the subject or in history, that the subject subsists only in his capacities, that he is a potential to be realized, not a truth to be deciphered; and that history is a myth since reality lies only in the environment that surrounds us, in the organized forms of our social relations which it is for us to modify according to the capacity change offers us to realize ourselves more fully; that therefore there is no truth other than the more or less successful fulfilment, in the here and now, of this double requirement. Between the economic and the social, between the private and the public, these techniques thus posit an intermediate plane of resolution through action designed to overturn the statutory position of the subject, that sort of juridical shelter for the reign of imagination, extraverting the subject towards a world of possibilities that exhaust imagination.

The cost of life

A similar postulation of the irrationality of the social–economic distinction acted as the point of departure for the health policies developed in the 1960s following the discovery of the alarming rate of growth of health insurance spending. Sound socioeconomic sense in the domain of employment means first of all assessing the relative cost of hiring an individual as against that of sacking one, and then adopting an appropriate coherent policy for employment and training. Does not similar good sense in the domain of health begin when one compares the cost of an individual in terms of the sum of social and health-care investment he embodies, the cost of his loss, and what he produces: that is to say, the gross value of his product? This of course means observing the distinction between the cost of a life (the sum of money technically necessary to preserve it) and its price (the sum actually spent in doing so). The only difference here from the case of employment is that, whereas there we had a right attributed to the individual whose realization depended on social mediation, here on the contrary we have a social instance, a central social plan, whose effectuation depends on a mobilization of the individual.

To introduce the principle of economy into health policy means asking two kinds of question about the allocation of priorities: a 'how' and a 'who' – selecting the most cost-effective modes of action, and deciding on the level of priority to be given to different categories of individual, in the light of the effect on the economy of their disability. Thus one gets a picture, in descending order of costs, of the impact of sickness on the economy, from adults where loss in terms of the cost of care is added to the lost value of their arrested productivity; children, expenditure on whom constitutes a short-term cost but a long-term investment; and lastly, the old, where illness has no incidence on production and the cost of care amounts to pure loss. From this observation there results an official policy aimed at keeping as many of the elderly as possible at home (by developing facilities for home help and home care), since this is what the elderly themselves prefer and, above all, because it is vastly cheaper. There also results an unofficial policy, not openly avowed but administratively practised, of rapidly excluding from state-insured medicine the treatment of elderly persons needing long-term hospital care, thereby obliging them to draw on their own assets to pay for what is often highly expensive treatment, and frequently obliging people to sell a house or apartment to which, once finally cured, they are then unable to return to live.[6] Such selection of priorities according to criteria of medical economy also means identifying those individuals for whom the most favourable relationship obtains between the cost of care and the corresponding benefit in health, those cases in other words where concerted treatment can make an actual saving in the cost of production of health care. This involves thinking in terms of target groups, classifying populations according to the modes of care specifically appropriate for them, thus enabling these modes of care to be more rationally distributed so as to forestall the most expensive consequences in subsequent individual treatment of illness.

The second main principle of medical economics is the selection of methods of care which carry the best rate of return on their cost. This is the origin of those 'integrated schemes' which enable a single initiative to address simultaneously a number of different objectives. The most successful example of this approach is that of maternity care and child protection, which entrusts to a single apparatus equipped with a range of medical, preventive and social resources the objectives of reducing perinatal mortality, advance detection of mental, physical and social handicaps, and family education in child-rearing techniques, allocating to each case appropriate levels of associated financial and technical support.

On a general level, prevention clearly comes to assume the highest priority, turning the national territory into a field for planned policies of vaccination, regulation and control, and making society into the site of mobilization of each individual for the management of his own health and promotion of community responsiveness to health problems (users' committees, collective self-help, etc.).

Thus it is as though the classical contract between doctor and patient comes to be backed by a second contract between the state and the individual for shared economic management of sickness and health. Sickness is the concern of the state, which knows its cost to society, its distribution in society, the social factors which tend to produce it and the means of its prevention, here enlisting the collaboration of its citizens; health is the concern of the individual, his efforts to stay healthy, his psychology. While still operating through the old doctor–patient contract, this new contract also casts a certain suspicion on it. Under the old contract, sickness confers a right and demands a remedy. Under the new contract, sickness has meaning only in terms of its cost, while health is made a matter of civic responsibility. The doctor–patient relationship is thus laid open to doubts regarding the patient's possible abuse of his rights and the doctor's perhaps inordinately prompt or accommodating intervention. So that the discourses on the crisis of medicine can be understood equally as programming the liquidation of a right in favour of a dual mechanism of anticipatory prevention and guidance, and as prescribing a therapeutic relationship designed to induce the subject to assume responsibility for his own health.

The crisis opened up by the alarming gap between the development of the economy and that of social expenditure, between work and 'happiness', thus comes to be blocked at both ends at once: by the creation with continued retraining of a new right which articulates the old, over-rigid system of social rights on to the demands of the economy; and by the introduction through the new health policies of an economic imperative in the management of those same social rights. To the old Keynesian concept of state administration of the social to promote economic equilibrium, there thus succeeds the neo-liberal idea of an economic administration of the social which links it up in a closed circular relationship with the economy. This does not, as has sometimes been claimed, signify the end of the social, but rather its transfiguration through the integration of an economic constraint which, by breaking down the juridicial status of the subject by the dual tactic of autonomizing the individual and returning responsibility to the collectivity, elevates the social instance to the status of a subject of history. The site of decision making – in full knowledge of the relevant facts – now comes to reside within the social instance. To give a single example: if in former times populationist discourses demanded more children in the sacred names of Family, Work and Fatherland, today's discourse enjoins on the subject nothing but autonomy and cold calculation in weighing up the maintenance of one's level of social benefits against the 'planned' conception of a third child.

CONCLUSION

We have been retracing two lines. The first of these was centred on the enterprise and the social costs exacted by productivity. It discovered the role of a major cause for the high, continuing and oppressive burden of these costs: the lack of meaning of work for the worker. Here the internal preoccupation of the enterprise with increasing productivity inspired the invention of formulae for working conditions which take increased account of an innate need for autonomous organization. The second line was centred on the state and its need to control the economic costs of the nation's social expenditure. It leads firstly to the adjustment of the regime of social rights to bring them into line with economic requirements by means of continued retraining techniques, and secondly the penetration of the economic register into this sphere of social rights through the new health policies and the thoroughgoing rationalization of social policy management.

The intersection of these two lines of transformation sets up a series of correspondences which operate on two distinct levels. On one level, by 'setting free' the worker's productive capacity *formation permanente* breaks down his retractile statutory posture *vis-à-vis* the logic of production. This helps to render the worker more amenable to schemes for enhancing working conditions to take account of his 'societal need', enabling these new formulae to be put into application according to their economic pertinence and the measure of assured certainty that they will serve not to enlarge the worker's margin of resistance to the logic of production, but on the contrary to make him participate in it more fully. On a second level, the new health policies convert the social audit of enterprises into instruments for socially mobilizing individuals towards savings in the cost of health care and collaboration in their pursuit. The lack of meaningfulness in work finds its compensation through the promotion of the civic meaning of prevention, the transferring of responsibility to the individual and the invitation to autonomy – objectives which are also promoted by *formation permanente*.

In this manner a principle of continuity, an unbroken circularity, is established between the register of production and productivity, and that of the sanitary and social administration of society. In principle this seems to match the idea of the corporatist state – but with a difference which the foregoing analysis has sought to measure and explain. It is not a question here of creating joy through work (nor joy despite work), but of producing pleasure *and* work, and, so as better to realize this design, of producing the one *in* the other. It is not a question of realizing the social through the economic (nor against the economic), but of conjoining the two, in the interests of their greater efficiency and lesser cost. Pleasure in work diverts people from individual egoism as much as from nationalistic hysteria, putting before them instead a model of happiness in an updated, corrected social domain, where attention to the social costs of technique and to techniques for reducing the cost of the social create the possibility and necessity for a new social concert, in which the effacement of the juridical status of the subject removes inhibitions about his participation.

What is the significance of the recent inflated social currency of psychological techniques and discourses? What is the signification of the dissolution of certainties which hitherto grounded the distinction between sickness and health? We can say, at least on the level at which we have been studying this problem here, that what is involved is a mobilization (in every sense of the word), rather than a reinforcement, of the psychological subject: the crucial factor is not so much a shifting of the frontiers between the normal and the pathological, as the making of these frontiers into items negotiable within society in terms of a pervasive reality-principle which weighs the meaning of life against its cost, in the presence of a state which proposes henceforth only to chair and animate the debate.

NOTES

1. Cf. Robert Castel, 'Vers une rénégotiation des frontières du normal et du pathologique', in *Résistance à la médecine*; and Robert Castel, *La Gestion des risques*, Paris, 1981. For earlier work by Castel. cf. the review articles by Peter Miller and Colin Gordon in *I&C* vols 2, 7 and 8.
2. Bourret and Wisner, *Revue français du travail*, 1972.
3. M. M. Dienesel, speech at a day-school on handicap sponsored by the city of Toulouse.
4. J. Carotte, 'Préparer, adapter, réadapter à la vieillesse', in *Revue français du travail*, 1973.
5. Cf. note 1.
6. François Forette, 'L'insécurité sociale des vieillards', *Le Monde*, 19 November 1980.

CHAPTER FOURTEEN

From dangerousness to risk

Robert Castel

In this chapter I would like to put forward a line of reflection on the preventive strategies of social administration which are currently being developed, most notably in the United States and France, and which seem to me to depart in a profoundly innovatory way from the traditions of mental medicine and social work.

To begin by putting it very schematically, the innovation is this. The new strategies dissolve the notion of a *subject* or a concrete individual, and put in its place a combinatory of *factors*, the factors of risk. Such a transformation, if this is indeed what is taking place, carries important practical implications. The essential component of intervention no longer takes the form of the direct face-to-face relationship between the carer and the cared, the helper and the helped, the professional and the client. It comes instead to reside in the establishing of *flows of population* based on the collation of a range of abstract factors deemed liable to produce risk in general. This displacement completely upsets the existing equilibrium between the respective viewpoints of the specialized professional and the administrator charged with defining and putting into operation the new sanitary policy. The specialists find themselves now cast in a subordinate role, while managerial policy formation is allowed to develop into a completely autonomous force, totally beyond the surveillance of the operative on the ground who is now reduced to a mere executant.

Furthermore, these practical implications may also have a political significance to the extent that, as I shall try at any rate to suggest, these new formulae for administering populations fall within the emerging framework of a plan of governability appropriate to the needs of 'advanced industrial' (or, as one prefers, to 'post-industrial' or 'post-modern') societies.

Like all important transformations, this one presupposes a slow preceding evolution of practices which, at a certain moment, passes a threshold and takes on the character of a mutation. Thus, the whole of modern medicine has been engaged in a gradual drift towards the point where the multiplication of systems of health checks makes the individualized interview between practitioner and client almost dispensable. The examination of the patient tends to become the examination of the patient's records as compiled in varying situations by diverse professionals and specialists interconnected solely through the circulation of individual dossiers. This is what Balint has called 'the collusion of anonymity'. The site of diagnostic synthesis is no longer that of the concrete relationship with a sick person, but a relationship constituted among the different expert assessments which make up the patient's dossier. Already here there is the shift from presence to memory, from the gaze to the objective accumulation of facts. The resulting situation might, if one chooses, be called a crisis of clinical medicine, a crisis affecting the personalized relation between professional and client; or it might be called a transition from a clinic of the subject to an 'epidemiological' clinic, a system of multifarious but exactly localized expertise which supplants the old doctor–patient relation. This certainly does not mean the end of the doctor, but it does definitely mark a profound transformation in medical practice.

Over the past twenty years or so, this redefinition of the medical mandate has been fuelling discussion of the evolution of medicine and the quest for solutions or palliatives to its negative side-effects (Balint groups, group medicine, attempts to revalorize general practice, etc.). In addition, the very precise objective conditions on which this whole evolution depends have themselves been studied often enough: the increasingly 'scientific' direction in which technologies of care have been evolving; the growing importance of the hospital as the privileged site of emergence and exercise of a technically advanced medicine; and so on. In mental medicine, however, the discussion has not progressed quite as far: it is still assumed that the crucial practical issues are those relating to the therapeutic relationship, whether they are seen in terms – as most of the professionals who operate it tend to think – of improving it, adapting it to more complex situations by enriching it with new resources, or else in terms of criticizing the non-therapeutic social functions, for example of repression or control, which denature it. It may be, however, that this problematic, while not completely outdated, is no longer able to keep pace with the most recent innovations currently transforming the field of mental medicine. This at least is what I would like to suggest, although I shall confine myself here to giving an outline of the route which over the last hundred years has led to the replacement of the notion of *dangerousness*, formerly used to designate the privileged target of preventive medical strategies, by the notion of *risk*.[1]

From dangerousness to risk: what does that signify historically, theoretically and practically?

THE PARADOXES OF DANGEROUSNESS

For classical psychiatry, 'risk' meant essentially the danger embodied in the mentally ill person capable of violent and unpredictable action. Dangerousness is a rather mysterious and deeply paradoxical notion, since it implies at once the affirmation of a quality immanent to the subject (he or she is dangerous), and a mere probability, a quantum of uncertainty, given that the proof of the danger can only be provided after the fact, should the threatened action actually occur. Strictly speaking, there can only ever be *imputations of dangerousness*, postulating the *hypothesis* of a more or less probable relationship between certain *present* symptoms and a certain act *to come*. Even where what one is talking about is a risk of recidivism, there still always exists a coefficient of uncertainty separating the diagnosis of dangerousness from the reality of the act. To say, for example, that someone is 'a monomaniac' or 'an instinctive pervert' already involves postulating a risk, one which in a paradoxical manner is supposed to dwell 'in' the subject even though it will often not yet have manifested itself in any act. Hence the special *unpredictability* attributed to the pathological act: all insane persons, even those who appear calm, carry a threat, but one whose realization still remains a matter of chance. 'Harmless today, they may become dangerous tomorrow.'[2] Faced with this besetting paradox of classical mental medicine, psychiatrists generally opted for the all-out prudence of preventive interventionism. When in doubt it is better to act, since, even if unfounded intervention is an error, it is one that will certainly never be known to be such; whereas if one abstains from intervening and the threatened act should still materialize, the mistake is obvious and the psychiatrist is exposed to blame. Hence the comment of one nineteenth-century alienist on reading one of those periodic news items smugly headlined in the newspapers, narrating the outburst of one such unpredictable act of violence: 'If we did not wait until lunatics committed some serious crime before we committed them, we would not have to deplore such accidents every day.'[3]

But is it possible to develop on this basis a fully-fledged policy for prevention? Only in a very crude way, since one could only hope to prevent violent acts committed by those whom one has already diagnosed as dangerous. Hence the double limitation arising from the fallibility of such diagnoses on the one hand, and the fact that they can only be carried out on individual patients one by one, on the other. This was why classical psychiatry was only able to make use of the correspondingly crude preventive technologies of confinement and sterilization. To confine signified to neutralize, if possible in advance, an individual deemed dangerous. In this sense it is not an exaggeration to say that the principal laws on compulsory confinement, such as the law of 1838 in France and the law of 1904 in Italy, are preventative laws, since, at the alarm signalled by the perception of a pathological symptom by the persons around him or her, the sick person is subject to forcible transplantation into a new environment, the asylum, where he or she will be systematically prevented from fulfilling the threat carried inside.

However, even apart from the moral or political reservations one might have about this strategy, it must be noted that *technically* it is not very satisfactory, since it has an arbitrary element which considerably limits its possible application. One cannot confine masses of people just out of simple suspicion of their dangerousness, if only for the reason that the economic cost would be colossal and out of all proportion to the risks prevented. Thus in a country like France the number of mentally ill persons confined in institutions has levelled off at around 100,000, which may seem a lot but at the same time is very few if one considers the number of dangers needing to be 'prevented'. These limits to confinement have become increasingly obvious as, through a line of development starting with monomania and 'madness without delirium', and progressively tracing the elaboration of a whole protean pathology of will and instinct, dangerousness turns into more and more of a polyvalent entity credited with unfathomable causes and unpredictable ways of manifesting itself. All those abnormal individuals, 'too lucid for the asylum, too irresponsible to imprison: are they not, above all, too harmful to be left at liberty?'[4] How, then, are they to be disposed of?

The more alert among the psychiatrists very soon realized the trap into which they risked falling through their propensity to treat dangerousness as an internal quality of the subject. Thus, as early as the middle of the nineteenth century the French psychiatrist Morel (better known as the discoverer of degeneracy) proposed a 'hygienic and prophylactic point of view' based on assessment of the *frequency* of mental illnesses and other abnormalities among the most disadvantaged strata of the population, and related this frequency to the living conditions of the subproletariat – malnutrition, alcoholism, housing conditions, sexual promiscuity, etc. In doing this, Morel was already arguing in terms of *objective risks*: that is to say, statistical correlations between series of phenomena. At the level of practices, he also suggested that the public authorities undertake a special surveillance of those population groups which might by this stage already have been termed 'populations at risk', those located (of course) at the bottom of the social ladder.[5] Morel was, incidentally, reactivating here the tradition of medical hygiene which had flourished in France in the late eighteenth century but from which alienism had distanced itself by concentrating the main part of its activities within the asylum.

But Morel was not able to go very far in this direction towards a genuinely preventive perspective, since he did not have at his disposal the specific techniques to achieve this. For him, to intervene still means to enter into contact with and take complete responsibility for particular individuals. Thus he talks of 'generalized moral treatment' as designating the new preventive practices he aims to promote, as though it were sufficient to extend and proliferate the same existing form of action, moral treatment, which at that time was established as the mandatory form of therapy for individual patients. He does draw the essential distinction between 'defensive prophylaxis' (internment) and 'preventive prophylaxis', but he is obliged to restrict the latter to:

> trying to modify the intellectual, physical and moral conditions of those who, on various grounds, have been separated from the rest of men; it must, before returning them to the social milieu, so to speak equip them against themselves, so as to reduce the rate of relapses.[6]

In other words, this 'preventive prophylaxis' is in practice still only applied to populations which undergo traditional confinement. For want of an adequate technology of intervention, Morel is unable to profit from his distinctly modern intuitions.

To be exact, one does find the emergence, in continuity from Morel and the discovery of degeneration, of the possibility of another kind of preventive strategy which culminates in the eugenic policies of the early twentieth century. Eugenics also starts to reason in terms of risks rather than dangers; the goal of an intervention made in the name of preservation of the race is much less to treat a particular individual than to prevent the threat he or she carries from being transmitted to descendants. Accordingly, the prophylactic measure of sterilization can be applied in a much more widespread and resolute preventive manner than confinement, since it can suppress future risks, on the basis of a much broader range of indications than those of mental illness strictly defined. Thus in 1914 a voice as authoritative as that of the President of the American Psychiatric Association declared:

> that a radical cure of the evils incident to the dependent mentally defective classes would be effected if every feeble-minded person, every imbecile, every habitual criminal, every manifestly weak-minded person, and every confirmed inebriate were sterilized, is a self-evident proposition. By this means we could practically, if not absolutely, arrest, in a decade or two, the reproduction of mentally defective persons, as surely as we could stamp out smallpox absolutely if every person in the world could be vaccinated.[7]

Indeed we often fail to remember that eugenic practices were widespread during the first third of this century, and that even in a country as supposedly 'liberal' as the United States special laws imposing sterilization for a wide range of deficient persons were enacted in almost all states.[8] But the interventions of eugenics were braked by the crisis affecting the 'scientific' basis which was held to justify them. Such interventions rely on the postulate that the hereditary character of the risks to be prevented, and of their mode of transmission, is scientifically established: something which in the majority of cases is far from having been proven. And then the monstrously grotesque version provided by Nazism helped both morally and politically to discredit eugenic techniques which, but for this tragic episode, would doubtless have had a fine future ahead of them. Besides, it was a French doctor who, as early as 1918, was so far as I know the first person to propose the setting up of an 'Institute for Euthanasia where those degenerates tired of life will be painlessly put to death by means of nitrous oxide or laughing gas'.[9]

But if the preventive path followed by eugenics thus finds itself (definitively or provisionally) discredited, how will it be possible to prevent without being forced to confine? There is a risk here of reverting to Morel's position: recognizing the need to act directly on the conditions liable to produce risk, but lacking the techniques with which to instrumentalize this requirement. A century after Morel, this ambiguity still characterizes the whole American tradition of preventive psychiatry founded on the works of Gerald Caplan.[10] Here again the question is one of *widening the intervention of the psychiatrist*, if need be by giving him or her new roles to play, making the psychiatrist into an adviser to ruling politicians or an auxiliary to administrative 'decision makers'. Take for example this programmatic text:

> The mental health specialist offers consultation to legislators and administrators and collaborates with other citizens in influencing governmental agencies to change laws and regulations. Social action includes efforts to modify general attitudes and behavior of community members by communication through the educational system, the mass media and through interaction between the professional and lay communities.[11]

On this basis, Caplan defines a first meaning of prevention, 'primary prevention', which is in fact a whole programme of political intervention.

But what is there that especially qualifies the psychiatrist to assume these new functions? What connection is there between the competence he or she can claim and that which is for instance needed to reform environmental policy or the school system? The specialist in mental medicine who, in Caplan's words, 'offers consultation' in these fields, runs a high risk of seeing his competence challenged, or at least of encountering strong competition from numerous other specialists, many of whom may seem better qualified than him. And so the hopes and fears which developed around an 'expansionist' psychiatry, and sometimes gave rise to denunciations of the risks of 'psychiatric imperialism', are doubtless somewhat exaggerated, at least at this level. They credit psychiatrists with quite exaggerated powers, in view of the actual position they occupy in society and the uncertain character of their knowledge: they represent psychiatrists as being able to intervent in a wide range of specifically social problems, despite the random social provenance of their classically individual clientele. Doubtless they can attempt to make their traditional therapeutic role a little more flexible. But they cannot variegate at indefinitely so long as they remain constricted by the relational character of their practice.

THE NEW SPACE OF RISK

The limitations are removed if one breaks this *direct* relation with the assisted subject which characterizes classical forms of treatment not only in psychiatry but in all the social work and care professions. In so doing, one makes an overt dissociation of the technical role of the practitioner from the managerial role of the administrator.

Such a shift becomes possible as soon as *the notion of risk is made autonomous from that of danger*. A risk does not arise from the presence of particular precise danger embodied in a concrete individual or group. It is the effect of a combination of abstract *factors* which render more or less probable the occurrence of undesirable modes of behaviour.

For example, in 1976 a general system for the detection of childhood abnormalities began to be installed in France, entitled the GAMIN (automated maternal and infantile management) system.[12] This involves making *all* infants subject to systematic examination (three examinations, in fact: at a few days, a few months and two years of age). These examinations detect all possible abnormalities of child and mother, whether physical, psychological or social. Among the kinds of data thus collected are: certain illnesses of the mother; psychological deficiencies; but also social characteristics such as the fact of being an unmarried mother, a minor, of foreign nationality, etc. These items of information can then be collated, thus grouping together types of factor which are totally heterogeneous. For instance, one may happen to be born of an unmarried mother who is less than seventeen years old, or more than forty, who has had a certain type of illness, or previous difficult pregnancies, who is a farmworker or a student, and so forth.

The presence of some, or of a certain number, of these factors of risk sets off an automatic alert. That is to say, a specialist, a social worker for example, will be sent to visit the family to confirm or disconfirm the *real* presence of a danger, on the basis of the *probabilistic and abstract* existence of risks. One does not *start from* a conflictual situation observable in experience, rather one *deduces* it from a general definition of the dangers one wishes to prevent.

These preventive policies thus promote a *new mode of surveillance*: that of systematic predetection. This is a form of surveillance, in the sense that the intended objective is that of anticipating and preventing the emergence of some undesirable event: illness, abnormality, deviant behaviour, etc. But this surveillance dispenses with actual presence, contract, the reciprocal relationship of watcher and watched, guardian and ward, carer and cared. This form of copresence, if only in the sublimated form of the observing gaze, was a requisite of all the classic disciplinary, benevolent and therapeutic techniques (cf. the model of the panopticon as analyzed by Michel Foucault).[13] Even in their most collective, impersonal and repressive forms, in barracks, factories, prisons, boarding schools and psychiatric hospitals, operations designed to detect and correct deviant behaviour retained this reliance on presence 'in the flesh' and, in short, on a certain form of individualization.

But now surveillance can be practised without any contact with, or even any immediate representation of, the subjects under scrutiny. Doubtless the police have long kept their secret files. But the logic of such subterranean dossiers now attains the sophisticated and proudly proclaimed form of 'scientific' predetection.

It seems to me that one has here a real mutation here, one that is capable of giving an extraordinary scope to the new technologies of surveillance. To intervene no longer means, or at least not to begin with, taking as one's target a given individual, in order to correct, punish or care for him or her (however one cares to interpret these latter forms of intervention – positively, according to the tradition of charitable, albeit muscular philanthropy, or negatively in line with the anti-respressive critical school of thought). There is, in fact, no longer a relation of immediacy with a subject *because there is no longer a subject*. What the new preventive policies primarily address is no longer individuals but factors, statistical correlations of heterogeneous elements. They deconstruct the concrete subject of intervention, and reconstruct a combination of factors liable to produce risk. Their primary aim is not to confront a concrete dangerous situation, but to anticipate all the possible forms of irruption of danger. 'Prevention' in effect promotes suspicion to the dignified scientific rank of a calculus of probabilities. To be suspected, it is no longer necessary to manifest symptoms of dangerousness or abnormality, it is enough to display whatever characteristics the specialists responsible for the definition of preventive policy have constituted as risk factors. A conception of prevention which restricted itself to predicting the occurrence of a particular act appears archaic and artisanal in comparison with one which claims to *construct* the objective conditions of emergence of danger, so as then to *deduce* from them the new modalities of intervention.

In brief, this generalized space of risk factors stands in the same relation to the concrete space of dangerousness as the generalized space of non-Euclidean geometries has to the three-dimensional space of Euclidean geometry; and this abstracting generalization which indicates the shift from dangerousness to risk entails a potentially infinite multiplication of the possibilities for intervention. For what situation is there of which one can be certain that it harbours no risk, no uncontrollable or unpredictable chance feature?

The modern ideologies of prevention are overarched by a grandiose technocratic rationalizing dream of absolute control of the accidental, understood as the irruption of the unpredictable. In the name of this myth of absolute eradication of risk, they construct a mass of new risks which constitute so many new targets for preventive intervention. Not just those dangers that lie hidden away inside the subject, consequences of his or her weakness of will, irrational desires or unpredictable liberty, but also the exogenous dangers, the exterior hazards and temptations from which the subject has not learnt to defend himself or herself, alcohol, tobacco, bad eating habits, road accidents, various kinds of negligence and pollution, meteorological hazards, etc.[14] Thus, a vast hygienist utopia plays on the alternate registers of fear and security, inducing a delirium of rationality, an absolute reign of calculative reason and a no less absolute prerogative of its agents, planners and technocrats, administrators of happiness for a life to which nothing happens. This hyper-rationalism is at the same time a thoroughgoing pragmatism, in that it pretends to eradicate risk as though one were pulling up weeds. Yet throughout the multiple current expressions of this tranquil preventive conscience (so hypertrophied at the moment in France, if one looks at all the massive national preventive campaigns), one finds not a trace of any reflection on the social and human cost of this new witch-hunt. For instance, there are the *iatrogenic aspects of prevention*, which in fact are always operative even when it is consumption of such 'suspect' products as alcohol or tobacco which is under attack.

PRACTICAL AND POLITICAL IMPLICATIONS

Even if one sets on one side the issue of these general implications, it is possible to begin to draw a certain number of practical and prosaic consequences. I shall limit myself here to two which seem to me to be particularly important.

*The separation of diagnosis and treatment, and the transformation of the caring
function into an activity of expertise*

Whether one thinks this a good or a bad thing, the tradition of mental
medicine, and more broadly of social work and assistance in general, has
until now been characterized by an aspiration to provide as complete as
possible a service of care for the populations for which it had
responsibility.

For psychiatry, this aspiration was initially realized in the clear, simple
form of internment: to be diagnosed as mentally ill amounted to being
placed in a special institution or asylum, where the way a person was
taken charge of was so total that it often continued for life. But in
modern psychiatry, in its community-based mode of operation, this
globalized vocation is taken over by the essential notion of *continuity of
care*: a single medico-social team, notwithstanding the diversity of sites in
which it operates, must provide the complete range of interventions
needed by a given individual, from prevention to after-care. This is
fundamental to the doctrine of the 'sector' which is official mental health
policy in France, and to the Community Mental Health Centers movement in the United States. One might add that even psychoanalysis is not
altogether foreign to this tradition, since, as we know, it follows the
client over many years through the various episodes of the cure and
punctuates his or her life with the rhythm of its sessions, thus in its own
way providing a continuity of care.

Today, this *continuous regime of assistance* has certainly not come to an
end, but it no longer represents a quasi-exclusive model of medico-
psychological practice. In a growing number of situations, medico-
psychological assessment functions as an *activity of expertise* which serves to
label an individual, to constitute for him or her a *profile* which will place
him or her on a *career*. But to actually take the individual into some kind of
care does not necessarily form a part of this continuity of assessment.

Such, for example, is the logic of the important law 'in favour of
handicapped persons' which was passed in France in 1975 and affects
around two million individuals.[15] A diagnosis of handicap makes it
possible to allocate subjects to various special trajectories, but these are
not necessarily medical ones. For example, a handicapped person may be
placed in a sheltered workshop or a Centre for Help through Employment (Centre d'aide par le Travail: CAT): that is to say, an establishment
which has nothing medical about it, where the handicapped person is not
so much 'cared for' as invited to work in a less competitive way than in
ordinary productive enterprises. One can call this 'demedicalization' or
'depsychiatrization' if one likes, but it is of a kind in which treatment is
replaced by a practice of *administrative assignation* which often intervenes

on the basis of a medico-psychological diagnosis. In France this law is encountering increasingly determined opposition from a majority of practitioners who realize that it carries a fatal threat to their professions. Nevertheless, the intervention of the practitioner remains an essential part of the functioning of the process, since it is the practitioner's expert assessment which seals the destiny of the handicapped individual. But this expertise no longer serves the same end: while remaining indispensable as an evaluation, it can become superfluous to the process of supervision. In other words, there are a growing number of subjects who continue to have to be *seen* by specialists of medico-psychological knowledge whose intervention remains necessary for assessment of their abilities (or disabilities). But individuals who are *seen* in this way no longer have to be *treated* by these same specialists. We have gone beyond the problematic of treatment (or, in critical nomenclature, that of repression and control). We are situated in a perspective of *autonomized management* of populations conducted on the basis of differential profiles of those populations established by means of medico-psychological diagnoses which function as pure expertises. Undoubtedly we have yet to take in the full moment of this mutation.

The total subordination of technicians to administrators

Conflict between administrators and practitioners is itself an old tradition of the mental health and social work professions. Indeed it is a leitmotif of the whole professional literature to regard administrative exigencies as the principal obstacle to the deployment of a therapeutic or caring activity worthy of the name: the administrator is always refusing the practitioner the resources needed for his or her work, obstructing initiatives by niggling regulations, imposing functions of control and repression, etc.

But in the classical system this conflict of viewpoints was acted out between two almost equal partners, or at least it left room for negotiation, compromise and even alliance on the basis of a division of responsibilities. One could set out to seduce or neutralize an administrator, to outflank or exploit a regulation, to influence or intimidate a manager, etc. Moreover, from the beginnings of psychiatry until today, policy for mental health has been the product of a confused interaction (or, if one prefers, a dialectical relation) between the respective contributions of practitioners and administrators. In the elaboration of policies, one can in spite of the disparities between different historical eras and geographical regions identify four common phases which follow on from one another with such regularity that one is entitled to conclude that it amounts to a genuine constitutive logic.[16]

An initial phase is dominated by the operators on the ground. Practitioners confronted with day-to-day problems gradually devise through trial and error a new formula for organizing the domain they have charge of. Thus one has the 'invention' of the asylum in France at the start of the nineteenth century, set against the background of the old *hôpital général*, and the geographical sectorization of the care of problem populations after the Second World War: to begin with these are more or less improvised reactions to concrete situations, which afterwards become progressively systematized.

During a second phase, which in fact starts very early on, these professionals make advances to the administrative and political authorities to request the officialization of their formula. Esquirol writes his famous 1819 report to the Minister of the Interior on the condition of hospitals for the insane and the reforms they require. In the post-war United States the modernizing professionals of the National Institute of Mental Health, and in France the progressive wing of the psychiatric profession of the 1950s, form their respective alliances with the Democrat administration and the progressive administrators at the Ministry of Health.

After a series of comings and goings, a shuttle operation which proceeds through mutual adjustments and compromises and may extend over years or even decades, an official decision is finally taken which definitively establishes the new mental health policy. This happens with the French 1838 law and 1960 ministerial circular on sectorization, and with the 1963 USA Community Mental Health Centers and Retardation Act, backed by the full authority of President Kennedy himself. On these administrative and medical foundations, a new formula for the management of problem populations is elaborated. The care of the mentally ill and other deviant persons no longer poses problems *of principle*; it is inscribed in a coherent scheme of administration constituting what is termed a policy.[17]

There then begins a fourth phase, generally marked by the disillusion of the professionals. There are cries of betrayal, charges that their humanist intentions have been distorted for the sake of bureaucratic or even repressive criteria. They denounce administrative sabotage, the ill-will of ministries, the denial of necessary resources. But the professionals tend to forget that a law does not actually need to be applied according to the letter in order for it to fulfil its essential function: that of providing conditions for the coherent management of a thorny problem at the administrative, juridical, institutional and financial levels of provision. They also forget that, even if they have been let down and their intentions distorted, their practice has furnished an essential element in the construction of the system.

Such has been the structure, schematically outlined and looked at in its political dimension, of the practitioner–administrator relationship up until now. Certain recent critiques of psychiatry have undoubtedly distorted the issue by treating mental health professionals as mere agents of state power. There is absolutely no question that these professionals are equipped with an official mandate, but this mandate is held on the basis of a practice which is not itself a straightforward instrumentalization of administrative–political decisions. The proof of this is that certain of these agents have been able to make use of their powers to redirect their mandate and effect a subversion of the previous juridical function, working on the basis of advances achieved in their own practice. The contribution of the Italian democratic psychiatry movement has provided just such an example, with their action culminating in 1978 in the passage by the Italian parliament of the famous Law 180,[18] in the history of which I think one would not have too much difficulty in recognizing the four phases identified above.

There is no doubt that this complex, conflict-ridden relationship is in the course of breaking up, with the coming of the new preventive technologies. Administration acquires an almost complete autonomy because it has virtually absolute control of the new technology. The operative on the ground now becomes a simple auxiliary to a manager whom he or she supplies with information derived from the activity of diagnosis expertise described above. These items of information are then stockpiled, processed and distributed along channels completely disconnected from those of professional practice, using in particular the medium of computerized data handling.

Here there is the source of a fundamental disequilibrium. The relation which directly connected the fact of possessing a knowledge of a subject and the possibility of intervening upon him or her (for better or for worse) is shattered. Practitioners are made completely subordinate to objectives of management policy. They no longer control the usage of the data they produce. The manager becomes the genuine 'decision maker'. The manager holds all the cards and controls the game. Among other consequences, this means an end to the possibility of those strategies of struggle developed over the last twenty or so years by progressive mental health operatives in Italy and, to a lesser degree, elsewhere.

TOWARDS A POST-DISCIPLINARY ORDER?

Finally one can wonder whether these trends do not inaugurate a set of new management strategies of a kind specific to 'neo-liberal' societies. New forms of control are appearing in these societies which work neither through repression nor through the welfare interventionism which grew up especially during the 1960s (with, in the field of psychiatry, the sectorization policy in France and the Community Mental Health Centers in the USA: here it was, in a nutshell, a question of covering the maximum amount of ground, reaching the maximum number of people, through the deployment of a unified apparatus linked to the machinery of the state). In place of these older practices, or rather alongside them, we are witnessing the development of differential modes of treatment of populations, which aim to maximize the returns on doing what is profitable and to marginalize the unprofitable. Instead of segregating and eliminating undesirable elements from the social body, or reintegrating them more or less forcibly through corrective or therapeutic interventions, the emerging tendency is to assign different social destinies to individuals in line with their varying capacity to live up to the requirements of competitiveness and profitability. Taken to its extreme, this yields the model of a 'dual' or 'two-speed' society recently proposed by certain French ideologists: the coexistence of hyper-competitive sectors obedient to the harshest requirements of economic rationality, and marginal activities that provide a refuge (or a dump) for those unable to take part in the circuits of intensive exchange. In one sense this 'dual' society already exists in the form of unemployment, marginalized youth, the unofficial economy. But until now these processes of disqualification and reclassification have gone on in a blind fashion. They have been uncontrolled effects of the mechanisms of economic competition, underemployment, adaptation or non-adaptation to new jobs, the dysfunctioning of the educational system, etc. The attempts which have been made to reprogramme these processes are more addressed to infrastructures than to people: industrial concentration, new investment sectors, closures of non-competitive concerns, etc. – leaving their personnel to adjust as well they may, which often means not particularly well, to these 'objective' exigencies.

But one has to ask whether, in the future, it may not become *technologically feasible* to programme populations themselves, on the basis of an assessment of their performances and, especially, of their possible deficiencies. Already this is what is being done with the handicapped, who are guided on to special careers in what is termed sheltered employment. But exactly the same could, for example, be done with the exceptionally gifted, who after all are only sufferers from a handicap of excess and could be guided and 'treated' to prepare them for careers in social functions which require very developed or specific aptitudes. In a more general sense, it would be possible thus to objectivize absolutely any type of difference, establishing on the basis of such a factorial definition a differential population profile. This is, thanks to the computer, technically possible. The rest – that is to say, the act of assigning a special destiny to certain categories defined in this way – is a matter of political will.

The fact that there has so far been no politically scandalous utilization made of these possibilities is not enough to allow complete peace of mind. In present circumstances for the majority of industrialized countries, among which Reagan's United States represents an extreme case, the crisis of the Keynesian state is causing not just a standstill but a contraction of welfare policies whose growth seemed until a few years ago inscribed in the course of history. Thus it has become extremely problematic in advanced capitalist societies to promote generalized welfare as a response to the penalties of economic development and political organization of society; but this does not mean that one reverts to *laissez-faire*.

In this conjuncture, the interventionist technologies which make it possible to *guide* and *assign* individuals without having to assume their custody could well prove to be a decisive resource. Traditional social policies have always respected, even if viewing with suspicion, what might be called a certain naturalness of the social: individuals are inscribed within territories, they belong to concrete groups, they have attachments, heritages, roots. Sometimes repressive, but progressively more and more welfare oriented in their character, social policies have until now worked upon this primary social material, canalizing untamed energies, pruning back the more bushy entanglements, weeding out here and there, occasionally transplanting. But all these measures, more corrective and reparative than preventive in function, shared a conception of individuals as previously assigned to some place within the geography of the social.

The profiling flows of population from a combination of characteristics whose collection depends on an epidemiological method suggests a rather different image of the social: that of a homogenized space composed of circuits laid out in advance, which individuals are invited or encouraged to tackle, depending on their abilities. (In this way, marginality itself, instead of remaining an unexplored or rebellious territory, can become an organized zone within the social, towards which those persons will be directed who are incapable of following more competitive pathways.)

More the projection of an order than an imposition of order on the given, this way of thinking is no longer obsessed with discipline; it is obsessed with efficiency. Its chief artisan is no longer the practitioner on the ground, who intervenes in order to fill a gap or prevent one from appearing, but the administrator who plans out trajectories and sees to it that human profiles match up to them. The extreme image here would be one of a system of prevention perfect enough to dispense with both repression and assistance, thanks to its capability to forward-plan social trajectories from a 'scientific' evaluation of individual abilities. This is of course only an extreme possibility, what one might call a myth, but it is a myth whose logic is already at work in the most recent decisions taken in the name of the prevention of risks.

NOTES

1. I have attempted a more systematic explanation of this new problematic in *La Gestion des risques*, Paris, 1981, especially chapter 3, 'La gestion prévisionnelle'.
2. Doctors Constant, Lunier and Dumesnil, *Rapport général à Monsieur le Ministre de l'Intérieur sur le service des alienes en 1874*, Paris, 1878, p. 67.
3. L. Lunier, 'Revue medicale des journaux judiciaires', *Annales medico-psychologiques*, vol. VIII, 1848, p. 259. The *Annales* had a regular section of these items, accompanied by 'reflections' that underline at once the discomfort of the psychiatrist faced with this situation, and the need for preventive vigilance.
4. P. Seriex and L. Libert, *Les lettres de cachet 'prisonniers de famille' et 'placements volontaires'*, Ghent, 1912, p. 12.
5. Cf. Morel's letter to the Departmental Prefect of Seine-Inférieur to solicit his aid in 'penetrating the interior of families, looking closely at the manners of life of inhabitants of a locality, getting acquainted with their physical and moral hygiene'. 'This is', he says (and one can understand his point), 'a delicate mission which can only suitably be carried out under the patronage of authority. I do not believe that one can otherwise succeed in establishing the statistics of this populous Department and thus providing the authorities with useful documents on the causes of the increase in lunacy and the most appropriate prophylactic and hygienic means of preventing so great an infirmity.' (Letter reproduced in *Le neo-restraint*, Paris, 1857, p. 103.)
6. B. Morel, *Traité des dégénérescences physiques, intellectuelles et morales de l'espèce humaine*, Paris, 1857, p. 691.
7. Carlos F. Macdonald, Presidential Address, *American Journal of Insanity*, July, 1914, p. 9.
8. For example, the law enacted in Missouri in 1923.
9. Dr Binet-Sangle, *Le Haras humain*, Paris, 1918, p. 142.
10. Gerald Caplan, *Principles of Preventive Psychiatry*, Boston, 1960.
11. *Ibid.*, p. 59.
12. In the United States, President Nixon sought advice as early as 1969 from the Secretary for Health, Education and Welfare on a report he had commissioned which proposed that 'the Government should have mass testing done on all 6–8 year old children . . . to detect [those] who have violent and homicidal tendencies'. Subjects with 'delinquent tendencies' would undergo 'corrective treatment' ranging from psychological counselling and day-care centres to compulsory enrolment in special camps. The minister replied, through the mouth of the Director of the National Institute of Mental Health, that the required detection technologies were not sufficiently

advanced for their results to be credible (quoted by Peter Schrag and Diane Divosky, *The Myth of the Hyperactive Child*, Harmondsworth, 1981). Where systematic tests are practised in the United States at present, they apply to limited groups perceived as carrying special risks. It seems that France's 'advanced' position in these matters results from the centralized structure of power, which makes readily possible the planned national implementation of administrative decisions. I should add that in June 1981 (the date is not fortuitious; it falls one month after the change of Presidential majority in France), a government commission on 'Computerization and liberties' gave a hostile verdict on the GAMIN system. But its condemnation applied only to the threat to individual liberties posed by breach of confidentiality in the system's procedures, and not to the technological apparatus itself.

13. Michel Foucault, *Discipline and Punish*, especially part III, chapter 3.

14. A conference was recently held on preventing the effects of earthquakes on the Cote d'Azur, at which serious indignation was expressed that this problem had not yet been accorded the attention it merited. One can see here how the *mise en scene* of a 'risk' which is after all perhaps perfectly real, but totally random in its effects, unpredictable in its occurrence and uncontrollable in source, can create a piece of machinery which for its part can also have a perfectly real existence, prompting the creation of a corps of experts, modifying norms and costs of construction work, influencing flows of tourism, and so on. Not to speak of the culture of fear, or at least of anxiety, provoked by this habit of digging up endless new kinds of risk in the name of a mythological representation of absolute security. But it is true that a culture of anxiety secretes a developing market for remedies for anxiety, just as the cultivation of insecurity justifies a muscular security policy.

15. The law of 30 June 1975 'in favour of handicapped persons' institutes new committees at Department level, one for children and one for adults, before which are brought the cases of the entirety of persons seeking, or for whom someone is seeking, a financial benefit and/or placement in a specialized institution. They work on dossiers built up by subordinate specialist technical committees. Representatives of the various administrative agencies are in the majority on the departmental committees, whereas the technicians are the majority on the specialized committees. The departmental committees have power of decision in questions concerning handicap. As the then Minister of Health, Mme Simone Veil, put it during the debate on the law in the Senate: 'In future those persons will be considered handicapped who are recognized as being such by the departmental committees proposed in Article 4 of the Bill, for minors, and Article 11, for adults' (*Journal Officiel*, 4 April 1975).

16. I have tried to demonstrate this for the 1838 law and the policy of the sector in France in *L'Ordre psychiatrique*, and for the American Community Mental Health and Retardation Act of 1963 in *The Psychiatric Society*, co-authored with Françoise Castel and Ann Lovell, 1982.

17. For example, the 1838 law removed the contradiction between the impossibility of juridical internment of mentally ill persons regarded as dangerous, since they were penally irresponsible, and the necessity of doing so to safeguard public order. The new medical legitimacy provided under the rubric of 'therapeutic isolation' allows for a sequestration which is as rigorous as imprisonment but justified henceforth by a therapeutic end. The insane person is provided with a civil and legal status, he or she is assigned a place in a 'special establishment', and even the financial details of his or her

custody are provided for in the framework of the law. But this complete apparatus, which henceforth makes possible a rational administration of madness, had been made possible by transformations of hospital practice extending over more than thirty years, starting with Pinel at Bicêtre and then Salpêtrière, and snowballing thereafter.

18. The Law 180 among other things provides for the closure of existing psychiatric hospitals, prohibits the building of new ones and stipulates that acute psychiatric crises must be treated in small care units integrated in the general medical hospitals.

Index